Planning for
Windows® 2000

New Riders Professional Library

Windows NT DNS
Michael Masterson, Herman Kneif, Scott
Vinick, & Eric Roul,
ISBN: 1-56205-943-2

Windows NT Registry
Sandra Osborne,
ISBN: 1-56205-941-6

Windows NT Performance
Mark Edmead & Paul Hinsburg,
ISBN: 1-56205-942-4

Windows NT TCP/IP
Karanjit Siyan,
ISBN 1-56205-887-8

Windows NT Terminal Server & Citrix
MetaFrame
Ted Harwood,
ISBN: 1-56205-944-0

Windows NT Network Management
Anil Desai,
ISBN: 1-56205-946-7

Implementing Exchange Server
Doug Hauger, Marywynne Leon, &
William C. Wade III,
ISBN: 1-56205-931-9

SQL Server Administration
Sean Baird & Chris Miller,
ISBN: 1-56205-955-6

Cisco Router Configuration &
Troubleshooting
Mark Tripod,
ISBN: 0-7357-0024-9

Developing Linux Applications
Eric Harlow,
ISBN: 0-7357-0021-4

Understanding Data Communications,
6th Edition
Gilbert Held,
ISBN: 0-7357-0036-2

Planning for
Windows® 2000

201 West 103rd Street,
Indianapolis, Indiana 46290

Eric Cone
Jon Boggs
Sergio Perez

Planning for Windows 2000

Eric Cone
Jon Boggs
Sergio Perez

Trademarks

Warning and Disclaimer

Publisher
David Dwyer

Executive Editor
Al Valvano

Acquisitions Editor
Stephanie Layton

Development Editor
Leah Williams

Managing Editor
Sarah Kearns

Project Editor
Alissa Cayton

Copy Editor
Audra McFarland

Indexer
Lisa Stumpf

Technical Editors
Desmond Banks
Scott Burgess
Marc Charney
Lori Sanders

Proofreader
Elise Walter

Book Designer
Ruth Harvey

Cover Designer
Brainstorm Design

Production
Liz Johnston

Contents

About the Authors

Eric K. Cone, MCSE, MCNE, is the Senior Technical Architect for the Infrastructure Services and Support practice of Metamor Technologies, Ltd., a partner level Microsoft Solution Provider in Chicago. He is responsible for the firm's deployment plans, product research, and consultant training. His breadth and depth of experience in Windows 2000 were recently shared in a presentation given to COMDEX Windows World attendees at the McCormick Center in Chicago. As a member of the Windows 2000 Rapid Deployment Program, he has been testing and evaluating all interim developer release builds of Windows 2000 (formerly NT 5.0) since early 1998.

Jon Boggs, MCSE, CNE, is a Consultant for the Infrastructure Services and Support practice of Metamor Technologies. He has provided consulting services to a number of nationally known corporations. An expert in automating administrative tasks under Windows NT/2000, he also excels at automating Windows NT deployments. Knowledge of SMS and Visual Basic round out his technical abilities. Jon graduated magna cum laude from Anderson University with a BA in Computer Science. He enjoys reading and biking in his spare time.

Sergio Perez is the Practice Manager for Networking Technologies at Metamor Technologies. He specializes in providing strategic solutions focused on the design, security, and management of complex multiprotocol internetworking environments. He has a BBA in Computer Information Systems and an MBA in Finance and Management from the University of Miami.

About the Reviewers

Desmond Banks is an MCSE and Novell Master CNE who has been working in the computer industry for more than 13 years. He has an extensive background in designing Windows NT and Novell Networks for large enterprises. He is currently designing a national NT infrastructure for a Fortune 500 company.

Scott Burgess is a Senior Systems Architect and Project Manager for New Technology Partners Consulting, Microsoft's number-one solution provider worldwide for 1997. Scott is an MCSE+I and is MCT certified to teach all current Microsoft products, including the new Windows 2000 curriculum. Mr. Burgess has multiple years of experience implementing and designing enterprise-wide LAN, WAN, NT, Exchange, and SMS environments. In addition, Scott is the lead for New Technology Partners Consulting rapid deployment program. RDP is made up of 69 solution providers worldwide with special focus on aiding corporate customers with integrating and migrating their current environments to Windows 2000.

Marc Charney has 12 years of experience in the computer industry. After receiving his degree from the University of California, Berkeley in 1987, Marc worked for the Federal Reserve Bank of San Francisco, where he helped design computer models of the United States economy. Marc then moved on to Sybase, where he helped develop its sales-office integration, automation, and networking strategy. In his next position at Delta Life & Annuity, Marc managed a complete overhaul of its network and systems infrastructure. Currently, Marc is an Internet security and intranet development manager at First Tennessee Bank. His efforts are focused on Web integration of current bank systems.

Lori Sanders owns iSolve Consulting Group, a company specializing in NT networking, I-net based client/server system design, and technology consulting. Lori is also a technical editor and trainer for Learning Tree International, focusing on the Windows 2000, Microsoft NT 4, and client/server arenas. Lori has been working with Windows 2000 since the first beta and has implemented the OS in several lab sites for her clients. Her 17-year background in the IS field includes project management, systems engineering, network administration, and tech support. Lori is based in Tennessee, where she lives happily (when she's not on the road!) with her most wonderful husband Wade, their six daughters, four beautiful grandchildren, and the cats. Lori can be reached at loris@isolveconsulting.com.

Acknowledgments

Eric K. Cone

For my very best friend, and dearly loved son Anthony (known by his friends and family as "Goose," age five). Thanks for allowing daddy to work so many hours on his "dumb book."

For my life-long soul mate and lasting love of my life Tamara. Your friendship, understanding, love, and support mean the world to me.

For my beloved mother and father, Sherman and Ellen Cone. Your wisdom, understanding, and principles are the foundation for my values, beliefs, and passions in life.

For my cherished mother and father-in-law Jack and Gloria Kerrill. Your love for life, for each other, and for family and friends is a blessing to me and to those that surround you.

For my long-time friend James Bodan. You are like the brother I never had.

Jon Boggs

Thanks to my parents for introducing me to computers and all your support. Leah, thanks for whipping my chapters into a form I'm proud to publish.

Sergio Perez

To Nicholas and Molly, everything is for you. To Mami, Papi, Abea, Cako, Cuca, and Pio, thanks for sacrificing everything for us and giving us the Cuban work ethics and morals.

Tell Us What You Think

As the reader of this book, *you* are our most important critic and commentator. We value your opinion and want to know what we're doing right, what we could do better, what areas you'd like to see us publish in, and any other words of wisdom you're willing to pass our way.

As the Executive Editor for the Networking team at New Riders Publishing, I welcome your comments. You can fax, email, or write me directly to let me know what you did or didn't like about this book—as well as what we can do to make our books stronger.

Please note that I cannot help you with technical problems related to the topic of this book, and that due to the high volume of mail I receive, I might not be able to reply to every message.

When you write, please be sure to include this book's title and author, as well as your name and phone or fax number. I will carefully review your comments and share them with the author and editors who worked on the book.

Fax: 317-581-4663
Email: newriders@mcp.com
Mail: Al Valvano
            Executive Editor
            New Riders Publishing
            201 West 103rd Street
            Indianapolis, IN 46290 USA

Introduction

There is no doubt that Windows 2000 is Microsoft's flagship operating system. With a host of powerful technologies such as Active Directory, Dynamic DNS, and Group Policy, Windows 2000 completely changes the way you should plan, design, and deploy Microsoft networks. Making your transition to Windows 2000 a success requires complete, practical, and competent planning direction. The aim of this book is to addresses the key requirements in every stage of your transition.

Who This Book Is For

This text contains invaluable information for administrators charged with transitioning from Windows NT to Windows 2000. The intended audience is familiar with administration and design concepts in Windows NT and is ready to take the next big step: transitioning to Windows 2000. *Planning for Windows 2000* provides experienced NT professionals with the tools necessary to design and deploy world-class Windows 2000 networks.

How This Book Is Organized

The organization of this book mirrors our recommended approach for transitioning your enterprise to Windows 2000. In Part I, "Preparing for Windows 2000," we explain the real challenges in your move from Windows NT to Windows 2000 and provide you with the essential tools and information to meet them. We offer labor-saving tips on key planning tasks, including inventory, standardization, and domain restructuring, that will simplify your eventual transition. The assessment of your critical applications and the preparation steps to clean up your NetBIOS-dependent services are then covered at length. In short, Part I will help you prepare for Windows 2000 by laying the groundwork for stability in your current and future environments.

In Part II, "Designing Windows 2000 Networks," we will help you begin tackling design objectives using a systematic, practical, and proven approach. We guide you through the steps for effective Active Directory design, highlighting the structural significance of sites, domains, and organizational units. Then we explain in detail how to plan your Dynamic DNS services, form your TCP/IP standards, and create a robust security plan. Often-overlooked topics are included, such as hardware planning and practical steps for simplifying everyday administration. In a nutshell, this section presents all critical Windows 2000 design topics in an easy-to-use, intuitive, and workable framework.

The focus of Part III, "Deploying Windows 2000," is to explain the Windows 2000 upgrade procedure in detail, with a constant eye to the technical. We will use examples from our own experiences, including typical scenarios and case studies along the way, to explain, punctuate, and add clarity to an otherwise-tangled procedure. To guide you step-by-step through each major turning point, this section also includes a unique series of checklists and planning templates. These will aid you in the collection and organization of all critical information required in your transition. In sum, Part III is a step-by-step examination of all crucial elements that will help guide you from the initial preparation steps to your eventual deployment.

We all hope that you find *Planning for Windows 2000* a useful tool in your upcoming transition. Please provide us with any feedback on the material we've covered, and share with us your Windows 2000 experiences. You can reach us by sending email to `windows2000@metamor.com`. Please check this book's home page at `www.newriders.com` periodically for any new information.

Conventions Used

You should be aware of the following typographical conventions when reading this book:

Element	Style	Example
Windows 2000/DDNS domain names	Monotype font	`lhtrucking.com`, `CHICAGO`
Domain controllers	All caps	PACPDCO1
Organizational units	All caps	BOSTON
Web sites	Monotype font	`www.microsoft.com`
Dialog boxes	Italic	the *Pre-Configure Verify Object* dialog box
Glossary terms	Italic	*certificate revocation list*
Selections	Bold	Select **Next** to continue

I

Preparing for Windows 2000

Windows 2000 Overview

WITH EACH NEW RELEASE OF WINDOWS NT, Microsoft gives you new and inventive technologies to build more useful, manageable, and scalable networks. Windows 2000 (formerly Windows NT 5.0) is no exception. In fact, it is the most innovative release to date. There are four separate products that form the Windows 2000 line of operating systems:

- **Windows 2000 Professional.** Replaces NT 4.0 Workstation. It is Microsoft's flagship desktop operating system.

- **Windows 2000 Server.** Replaces NT 4.0 Server. For new installations, it supports two-way symmetric multiprocessing (SMP). Upgrades from NT 4.0 Server support four-way SMP.

- **Windows 2000 Advanced Server.** Replaces NT 4.0 Server Enterprise Edition. New installations support four-way SMP. Upgrades from NT 4.0 Server Enterprise Edition support eight-way SMP. Like its predecessor, Advanced Server supports large physical memories, clustering, and load balancing.

- **Windows 2000 Datacenter Server.** A new Microsoft offering. It supports sixteen-way SMP, up to 64GB of physical memory, clustering, and load balancing.

Each of these products includes key advancements that change how you plan, design, and deploy Microsoft networks. To employ such groundbreaking features as Active Directory, Dynamic DNS (DDNS), and IntelliMirror, you will need to plan ahead. To help you build your roadmap from Windows NT to Windows 2000, this chapter offers an overview of the key Windows 2000 technologies and services. These advances are detailed in the sections that follow:

- Active Directory
- Security
- Storage
- Networking
- Enterprise Management

Active Directory

Can you effectively manage every resource in your network with a single logon? Do your users have a meaningful view of these resources? Was it easy for you to build a large, complex, international network with Windows NT? If you're bound by the limits of *downlevel* (NT 3.x–4.0) networks, your answer is probably no—at least not without some headaches.

Microsoft networks that are built with Active Directory can help you meet these challenges. Unlike downlevel directory services, which are flat, Active Directory is hierarchical. Active Directory stores each of your company's resources logically, forming a Tree structure that mirrors your enterprise. Every resource in even the largest networks is easy to find and manage.

Planning for Active Directory is one of the most important tasks in your company's transition to Windows 2000. If your Active Directory design is good, you'll be able to leverage all its benefits. To help you create the best directory for your company, we'll cover the fine points of planning and design in Chapter 6, "Designing the Active Directory." The building blocks of networks built with Active Directory include the following:

- Domains
- Organizational units (OUs)
- Trees
- Forests
- Sites
- The global catalog

Domains

Domains that are built with Active Directory can store millions of objects. The types of objects that can be stored in Active Directory domains are those considered *interesting* to the networked community. For example, an interesting object can be a user, a group, a printer, and so on.

The types of objects that can be stored in Active Directory domains are defined in the *schema*. The Active Directory schema is extensible. You can extend it to support objects and properties that are unique to your company[1]. This flexibility gives you the option to store additional types of data in Active Directory to make it more useful, such as an employee hire date or other information.

Replication

In NT 3.x–4.0 networks, the SAM database is replicated between primary domain controllers (PDCs) and backup domain controllers (BDCs). This type of replication relationship is known as *single master replication*. In this relationship, the PDC is the master. It has a Read/Write copy of the SAM. The BDC has a Read-Only copy.

There is not a master-slave replication relationship in Windows 2000. The servers in your network are either domain controllers (DCs) or member servers. A Windows 2000 domain is a *partition* in the Active Directory. This partition holds the values for every interesting object and each of its properties. The domain controllers in each of your domains replicate this partition to share changes. The replication relationship between domain controllers in Windows 2000 is multi master. Every domain controller is a master in this relationship. They each have Read/Write copy of the partition for the domain.

Trusts

To share resources from one domain with another, you need a trust relationship between them. Downlevel networks support one-way trust relationships. For example, if you have three NT 3.x–4.0 domains that need to share resources, you must manually create six one-way trusts. In Windows 2000, all trust relationships are created auto-matically, allowing you to share resources with every domain in your network. This is because the default trusts in Windows 2000 are *transitive* (you can also create one-way trusts in Windows 2000). In a trust relationship that is transitive, when DOMAINA trusts DOMAINB and DOMAINB trusts DOMAINC, DOMAINA will trust DOMAINC. Transitive trusts in Windows 2000 simplify resource sharing, and eliminate the hassle of configuring and managing many one-way relationships.

---

1. Each new object and property that you add to the schema requires a unique object identifier (OID). You can obtain a root OID for your organization from the American National Standards Institute (ANSI) at www.ansi.org.

Permissions

Transitive trusts let you *share* resources, but to *access* resources, you must have permissions. Every object in Active Directory has an *Access Control List (ACL)*. These ACLs contain *Access Control Entries (ACEs)*, which define users or groups with permissions for the object. You can grant permissions for objects to users, domain local groups, global groups, and universal groups. To keep your assignments manageable, you should always grant these permissions to groups instead of users. Each group in Windows 2000 has a scope that defines where it can be used on your network:

- **Domain local groups.** Can contain members from any domain, and can be granted permissions on member servers and domain controllers.

- **Global groups.** Can contain members from the same domain, and can be granted permissions in any domain.

- **Universal groups.** Can contain members from any domain, and can be granted permissions in any domain.

A Windows 2000 domain can operate in native mode or mixed mode. In *mixed* mode, you can replicate the domain partition to NT 3.x-4.0 backup domain controllers. In a *native* mode domain, multi master replication is enabled, and downlevel support for replication of the directory database is turned off. These details are discussed further in Chapter 12, "Windows 2000 Upgrade and Migration."

When your Windows 2000 domain is in native mode, you can nest groups. This lets you exceed a group's 5,000-member maximum, or in smaller networks, simplify permission assignments—a complex set of permissions from one group can be easily added to another. The following rules apply to nested groups:

- Domain local groups in native mode domains can contain users, universal groups, and global groups from any domain and other domain local groups from the same domain. When created in mixed mode domains, users and global groups from any domain are allowed.

Main Differences Between the NT 3.x-4.0 SAM and Active Directory

The Security Accounts Manager (SAM) database is used to store the objects in Windows NT 3.x-4.0 domains. It is recommended that you limit the SAM database to a maximum size of 40MB. This recommended limit allows you to group approximately 40,000 users in a single NT 3.x-4.0 domain (the maximum user count will vary depending on how groups and computer accounts are used). Active Directory domains, on the other hand, can be up to 17TB in size. A domain that is 17TB can support millions of objects.

- Global groups in native mode domains can contain users and other global groups from the same domain. If created in mixed mode domains, users from the same domain are allowed.

- Universal groups in native mode domains can contain users, other universal groups, and global groups from any domain. In mixed mode domains, universal groups cannot be created.

You can use these groups (or users) to assign permissions to objects as a whole or to select object properties. These permissions allow or deny specific actions. Because permissions can be defined at a fine-grained level, you can let a user read one property of an object, and write to another. This topic is covered in more detail in the next section, "Organizational Units (OUs)." In NT 3.x–4.0, controlling access with this level of granularity was impossible. This capability, along with other improvements in Windows 2000 domains, helps you build scalable, extensible, and manageable networks.

Organizational Units (OUs)

Domains are the smallest units you can use to group resources in downlevel networks. In Windows 2000, an *Organizational Unit (OU)* is the smallest division. OUs are created to further delineate the domain namespace. This lets you group users, groups, file shares, and other information into a usable hierarchy.

The most significant benefit of configuring OUs in your domains is gained when delegating administrative tasks. This benefit is illustrated in the following example. The Windows 2000 domain in Figure 1.1 has three OUs: US, MKTG, and SALES. Hundreds of users are added each spring in the SALES OU to accommodate the seasonal rush for mycompany.com. Each new user needs access to the company's sales material and permission to use and manage shared printers. Company executives have asked you to let Susan Jones handle creating users and providing them the access they require. They've also requested that you prohibit Mrs. Jones from managing any resources in the US and MKTG OUs. In NT 3.x–4.0 networks, providing this level of administrative authority would not be possible without creating multiple domains. With Windows 2000, however, you can easily meet this request.

To give Susan Jones the authority she requires, you must complete the following:

1. Assign Susan the Create User Objects permission in the SALES OU.

2. Create a new group in the SALES OU (called SALESUSERS) with permissions to access the sales material and to use and manage shared printers.

3. Grant Susan the Write permission to the Members property of the new SALESUSERS group.

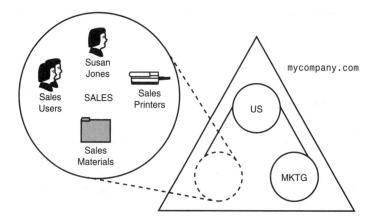

Figure 1.1   You can easily delegate a limited set of abilities to a sub-administrator, such as
Susan Jones, in Windows 2000 domains.

After you assign these permissions, Susan is able to create new users in the SALES
OU and add them as members to the SALESUSERS group. Because you've just
assigned her a limited set of permissions, these are the full scope of her abilities in the
domain. By granting her a granular level of administrative authority in the SALES OU,
you've met the company's original request: She is not able to perform administration
in the US or MKTG OUs. Further, if she attempts to complete a task that requires
permissions beyond what you've assigned (such as deleting a user), she is denied.

What if Susan were asked to add accounts in US, SALES, and MKTG? One way
to fulfill this request is by granting the Create User Objects permission in each OU
separately. However, this would require three distinct permission assignments. Rather
than granting these permissions three times, you can assign them once, and allow
them to be inherited. By default, all objects that are below others in Active Directory
inherit permissions from their parents. Because the US OU is a parent of the SALES
and MKTG OUs, the Create User Objects permission can be assigned at the US OU
and flow down the hierarchy. You must select the behavior of inheritance when
assigning permissions. When you set permissions on an OU, you can specify to which
objects they apply:

- To this object only
- To this object and all subobjects
- To objects and/or containers within this container only
- To subobjects only

To give Susan the authority she requires in the second scenario, you must grant the
Create User Objects permissions at the US OU, and specify that they are applied to
this object (US) and all subobjects (SALES and MKTG). Keep in mind that you

should always grant object permissions at the uppermost level in Active Directory to leverage inheritance. By following this rule, you'll end up with fewer assignments to manage than with explicit assignments.

Trees

Like OUs, you can use Trees to further define the Active Directory namespace. A *Tree* is a hierarchy of Windows 2000 domains, each represented by a partition in Active Directory. Your first Windows 2000 domain forms the root of this Tree. Every domain created after it becomes its child. Those children in turn may have child domains of their own, which creates a parent-child relationship.

One of the advantages of this parent-child relationship is that children inherit some of the attributes of their parents. For example, when a new domain joins the Tree, it is automatically configured with its parents' common configuration, global catalog, and schema. This information binds the new domain to your Tree. After joining the Tree, your domain maintains its own security. Just as with NT 3.x–4.0, domains in Windows 2000 are still a security boundary. Parent domain administrators aren't given authority over child domains. However, this doesn't mean that you can't implement a Tree that is centrally administered—Trees can be configured for decentralized or centralized administrative needs.

A simple Tree of Windows 2000 domains is shown in Figure 1.2. Notice that the Tree forms a contiguous namespace. Just as in Domain Name System (DNS) standards, the fully qualified name of each child in the Tree is the concatenation of its name and the name of its parent. Windows 2000 domain names *are* DNS names. In Figure 1.2, us.mycompany.com is a child domain and the mycompany.com domain is its parent.

Whereas Windows 2000 domains are grouped in Trees, downlevel domains are organized in one of several domain models. Each of these domain models outlines the relationship between resource domains and account domains. For example, in the single master domain model, resource domains are configured to trust account domains. This model lets you delegate administrative authority for resource domains, while retaining control over account domains. If an account domain grows larger than 40MB, you should consider using the multi master domain model. This will allow you to comply with recommended limits of the SAM database. In the multi master domain model, you can create multiple account domains. Each of these account domains trusts the other, and every resource domain in the domain model trusts the account domains. In a network that uses two account domains and 10 resource domains, 22 one-way trusts are required.

There is no reason to create these types of domain models with Windows 2000. By leveraging granular access control, you can delegate administrative tasks to sub-administrators for objects in a portion of your domain while retaining control of others. You don't need a resource domain in Windows 2000 for every sub-administrator. Additionally, you aren't forced to create a second account domain when the directory database exceeds 40MB. Windows 2000 domains can store millions of objects. Instead of spending your time working around limits, with these improvements you can focus on more important issues, such as user needs and reliability of service.

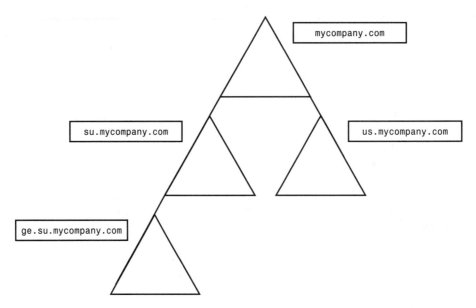

Figure 1.2   The Active Directory domain namespace in Windows 2000 mirrors the DNS namespace.

Forests

If you decide to create your Windows 2000 network with more than one Tree, you can form a Forest. A *Forest* is a collection of two or more Trees, each with its own distinct namespace. When you create a Forest of Trees, a transitive trust relationship is established between the root domains in each Tree. Because this trust is transitive, every domain in the Forest can automatically share resources. Each Tree in a Forest has a common configuration, schema, and global catalog. In Figure 1.3, mycompany.com and yourcompany.com form a Forest. Note that a contiguous namespace is formed only in each Tree.

Sites

Sites give domain controllers and other computers in a Tree or Forest information to identify areas of good network connectivity. When a site is configured in Active Directory, it is assigned one or more TCP/IP subnets. The subnets that you choose for a site should share a high bandwidth link; the connection between subnets should be at least 512Kbps. Each site in Active Directory can contain multiple domains, and single domains can be members in more than one site.

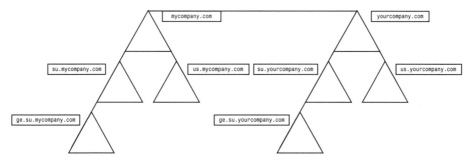

Figure 1.3 In a Forest of Trees (like this one formed by mycompany.com and yourcompany.com), the
Active Directory namespace is not contiguous.

The three sites in Figure 1.4 (Los Angeles, New York, and Dallas) distinguish areas
that are connected by low-bandwidth links. Because the mycompany.com domain spans all
three sites, every site has a domain controller as a member. To keep the partitions in the
domain up to date, each domain controller replicates its changes with the others. This
means that partition traffic must travel from site to site, across low-bandwidth links.
Among other capabilities, sites let you define replication schedules for the partitions in
Active Directory. This lets you throttle intrasite and intersite replication traffic.

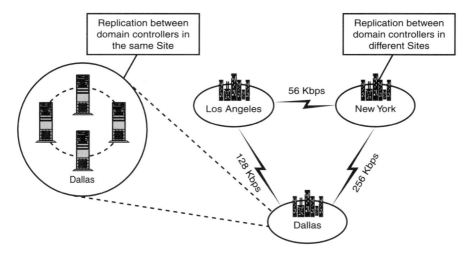

Figure 1.4 You should configure the replication schedule between domain controllers divided
by slow WAN links differently than you do the replication schedule for
domain controllers on your local network.

The Global Catalog

Each domain exists as a separate partition in Active Directory. A domain's partition stores every object in the domain and in each of its properties. The objects that are contained in one domain aren't replicated to another domain. How then does Active Directory provide information on all objects in a Tree or Forest to every user in your network? What must you do to discover the details of objects and properties in other domains? The answer to these questions is to use the global catalog.

The *global catalog* is built automatically by Active Directory. It has an entry for every object and property that exists in a Tree or Forest. The global catalog is not simply a merged version of every domain partition—every value for each property in a Tree or Forest is not stored in the global catalog. Instead, it contains the values for a subset of object properties that are useful to the global community. These are values such as the Logon Name property for a user or the Members property in a universal group.

If you request the value of an object that is not in the global catalog, you are returned the object's *distinguished name (DN)*. The DN gives you enough information to find a domain controller containing the partition holding that particular object and its values. The information that is returned by the global catalog is known as a *referral*. Referrals are valid only for the domain partitions in a single Tree. Any referrals from the global catalog to partitions in other Trees are not searched. This means that you need to closely examine object search and retrieval requirements when building a Forest.

The objects and properties that are stored in the global catalog are identical to the objects and properties in source partitions. When you update the value of an object in Active Directory, the object change operation is atomic—the update succeeds or fails based on the success or failure to update both the partition and the global catalog. Objects and properties that are replicated to the global catalog inherit the same permissions as in source partitions. This ensures that data in the global catalog is secure. In today's networks, security is a growing concern. Fortunately, Windows 2000 and Active Directory were built with this in mind.

Security

The cornerstone of Windows 2000 security is Active Directory. Its support for granular access control, inheritance, and delegation of administrative tasks gives you the flexibility to secure resources without compromising your network's purpose. Fine-grained access control is not offered in NT 3.x or 4.0. This often forces you to assign permissions that give either too little or too much control. Although Active Directory should be a significant piece of your Windows 2000 security strategy, it cannot deliver complete enterprise security by itself. Windows 2000 networks include several key improvements to security that are provided by the following:

- Security Configuration Editor (SCE)
- Security Configuration Manager (SCM)

- Windows NT LAN Manager (NTLM)
- Kerberos
- Public Key Cryptography

Security Configuration Editor (SCE)

How do you configure security settings for the computers in your network? If you're like most NT administrators, it's not uncommon to have to move from User Manager to Explorer, and then to the command line to make even simple security changes. Unless you've configured the early release version of Security Configuration Editor for use in NT 4.0, you have no other option.

The Security Configuration Editor consolidates the management of Windows 2000 security settings in one easy-to-use interface. The values of each security parameter listed in this interface can be stored in a template file. When you view this template file, you see a Tree-like structure that is made of nodes, sub-nodes, and items—each containing attributes that represent an aspect of system security. You will find the following nodes in a Security Configuration Editor template:

- Account policies
- Local policies
- Event logs
- Restricted groups
- System services
- Registry
- File system
- Active Directory objects

The Security Configuration Editor makes configuring security a whole lot simpler. Consider the process in Windows NT 3.x or 4.0 to secure the Registry, event log, and file system. With the Security Configuration Editor, this is a simple task. You just navigate to each node, in one interface, and make the appropriate changes. No other tools are needed. The Security Configuration Editor is even more useful as an enterprise configuration management tool. We'll cover this topic at length in Chapter 10, "Creating a Security Plan."

Security Configuration Manager (SCM)

Once you've created a security template, you need some way to apply it to a computer. To make use of this template file, you must use the Security Configuration Manager. The Security Configuration Manager uses your template to configure and analyze the parameters it contains. To configure a particular computer, it processes each instruction in the template. This makes intricate and complex changes to system security simple.

The real benefit of the Security Configuration Manager is more evident when it is used to analyze security. You can use it to compare the security parameters of any Windows 2000 computer to settings stored in a template and report the differences. When a security item matches the baseline that is stored in your template, it is tagged with a green checkmark. Any red *X* that you see is a warning. These are shown next to items that don't match your template. As you can see, the Security Configuration Editor and Security Configuration Manager are quite powerful. Security-related tasks that once took several hours to complete now take just a few minutes.

Windows NT LAN Manager (NTLM)

Windows 2000 supports two core authentication protocols: Windows NT LAN Manager (NTLM) and Kerberos. Kerberos is now the preferred protocol for authentication. If you're running an NT 3.x–4.0 network, on the other hand, NTLM fulfills this vital role. It validates your access to shared resources. Because Windows 2000 supports NTLM and Kerberos, downlevel clients (such as Windows for Workgroups) can continue to use NTLM for authentication purposes.

Transparent support for multiple authentication protocols makes Windows 2000 extremely versatile. Because you can support NTLM and Kerberos simultaneously, you can implement a staged desktop migration to Windows 2000—you aren't forced to replace all downlevel operating systems if you upgrade your servers. When downlevel users authenticate to a native mode Windows 2000 domain controller, they gain a key benefit: transitive trusts. These trusts allow them access to every resource in your enterprise network (if these users have the appropriate permissions).

Kerberos

As you learned earlier, in Windows 2000 networks, Kerberos is the preferred authentication protocol. It has the following advantages over NTLM:

- It's a platform-independent, widely implemented security protocol (NTLM is still largely proprietary).
- It can establish sessions with other computers much faster than NTLM can.
- Its trust relationships are all transitive.
- It supports delegation of authentication.
- It's a shared-secret, identity-based protocol that uses symmetric (or secret) cryptography.

Session Establishment

One of the advantages Kerberos has over NTLM is that it can establish sessions with application servers much faster than NTLM can. An NTLM-based application server must validate your credentials with the help of a domain controller. Because this server is unable to confirm your credentials by itself, session establishment traffic must traverse your network. Upon arrival at your domain controller, it must contend for priority. In the Kerberos authentication process, contact with a separate entity is not required. A Kerberos-based application server can authenticate your credentials directly.

Transitive Trusts

The central component in Kerberos security is the *Key Distribution Center (KDC)*. Every KDC issues tickets. Your Kerberos clients use these tickets to access shared resources. The tickets that are issued by a KDC are valid in any domain. This is how Windows 2000 supports transitive trusts. Transitive (or *Kerberos*) trusts allow you to share resources with each domain in a Tree or Forest. Your Kerberos clients will always benefit from these trust relationships. However, your NTLM clients will not. These clients can take advantage of transitive trust relationships only in a native mode domain.

Keep in mind that downlevel servers have no awareness of transitive trusts. They support only NTLM (or one-way) trust relationships. In a mixed mode domain, changes to Active Directory can be replicated to downlevel domain controllers. In this arrangement, both Windows 2000 domain controllers and downlevel domain controllers have the authority to authenticate users. An NTLM user might contact a Windows 2000 domain controller for authentication one day, and a downlevel domain controller (that can't see transitive trusts) another day. If Microsoft allowed transitive trusts for NTLM clients in mixed mode domains, these clients would have inconsistent behavior—depending on the version of the domain controller that is contacted, the NTLM clients might or might not see transitive trusts.

Delegation of Authentication

The Kerberos protocol supports delegation of authentication, another key advantage over NTLM. This lets a server impersonate your identity to connect to other computers in your network. To do this, it obtains a session ticket from the KDC on your behalf. The server then uses this ticket to validate your access to another computer. Delegation of authentication is not supported by NTLM. An NTLM client must always authenticate directly with each computer. Delegation of authentication can greatly benefit multi-tiered applications. Kerberos clients aren't required to pass transactions from server to server. The first server that is contacted can simply impersonate the clients and work with each other tier directly.

Symmetric Cryptography

The Kerberos network authentication protocol is very well-known and widely accepted. It safeguards client-to-server authentication traffic with *symmetric* (or *secret*) cryptography, an improvement over its NT 3.x–4.0 predecessor, NTLM. In a symmetric cryptographic algorithm, a single key is used for encryption and decryption purposes.

Many other forms of cryptography use multiple keys. The next section discusses Public Key (PK) cryptography, which requires two keys: a public key and a private key (collectively called a *key pair*).

Public Key Cryptography

The universal property in all forms of public key cryptography is the use of a key pair. One of these keys is kept private; the other is made public. If you are a frequent user of the Internet, you'll immediately recognize the value of public key cryptography. The Web sites you visit that use ActiveX controls usually *sign* these controls. They do this with a public key technology known as a *digital signature*. (See the ActiveX control in Figure 1.5, which is signed with a digital signature.). When an ActiveX control or any other code is signed, its origin and authenticity are guaranteed by the publisher. A few steps illustrate this process:

1. The code is run through a one-way hash function. This function produces a unique, fixed-length piece of data (known as a *digest*).

2. The publisher encrypts this digest with its private key.

3. When you get the code, you decrypt the digest with the publisher's public key.

4. You verify that this key is valid by using the publisher's certificate (see Figure 1.6).

5. The same hash function run by the publisher to create the digest is used to create a second copy of the digest.

6. The original digest created by the publisher and the second digest are compared.

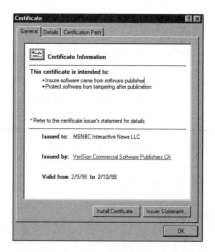

Figure 1.5   The MSNBC News Menu 3.0 ActiveX control is presumed safe to download because it is signed with a digital signature from VeriSign.

Figure 1.6   The digital certificate issued to MSNBC guarantees the origin and authenticity of the MSNBC News Menu 3.0 ActiveX control.

If the code you now have and the code used by the publisher to create the original digest are the same, the second digest will match the first. This guarantees that it is authentic—that it wasn't modified in any way since it was signed. The origin of the code is also known. The certificate guarantees that it came from this publisher. This guarantee is made by a trusted entity called a *certificate authority (CA)*. The following sections explain public key cryptography and certificates in more detail. These sections include the following:

- Microsoft Certificate Services
- Smart Cards
- IP Security
- Authentication of External Users
- Encrypting File System (EFS)

Microsoft Certificate Services

Windows 2000 includes the tools to build a robust, scalable, standards-based *public key infrastructure (PKI)*. To build your PKI, you can use Microsoft Certificate Services. Figure 1.7 shows the core components in the Microsoft PKI. To enable widespread use of public key cryptography, you must deploy one or more certificate authorities (CAs). Your CA is a service that lets you issue and manage certificates.

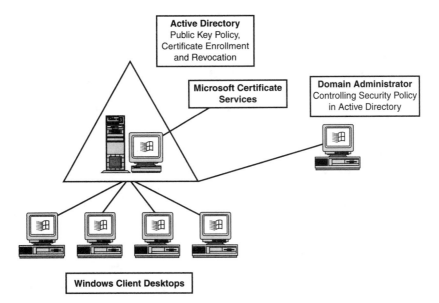

Figure 1.7   The Windows 2000 public key infrastructure can use Active Directory to issue and revoke certificates.

The publisher in Figure 1.7 is using a certificate to guarantee the origin and authenticity of its ActiveX control. This is one of the many ways to use certificates. They can also be used as user credentials. For example, if your intranet needs a higher level of security, you can use your CA to create a certificate. You can then only allow users who possess your certificate to enter.

Smart Cards

Smart cards are secure, physical media that store private user credentials, system passwords, and other sensitive information. Smart cards can store certificates issued by your CA to support logon (see Figure 1.8). Because of smart cards' tight integration with the Windows 2000 PKI, smart card users can start the secure attention sequence. This means that the insertion of a smart card has the same effect as pressing **Ctrl+Alt+Del**, except that instead of entering a username and password, a smart card user uses a certificate and PIN. Smart cards let you implement extremely tight security—you can block traditional logon for all smart card users. If the users don't have their cards, they can't log on. Of course, neither can anyone else. For more details on smart card use in Windows 2000, see Chapter 10.

IP Security

Another benefit of the Microsoft PKI is support for the Internet Engineering Task Force (IETF) IP Security standard. This standard outlines the framework for *secure networking*—the exchange of data on a public or private network using a cryptographic defense. Windows 2000 implements IP Security below the TCP/UDP transport layer in the OSI model. Because IP Security resides at such a low level (below the transport, session, presentation, and application layers) its use is transparent. No special training is required for IP Security users, and all applications can immediately benefit from its use.

However, by default, IP Security is disabled. To take advantage of its features, you must configure policy in Active Directory. The policy you set in Active Directory will define the behavior for IP Security. One of the parameters that you can set in policy for IP Security is dependent on your PKI. IP Security can use a certificate to authenticate the trust between two hosts. You can create this certificate with your own CA. To secure host-to-host communications, IP Security uses industry-standard hash functions, as well as public and symmetric key cryptography. For more details on how to use IP Security, see Chapter 10.

Smart Card Use in Windows 2000

Smart card use in Windows 2000 is permitted when following specifications formed by the Personal Computer Smart Card (PC/SC) Workgroup—a consortium of leading smart card and PC companies. The PC/SC was formed to further the development of smart card functionality for use in the PC industry. Members of the PC/SC, including Microsoft, Hewlett Packard, Gemplus, Sun Microsystems, and Schlumberger, based their implementation on International Standards Organization (ISO) 7816 standards. To use smart cards in Windows 2000, compliance with ISO standards 7816-1, 7816-2, and 7816-3 is required.

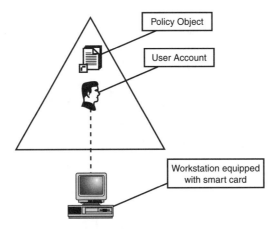

Figure 1.8 Policy stored in Active Directory controls whether or not smart card logon is allowed.

Authentication of External Users

The Microsoft PKI can also help you to securely authenticate external users. You can accomplish this by controlling access to internal resources with a certificate from your CA. You permit this kind of access by mapping the subject name of a certificate to an account in Active Directory. This flexibility can make your relationships with temporary employees or vendors much easier to manage. An account can be associated with more than one certificate, simplifying the administration and management of access control for external users.

Encrypting File System (EFS)

You can also implement a recovery policy for the Encrypting File System (EFS) with your PKI. EFS enables security-conscious organizations to use file and directory level-encryption for added privacy. Unlike other third-party solutions, EFS works transparently, encrypting and decrypting files during normal read and write operations. Your applications use encrypted and unencrypted files the same way. In day-to-day use, you will see no visible difference between encrypted and decrypted files.

Two sets of keys are used to implement an EFS recovery policy: a *user* key pair (generated locally), and a key pair that is issued by your CA (*recovery* key pair). A random key called a *File Encryption Key* (FEK) is used to encrypt each file. Two FEKs are created for every encrypted file. One FEK is created with the user's public key, and the other is created with the recovery public key.

Users' private keys can decrypt FEKs created with their public keys. The enterprise-wide recovery private key cannot decrypt the users' FEK. It can only decrypt a FEK created with its public key. Because either key can decrypt its own FEK, just one is needed to decrypt the file. Figure 1.9 illustrates this process.

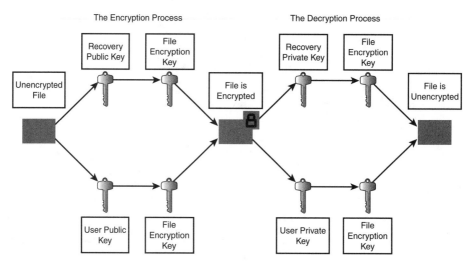

Figure 1.9   If a user loses his private key, an administrator can decrypt the user's files with the recovery private key. This keeps the user's keys confidential; they are not required to decrypt the file.

By implementing a well-planned PKI, you can take advantage of every PK technology in Windows 2000. How will you deploy the CAs in your enterprise to best suit your needs? What measures can you take to provide fault-tolerance for your PKI? How many CAs should you implement? These are a few of the questions that are answered in Chapter 10.

Storage

The Encrypting File System (EFS) would not be possible without extensions to NTFS. New Technology File System (NTFS) 5.0 is the foundation for several storage enhancements in Windows 2000. Sharing and managing your company's data is a top priority. You must gain complete control of storage to be a successful administrator. Further, your company's data must be available, reliable, and useful. The following improvements to network storage make Windows 2000 the logical choice for next-generation networks:

- Dynamic disks
- Disk quotas
- Remote Storage Service (RSS)
- Distributed File System (DFS)

Dynamic Disks

What happens when you run out of disk space? You probably delete unused files, compress a drive or two, or route your users to a different server. This is a temporary fix; when your users are gone for the day, you can down the server and add more disk space. What if you could add space to your server without taking it offline, and expand the size of the volume without enduser interruption? You can complete each of these tasks in Windows 2000 using *dynamic disks*. Dynamic disks have no partitions or logical drives. They are organized in volumes. *Dynamic volumes* can be expanded while your server is online. This allows you add disk space as needed. These disks and volumes also support moving from one computer to another. If your server suffers a hardware failure, you can move its disks to another system to bring them online.

Disk Quotas

You can implement more proactive disk space management practices than offered by dynamic disks with native disk quotas. With *disk quotas*, you set quota limits and thresholds to control users' disk space. With this level of control, you can prevent common storage problems (such as running out of space) before they happen.

Windows 2000 calculates quota limits and thresholds by file ownership. These calculations are made on a per-user per-volume basis. The *quota limit* defines the maximum value of space allocated to a user. When this limit is reached, one of two actions occurs—either an entry is made in the event log, or write operations are halted. Halting write operations is the most restrictive of these options. You'll want to use this in situations where disk space is limited. If you just need to monitor disk space, you can configure quota limits to record violations in the event log. However, this option allows users to exceed their quota limits. It is best used for reporting purposes only.

Like a quota limit, a *quota threshold* has a maximum value. When a threshold is met, a warning is listed with the user's quota entries and written to your event log. By using limits and thresholds effectively, you can increase your ability to anticipate and resolve disk space issues.

Remote Storage Service (RSS)

Reparse points, another Windows 2000 innovation, make low-level disk space management possible. They allow a piece of code to execute when a file or directory is accessed. This code and its control information are stored in a reparse attribute. Reparse points are the underpinnings for *Remote Storage Service (RSS)*, which moves infrequently used files to nearline storage devices. When RSS moves a file, it writes its new location to the reparse attribute. A file migrated by RSS looks like any other file.

When a user lists a directory moved by RSS, its files appear available. When one of these files is accessed, the RSS file system filter brings it back from the nearline storage device. A delay in access is the only drawback. This delay is proportional to the size of the file and limited by the speed of your nearline device. With RSS, you can provide your company with turnkey disk management.

Distributed File System (DFS)

So far, we've been discussing several key improvements to storage management. Early in this section, we mentioned that sharing your company's data effectively should be a top priority. To improve data sharing, Windows 2000 includes a new version of the Distributed File System (DFS). This release includes improvements made possible by Active Directory. The first version of DFS was released for Windows NT 4.0. It solved the following problems:

- Large NT shops have more shares than their clients have drive letters.
- Shares are not usually organized in a meaningful way to users.
- Shares offer no fault-tolerance or load balancing.

The NT 4.0 and Windows 2000 versions of DFS are used to create a logical view of your shared resources. Your users can connect these resources through a DFS root using a single drive letter. DFS roots can contain multiple child nodes that represent shared resources from different physical locations. This presents users with a meaningful, familiar, directory-like view of resources organized in a single namespace. A DFS root is accessed using its Universal Naming Convention (UNC) name, as shown in the following example:

```
NET USE * \\Server Name\DFS Root Name
```

A child node in DFS can be replicated to more than one server. Child nodes are often replicated to offer fault-tolerance and load balancing for the data they contain. The NT 4.0 version of DFS has two main limitations. If the server hosting the DFS root goes down, your users will have no mapping to its resources. Further, if multiple replicas are configured for a child node, nothing guarantees which replica will be used. This could send your users to a replica located across a slow WAN link.

In Windows 2000, DFS addresses these flaws with root replication and child-node selection based on site membership. A fault-tolerant DFS root can replicate its topology to more than one server. This version of DFS is domain specific: its UNC name is a domain name. If one server becomes unavailable, your users are directed to another.

The replication vehicle for the DFS topology is Active Directory. Active Directory provides replication services for DFS using the schedule defined by your sites. When you configure multiple child node replicas, your DFS users will choose a replica in the same site. Your site configuration guarantees that child node replicas are effective for fault-tolerance and load balancing.

If you didn't use DFS in NT 4.0, don't make the same mistake twice. DFS provides faster, more reliable, meaningful data sharing—something everyone can benefit from. Innovations to Windows 2000 storage dramatically change how you share and manage data. You can implement Windows 2000 without leveraging some of these benefits, but with them, your infrastructure will be much more stable, usable, and meaningful.

Networking

Storage innovations give you improved tools to manage and share resources. The improvements to networking in Windows 2000 are equally groundbreaking. For example, you have the opportunity in Windows 2000 to remove all NetBIOS traffic from your network. The Dynamic Domain Name System (DDNS) can entirely eliminate your dependence on NetBIOS and WINS. Also, you can now build more secure Virtual Private Networks (VPNs) that leverage PK cryptography. Further, support for Quality of Service (QoS)—a policy-based bandwidth management technology—is added. Some of the topics covered in this section are new in Windows 2000; others represent improvements to existing technologies. These additions and improvements include the following:

- NetBIOS name resolution
- Dynamic Domain Name System (DDNS)
- Windows Internet Name Service (WINS)
- Dynamic Host Configuration Protocol (DHCP)
- Quality of Service (QoS)
- Protocol support

NetBIOS Name Resolution

Downlevel (NT 3.x–4.0) Microsoft networks use NetBIOS names to identify and locate resources. In Windows 2000, you can eliminate all NetBIOS traffic. To make this transition, use Dynamic DNS (DDNS)—a DNS server that supports dynamic update. However, before examining DDNS in detail, take a moment to review the fundamentals of NetBIOS name resolution.

Using LMHOSTS to Resolve NetBIOS Names

On pure NetBIOS networks, name resolution is broadcast-based and inefficient. To resolve a name to a TCP/IP address, you send a broadcast to the local subnet. Most of today's routers block these broadcasts, limiting your view of resources. To view resources on routed networks, you can use LMHOSTS files. *LMHOSTS* allows you to resolve NetBIOS names by referencing its local entries. This solution may be sufficient for you if you use static TCP/IP addresses; however, if you use dynamic addresses, LMHOSTS files will quickly become unmanageable. They will require a change each time a computer gets an updated TCP/IP address. To address this shortcoming, Microsoft introduced the Windows Internet Name Service (WINS) in NT 3.5.

Using WINS to Resolve NetBIOS Names

The *Windows Internet Name Service (WINS)* is a distributed database that stores NetBIOS name-to-IP address mappings. The Microsoft WINS server is compliant with the definition of a NetBIOS Name Server as outlined in RFCs 1001 and 1002. WINS supports *dynamic name registration*, which means that each time a WINS-enabled client is started, it updates the server with its current TCP/IP address. Because clients update the WINS database periodically, dynamic TCP/IP addresses are easier to support.

Microsoft addressed many of the limitations in NetBIOS networks with WINS. Unfortunately, WINS and other NetBIOS name servers are not widely accepted. The Domain Name System (DNS) is the accepted name resolution service in mainstream heterogeneous networks. This is illustrated best by considering the Internet: Its basis for name resolution is DNS.

One of the reasons Microsoft chose WINS over DNS was for dynamic name registration support. Dynamic name registration is critical to networks that rely on dynamic TCP/IP addresses. Because the records in downlevel DNS servers are static, dynamic registration is not supported. The core DNS specifications are defined in RFCs 974, 1034, and 1035.

Dynamic Domain Name System (DDNS)

A recent DNS standard defined in RFC 2136 outlines rules that allow DNS to update its records dynamically. This new standard is known as *dynamic update*. The DDNS Server included with Windows 2000 supports this standard. To support downlevel users, Windows 2000 computers can register two name types: a NetBIOS name and a DDNS name. This makes implementing Windows 2000 much easier in mixed environments. However, your long-term goal should be to remove NetBIOS from your network entirely—DDNS is much more efficient (see Chapter 5, "Removing NetBIOS," for more details). In the meantime, your downlevel users can continue to use WINS. The implications of DDNS are covered at length in Chapter 7, "Planning a Dynamic DNS Structure."

Windows Internet Name Service (WINS)

A WINS server stores a database of NetBIOS name-to-IP address mappings. WINS provides a solution to the problems that NetBIOS has in routed networks. In addition, it significantly reduces NetBIOS broadcast traffic. DDNS will help Windows 2000 users find domain controllers, but downlevel users will still need WINS. These users have no awareness of DDNS or Active Directory. WINS will be around until all downlevel clients are removed from your network. Expecting this, Microsoft includes the following new features in the Windows 2000 WINS server:

- You can tombstone WINS records on one server, and they will be marked for deletion in all others.

- WINS servers now maintain persistent connections with their partners. This speeds up replication and eliminates the burden of opening and closing connections.

- Records in WINS can be checked for consistency. This alerts you to any discrepancies between one or more WINS servers.

- You can search your WINS database for records matching a string or a NetBIOS name type.

- WINS now supports re-registration. This lets clients register records in WINS without rebooting.

- The WINS Manager console is now multithreaded.

- WINS records can be exported from the database to a comma-separated text file.

Don't think of these improvements as a reason to delay your migration to DDNS. DDNS offers the best solution to name resolution in Windows 2000 networks.

Dynamic Host Configuration Protocol (DHCP)

WINS is essential in networks supporting downlevel clients. The Windows 2000 Dynamic Host Configuration Protocol (DHCP) server also plays a role. You can use DHCP to support dynamic TCP/IP addressing. With DHCP, your users get leased TCP/IP addresses from a central authority. This greatly simplifies day-to-day IP address management. A series of exchanges in RFCs 2131 and 2141 detail the DHCP standard.

The Windows 2000 DHCP server can update DDNS with the address of any downlevel client. If this client is using WINS, a record is also to the WINS database. This lets you find resources with NetBIOS names or DDNS names. You can also configure DDNS for WINS lookup to forward unsuccessful DDNS queries to WINS. In addition to downlevel support, the new DHCP server offers several enhancements:

- It is now cluster-aware. Scopes can be instantiated on one cluster member if the other goes down.

- Static address entries can be stored in Active Directory. This offers a level of fault tolerance and quick recovery.

- It includes Rogue DHCP server detection support. DHCP servers must be authorized in Active Directory to offer their services.

- It can now supply multicast addresses to clients or to applications.

- RFC 2132 vendor classes are supported. This permits a custom IP configuration to be associated with a vendor class.

- DHCP now supports user classes. These are similar to vendor classes. For example, you can configure a user class for laptop users. This might give laptop users a shorter lease on their IP address.

DHCP is a good example of a protocol standard that simplifies administration. Instead of walking from desktop to desktop, reconfiguring TCP/IP addresses whenever a change is needed, you can use a centrally managed DHCP server.

Quality of Service (QoS)

Like DHCP, Quality of Service (QoS) technology benefits day-to-day administration. Whereas DHCP solves TCP/IP configuration management issues, QoS resolves a more critical administrative problem: network bandwidth allocation and availability. With the advent of applications such as real-time audio/video, IP telephony, and conferencing comes the need to better manage and prioritize network traffic. For example, the applications that run your business should have a higher priority than those that don't. No single user should be able to squander a significant percentage of your network resources. The QoS technology in Windows 2000 helps you accomplish the following:

- Allocate network resources differently for high- and low-priority traffic.

- Limit the amount of traffic for any user or group on a certain subnet during a specific time period.

- Guarantee resources for a particular user.

- Deploy QoS-enabled applications, which provide their requirements to Admission Control Services (ACS).

- Implement traffic control for applications that are unable to do so on their own.

The central component in QoS is *Admission Control Services (ACS)*. ACS is based on the IETF Subnet Bandwidth Management (SBM) platform. ACS adds support for QoS policy stored in Active Directory. Because QoS technology is central to network reliability, this topic is covered in detail in Chapter 8, "Forming TCP/IP Standards."

Protocol Support

If you're building a mixed environment, support for multiple network protocols is always essential. Any network operating system (NOS) that uses proprietary protocols or services has limited use. Like its predecessors, Windows 2000 includes broad protocol support. These supported core protocols include the following:

- TCP/IP
- NWLink
- AppleTalk
- DLC
- NetBEUI

With extensive support for industry-standard core network protocols, Windows 2000 provides transparent connectivity with leading platforms. It can share resources and/or applications with Novell NetWare, Apple Macintosh, UNIX, LAN Manager, OS/2, and IBM mainframes.

Added in Windows 2000 is support for the *Layer 2 Tunneling Protocol (L2TP)*. (Although it is not a core network protocol, L2TP is a replacement for Point to Point Tunneling Protocol [PPTP].) LT2P is an industry-standard Internet protocol used to build Virtual Private Networks (VPNs). Like PPTP, L2TP is used to build secure tunnels across internetworks. To ensure confidentiality and data protection, L2TP can leverage public key certificates and IP Security. This provides you with the tools to build secure VPNs that traverse public networks (such as the Internet).

Another innovation in Windows 2000 is support for *Asynchronous Transfer Mode (ATM)* transmission services. ATM is a technology that packetizes data, voice, and video simultaneously over high-bandwidth circuits. ATM hardware and software form an architecture based on switching and forwarding small fixed-length units of data called *cells*. These cells are exactly 53 bytes in length. As a result, the process of directing and managing traffic is simplified. ATM permits transmission speeds ranging from 25Mbps (megabits per second) to 4.8Gbps (gigabits per second). With ATM, you can easily support the demanding requirements of next-generation applications.

Enterprise Management

Along with its advances in directory management, security, public key cryptography, storage, and networking, Windows 2000 includes improvements in enterprise management. Total Cost of Ownership (TCO) is a leading concern shared by many companies. After you deploy a particular technology, a TCO study will consider the cost of maintaining (or owning) it. In corporate networks, most TCO efforts are aimed at reducing the expense of managing desktops. Windows 2000 includes several new enterprise management tools to help you lower desktop TCO:

- IntelliMirror
- Remote Installation (RI) Service
- Group Policy

IntelliMirror

You can use IntelliMirror to reduce day-to-day desktop management costs. To leverage all of its benefits, Windows 2000 is a requirement for both servers and desktops. IntelliMirror consists of three core technologies:

- User Document Management
- User Settings Management
- Software Installation

User Document Management

User Document Management provides two services: user data mirroring and client-side caching. When you configure a roaming profile for a Windows 2000 user, that user's My Documents folder is mirrored to the network. This is similar to profile behavior in NT 4.0. There are two key differences between Windows 2000 profiles and downlevel profiles. First, with Windows 2000 profiles you can specify any location to mirror your users' My Documents folders. This location can be on any server, and can be separate from the profile itself. Second, with Windows 2000 profiles you can add new files and folders to the mirror list. This gives you the flexibility to make all critical documents available to your roaming users.

To take advantage of client-side caching you must use offline folders. An *offline folder* is a network share that is cached locally. When the network is not available, your users can continue to work on files that have been previously cached. After your users connect to the network, their cached files are automatically synchronized. Any new files replace old ones. Several choices are available when configuring offline folders on the server. You can specify any of the following:

- Documents are automatically cached.
- Programs are automatically cached.
- Document or program caching must be configured manually.
- Caching of documents and programs is not allowed.

When you create a new shared folder, caching is allowed by default. This lets your users manually cache its contents. If you want folder caching to be automatic for your user, you must establish this at the shared folder.

User Settings Management

User Settings Management is another IntelliMirror technology. It helps you maintain standard desktop configurations for your networked users. Windows 2000 user settings are similar to policies in NT 4.0. In Windows 2000, these settings define behavior for the following:

- Control Panel
- Desktop
- Folder redirection
- Network
- Printers
- Scripts
- Security settings
- Software installation
- Start menu and taskbar
- System
- Windows components

Most user settings are restrictive. For example, you can prevent users from changing share-caching behavior, or from running the Registry Editor. Windows 2000 user settings are applied at logon and are mirrored to the network. Because these settings are mirrored, they follow roaming users to any desktop. This helps you provide a consistent computing environment for roaming users.

Software Installation

Software Installation, another key IntelliMirror technology, cuts the cost of installing and maintaining corporate applications. It lets you assign and publish applications to Windows 2000 users using Active Directory. Applications that are assigned are automatically installed for users during logon. Assignments are used to distribute mandatory applications. Optional applications can be published. Rather than automatically installing, a published application will appear in a user's Add/Remove Programs applet. You can also configure a published application to install based on document activation. This will be useful, for example, when your users open a file without an appropriate viewer installed. Windows 2000 Software Installation also supports upgrade and uninstall capabilities. With these features, you can require clients to upgrade older packages or uninstall those that are outdated, all automatically.

Each component in IntelliMirror helps to reduce desktop management costs. To take advantage of all of these technologies, you need Windows 2000 on the server and on the desktop. The container for all IntelliMirror settings is Active Directory. It's important to consider how you use this technology to understand its effect on your network. To make this clear, we'll discuss IntelliMirror again in Chapter 11, "Simplifying Administration."

Remote Installation (RI) Service

Another addition to Windows 2000 aimed at reducing TCO is the *Remote Installation (RI) service*. The RI service helps you reduce the cost of deploying operating systems. During installation, the RI service asks for the location of any operating system installation files. It then copies these files from the source, such as a CD-ROM, to a location on the RI server. These files can then be used for client installations. After a successful copy of these files to the RI server, your installation routine is given a name and description.

The Windows 2000 RI service is a *boot server*. This is a server that responds to client requests for boot images. The RI service will work with clients supporting Pre-Boot Execution Environment (PXE) architecture. Some non-compliant systems can emulate a PXE client using a boot disk. Either way, when the PXE client boots, it gets two TCP/IP addresses from DHCP: one for itself, and another indicating its boot server. To download the boot image, the client uses Trivial File Transfer Protocol (TFTP).

When started for the first time, a PXE client will see a welcome screen, which can be customized based on the environment. This welcome screen is a good place for you to provide any additional installation instructions. The PXE client must then log on. After authenticating to Active Directory, an installation menu called *OSChooser* is shown to the user. This menu is customized by the RI service after evaluating which options the user should have access to based on their permissions. A user with full permissions will see four options:

- Automatically setup this computer
- Customize the setup of this computer
- Restart a previous setup attempt
- Maintenance and troubleshooting tools

If this user selects **Automatically setup this computer**, she will see the name and description of any operating system installations you've made available. You can offer multiple installation choices based on the same set of source files. To do this, you configure several unattended installation scripts, each meeting separate requirements. You can then associate a meaningful name with these scripts, such as Windows 2000 Setup for Human Resources.

After the user selects an option from the menu, installation of the operating system proceeds automatically. The machine name and computer account location is generated by the RI service. They are based on the installer's user name and RI service settings. To set up a computer for another user, you select **Customize the setup of this computer**. This gives you more control over the installation process. If the installation fails, choose **Restart a previous setup attempt**. The final option, Maintenance and troubleshooting tools, is extensible by ISVs and OEMs. To make this menu choice useful, they will provide tools to troubleshoot and update client computers. By con-figuring the RI service for helpdesk personnel and savvy users, you significantly reduce the cost of installing operating systems.

Group Policy

Throughout this chapter, you've learned that computers get *policy* from Active Directory. To configure this policy, you must use the Group Policy editor. Each policy you create is stored in a Group Policy Object (GPO). GPOs can be associated with sites, domains, and organizational units (OUs). Many of the topics we've covered in this chapter need Group Policy to define their behavior. These include the following:

- Microsoft Certificate Services
- IP Security
- Encrypting File System
- Quality of Service

- User Document Management
- User Settings Management
- Software Installation

The way you configure and manage Group Policy will impact every user in your network. You should determine this impact up front to make informed design and implementation decisions. Because GPOs are inherited and cumulative, Active Directory and Group Policy have a direct relationship. The details of Group Policy design are discussed in Chapter 11.

2

Restructuring Downlevel Domains

Restructuring your Windows NT 3.x–4.0 domains can be challenging. The process will involve moving applications and services from one domain to another, combining two domains into one, or combining multiple domains. In your transition to Windows 2000, you may decide to restructure domains for several reasons. Most often, your motivation will be to simplify the transition from old to new.

In this chapter, you will examine the different types of downlevel (NT 3.x–4.0) domains and the reasons companies create them. You will then study the ideal downlevel domain model. This is a domain model that will best position you for your transition to Windows 2000. You may need to restructure some of your existing domains to conform to this model. With the help of this chapter, you will be able to determine what the scope of your restructuring efforts should be, if any are necessary.

You will then address when you should begin this process. Some domain reorganization tasks should be executed prior to implementing Windows 2000; others should be executed after your transition. Then you will take an in-depth look at the details you need to understand to successfully make your changes. Tools you can use to more easily complete this process are then covered at length.

Finally, you'll learn about each of your options in detail. You'll get step-by-step instructions to help you complete this challenging but rewarding process. The contents of this chapter are aimed at companies transitioning to Windows 2000. However, simplifying the Windows 2000 transition process is not its only use. Consider what must happen when two companies with established domain models merge. They will most likely be forced to combine two or more of their existing domains. Any company that must reorganize their domains can use this chapter to guide them.

Typical Downlevel Domain Models

In Windows NT 3.x–4.0 networks, we create multiple domains to meet varying requirements. Most often, our additional domains are created to delegate administrative tasks. In much larger networks, we also create multiple domains to comply with limits of the Security Accounts Manager (SAM) database. In Windows 2000, our criterion for creating multiple domains changes dramatically. As a step in your transition from Windows NT to Windows 2000, you should evaluate your company's current domain model. In the sections that follow, we will take a look at some of the common domain models used in downlevel networks, which will illustrate where and when multiple domains are typically used. We will then close this section by examining the ideal domain model.

The Single Master Domain Model

The *single master domain model* is widely implemented. This domain model consists of two domain types. One of these is the *master user domain*, a domain created to house and maintain a company's user accounts. The second type of domain in the single master domain model is the *resource domain*. Resource domains are used to house resources that are often managed by a separate set of administrators. In the single master domain model, resource domains must trust the master user domain. This domain model can accommodate many resource domains; however, just one master user domain is allowed.

The single master domain model is often used to delegate administrative tasks. Consider the domain structure shown in Figure 2.1. The master user domain contains all of the company's user accounts, and each resource domain contains the company's distributed resources. These are the resources you would commonly find on a company's servers, including file shares, printers, and various applications. The number of resource domains used in the single master domain model varies. This number is defined by a company's administrative requirements. For example, a resource domain is often created for each set of a company's administrators. This gives each group of administrators control over their local applications and services—the resources—in their resource domains. These administrators are often best prepared to manage these resources because they are physically closest to them.

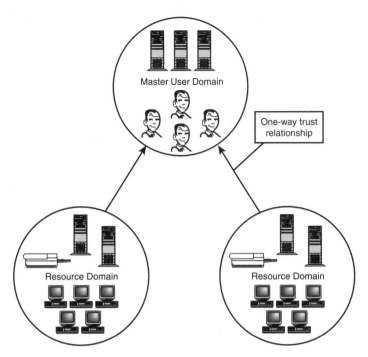

Figure 2.1   The single master domain model is the most popular because it mirrors the way most companies are arranged.

The number of domains created in the single master domain model is driven by the number of distinct administrative boundaries in an organization. However, the number of domains created in the multi master domain model is driven by additional factors.

The Multiple Master Domain Model

Like the single master domain model, the *multi master domain model* forms an administrative hierarchy. The resource domains that are created in a multi master domain model serve the same purpose as resource domains in the single master domain model. They are most often created to delegate administrative tasks. The only difference between the single and multi master domain models is the number of master user domains they permit.

The Single Domain Model

You may have noticed that this chapter doesn't cover the single domain model. That's because this domain model permits only a single domain. An organization that has just one domain has no need for restructuring in preparation for Windows 2000.

Think of the multi master domain model as a large single master domain model. The number of master user domains used in the multi master domain model is driven by recommended limits of the SAM database. The SAM should never be larger than 40MB. Several master user domains can be created to divide the excessive size of a company's SAM. Any company with a large number of users, groups, and computers will have a large SAM. The following objects determine the overall size of the SAM:

- User accounts require 1,024 bytes (1KB) each.

- Computer accounts require 512 bytes (0.5KB) each.

- Global group accounts require 512 bytes (0.5KB), plus 12 bytes per member.

- Local group accounts require 512 bytes (0.5KB), plus 36 bytes per member.

As you can see, companies with between 20,000 and 40,000 users can often reach this limit. This number varies from one company to another, depending on how user, group, and computer accounts are used.

The multi master domain model is shown in Figure 2.2. This example shows two master user domains and four resource domains. This particular configuration can support between 40,000 and 80,000 users. Note that the multi master domain model permits more than two master user domains. Each master user domain stores a portion of the company's user and group accounts. Like in the single master domain model, resource domains in the multi master domain model are often used to delegate administrative tasks.

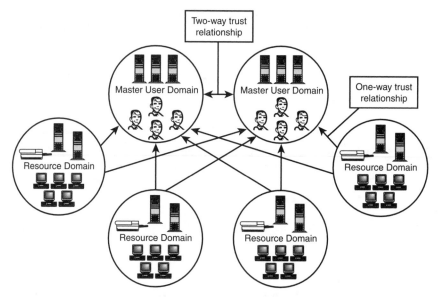

Figure 2.2   In the multi master domain model, the master user domain contains the company's user accounts, and one or more resource domains contain resources such as servers, workstations, and printers.

The biggest difference between the single and multi master domain models is where they are typically used. The multi master domain model is most often used in relatively large companies, with many users, computers, and groups. The single master domain model is more common in small- and medium-sized organizations. You may see the multi master domain model implemented for another valid reason. When two companies using single master domain models merge, often the simplest way to combine them is by forming a multi master domain model. This can be set up in a relatively short time frame by creating additional trust relationships between the existing domains.

While the multi master and single master domain models are common, the complete trust domain model, which is discussed in the next section, is not.

The Complete Trust Domain Model

The complete trust domain model has few benefits. Single master and multi master domain models form distinct administrative hierarchies. The greatest level of administrative control in these two domain models is at the top of these hierarchies, in the master user domains. The complete trust domain model has no such hierarchy. Consider the domains shown in Figure 2.3. Each domain in the complete trust model is a peer, and all are configured with two-way trusts between them. This model forms a web of trust relationships that is both difficult to control and manage. User accounts are created in each independent domain, and all domains contain both users and resources.

This domain model exists to support organizations that require completely decentralized administration. This would be an organization, for example, with no central IT department. The company's IT staff would most likely exist in each different location. The only reason trust relationships are established between independent domains in the complete trust model is to support resource sharing. What makes the complete trust model uncommon is its unique set of requirements. Organizations that must share resources across many independent domains are usually large enough to centralize IT services. Nevertheless, meeting the unique requirements of the complete trust model is another reason that companies create multiple domains.

The Ideal Domain Model

You've looked at the typical downlevel domain models and the common reasons for companies to create multiple domains, but you haven't yet discovered the ideal domain model. If you've read much about Windows 2000, you may be aware of Microsoft's recommendation for this. In a white paper titled "Planning Windows NT Server 4.0 Deployment with Windows NT Server 5.0 in Mind," Microsoft makes the case for fewer and larger domains. Simply put, Microsoft states that fewer domains created means fewer domains to migrate. Using fewer, larger domains is a key element in what is defined as the ideal domain model. But it is certainly not the only element.

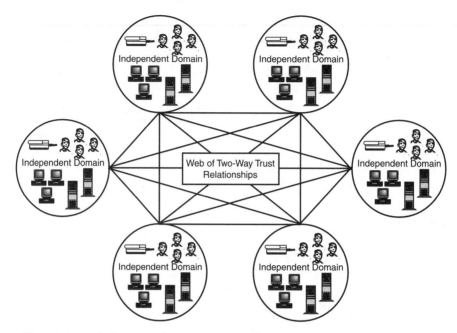

Figure 2.3 Each domain in the complete trust domain model houses autonomous users, groups, computers, and administrators.

An ideal domain model is one that mirrors your design for Active Directory. This domain model will upgrade to the domains defined in your Active Directory design without a hitch. Suppose your Active Directory design calls for two domains to support international differences. If you currently have three domains, this is not ideal. For part of your transition to Windows 2000, you must consider eliminating the extra domain. The simplest upgrade path to an Active Directory with two domains is from a downlevel domain model of two domains.

Every NT 3.x–4.0 domain model can technically be upgraded to Windows 2000 and Active Directory. If your goal is to simply complete an upgrade, it doesn't matter what you do beforehand. Based on the limited scope of this goal, you'll be successful. If you design a simple upgrade procedure, however, you'll not give yourself the opportunity to make the most of Active Directory. Designing an upgrade procedure and designing a plan to transition to your vision and design for Active Directory are vastly different.

When you design your company's Active Directory, you should decide the position of sites, domains, organizational units, and other related components based on one purpose: to best meet your company's administrative, organizational, and technical needs. This may mean that your Active Directory design plan will contain fewer domains than defined in your existing domain model. To mirror your plans for Active

Directory and to make your transition much simpler, you might have to restructure your current domains. You'll examine the options you have for making this transition simpler in the section that follows.

You now know that an ideal domain model is one that mirrors your Active Directory design plan. At this stage in your transition to Windows 2000, however, you probably haven't had time to form this plan. The many details of your plans for Active Directory will only be clear to you after you perform a rigorous design process. To form your design plan for Active Directory, you must read Chapter 6, "Designing the Active Directory." Chapter 7, "Planning a Dynamic DNS Structure," will also be helpful. You must know where you're headed before you can create an effective plan to get there.

Understanding Your Restructuring Options

After designing your company's Active Directory, you should evaluate the pros and cons of your domain restructuring options. This chapter covers two options for restructuring your company's domains:

- Restructuring domains before your upgrade
- Restructuring domains after your upgrade

It may be best to combine your domains before your upgrade to Windows 2000. Combining two or more NT 3.x–4.0 domains beforehand is often more difficult than combining them afterwards. The benefit of this additional work, however, can often be worth the effort.

Combining domains after your Windows 2000 upgrade is the least difficult option. This strategy will be used to eliminate resource domains in the single and multi master domain models using the process detailed in Chapter 13, "Removing Resource Domains." In most cases, the only work required in the resource domains beforehand will be the task of moving applications and services from domain controllers to member servers. If you complete this work in advance, combining domains after your upgrade using the process in Chapter 13 will be less difficult.

To determine whether to combine domains before or after your Windows 2000 upgrade, you need to consider the number of domains you plan to eliminate and your available resources. For example, if you need to combine a large number of domains to mirror your design for Active Directory, you should consider combining some of them before your upgrade. However, you should carry out a large scale restructuring project only if you have the available resources. Some organizations will have resources available to combine domains before their upgrade, but others will only have resources afterward. Given that the start time for your restructuring efforts will rely heavily on your available resources, it is difficult for us to offer exact recommendations for how you should proceed.

However, you can use the following practical guidelines:

Restructuring Option	**When to Start**
Combining more than thirty percent of your existing domains	Before your Windows 2000 upgrade
Combining fewer than thirty percent of your existing domains	After your Windows 2000 upgrade

You will face some interesting challenges if you choose to combine domains before your upgrade. Perhaps the greatest hurdle to clear is with NT itself. Unlike Windows 2000, Windows NT includes no tools that allow you to move objects from one domain to another. To move an object, such as a user or group, to another NT domain, you must use either utilities from the resource kit or a separate third-party tool. Combining several domains before your Windows 2000 upgrade will almost always be more difficult than combining them afterward. On the other hand, there is no magic formula that makes combining domains after your upgrade simple.

Restructuring Domains Before Your Upgrade

As stated previously, if you must get rid of more than thirty percent of your domains to mirror your Active Directory design plan, it may be best to combine some of them beforehand. Your transition to Windows 2000 will be complex even if you don't have to combine any existing domains. Some weighty issues that aren't directly related to combining domains may determine how and when you should proceed. For example, designing and implementing Active Directory and Dynamic DNS (DDNS) will require considerable effort and resources. Instead of adding the requirement of combining more than thirty percent of your current domains to a visibly complex transition process, you may be better off breaking these tasks into separate projects. This can make your Windows 2000 upgrade a whole lot simpler.

Before you decide to combine domains before your upgrade, consider the following issues:

- You should never combine domains if their united SAM databases will be greater than 40MB. 40MB is the recommended size limit of the SAM.

- When you combine one domain with another, you increase its SAM size. Even if the combined SAM of two or more domains is less than 40MB, you will increase SAM replication traffic in the domain. You must verify that your network can handle this added traffic.

- You may have certain domains that were created to delegate administrative tasks. If you eliminate these domains, you will break your company's current administrative model.

Some of these issues will force you to combine domains after your Windows 2000 upgrade. There is one issue, though, that you can likely overcome. As indicated, combining domains can cause you to break your company's administrative model. You may have created a resource domain in order to delegate certain tasks to a group of administrators. If you eliminate this resource domain by combining it with another, you'll no longer be able to delegate the same tasks. To delegate these tasks to your administrators, you were originally forced to create two separate domains. Windows NT 3.x–4.0 domains do not permit a granular level of access control. To mimic your original administrative model, you can use a third-party delegation tool. These products allow you to leverage a granular level of access control within Windows NT 3.x–4.0 domains.

If you are unprepared, combining domains before your upgrade can be a daunting task. To be successful in your restructuring effort, you must plan each step carefully. Here are the suggested steps for combining domains before your upgrade:

1. Migrating user accounts

2. Migrating global groups

3. Updating local group memberships

4. Updating permissions

5. Updating user rights

6. Migrating computer accounts

7. Moving domain controllers

8. Moving member servers

9. Moving workstations

This process is covered at length in the section "Combining Domains Before Your Upgrade." Combining domains with these steps requires careful planning and attention to detail. This additional work is often worth the reward, however, because combining domains can make your transition to Windows 2000 and Active Directory easier. The added work that is required to combine domains after your upgrade is also worthwhile.

Third-Party Delegation Tools

Many popular third-party delegation tools give your Windows NT 3.x–4.0 domains more administrative depth. Some of the more prevalent tools even have reporting capabilities. Third-party delegation tools will help you create simpler, flatter, and more flexible NT 3.x–4.0 networks. Some of these well-known tools include the following:

Enterprise Administrator from Mission Critical Software (www.missioncritical.com)

DM/Administrator from FastLane Technologies (www.fastlanetech.com)

Virtuosity Enterprise from Aelita Software (www.aelita.com)

Restructuring Domains After Your Upgrade

If you plan to combine several domains after your upgrade, you should consider moving applications and services from domain controllers to member servers in the domains you will eliminate. This approach works best if you eliminate fewer than thirty percent of your domains by combining them. It is always a good idea to move applications and services to member servers prior to your upgrade. If you don't take this necessary step, you can run into some very serious problems.

For example, consider the single master domain model shown in Figure 2.4. The master user domain, SMALLCORP, contains two servers, SCPDC and SCBDC. SCPDC is the SMALLCORP primary domain controller, and SCBDC is the SMALLCORP backup domain controller. The resource domain, FIELDDOM, contains three servers: FDPDC, FDBDC, and FDMEM. FDPDC is the FIELDDOM primary domain controller, FDBDC is the FIELDDOM backup domain controller, and FDMEM is the FIELDDOM member server. FDPDC is running WINS, DNS, and DFS services. FDBDC is running SQL Server. FDMEM is an Intranet server running IIS.

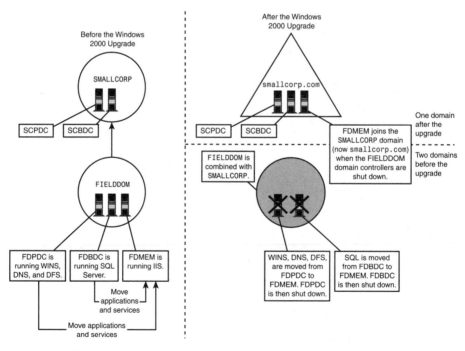

Figure 2.4 The FIELDDOM and SMALLCORP domains can be combined after the company upgrades to Windows 2000.

Suppose you plan to use the procedures in Chapter 13 to combine the FIELDDOM resource domain with SMALLCORP after your Windows 2000 upgrade. The final step in removing resource domains after an upgrade to Windows 2000 is to shut down domain controllers in the resource domain. This means that you must take FDPDC and FDBDC offline. The problem with taking these servers offline should be obvious. If you shut down FDPDC and FDBDC, you will lose critical applications and services, including WINS, DNS, DFS, and SQL Server. IIS will not be affected because it resides on your member server, which will simply join the SMALLCORP domain. This should make it very clear why moving applications and services from domain controllers to member servers before your upgrade is always the best choice. By moving these resources beforehand, you can avoid a would-be disaster.

The process for migrating any one of the thousands of applications and services that NT supports from a domain controller to a member server varies. In spite of this, there are some universal guidelines. The recommended process for migrating these resources is outlined here:

1. Design your migration plan.
2. Form your back out procedures.
3. Test your migration plan.
4. Execute your migration plan.
5. Perform acceptance testing.
6. Remove the source domain.

The challenges you face when combining domains after your upgrade are not easy to predict. Some applications and services are easier to move from domain controllers to member servers than others are. Each migration will present a unique challenge. Later on, you'll cover these steps in more detail.

You should now have an understanding of the options you have when preparing for Windows 2000, as well as a sense of the steps involved in combining domains both before and after your upgrade. Many of these steps are tough to complete without the right tools, and certain tools will definitely help you more than others.

Choosing the Right Tools for Combining Domains

You can use a number of tools to combine your existing domains. Some of these tools cost next to nothing, such as those in the Resource Kit, whereas others can be quite costly. To help you make an informed choice, this section will review two tool sets. You will first examine a number of utilities in the Resource Kit. Combining domains with these simple but affordable utilities is a manual process. After that, you will examine the Domain Reconfiguration Tool from FastLane Technologies. It is specifically designed to help you combine two or more NT 3.x–4.0 domains. Combining domains with most third-party consolidation tools is an automated process.

Resource Kit Utilities

As you might imagine, combining domains with Resource Kit utilities is not for the faint of heart. With the exception of the Security Migration Editor, all of these utilities run from the command line. Further, this motley collection of tools was not designed to help you combine domains. Nonetheless, these tools can work together to help you get the job done. In some companies, approving the purchase of a third-party domain consolidation tool will be easy. This is by far your best option and the easiest way to combine several domains. For those of you who aren't able to get your hands on one of these tools, combining domains with the Resource Kit is your best (and likely your only) option. This section covers the following Resource Kit utilities:

- ADDUSERS.EXE
- The SIDWalker Tools
- NTRIGHTS.EXE
- NETDOM.EXE
- SHUTDOWN.EXE

ADDUSERS.EXE

ADDUSERS.EXE is a command line user account administration tool included with the Windows NT 4.0 Server Resource Kit. Using a comma-delimited file as input, ADDUSERS.EXE can create, modify, and delete users, global groups, and local groups. ADDUSERS.EXE requires that each section in its comma-delimited input file have a heading. Each heading in this file defines the type of information that follows. These headings include User, Global, and Local. Coupled with the ability to create user and group accounts, ADDUSERS.EXE supports the dump accounts switch. This switch lets you create a comma-delimited file containing the users, global groups, and local groups in a particular domain. ADDUSERS.EXE supports the following syntax:

```
addusers [/?] [\\computername [/p] [[/c ¦ /d ¦ /e] filename]] [/s:?]

    /c    Create accounts specified in the file.
    /d    Write current accounts to the specified file.
    /p    When creating accounts, don't expire passwords.
    /e    Erase user accounts specified in the file.
    /s:?  Sets the separator character for the input/output file.  Replace
          ➥the ? with the character to be used for separating fields.
          ➥(eg /s:~)
          Note: The separator character is a comma ',' by default.
```

If you must combine domains manually, ADDUSERS.EXE will help you complete the following three steps:

1. Migrating user accounts

2. Migrating global groups

3. Updating local group memberships

The SIDWalker Tools

The SIDWalker Tools, included with the Windows 2000 Resource Kit, can help you migrate permissions from one domain to another. This task composes step four (updating permissions) in the process for combining your domains. The SIDWalker Tools consist of three separate utilities: SHOWACCS.EXE, the Security Migration Editor, and SIDWALK.EXE (affectionately called SIDWalker).

SHOWACCS.EXE

SHOWACCS.EXE is used to create a comma-delimited file known as the access-profile file. The access-profile file lists all the permissions for a computer's files, file shares, printers, local groups, and Registry. SHOWACCS.EXE also creates a mapping file, which lists the users and groups that appear in a particular computer's access control lists (ACLs). This file is used as input for the Security Migration Editor. SHOWACCS.EXE supports the following syntax:

```
showaccs <access profile file> [/f [<path>] /r /s /p /g /m <map file>
➥/nobuiltins]
<access profile file>  path of the .csv file to be generated
/f   [<path>]          for all NTFS files
/r                     for Registry
/s                     for File Shares
/p                     for Printer Shares
/g                     for local groups
/m                     generate a map file
<map file>             map file path for /m option
/nobuiltins            for no builtin groups
```

Security Migration Editor

The Security Migration Editor is an MMC snap-in that maps old users and groups in a mapping file created with SHOWACCS.EXE to new users and groups. Selecting several new user and group accounts in your target domain completes the mapping from any users and groups in your source domain. After the mapping is complete, the Security Migration Editor is used to update the mapping file so that it can be used as input for SIDWALK.EXE.

Third-Party Domain Consolidation Tools

You should evaluate several domain consolidation tools before choosing one. Some of the more popular consolidation tools include the following:

The Domain Reconfiguration Tool from FastLane Technologies (www.fastlanetech.com)

Enterprise Administrator with the Domain Consolidation Module from Mission Critical Software (www.missioncritical.com)

Virtuosity Enterprise with the Domain Migration Wizard from Aelita Software (www.aelita.com)

DirectManage and DirectScript from Entevo (www.entevo.com)

SIDWALK.EXE

SIDWALK.EXE uses the updated mapping file as input to either delete or replace the security identifiers (SIDs) on a particular computer. It is used to complete the final step in migrating permissions from one domain to another. SIDWALK.EXE supports the following syntax:

```
sidwalk <profile file> [<profile file> ..] [/t /f /r /s /p /g /l <file>]
<profile file>  path of the .csv file(s)
/t              test/dry run
/f              for all NTFS files
/r              for Registry
/s              for File Shares
/p              for Printer Shares
/g              for local groups
/l              generate a Converter log file
<file>          log file path for /l option
```

NTRIGHTS.EXE

NTRIGHTS.EXE is a utility in the Windows NT 4.0 Server Resource Kit that allows you to modify user rights from the command line. You can use NTRIGHTS.EXE to complete step 5, updating user rights. NTRIGHTS.EXE supports the following syntax:

```
ntrights +r¦-r <userright> -u <username> -m <machinename>
+r                    grant user right
-r                    revoke user right
<userright>           user right to grant or revoke
<username>            user name to grant or revoke user right
<machinename>         machine to grant or revoke rights on
```

NETDOM.EXE

NETDOM.EXE is another utility included in the Windows NT 4.0 Server Resource Kit. It lets you manage NT domains from the command line. You can use NETDOM.EXE to complete step 6 (migrating computer accounts) and a portion of step 9 (moving workstations). NETDOM.EXE supports the following syntax:

```
netdom [/d /u /p] [<command>]
/d:<domainname>       performs operation on <domainname> PDC
/u:<username>         user account to connect with
/p:<password>         user account password
<command>             [ BDC ¦ HELP ¦ MASTER ¦ MEMBER ¦ QUERY ¦ RESOURCE ]
```

SHUTDOWN.EXE

SHUTDOWN.EXE is yet another useful tool in the Windows NT 4.0 Server Resource Kit. It is an easy-to-use command line utility that lets you remotely shut down or reboot an NT computer. SHUTDOWN.EXE can be used with NETDOM.EXE to complete step 9 (moving workstations) in the process to combine domains. SHUTDOWN.EXE supports the following syntax:

```
shutdown [/?] [\\computer] [/l] [/a] [/r] [/t:xx] ["Msg"] [/Y] [/C]
```

```
\\computer      Specifies a remote computer to shutdown.
/l              Specifies a local shutdown.
/a              Aborts a system shutdown. This is only possible during the
                ➥timeout period.
                If this switch is used, all others are ignored.
/r              Specifies that the machine should reboot after shutdown.
/t:xx           Sets the timer for system shutdown in seconds [20 sec.
                ➥default].
"msg"           Specifies an additional message
/y              Answers all following questions with yes
/c              Forces running applications to close.
```

This should give you a good introduction to the tools you will use to combine domains manually. One of the easier ways to combine domains, however, is to use the Domain Reconfiguration Tool from FastLane.

The Domain Reconfiguration Tool

The Domain Reconfiguration Tool from FastLane Technologies offers many advantages over its command line competitors. For example, it keeps a log of all changes you make in a domain, allowing you to review your steps later for completeness and accuracy. It also allows you to reverse certain tasks when combining domains, such as migrating user and group accounts. Its ability to preserve passwords when combining domains will also be valuable. Most importantly, if you plan to use the Distributor, you can significantly shorten the time it takes to combine several domains. And by saving a little time, you may just be able to justify purchasing a third-party consolidation tool.

With the Domain Reconfiguration Tool, you can combine several domains using an automated, graphically driven process. Because this particular tool is widely known, this chapter covers its use in detail. However, there is not enough space in this chapter to cover each domain consolidation tool on the market.

The Domain Reconfiguration Tool consists of three core components:

- The Phoenix Application
- The Distributor
- The Phoenix Resource Kit

The Phoenix Application

The Phoenix application lets you migrate users, global groups, and computer accounts from one domain to another. It also allows you to update local groups in your source domain and to update file permissions and user rights on computers that move from your source domain to your target domain. The Phoenix application will help you complete the majority of the steps in the process to combine your domains. These include:

1. Migrating user accounts
2. Migrating global groups
3. Updating local group memberships
4. Updating permissions
5. Updating user rights
6. Migrating computer accounts

The Distributor

Perhaps the Distributor is the most valuable component. It lets you distribute the tasks that must be performed when you combine domains. Instead of running all the tasks to combine domains from a central location, the Distributor installs a secure scheduler on every computer. This scheduler lets each computer process its own resource updating tasks locally. The Distributor drastically reduces the amount of network bandwidth that is required to update resources when you combine domains. It can significantly reduce the time it takes you to complete the following steps: updating local group memberships (step 3), updating permissions (step 4), and updating user rights (step 5).

The Phoenix Resource Kit

The Phoenix Resource Kit includes several utilities to help you combine your domains. These utilities can be used in two phases of your project: pre-migration and post-migration.

The pre-migration toolkit consists of two utilities: AdminChecker and NTReporter. The AdminChecker utility saves you some time by verifying that you have adequate permissions to perform certain tasks. The NTReporter utility can be used to produce a detailed inventory of your NT network.

The post-migration toolkit can also be helpful when you combine domains. It consists of five utilities: DCMover, CompMover, CopyPassword, Profile Updater, and the Exchange Updater. The following list provides details on each of these utilities:

- **DCMover.** Allows you to automate moving domain controllers from one domain to another. This fairly unique utility can help you complete step 7 (moving domain controllers) in the process to combine domains.
- **CompMover.** Automates the task of moving computers from your source domain to your target domain. It is used in step 9, moving workstations.

- **CopyPassword.** Allows you to retain passwords from your source domain when creating accounts in your target domain.

- **Profile Updater.** Lets you update the NT profiles on computers to provide endusers with the same profiles they had as members of your source domain when you move them to your target domain.

- **Exchange Updater.** This utility performs an advanced function. It is not covered here because its use is beyond the scope of this chapter's subject material. (See `www.fastlanetech.com` for more details on the Exchange Updater.) You might look into using this tool if you need to update Exchange mailboxes after combining several domains.

Each of these utilities can be used in the process of combining domains before your upgrade. Now that you have an understanding of their function and capabilities, you're ready to examine that process more closely.

Combining Domains Before Your Upgrade

You should approach the process of combining domains with respect for its complexity. This process involves making significant changes to your existing environment, which includes modifying user and group accounts, file permissions, user rights, and more. Most of the components in the source and target domains you combine will be affected in this process. It is important to understand the impact of each step in this process before you start. The order in which you combine your domains is also important.

The method you use to combine two domains will be different from the method you use to combine more than two. Combining two of your existing domains is certainly much less challenging than combining several of them. To combine two domains, you will collapse the resources of a source domain into a target domain. For example, suppose that you administer the three domains shown in Figure 2.5: DOMAINA, DOMAINB, and DOMAINC. DOMAINA is your master user domain, and both DOMAINB and DOMAINC are resource domains. If your plan is to eliminate DOMAINB by combining it with DOMAINA, DOMAINB is your source domain, and DOMAINA is your target domain. Choosing the order in which to combine these two domains in is not difficult as there are only two domains.

Combining several domains (more than two, to be specific) is a little trickier. First, the more domains you combine, the greater the possibility of finding duplicate user and group accounts. When you combine more than two domains into one, you will probably have to rename a few more user and group accounts. Furthermore, the order in which to combine more than two domains is not clear cut. For example, suppose you still administer DOMAINA, DOMAINB, and DOMAINC, but instead of combining DOMAINA and DOMAINB, you decide to combine them all. You would like to combine the resources in all of these domains into DOMAINA, your master user domain. To combine these three domains, you can proceed in either of two ways:

- You can first combine DOMAINC with DOMAINB, and then finish by combining DOMAINB and DOMAINA. This is not the best method, however, because it is inefficient.

- You can eliminate a redundant step in the preceding example. When you combine more than two domains, you should combine each domain directly with its ultimate target. In this example, you should combine both DOMAINB and DOMAINC directly with DOMAINA.

Take some time in the early stages of this process to plan the order in which you will combine your domains. You can save a whole lot of time and effort by closely examining all of your options.

In the following sections, you will walk through step-by-step instructions for combining two or more domains. You will first see how to combine domains using utilities from the Resource Kit. After that, you will look at the steps for combining domains with the Domain Reconfiguration Tool. Whether you use the Resource Kit or the Domain Reconfiguration Tool, the steps in this process must be completed sequentially. If you perform these steps in no particular order, several steps in this process will fail.

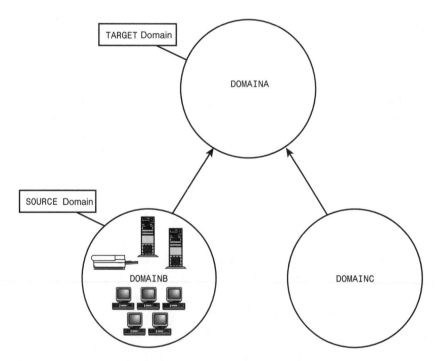

Figure 2.5 Resources in DOMAINB, including servers, workstations, and printers, will move to DOMAINA when they are combined.

Using the Resource Kit

Combining domains with Resource Kit utilities is workable, but challenging. Most of the steps in this process must be executed from the command line. No logs are generated, no status is reported, and no check is performed before you carry out a step to verify that every prerequisite step is complete. In addition, several of the steps in this process are extremely resource intensive. For example, when you update the file permissions on a particular computer, its CPU and disk will be heavily taxed. As a result, you must combine your domains during off-peak hours or, better yet, during scheduled downtime.

For you to execute most of the steps in this process, your target domain must trust your source domain. Without this trust relationship, you can't complete steps 3, 4, and 5. When you combine your source and target domains, some resources will be temporarily unavailable in your source domain. In particular, if you will need to move any domain controllers or member servers from your source domain to your target domain, make sure that their resources can be offline briefly.

Another word of caution: You should test each step in this process thoroughly. Assemble a lab that is representative of the computers in your company's environment. Then test each of the steps you will use to combine your domains in the lab first. This will give you a real-world look at the flow and timing of this process.

Step 1: Migrating User Accounts

As the first step, you must migrate users from your source domain to your target domain. To complete this step, you must create a new user in your target domain for every user that exists in your source domain.

You will use ADDUSERS.EXE to migrate these user accounts. You must first dump the users and groups from your source domain to a comma-delimited text file. To do this, execute the following command:

```
addusers.exe \\computername /d filename
```

Then open your comma-delimited file in a text editor, such as Notepad. Notice that this file contains three main headings: Users, Local, and Global. Each of these sections lists accounts from your source domain by heading type. You will have to make a few changes to this file for it to be useful. You will make these changes in steps 1.1 through 1.3. Then in step 1.4, you will write these changes to your target domain. Proceed with the following steps:

1.1   Make a backup copy of your original comma-delimited file. You will need a clean copy of this file in a later step. When you back it up, give it an easy-to-remember name, such as ORIGINAL.TXT, and store it in a safe location. Then save your working file with another name, such as STEP1.TXT. Perform the remaining steps in this section using STEP1.TXT.

1.2 Before you can proceed, remove two sections from STEP1.TXT: Local and Global. Because you are using ADDUSERS.EXE to migrate user accounts from your source domain to your target domain, the local and global groups listed in the file must be removed.

1.3 Compare the user accounts that are listed in STEP1.TXT with the user accounts in your target domain. (You may want to dump the accounts from your target domain to a separate text file to make this comparison easier.) You must then resolve any identical usernames between the users listed in STEP1.TXT and those in your target domain. If two user accounts have the same name, you should rename the user from your source domain. To do this, simply change the username listed beneath the Users heading in STEP1.TXT.

1.4 Create each of the users from your source domain that are listed in STEP1.TXT in your target domain. To perform this task, you must execute the following command, where *computername* is a domain controller in your target domain:

```
addusers.exe \\computername /c step1.txt
```

When the user accounts from STEP1.TXT are created in your target domain, their password properties will be left blank. You should change this property to reflect your company's security requirements. Most other user properties, such as Home Drive, Home Path, Profile, and Logon Script, are populated with values from the accounts in your source domain. Depending on your standards for user accounts in your target domain, you may need to change these properties to make them compliant.

Step 2: Migrating Global Groups

Your next step is to migrate the global groups from your source domain to your target domain. The first stage in this task is to create a global group in your target domain for each global group that exists in your source domain. The second stage is to then populate these groups with members.

You will use ADDUSERS.EXE to migrate the global groups in your source domain to your target domain. This process consists of the following steps:

2.1 Retrieve your original dump file. This is the file you named ORIGINAL.TXT and placed in a safe location in step 1.

2.2 Because you are migrating the global groups from your source domain to your target domain, you must modify the dump file's contents. Before you make any changes to the original dump file, create a second copy and give it an easy-to-remember name, such as STEP2.TXT. Then perform the remaining steps in this section using STEP2.TXT.

2.3 Remove two main sections from STEP2.TXT: Users and Local. After you remove these sections, only the Global section remains. The Global section lists all the global groups in your source domain.

2.4 Each entry in the Global section of STEP2.TXT contains the name of your source domain. In STEP2.TXT, replace each reference to your source domain with the name of your target domain. Additionally, because you are using a copy of your original dump file, any of the users you renamed in STEP1.TXT are not renamed in STEP2.TXT. You must be sure to update STEP2.TXT to reflect any users you renamed in step 1.

2.5   Compare the global groups that are listed in STEP2.TXT with the global groups in your target domain. (You may want to dump the group accounts from your target domain to a separate file to make this comparison easier.) Then resolve any duplicates between the global groups listed in STEP2.TXT and those in your target domain. If two global groups have the same name, you should rename the group account in your source domain. To so this, simply change the name that is listed under the Global heading in STEP2.TXT.

2.6   Finally, create each of the global groups from your source domain that are listed in STEP2.TXT in your target domain. To perform this task, execute the following command where *computername* is replaced with the name of a domain controller in your target domain:

```
addusers.exe \\computername /c step2.txt
```

Step 3: Updating Local Group Memberships

In this step, you will add the users and global groups from your target domain as members of local groups in your source domain. These local groups can exist on domain controllers, member servers, and NT workstations in your source domain. You must update these groups to preserve access control on any computers that will move to your target domain.

To update these groups, you can use ADDUSERS.EXE. Updating your local groups requires the following steps:

3.1   Use ADDUSERS.EXE to create a dump file for each computer in your target domain that will move to your source domain. To complete this step, you will execute the following command, where *computername* is the name of each domain controller, member server, and NT workstation that will move from your source domain to your target domain:

```
addusers.exe\\computername /d filename
```

When you are finished, you should have a dump file for each computer in your source domain that will move to your target domain. If 300 computers in your source domain will move to your target domain, you should have 300 dump files. To keep track of these dump files, you should give them intuitive names, such as *MACHINENAME.TXT*, where *machinename* is the name of each computer.

3.2   Create a directory to hold backup copies of these dump files. Before you make any changes to the dump files, make a second copy of each and place the copies in this backup directory.

3.3   For each dump file you have, complete the following tasks. Open the dump file in a text editor, such as Notepad. Then remove two main sections from the file: Users and Global. Leave the Local section intact. Then, in the dump file, replace every reference to the name of your source domain with the name of your target domain. After making these changes, your dump file should look somewhat like the following example:

```
[Local]
Administrators,Members can fully administer the
➥computer/domain,WKS01\Administrator,TARGETDOM\Domain Admins
Backup Operators, Members can bypass file security to back up
➥files,TARGETDOM\WKSBACK
Guests,Users granted guest access to the computer/domain,WKS01\Guest
Replicator,Supports file replication in a domain
```

3.4 Take a close look at the local group members listed in this dump file. If you renamed any of the user or global group accounts in steps 1 or 2, you must update the dump file to reflect those changes. For example, consider the contents of the dump file already listed. If you renamed the WKSBACK user to WKSBACK2, you will need to change your dump file to reflect the user's new account name.

3.5 Run ADDUSERS.EXE once for every dump file. For example, if you were updating the local groups on three of your computers (PDCDOMA, MEMDOMA, and NTWKDOMA), you would execute the following commands:

```
addusers.exe \\PDCDOMA /c pdcdoma.txt
addusers.exe \\MEMDOMA /c memdoma.txt
addusers.exe \\NTWKDOMA /c ntwkdoma.txt
```

When you finish running ADDUSERS.EXE for each dump file, you have updated all the local groups in your source domain.

Step 4: Updating Permissions

In this step, you will update the permissions for resources in your source domain to reflect accounts in your target domain. These are the permissions for files, shares, and directories on computers in your source domain that will move to your target domain. Perhaps preserving these permissions is the most challenging step.

Like local groups, permissions can exist on domain controllers, member servers, and NT workstations. Without permissions for resources, the users and groups you've created in your target domain are useless. Those security identities have no access to objects such as files, shares, and directories. To give the accounts in your target domain the proper permissions, you must assign permissions to accounts in your target domain equivalent to those in your source domain.

What makes this step the most challenging is its broad scope. For example, to preserve NTFS permissions, you must search for and either append to or replace file system access control lists (ACLs) on every domain controller, member server, and NT workstation in your source domain that will move to your target domain. To complete this step you will use the SIDWalker Tools.

The SIDWalker Tools, which are included with the Windows 2000 Resource Kit, consist of three separate utilities: SHOWACCS.EXE, the Security Migration Editor, and SIDWALK.EXE (each of which was discussed in depth in the previous section,

"Resource Kit Utilities"). Each of these tools must be run locally on the computer where permissions will be updated.

The process for updating these permissions consists of the following steps:

4.1 Run the SHOWACCS.EXE utility on the local computer. SHOWACCS.EXE examines and documents access permissions. You will use it to create two separate files: an access-profile file and an account mapping file. To create these files, execute the following command:

```
showaccs.exe AccessProfileFile /f /r /s /p /g /m AccountMappingFile
```

Each account with permissions to resources on this particular computer will then be written to the account mapping file. This file will be used by the Security Migration Editor to map the accounts from your source domain to the accounts in your target domain.

4.2 Load the account mapping file into the Security Migration Editor snap-in. This allows you to map the accounts in your source domain to those in your target domain. To do this, you will make a selection from the list of user and group accounts in your target domain for each user and group account in your source domain. You have two options for each mapped user and group account: Ignore in ACL or Delete in ACL. You should choose Ignore in ACL to append new permissions to the existing access control lists. To replace the existing permissions in an access control list with new permissions, you should select **Delete in ACL**[1]. Once you create the appropriate mapping between these accounts, use the Security Migration Editor to update the mapping file.

4.3 Use this updated mapping file as input for the SIDWALK.EXE utility. SIDWALK.EXE will be used to write every change in your mapping file to the local computer. The parameters that you pass to SIDWALK.EXE define which user and group accounts on the local computer to update. To make your changes final—which will update the files, directories, and file shares on the local computer—run the following command, where *AccountMappingFile* is the mapping file created in step 4.1:

```
sidwalk.exe AccountMappingFile /f /s /l
```

You can also use the SIDWALK.EXE utility to perform a test run. To perform a test run beforehand, simply execute the following command:

```
sidwalk.exe AccountMappingFile /t /f /s /l
```

Remember that the SIDWalker Tools are very resource intensive and must be run locally on each computer. This will include every domain controller, member server, and NT workstation that is slated to move from your source domain to your target domain.

---

1. If the two domains you combine will coexist for some period, it is best to append your new permissions to the existing permissions. This allows the users and groups in your source and target domains to simultaneously access the resource.

Step 5: Updating User Rights

Next, you must update the user rights on computers in your source domain to reflect the accounts in your target domain. Updating these rights consists of changing user rights on every domain controller, member server, and NT workstation that will move from your source domain to your target domain.

You can use NTRIGHTS.EXE to update these rights. The NTRIGHTS.EXE utility allows you to update any user right from the command line. Unlike the SIDWalker Tools, NTRIGHTS.EXE can be run from a central location. To update the user rights on computers in your source domain, you can create a script file for NTRIGHTS.EXE. You can create this script using a simple text editor, such as Notepad. You can use the following sample script as a template to build your own:

```
NTRIGHTS -U TARGETDOM\USER -M \\MACHINENAME +R
➥SeAssignPrimaryTokenPrivilege
;Replace a process level token
NTRIGHTS -U TARGETDOM\USER -M \\MACHINENAME +R SeAuditPrivilege
;Generate security audits
NTRIGHTS -U TARGETDOM\USER -M \\MACHINENAME +R SeBackupPrivilege
;Back up files and directories
NTRIGHTS -U TARGETDOM\USER -M \\MACHINENAME +R SeBatchLogonRight
;Logon as a batch job
NTRIGHTS -U TARGETDOM\USER -M \\MACHINENAME +R SeChangeNotifyPrivilege
;Bypass traverse checking
NTRIGHTS -U TARGETDOM\USER -M \\MACHINENAME +R SeCreatePagefilePrivilege
;Create a pagefile
NTRIGHTS -U TARGETDOM\USER -M \\MACHINENAME +R SeCreatePermanentPrivilege
;Create permanent shared objects
NTRIGHTS -U TARGETDOM\USER -M \\MACHINENAME +R SeCreateTokenPrivilege
;Create a token object
NTRIGHTS -U TARGETDOM\USER -M \\MACHINENAME +R SeDebugPrivilege
;Debug programs
NTRIGHTS -U TARGETDOM\USER -M \\MACHINENAME +R
➥SeIncreaseBasePriorityPrivilege
;Increase scheduling priority
NTRIGHTS -U TARGETDOM\USER -M \\MACHINENAME +R SeIncreaseQuotaPrivilege
;Increase quotas
NTRIGHTS -U TARGETDOM\USER -M \\MACHINENAME +R SeInteractiveLogonRight
;Log on locally
NTRIGHTS -U TARGETDOM\USER -M \\MACHINENAME +R SeLoadDriverPrivilege
;Load and unload device drivers
NTRIGHTS -U TARGETDOM\USER -M \\MACHINENAME +R SeLockMemoryPrivilege
;Lock pages in memory
NTRIGHTS -U TARGETDOM\USER -M \\MACHINENAME +R SeMachineAccountPrivilege
;Add workstations to domain
NTRIGHTS -U TARGETDOM\USER -M \\MACHINENAME +R SeNetworkLogonRight
;Access this computer from the network
```

```
NTRIGHTS -U TARGETDOM\USER -M \\MACHINENAME +R
➥SeProfileSingleProcessPrivilege
;Profile single process
NTRIGHTS -U TARGETDOM\USER -M \\MACHINENAME +R SeRemoteShutdownPrivilege
;Force shutdown from a remote system
NTRIGHTS -U TARGETDOM\USER -M \\MACHINENAME +R SeRestorePrivilege
;Restore files and directories
NTRIGHTS -U TARGETDOM\USER -M \\MACHINENAME +R SeSecurityPrivilege
;Manage auditing and security log
NTRIGHTS -U TARGETDOM\USER -M \\MACHINENAME +R SeServiceLogonRight
;Log on as a service
NTRIGHTS -U TARGETDOM\USER -M \\MACHINENAME +R SeShutdownPrivilege
;Shut down the system
NTRIGHTS -U TARGETDOM\USER -M \\MACHINENAME +R
➥SeSystemEnvironmentPrivilege
;Modify firmware environment values
NTRIGHTS -U TARGETDOM\USER -M \\MACHINENAME +R SeSystemProfilePrivilege
;Profile system performance
NTRIGHTS -U TARGETDOM\USER -M \\MACHINENAME +R SeSystemtimePrivilege
;Change the system time
NTRIGHTS -U TARGETDOM\USER -M \\MACHINENAME +R SeTakeOwnershipPrivilege
;Take ownership of files or other objects
NTRIGHTS -U TARGETDOM\USER -M \\MACHINENAME +R SeTcbPrivilege
;Act as part of the operating system
NTRIGHTS -U TARGETDOM\USER -M \\MACHINENAME +R
➥SeUnsolicitedInputPrivilege
;Read unsolicited input from a terminal device
```

If your environment is fairly standardized, the user rights across your computers will be well-known and documented. They should not differ too much from one computer to the next. If that's the case, a unique script file is not required for each computer in your source domain that will move to your target domain; one script containing the same parameters can be shared. To update user rights in your source domain, simply execute this script once for each computer after modifying it to suit your environment.

Step 6: Migrating Computer Accounts

You need to create new computer accounts in your target domain in order for computers in your source domain to join your target domain. This means that you should create a computer account in your target domain for every computer that will move from your source domain.

To migrate these computer accounts, you can use NETDOM.EXE and a simple text editor.

This process consists of the following steps:

6.1 Run the following command to pipe the computer accounts in your source domain into a text file. In this command, replace *DomainName* with the name of your source domain and replace *TextFileName* with the name of the text file to store these accounts:

```
netdom.exe /domain:DomainName member >TextFileName.txt
```

After running this command, you will have a text file with entries in it similar to the following:

```
Member    1 = \\WKS01
Member    2 = \\SRV01
Member    3 = \\WKS02
Member    4 = \\SRV02
Member    5 = \\WKS03
```

6.2 Load this text file into a text editor, and then replace the text and equal sign preceding the computer name with the `net computer` command. Finally, append /add to the end of each line that is listed in the text file. Your file will then contain a listing of `net` commands that will add each computer account from your source domain to your target domain. The following is an example of the file that is produced from these steps:

```
net computer \\WKS01 /add
net computer \\SRV01 /add
net computer \\WKS02 /add
net computer \\SRV02 /add
net computer \\WKS03 /add
```

6.3 Save this text file with a .bat or .cmd extension and run it while attached to your target domain. When you execute this .bat or .cmd file, each computer account that is listed in the file is created in your target domain.

Step 7: Moving Domain Controllers

You now have the option of moving domain controllers from your source domain to your target domain. If a domain controller, such as a source domain PDC or BDC, has the sole purpose of authenticating logons, you don't need to move it to your target domain. You can always use this PDC or BDC for another purpose. Furthermore, you should leave the PDC running in your source domain until all the member servers and workstations move to your target domain.

Before proceeding, make sure you've completed steps 1–6. If you haven't completed these steps, the permissions and user rights on your domain controller will not reflect the accounts in your target domain.

To move a domain controller from your source domain to your target domain, perform the following steps:

7.1 Make a full backup of your domain controller before you go any further. In addition, make sure that you record the permissions on the domain controller either with your backup software or with a simple utility, such as CACLS.EXE. If you take this precaution, you will be able to reverse the migration process if you run into any trouble.

7.2 Create domain local groups in your target domain to mirror the domain local groups in your source domain. You will give your new domain local groups the same members and permissions after you reinstall the operating system. (Mirroring these groups is required to preserve permissions. When you reinstall NT on your domain controller, you will lose all of the permissions assigned to domain local groups in your source domain.)

7.3 Reinstall the NT operating system on the domain controller. Make the domain controller from your source domain a BDC in your target domain. During the reinstallation process, be sure to specify that you are replacing the existing operating system, not upgrading it. Your domain controller's file and directory permissions are stored with the file system, so after the reinstallation procedure, all permissions (except those assigned to domain local groups in your source domain) are still valid.

7.4 When the reinstallation process is complete, reboot the domain controller and examine the permissions and user rights. Instead of domain local groups from your source domain, this new BDC now has the domain local groups from your target domain. You should now mirror the permissions from domain local groups in your source domain to those in your target domain. You should also reapply any service packs or hot fixes to the domain controller because this is a fresh installation of the operating system.

7.5 Make sure the applications and services on the domain controller are running as expected. In almost all cases, a few of your applications and services will have to be reinstalled in order to function properly.

This process is not extremely fast or automated, but it is certainly effective. After you perform these steps, the domain controllers in your source domain are domain controllers in your target domain.

Step 8: Moving Member Servers

Moving the member servers from your source domain to your target domain is not complicated. Before you begin, verify that you've completed steps 1–6. If you skipped any of these steps, the permissions and user rights on your member servers will not reflect the accounts in your target domain.

To move your member servers, perform the following steps:

8.1 Create a full backup of the member server before you start. Additionally, you should record the permissions on your member server with your backup software or with CACLS.EXE. This will enable you to back out of the move procedure if you run into problems.

8.2 Then join your target domain. You can join your target domain from the server's Network Identification tab or by running the NETDOM.EXE utility, as with the following command:

```
netdom.exe /domain:TargetDomainName member %computername%
➥/joindomain
```

8.3 As a precaution, you should verify that the applications and services on your member server are still functioning properly. Since you haven't reinstalled the operating system in this procedure, you should not run into any problems.

After you carry out these three steps, the member servers in your source domain will be members in your target domain. At this stage, you are just one step away from completing the process of combining your domains.

Step 9: Moving Workstations

The final step in combining your domains is to move workstations from your source domain to your target domain. Like moving your member servers, moving your workstations will be straightforward. If you are running NT workstation on your company's desktops, first verify that you've completed steps 1–6. If you skipped any of these steps, the permissions and user rights on your NT workstations will not reflect the new accounts in your target domain.

This process consists of the following steps:

9.1 To complete this step, your workstations must join your target domain. This task is simple if you have only a few NT workstations. You can manually move a small number of workstations by accessing the Network Identification tab on each of them. If you do that, you can stop here.

If you have a large number of workstations, however, it may be more practical to automate this process. In that case, proceed with the remaining steps.

9.2 To automate joining your target domain, use the NETDOM.EXE and SHUTDOWN.EXE utilities. First copy NETDOM.EXE and SHUTDOWN.EXE to the NETLOGON share on the PDC in your source domain. Then modify the domain logon script in your source domain to run the following commands:

```
.\netdom.exe /domain:TargetDomainName member %computername% /
➥joindomain
.\shutdown /l /r /t:30 "You have joined the DomainName domain." /
➥y /c
```

When you run this logon script, NETDOM.EXE automatically changes the domain membership of %computername%, an environmental variable that stores the value of each computer's computer name. Keep in mind that this example is just a generic script. If you log in to the source domain from a member server, this script will definitely run. To prevent this from happening, you should qualify the script's execution.

For example, to add some logic to the script, you can check the value of `%computername%` before running it. If `%computername%` equals the name of any member server, you can halt its execution.

The SHUTDOWN.EXE utility runs in the second half of this script. It displays the message that is enclosed in quotes, and after thirty seconds, it forces a reboot of the computer. The next logon from an NT workstation that runs this script will be to your target domain.

9.3 Don't forget about your other desktop clients in the source domain, such as those running Windows 3.x, Windows 95, or Windows 98. These computers must be configured to log in to your target domain as well. If you're not using policy files, you'll have to complete this task manually. Before shutting down your source domain, make sure that each desktop client moves to your target domain.

When you've moved all your client computers to your target domain, the process of combining your domains is complete. You now have a simpler, flatter, and more manageable domain model. If you've flattened your existing domains to mirror your Active Directory design, your upgrade to Windows 2000 will be much less complicated.

Using the Domain Reconfiguration Tool

Consolidating your domains with FastLane's Domain Reconfiguration Tool is an automated, graphically driven process. For the most part, it is also pleasurable—if you find pleasure in this sort of thing. However, several steps in this process are extremely resource intensive. For example, when you execute step 4 (updating permissions in your source domain), the computers' CPUs and hard disks will be heavily strained. In view of this, you must plan to combine your domains during off-peak hours or, better yet, during scheduled downtime.

The steps for combining domains using the Domain Reconfiguration Tool and the Resource Kit are similar to a large extent. In this process, your target domain must trust your source domain. Without this trust relationship, you can't complete steps 3, 4, and 5. In addition, when you combine domains, some of the resources in your source domain will be briefly unavailable. If you will need to move domain controllers or member servers from your source domain to your target domain, make sure that their applications and services can be temporarily taken offline.

FastLane's DM/Manager Tool

By the time this book is released, FastLane Technologies will have released its next domain consolidation tool: DM/Manager. This tool will not be an entirely new product. It will have its roots in it predecessor—the Domain Reconfiguration Tool. It will, however, offer the following improvements:

- An intuitive drag-and-drop interface for ongoing administration

- Faster updating for local groups and profiles

- Fewer network bandwidth requirements

- More robust movement of computers from one domain to another

Another word of caution: You should test each step in this process beforehand. Create a lab environment representative of the computers in the domains you will combine, and then test every step of combining them in the lab first. This will give you a firsthand look at the flow and timing of this process.

Step 1: Migrating User Accounts

The first step in combining your domains is to migrate the users in your source domain to your target domain. Your source domain is the domain you plan to eliminate, and your target domain is the domain that will remain after you combine the two. For example, if you are dissolving resources from a resource domain into a master user domain, the resource domain is the source, and the master user domain is the target.

You need to start the Phoenix application to migrate user accounts from your source domain to your target domain when combining domains with the Domain Reconfiguration Tool. Once you've started Phoenix, your first step is to create a new project.

To create a new project, you must perform the following steps:

1.1 Select **File**, **New Project** from the main window in the Phoenix application.

1.2 Enter an intuitive name for your project in the **Project Name** field. Then specify the path for your project files in the **Project Path** field. Optionally, add a brief description for your project in the **Project Description** field.

1.3 To finish creating your project, select **Create Project**.

Three files will be created for each project. The first file will have a .prj extension. This is your project file, which contains the details you entered when creating the project, as well as some status information. The second file that is created will have a .suf extension. This is your working file. The final file that is created is named PHOENIXERRORS.TXT. This is your error log, which can be a useful reference during the remaining steps in this process.

On the User tab in the Phoenix application, you should see four selections. Three of these—Create Mapping File, Pre-Process Users, and Migrate Users—are used in the user migration process. The fourth selection—Undo User Migration—is used to reverse the migration. To migrate the users from your source domain to your target domain, perform the following steps:

1.4 Create a mapping file first by selecting **Create Mapping File**.

1.5 You will then be presented with a dialog box, *Select Source and Target Domains*. Select the source and target domains you are combining.

1.6 You can now further define your migration options by selecting **Migration Options**. This allows you to change global migration settings, such as whether or not to copy logon hours or to standardize on a particular home drive when migrating user accounts. When you finish setting your migration options, select **Create Mapping File**.

1.7   From the main Phoenix application, select **Pre-Process Users**. This starts a comparison of the users in your source domain to those in your target domain. If any duplicate names are detected, you will be prompted for action. To resolve any name collisions, you can select one of four options: **Do Not Migrate User**, **Delete User on Target Domain**, **Merge IDs**, or **Modify User Name**.

1.8   To finish migrating these users, select **Migrate Users** from the main Phoenix application. Each of the users from your source domain is created in your target domain.

After you perform these tasks, your project directory will contain three new files. The first file has a .r1 extension. This is your user migration status report. The second file has a .run extension. This is your migration mapping file, which contains the mappings between user accounts. This mapping file is very useful in the migration process because it can be modified to reflect specific user naming conventions that are required in your target domain.

Remember that at any time you can reverse the user migration by selecting **Undo User Migration**.

Step 2: Migrating Global Groups

To migrate the global groups in your source domain to your target domain using the Phoenix application, you must first open your project file (if it's not already open). As a reminder, the steps in this process must be completed sequentially. If you haven't completed step 1, you should go back right now to finish it.

The process for migrating the global groups from your source domain to your target domain consists of the following steps:

2.1   From the Global Groups tab in the Phoenix application, select **Pre-Process Global Groups**. The *Global Group Pre-Process* dialog box appears. From this dialog box, you select the mapping file you created in step 1. By default, it is already selected for you. To continue, choose **Select This Mapping File**.

2.2   Decide whether to merge any duplicate global groups or give all new global groups a prefix in your target domain (such as SRCDOM). If you choose a prefix such as SRCDOM, all the global groups from your source domain will be created in your target domain with SRCDOM as a prefix (in this example, global group names would have the format SRCDOM-*GlobalGroupName*). If you choose to merge any duplicate global groups, the members from your source domain will be added as members of the merged group in your target domain. The permissions associated with the groups in your source domain will then be merged with those in your target domain.

2.3   Select **Pre-Process Global Groups** to continue. You should then review the global group migration report to verify the pre-process step. This report shows you the tasks that will be executed during the migration of your global groups.

2.4 When you finish reviewing the global group migration report, select **Migrate Global Groups**. The global groups from your source domain will be created in your target domain.

After you execute these tasks, your project directory contains another new file, which has an .r2 extension. This file is your global group migration status file.

As a reminder, you can always reverse the migration of your global groups by selecting **Undo Global Groups**.

Step 3: Updating Local Group Memberships

One of the advantages of using the Domain Reconfiguration Tool is that it can divide tasks in this process among several computers. When you update the local groups, permissions, and user rights in your source domain, you can use the Distributor. The Distributor enables you to minimize network traffic and save valuable time when you combine domains. For the remaining steps, however, this chapter will explain the centralized process for combining domains. You should look further into using the Distributor only if you must combine domains that consist of a large number of computers.

To update your local groups, first open your project file (if it's not already open). You need to update local groups on the computers that will move from your source domain to your target domain to preserve access control. The following steps outline the process for updating these groups:

3.1 From the Local Groups tab in Phoenix, select **Create Server List**. The *Server Selection* dialog box appears. Once again, verify that the mapping file listed is correct. Then select **Create Server List**. All the computers in your source domain are then listed.

3.2 You can choose to update any number of computers from your source domain with permissions from accounts in your target domain. If you know that a computer in your source domain, such as a primary domain controller, will not move to your target domain, you should remove it from the computer list. If all the computers in your source domain will move to your target domain, choose **Select All**. When the list of computers is correct, select **Accept Server List**.

3.3 Select **Pre-Process Local Groups**. The computers in the computer list are processed sequentially. In the pre-process stage, access to remote computers is verified, as are the instructions to update the local groups in your source domain.

3.4 To finish updating the local groups in your source domain, select **Update Local Groups**. Each of the local groups in your source domain will then be updated with members from your target domain.

After you perform these tasks, your project directory will contain another status file. This file is the local group processing status file, which has an .r3 extension.

Step 4: Updating Permissions

In this step, you will update the permissions on computers in your source domain to reflect the accounts in your target domain. These are the permissions for files, shares, and directories on computers that will move from your source domain to your target domain. During this step, you change the permissions on every computer that will move to your target domain. The source domain permissions will either be appended to or replaced with permissions from your target domain.

To start updating these permissions using the Phoenix application, you must first open your project file. Then execute the following steps:

4.1   From the Phoenix application, select the **ACLs** tab. First verify that the listed mapping file is correct, and then choose **Create Server List**. The computers in your source domain will be listed.

4.2   You can now specify which computers in the list will be processed. If one of these computers will not move to your target domain, remove it from the list. If every computer from your source domain will move to your target domain, choose **Select All**. When the list of computers is correct, select **Accept Server List**.

4.3   Select **Pre-Process ACLs**. At this stage, you must verify once again that the listed mapping file is valid. The computers you selected to process in step two are then listed.

4.4   You must now make an important decision. You have the option of pre-processing all file shares or only the drive shares (such as C$, D$, E$, and so on). To accelerate this process and guarantee that you update all file permissions, you should select the drive shares. This ensures that every share on a particular computer is processed (since all other shares exist beneath a computer's root drive shares).

When you have made your selection, select **Pre-Process ACLs**. During the pre-process stage, the computers in the computer list are processed sequentially. Basic access to remote computers is also verified, as are the instructions to update permissions.

4.5   To finish migrating permissions, select **Update Source ACLs**. Once again, verify that the mapping file named in the *ACL Migration* dialog box is correct. Then select **Update ACLs**. A progress indicator appears, showing you the status of the permissions update process.

After you update your ACLs, a status file with the .r4 extension is written to your project directory.

Step 5: Updating User Rights

You must now update the user rights in your source domain to reflect the new accounts in your target domain. You must update the user rights on every computer that will move from your source domain to your target domain. To start this process, you must first open your project file (if it's not already open).

To update the user rights on computers in your source domain, perform the following steps:

5.1 From the Phoenix application, select the **Rights** tab. The *Server Selection* dialog box appears; it is identical to the dialog box you saw during local group, and ACL processing. As you did in previous steps, verify that the named mapping file is correct, and then select **Create Server List**. The computers in your source domain will be shown in the list.

5.2 Specify which computers from your source domain to process. If a computer in the computer list will not move to your target domain, remove it from the list. If all computers from your source domain will move to your target domain, choose **Select All**. When the computer list is correct, select **Accept Server List**.

5.3 Select **Pre-Process User Rights**. Again, verify that the named mapping file is correct. The computers from your source domain that you selected in step 2 will now be shown.

5.4 When you finish, select **Pre-Process User Rights**. In this step, access to remote computers is verified, as are the instructions to update user rights on computers in your source domain.

5.5 To finish updating user rights on the computers in your source domain, select **Update User Rights**. Verify that the mapping file named in the *User Rights Migration* dialog box is correct. If it is, select **Update User Rights** to start the update process.

After you perform these tasks, your user rights migration status file is written to your project directory. This file has an .r5 extension.

Step 6: Migrating Computer Accounts

Your target domain must have a computer account for each computer that will move from your source domain. To create these accounts using the Phoenix application, first open your project file. Then perform the following steps:

6.1 Within the Phoenix application, select the **Computers** tab. The *Create Server List* dialog box appears. To populate this list, select **Create Server List**.

6.2 Verify that the listed mapping file is correct. Then select **Create Server List**.

6.3 Choose the **Computers to Process**. A list will show the computer accounts from your source domain that will be created in your target domain. Select **Accept Server List** to continue.

6.4 To finish migrating your computer accounts, select **Migrate Computers**. Verify once again that the named mapping file is correct. Then select **Migrate Computers** again. Each computer account from your source domain is created in your target domain.

After you execute each of these steps, your computer migration status file is added to your project directory. This file has an .r6 extension.

Step 7: Moving Domain Controllers

You now have the option of moving domain controllers from your source domain to your target domain. If a PDC or BDC in your source domain is used only to authenticate logons, you can shut it down or use it for another purpose. The Phoenix Resource Kit contains the DCMover utility, which can help you move a domain controller from one domain to another. You can use DCMover to move domain controllers (both PDCs and BDCs) from your source domain to your target domain. The DCMover utility can even move domain controllers that weren't selected in steps 1–6.

The following process for moving domain controllers assumes that the domain controller was not selected in steps 1–6. If you did select your domain controllers in steps 1–6, steps 7.4 and 7.5 will be completed already.

To move domain controllers from your source domain to your target domain using the DCMover utility, perform the following steps:

7.1 Make a full backup of your domain controller before you start. In addition, make sure you record the domain controller's permissions either with your backup software or with a simple tool, such as CACLS.EXE. Doing so enables you to reverse the migration process if you run into trouble.

7.2 Start the DCMover utility from your Phoenix application group and create a new project file. You will be prompted for the names of your source and target domains. When you have made the proper selection, select **Pre-Process Local Groups** from the Local Groups tab.

7.3 Choose which local groups you want to migrate from your source domain to your target domain. Additionally, you must specify whether to merge these groups or add a prefix to them (as you did with global group accounts in step 2). When you finish, select **Pre-Process**.

7.4 When the preprocessing stage is complete, select **Copy** from the Local Groups tab. Then verify that the listed mapping file is correct. The local groups you selected in the previous step are then copied to the PDC in your target domain.

7.5 Select the **Update PDC** tab to continue. A dialog box appears, containing a list of NTFS directories. Select the directories you want to process and select **Update ACLs.**

7.6 After updating the PDC, select the **Update BDCs** tab. Again, a dialog containing a listing of NTFS directories appears. Select the directories you want to process for each BDC, and then select **Update ACLs**.

7.7 Select the **Share Snapshot** tab and select **Pre-Process**. In the *Pre-Process Shares* dialog box, select the PDC and/or BDC where you will re-create file shares. Select **Pre-Process**, and the permissions on each share are processed and updated.

7.8 When the pre-processing stage is complete, select **Store Data** to save your ACL data. Choose which servers you will save the share ACLs on, and then select **Store** to finish.

7.9 Reinstall the NT operating system on the domain controller. Make this domain controller a BDC in your target domain. Note that your PDC and any BDCs that move to your target domain must have the same names they did in your source domain. During the reinstallation of the operating system, be sure to specify that you are replacing the existing operating system, not upgrading it.

7.10 After reinstalling NT, bring up the operating system and examine your permissions and user rights. Instead of domain local groups from your source domain, this new BDC will have domain local groups from your target domain.

You should reapply any service packs and hot fixes to the domain controller at this time because this is a fresh installation of the operating system.

7.11 To re-create the file shares on your domain controller, select the **Re-Create Shares** tab. In the *Re-Create Shares* dialog box, select the servers from this list and select **Process** to re-create all your shares.

7.12 Finally, test the applications and services on your new BDC. In most cases, a few applications and/or services will have to be reinstalled in order to function properly.

Step 8: Moving Member Servers

Moving the member servers from your source domain to your target domain should be straightforward. Verify that you've completed steps 1–6 before you start. If you've passed over any of these steps, the permissions and user rights on your member servers will not reflect the new accounts in your target domain.

To move these servers, complete the following steps:

8.1 Create a full backup of your member server beforehand. In addition, you should record the permissions on member servers with your backup software or with a simple utility, such as CACLS.EXE. This enables you to reverse the move procedure if you run into trouble.

8.2 Every member server in your source domain must join your target domain. You can complete this step manually from the member server's Network Identification tab or automatically by using the NETDOM.EXE utility (from the NT Resource Kit), as with the following command:

```
netdom.exe /domain:TargetDomainName member %computername%
➥/joindomain
```

8.3 After joining your target domain, you should verify that the applications and services on your member server are functioning properly. Because you haven't reinstalled the NT operating system, you should not run into any problems.

After you complete this process, the member servers from your source domain will be members in your target domain. At this stage, you are just one step away from combining your domains.

Step 9: Moving Workstations

The final step in combining domains is to move workstations from your source domain to your target domain. Like your member servers, moving your workstations will not be complicated. If your company is using NT workstation on the desktop, verify that you've completed steps 1–6 before you start. If you passed over any of these steps, the permissions and user rights on your workstations will not reflect the accounts in your target domain.

The process of moving workstations consists of the following steps:

9.1 Your NT workstations must join your target domain. This is a simple step if you have only a few workstations to worry about. You can manually move them by accessing their Network Identification tabs. If you do that, you can skip the remaining steps in this process.

Sometimes, however, it will be better to automate this process. To do so, you can use the Computer Mover utility. Proceed with the remaining steps.

9.2 Start the Computer Mover utility from the main Phoenix application group. Select your source domain from the **Select a Source Domain** list and your target domain from the **Select a Target Domain** list.

9.3 Select the computer accounts that will move from your source domain to your target domain. With the Computer Mover utility, you also have the option of rebooting these computers. If you don't choose this option, you will have to manually reboot all the computers you move.

When you've decided whether to automatically reboot these computers, select **Move**. The computers from your source domain are moved to your target domain. If you selected to reboot these computers from within Computer Mover, they are rebooted immediately. After the computers reboot (either automatically or manually), their next logon will be to your target domain.

9.4 Don't forget about your other desktop clients, such as those running Windows 3.x, Windows 95, or Windows 98. These desktops must be configured to log in to your target domain as well. If you're not using policy, you'll have to complete this step manually.

When you move your clients from your source domain to your target domain, the process for combining domains is complete. You now have a flatter, simpler, and more manageable domain structure. If you simplified this structure to prepare for Windows 2000 and Active Directory, your upgrade will be much easier.

Early on, you learned that you can also combine domains after your Windows 2000 upgrade. This process is further detailed in the following section.

Combining Domains After Your Upgrade

If you plan to combine your domains after upgrading to Windows 2000, you should move applications and services from domain controllers to member servers first. The process to combine domains after your upgrade is further detailed in Chapter 13, "Removing Resource Domains."

The last step in this process is to shut down domain controllers in the domain. To prepare for this, you should move any applications and services from your domain controllers to member servers in a domain you will eliminate. This process is detailed in the following sections.

Step 1: Designing Your Migration Plan

You must first design your application and/or service migration plan. To design this plan, you should build a lab that is representative of the computers in your current environment. Your objective in this step is to capture the scope of your migration effort.

For instance, you should determine what is affected when your application and/or service moves from a domain controller to a member server. Establish what, if anything, ties the application and/or service to this particular computer. Maybe its data resides in a local SQL database. Perhaps special permissions and user rights are required for it to function. When you have an understanding of the scope of what will be affected during the migration, design your migration plan. Detail each necessary step to move the application and/or service from a domain controller to a member server. To accelerate the development of this plan, consider contacting the application and/or service vendor. They may be able to offer you proven methods for getting the job done.

Step 2: Forming Your Back Out Procedures

After you design your migration plan, you should form back out procedures. Although the preliminary tests in your lab or the steps given to you by your vendor may look bulletproof, you may encounter a serious hang-up during the actual migration. Your back out plan is simply a plan for backing out of the migration and reversing your migration steps. With your back out plan, you must be able to restore your domain controller to the exact state it was in prior to the migration. You must add an additional component to this plan, however—an acceptance test plan.

With an acceptance test plan, you establish what signifies whether the migration is successful. This can be a series of practical system checks or something as simple as an enduser usability test. Either way, this acid test must confirm that the migration was carried out as planned.

You must also determine what must go wrong in your migration for you to back out of it. To do this, consider the length of time it will take to execute your back out plan, as well as the time window you're working in. For example, suppose you have four hours to move your accounting application. You know that your back out plan can reverse the migration in two hours. You might characterize the migration as unsuccessful if it isn't complete after an hour and forty-five minutes.

Step 3: Testing Your Migration Plan

Next, you must test both your migration plan and your back out plan in your lab. Go over your procedures to see if you missed anything. Make sure the steps you created are clear, especially if you will execute your migration late in the evening. You may find that at 2 a.m. your thoughts are not as clear as when you started.

When your plans are rock solid, you should consider improving them. Fine-tune every step. Optimize your migration plan, and make your back out plan more fault-tolerant. If you change your migration plan, test it again. You don't want to find out later that a tweak in your migration plan caused other problems.

Step 4: Executing Your Migration Plan

The best way to ensure that your migration goes well is to be thoroughly prepared. If you've worked through all the previous steps without omitting any details, you'll be right on track. You should be ready to carry out your plan.

Before making changes to any of your computers, however, you should make a full backup. This is your last line of defense in the event of a serious problem. Use your backup to reverse the migration if your back out plan fails. Then execute each of your application and/or service migration steps.

Pay attention to the details you've already worked out in the lab. Follow your plan verbatim, and do not deviate from it. If you've done a good job in your lab, all should go well. If not, fortunately, you have your back out plan and a full backup of the computer as insurance.

Step 5: Performing Acceptance Testing

After you've executed the migration, perform your acceptance test plan. Use this plan to substantiate what you hopefully already know—that your migration was successful.

Suppose you've migrated a financial application from your domain controller to your member server. When you finish, you execute your acceptance test plan. This consists of verifying permissions for the application and performing some enduser testing. Performing this type of plan often pays off. For example, if one of your endusers finds out that employee salary data in the application is exposed to everyone, you'll thank him many times over for catching your slip-up. Instead of publishing this sensitive information for all to see, you can lock it down beforehand.

Step 6: Removing the Source Domain

After moving the applications and/or services from domain controllers to member servers in your source domain, you can safely combine the source domain with your target domain. To do this, you should follow the process detailed in Chapter 13. If you move these critical applications and services from domain controllers to member servers beforehand, eliminating this domain is much easier.

3

Implementing Standards

WHEN YOU GET A NEW TOY, you probably take it home, rip open the package, and start having fun. The manual, if there is one, is quickly cast aside (along with the warranty registration card) as one more obstacle between you and the cool new toy. Someday operating systems (OS) may install and administer themselves (which would likely force quite a few of us into a new line of work). Unfortunately, Windows 2000, despite its futuristic-sounding name, does not belong in this category of OS. Although that childlike fly-by-the-seat-of-the-pants approach would work (although not very well) in some Windows NT 4.0 installations, the increased complexity of Windows 2000 significantly reduces your chance of success if you try such an approach. Standards are a key to your successful deployment of Windows 2000.

This chapter shows you how to standardize your installation. First, you'll examine some of the reasons standardization is worth the effort. Then you'll move into a description of the standards formation process and examine each part of that process, beginning with determining your current status. The major focus of this section is creating a comprehensive inventory. Once you know your current status, you'll discover a number of uses for the inventory information. After that, you will study the process of creating and maintaining the standards documentation and how to maintain the standard. Finally, the chapter closes on the subject of reviewing the standard.

Why Standardize?

Just as driving according to accepted standards prevents accidents, creating a standard computing environment will greatly smooth the migration to Windows 2000. Although significant cost is associated with creating and maintaining standards, the effort is certainly worth it. You may already know the benefits of standardization, but this section should help you justify these advantages to management. You should use standards in your environment for four reasons: to reduce the Total Cost of Ownership, simplify the environment, establish a precedent, and manage Windows 2000.

Reducing the Total Cost of Ownership

The two best ways to achieve a reduction in Total Cost of Ownership (TCO) are via systems management and standardization. TCO has become a buzzword over the past few years in the computing industry. Executives seek to achieve savings in TCO for each computer. Saving just a few dollars per computer can result in significant cost reductions when you add up the savings from all machines. A standardized environment also reduces the TCO because it's easier to support. Additionally, new hardware, OSes (such as Windows 2000), and software can be deployed more cheaply because fewer surprises will be encountered in a standardized environment than in a nonstandardized environment.

Simplifying the Environment

By standardizing the computing environment, you simplify it. For instance, instead of supporting five different word processor applications, standardizing on one will considerably simplify the environment and its administration. Users no longer face problems with exchanging documents in different file formats, and the help desk staff no longer has to be knowledgeable in four different applications. Additionally, simplification makes troubleshooting easier in the following ways:

- The simpler the environment, the less likely that problems will occur.
- When problems occur, tracking them to their source is easier because there are fewer potential causes of the problem.
- Because some elements of the environment have been eliminated, it is easier to focus your skills on the remaining items.

Besides easing the work of troubleshooting, simplification eases the burden of administration. When contemplating a change to an environment, the potential impact of the change is easier to grasp in a simple environment than in a complex one. Compare Figures 3.1 and 3.2 and decide which would be easier to implement changes in. Additionally, making a change in a simple environment is less likely to cause a problem. Finally, when staff changes occur, the new staff can get up to speed much more quickly in a standardized environment.

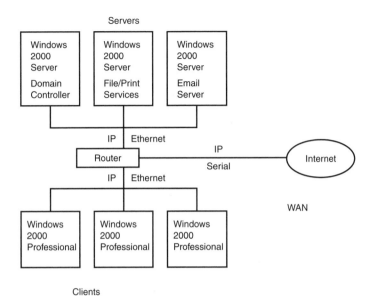

Figure 3.1 A simplified network is easier to troubleshoot, manage, and change.

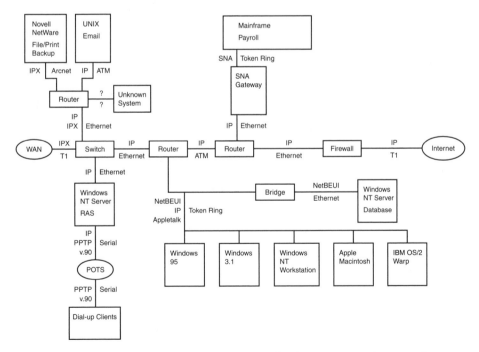

Figure 3.2 It's hard to determine the impact of a change in a complex network.

Establishing a Precedent

Another benefit of standardization is the precedent that it sets. Although your Information Technologies (IT) staff no doubt has some common operating principles, do you have a document that you can hand to new hires describing these procedures? Going through the process of creating a standard allows you to formalize the staff's procedures for operation. By laying out the standard, you establish a precedent that the staff should follow as they perform their duties. As a result, identical processes performed by different people should produce identical or nearly identical results.

For instance, everyone has his or her own ideas about what size the Windows NT/2000 pagefile should be. As a result, the pagefile size on systems in your organization will vary by RAM (as it should) and by the individual who set it up (which it shouldn't). If you create a standards document, the staff will have an agreed-upon setting for this and many other items.

The staff should be expected to abide by the standard, or it will fall apart. Although some may claim that they have a better way to do something, the standard should be upheld, at least until the change can be evaluated for merit. If a review of the suggested change reveals performance or cost improvements, the standard should be modified to include it.

Managing Windows 2000

Given this book's subject, the chief reason to standardize is the positive impact of standardization on managing Windows 2000. If you've read Chapter 1, you should have a feel for the immense number of new features in Windows 2000. The chapter's many pages mostly describe new features and only touch on a few features that have been upgraded from prior versions. Now imagine implementing a number of Windows 2000 systems without regard to standards. The result would be chaos.

The best example of a feature that should be managed with the help of standards is the Active Directory (AD). Of all the new features in Windows 2000, AD is the most important. The quality of the overall Windows 2000 rollout will be directly proportional to the quality of your AD implementation. Standards must be employed when implementing and managing AD for two reasons. First, a standard will ensure that users interact with the AD in a uniform manner across the organization. Second, and more importantly, developing the standard will force you to think about AD's implementation ahead of time, rather than slapping it together at the last moment. (See Chapter 6 for more information on creating a well-designed AD.)

Standardization Process Overview

Unfortunately, you can't go down to the local bookstore and buy a pre-written standard for your computing environment. Because each organization is different, no two standards will be identical. This chapter can serve as your guide for creating your organization's standards.

The process for creating each standard follows the same format:

1. **Discover current status.** Creating an inventory of your current environment is the first step in the standards process. It allows you to determine any de facto standards currently in place, shows you which areas must be adjusted once a standard is implemented, and probably brings to light issues about which you were previously unaware.

2. **Establish a standard.** Utilizing the inventory, you can work with management and the user community to create a standard that is acceptable within your environment. Numerous elements can be included in a standard, but most minutiae need not be present. The section devoted to this step describes the most common elements written into a standard.

3. **Document the standard.** When an agreeable standard has been selected, it must be documented. This allows everyone to reference it easily and also is helpful when staff turnover occurs.

4. **Bring the environment into compliance.** Again, utilizing the inventory information you created in the first step, you should bring items currently not in compliance into the standard. The section devoted to this step introduces the important topic of change control and addresses when to violate the standard.

5. **Maintain and review the standard.** As time passes, you must make sure current systems do not deviate from the standard. This can best be accomplished by repeating the systems inventory at regular intervals. New systems should also adhere to the standard. Just as new systems must comply with the standard, the standard should be reviewed to ensure that it remains relevant. Portions should be deleted, added, or changed as needed.

Step 1: Discovering Current Status

The first step in creating a standard is to determine the current status of the environment. Although the goal is for your systems to emerge into a standardized Windows 2000 environment, it's impossible to begin this process without knowing the current condition of the enterprise.

Inventory

In order to discover the current status of your environment, you must conduct a sweeping inventory. Although you may be able to recite a good deal about the environment from memory, that isn't good enough for the purposes of the standard. The goal of this inventory is to be complete. Because this is the first inventory for the standard, it's important that you try to get as much information as possible about the environment. This is doubly important if there has been staff turnover since the last major rollout because it's likely that knowledge has been lost regarding one or more areas of the environment. Be prepared for surprises, and double-check any especially odd results.

In all likelihood, users of the current, nonstandard environment have installed extra software on their systems. These products may be very helpful in solving particular business needs, or they may be rather superfluous. For example, some users will have installed software to connect to their Internet provider, such as AOL. Without the inventory, these items would be overlooked. Yet, if those programs provide a benefit for the organization, they should be included in the standardization process.

Tools

To inventory the environment, you will need to use several tools. A number of automated tools are available that can significantly reduce the amount of labor required to complete this task. However, where they fall short, you will need to perform certain parts of the inventory manually.

This section discusses several of the automated tools that can provide inventory information. Besides discussing the relevant features of each, it emphasizes which tool is most appropriate in various situations. See Table 3.1 for a comparison of each technique.

Table 3.1 **Tools for Inventorying Your Environment**

Category	NetCensus	Phoenix Domain Reconfiguration Tool	SMS	Manual
For small organization.	Good. Diminished returns for 25 or fewer clients.	Poor.	Cost-prohibitive.	Excellent. Time-consuming as number of clients increases.
For medium organization.	Good for occasional inventories.	Cost-effective if domains require reconfiguration.	Cost-effective if organization is dedicated to standardizing the environment.	Poor.
For large organization.	Poor. Not an enterprise-class utility.	Good. Most large organizations have a number of domains that will need reconfiguration.	Excellent. Most organizations of this size utilize inventory and software metering and require software distribution due to their size.	Cost-prohibitive.

Category	NetCensus	Phoenix Domain Reconfiguration Tool	SMS	Manual
Customization.	Good. Can be customized to detect new applications and hardware.	None.	Excellent. Wide variety of customization and third-party add-ons available.	Excellent. Manual processes are inherently customizable.
Other features.	None.	Domain reconfiguration.	Software distribution, software metering, and remote control.	Anything required.
Administration required.	Medium. Inventory collector must be created and distributed. Reports must be processed.	Medium. BackOffice inventory information must be generated and then exported.	Excessive. Requires dedicated administrator. Large time investment required.	Not applicable.

NetCensus

One useful tool for inventorying client computers is NetCensus by Tally Systems. NetCensus takes a complete hardware inventory and recognizes a good deal of the software programs in use today. While it's good at reporting mainstream applications, it may not list a version or sub-version. If desired, an organization can customize NetCensus to include applications not currently listed in its database, such as software developed in-house. Inventory information can be reported to a centralized location, where the program can add each report to its database. The database can be exported to other database systems for custom reporting, although a report generator is included in the administrative interface. NetCensus is most useful in smaller environments, in which SMS is cost-prohibitive or the inventory will be conducted infrequently.

Phoenix Domain Reconfiguration Tool

Although its main purpose is to restructure domains, the Phoenix Domain Reconfiguration Tool can also inventory Microsoft BackOffice applications. Additionally, the tool can provide inventory information about your domain setup, including the names of the domain controllers, member servers, and Windows NT workstations. Lists of file shares, users, and permissions are also available. However, you should not buy this tool merely for inventory because that is not the focus of the tool, but rather a side benefit. If the tool is being utilized as part of a domain restructuring, this inventory capability can be an asset; however, that should not be the motivating factor for purchasing the tool.

Microsoft Systems Management Server (SMS)

One tool you might want to seriously consider using is Microsoft's Systems Management Server (SMS). SMS 2.0 provides a complete hardware and software inventory for all of its clients. Included in this information are the services and devices that Windows NT/2000 clients are running. SMS is capable of encapsulating the information gathered by NetCensus into its own powerful database and query system. Inventory reports can be generated by a number of tools, including Crystal Reports, Microsoft Access, and Visual Basic.

SMS is the most expensive of the tools listed here, and in many cases, it requires a part-time administrator. Therefore, SMS is not recommended for a company that can't commit at least half of one person's time to SMS management. However, if the organization is dedicated to the standards process, SMS can be cost effective, especially when it's used to provide ongoing inventory reports. You can decrease TCO even more by taking advantage of SMS's other features. These include software distribution, software metering, and remote control of clients. Outside of the standardization process, these other features can be compelling by themselves.

SMS: Never Leave Your Desk Again

The most popular feature of SMS is its ability to distribute software in an automated fashion. Instead of you visiting each desktop to deploy a new application or patch, SMS can perform that task for you. For example, one of my recent clients had major virus problems because their desktop antivirus software was several years out of date. In addition, they needed to deploy the latest Web browser to access their intranet. In three months, we deployed SMS, created the needed software distribution packages, and deployed those packages across their multi-site organization. Aside from troubleshooting the occasional problem, there was never a need to visit the client desktops.

Besides updating client software, the remote control feature can be a great assistance to your help desk staff. It allows them to see what the user is seeing, rather than relying on a phone description or visiting the user. Additionally, they can take control of the mouse and keyboard to assist the user with the needed task or perform advanced troubleshooting.

Finally, SMS 2.0 introduced the capability to monitor software usage. Activity can simply be monitored, or licensing limits can be enforced. If desired, unauthorized applications can be terminated when they are launched.

If you become an SMS administrator, you should have a health club membership included in your benefits package to ensure that you get some exercise—because you won't get it running from desk to desk!

Manual Tools

Although automated tools can greatly reduce your workload, a certain amount of manual work is required. To fill in the gaps left by the automated tools, you will want to use two manual techniques. First is the manual inventory. Go to the computer in question and determine its configuration. Although this will be a time-consuming process, try to be as complete as possible. If the inventory is not complete, you might miss something that may become critical later in the inventory process. Even if you need to manually inventory only one computer, you should develop a form to write down what you find. For multiple machines, it's best to then enter your findings into a database for easier retrieval later.

The second manual technique is interviewing the users. This shouldn't be used in most cases for a reliable hardware inventory (what administrative assistant knows the version number of his system's BIOS?), but the user can always tell you what applications he or she uses most. This technique should be used for the following reasons:

- Custom applications or those that were developed in-house will not be well detected by the automated inventory tools. In this case, you will need to find out more information from the user.

- Talking to the users will enable you to determine what the users' critical applications are. Assessing these critical applications will be the topic of Chapter 4.

Leveraging the Inventory

When the inventory is complete, you should have a comprehensive snapshot of the enterprise's computing systems. Hopefully, the results of the inventory can be combined into a central database, which will make querying much easier. If the snapshot is spread between multiple databases and paper reports, it's much too easy to overlook an item when extracting information from the inventory.

The inventory snapshot can be put to a number of excellent uses. Some of its benefits relate to Windows 2000, but additional unrelated benefits may be of equal or greater value.

Windows 2000-Related Benefits

The inventory snapshot can be leveraged for two important purposes with regards to a planned Windows 2000 rollout:

- **Baseline for standards.** The snapshot provides a baseline that will be used to establish standards. For instance, if two different computer naming schemes are equally valuable as a standard, you can query the snapshot database to find out which scheme is currently more widespread, and then you can adopt it as the standard. Without the snapshot, you might know that two schemes were in use, but you might select the lesser-used scheme as the standard, which would cause more work when you start to bring the environment into compliance with the standard.

- **Upgrade planning.** The snapshot will be of great assistance when you begin budgeting for upgrades that are required before the rollout can occur. With a centralized snapshot database, it's easy to determine which machines don't meet your minimum hardware standards for Windows 2000. Similarly, computers hosting applications that are Windows 2000-incompatible can be discovered quickly.

Benefits Unrelated to Windows 2000

The Windows 2000-related benefits of a snapshot stand on their own merit. However, there are a number of other important benefits. They would normally fall outside the scope of this book but are included here because of their importance. These additional benefits may provide the impetus required for your manager to authorize a standardization project:

- Licensing
- Asset management
- Year 2000 readiness

Licensing

The first of these benefits is in the area of licensing. Very few organizations track licenses as they should. Additionally, unless your enterprise is running in a locked-down Windows NT desktop environment, employees may be installing dubiously licensed software of their own choosing. Because the company owns the hardware, it will be responsible for any fines should the Software Publisher's Association (SPA) make a raid. With a snapshot of the current computing environment, it is easy to create reports listing all the software installed across the enterprise desktops by quantity and computer name.

Asset Management

A second benefit of using the snapshot is in asset management. The snapshot allows you to determine just what the enterprise has installed at the time of the snapshot. This information can be valuable both for insurance purposes and for tracking depreciation. Also, if additional snapshots are taken at regular intervals, the snapshots can be compared for differences, such as a desktop having more RAM or a larger hard drive in an older snapshot than in the latest one. This loss-prevention technique is an often-overlooked part of asset management.

Year 2000 Readiness

Finally, the snapshot can be leveraged as a part of your Year 2000 (Y2K) preparations. Unfortunately, the inventory is one of the first items needed in a Y2K review, so hopefully your organization has already moved past that point in their review. If an application is not Y2K compliant, it will only function for a short time on Windows 2000, if at all.

Step 2: Establishing a Standard

Now that you know the current state of your computing environment, a standard can be established. Although a wealth of items can be included in the standard, the items that should be seriously considered for inclusion are those that are typically customized, such as computer names, pagefile sizes, and standard software suites. This section covers the most common items included in a standard:

- Hardware
- Platform standardization
- Applications
- Services
- Hot fixes/patches
- Naming schemes
- Network protocols
- User rights and permissions

Hardware

Including hardware in your standard is a must. Hardware is one of the most difficult areas in which to establish standards, because a hardware standard is typically out of date within three months. For this reason, a hardware standard should try to avoid requiring exact configurations. Rather, the standard should attempt to establish a minimum hardware requirement. Your standard should include these items:

- Basic hardware information, including the following:

    CPU type
    Amount of RAM
    Hard drive size and interface (SCSI or IDE)
    Graphics card type
    Network card type

- BIOS version
- System drivers

Year 2000 Assessment

If your organization has not performed a Year 2000 assessment, put this book down right now and go do it. You will be surprised by the results. Without a doubt, hardware and software in your environment will fail. The severity of these failures and their impact on your organization are up to you to discover.

Basic Hardware Information

Information such as the CPU type, RAM size, and hard drive type and size are straightforward. However, the graphics and network cards require a bit of additional explanation. As far as graphics cards are concerned, the standard should specify a card manufacturer or card family rather than a specific card. This is due to the speed of change within the graphics world. On the other hand, the network card type should be specified. Network cards typically do not evolve as quickly as other hardware components, and simplifying the environment can best be achieved by selecting a good network card and sticking with it. Some managers may like to save a few dollars by taking shortcuts with hardware, but if you have a minimum standard for hardware, it is easier to force them into a modicum of compliance.

It may be desirable in your organization to specify additional levels of hardware beyond the minimums. These categories might be called "standard" and "preferred." While these categories will be harder to maintain than the minimum category, the extra work is probably worth it. When possible, try to avoid changing hardware standards more than twice a year, or you may end up with fifteen different "standard" hardware platforms! This would, of course, eliminate the benefits of the standard.

BIOS Version

Several additional items should be specified in the hardware standard. The first is the BIOS version used in the various systems. Windows 2000 supports a number of new technologies, such as ACPI, that current hardware may not support. In a number of cases, a BIOS upgrade will add the needed capability. At the very least, upgrades might fix incompatibilities with Windows 2000 should your hardware have any. When these upgrades are released, it's important that you know what BIOS version your systems currently have. Possibly, the BIOS vendor may simply say that Windows 2000 compatibility exists in a currently shipping version of the BIOS. In this case, having a standard helps you to know almost instantly whether any BIOS upgrades will be required.

System Drivers

In a similar fashion, system drivers should be standardized. Although the drivers are really software components, they are included here due to their interaction with hardware. Driver updates represent one area in which having the latest version is not of critical importance. Of course, if a problem is discovered with the current edition, updating to the latest version is typically the best course of action.

For each hardware item that requires a driver (such as SCSI adapters, network adapters, and video cards), include a driver version as part of the standard. Drivers for current products are typically updated quarterly, which places them somewhere between hardware and software in terms of speed of change. Continually updating drivers to the latest version isn't usually necessary. A better course of action is to monitor vendor Web sites to see if a driver offers a major improvement over the current standard, and then to implement it if that is the case. Most of the time, the best approach to take with drivers and BIOS updates is this: "If it's not broken, don't fix it."

Platform Standardization

Microsoft has a clear message for those planning a Windows 2000 migration: streamline, update, and plan. These are the three keys to a successful Windows 2000 rollout. Standardization of your existing platforms addresses the requirements of streamlining and updating. There are two objectives:

- Standardize your existing platforms
- Update your environment so it will be ready for Windows 2000

Mixed OS Environments

Many organizations have mixed platforms for servers. This is especially common in larger organizations. In mixed server environments, a number of Windows NT, Novell NetWare, UNIX, and occasionally Apple Macintosh or IBM OS/2 servers typically provide various functions. It is possible to standardize these disparate environments, but a better alternative is to streamline and simplify where possible.

For example, an OS/2 machine sharing files or a NetWare box serving Web pages can easily be replaced by one running Windows NT/2000. While this may introduce some cost savings or performance gains, the biggest impact will be lowered TCO. Most of these savings are achieved because fewer specialists will be required. Instead of having a Windows NT/2000 expert, a NetWare expert, a UNIX expert, and a Macintosh expert, one or more Windows NT/2000 experts can be used. In addition, when you select a single OS as the standard, vendor support becomes easier.

For instance, imagine you have a communications problem between two Windows 2000 machines. Microsoft should be able to help you resolve the problem. However, if the problem is between a Windows 2000 machine and a UNIX box, the vendors may point at each other instead of helping you arrive at a solution. In addition, a standardized server that is having problems can likely be fixed quickly, whereas one for which you have only one expert may be down quite a while if that expert is on vacation or out sick.

Before you begin to think that the Microsoft propaganda department wrote this section, you should know that some environments should not standardize on a single platform of Windows NT or Windows 2000. Certainly, NetWare, UNIX, and mainframes all have their places in an organization's environment, and it may not be cost effective to replace them, even considering the savings inherent in standardization.

You need to consider two things when evaluating whether platform simplification will benefit your organization:

- **Is there currently redundancy in the environment?** Often, both NT and NetWare perform file sharing and printing duties. Even if NT cannot replace NetWare, it would be beneficial to standardize on one platform for file and print sharing. This can reduce complexity for troubleshooting and create modest TCO savings.

- **What does the existing system offer that Windows NT or Windows 2000 can't?** Certainly, you don't want to run a nuclear plant on a Microsoft OS, because it's not designed for that. However, Windows 2000 can fill the roles of a number of its competitors quite well. These areas include file and print sharing, Web and database serving, and directory services.

Windows NT Environment

Even if your organization runs Windows NT on all of its servers, several areas should be evaluated prior to the move to Windows 2000. First, are all the servers on Windows NT? 4.0 NT 4.0 provides the simplest migration path to Windows 2000. Where possible, servers running older versions should be upgraded to 4.0 for easier management now and a smoother migration to Windows 2000. Second, have all the servers had the same service packs and hot fixes installed? Unless a critical application has a known issue with a particular service pack, try to keep all servers on the latest service pack and implement hot fixes only on an as-needed basis.

Server Hardware

Another area of platform standardization you must address is that of server hardware. The hardware used for servers is one area in which everyone has their own opinion. While everyone would agree that a four-way Xeon CPU, 4GB RAM server with a large Fibre Channel RAID disk array should be able to handle most needs, few organizations can afford such extravagance for every server in the organization. (For comprehensive coverage of server hardware needs, see Chapter 9.) Opinions differ as to what hardware should support what load of services.

Fortunately, Microsoft has created the "Windows 2000 Ready" program, which enables the public to purchase hardware that is ready for Windows 2000. Note that this program is for Windows 2000 Professional, so these requirements should not be applied to servers without adding resources, especially RAM; but few servers should have less than 128MB. Here are the requirements for labeling a system as Windows 2000 Ready:

- Must be running Windows NT 4.0 with SP3 and the OPK supplement
- 64MB of RAM
- Meets the Windows NT Workstation 4.0 and Windows 98 Designed for Windows logo requirements (PC97 spec or higher)
- Laptops must support ACPI for power management and run at 233MHz or faster with 256KB or more L2 cache
- Desktops must run at 300MHz or faster with 256KB or more L2 cache

Probably the biggest change for server hardware is that it should now support Plug and Play (PnP). Because most server operating systems didn't support this previously, most server BIOSes don't support it.

Applications

While having a hardware standard is important, a software standard is more important for your preparation for a Windows 2000 rollout. The reason for this is the variety of conflicts that software can have with Windows 2000 (see Chapter 4 for more information). Software does not evolve at the torrid pace of hardware, and as a result it's much easier to achieve a standard.

Standardizing software may be more painful than standardizing any of the other components in a good standard. Once users have learned how to use an application, they might be reluctant to change to a new application of the same type. Additionally, enterprises that charge departments for software may face significant hurdles if you move to a software standard because of the departments' investment in nonstandard software. Fortunately, two factors reduce the pain of standardizing: the infrequent use of nonstandard programs and the limited range of the users' use of applications.

Most organizations already have an informal software standard in place. Few, if any, desktops in such organizations run a nonstandard office suite or email program, for example.

Similarly, a typical user does not run a wide range of applications. A standard desktop usually includes a word processor, spreadsheet, database manager, email, and Web browser, and hopefully such utilities as an antivirus program and disk defragmenter.

Choice of Application

Whenever possible, standardize all the commonly used software in your environment. Office suites and email programs are typically standardized even without a formal standard in place, but other applications need to be standardized as well. This includes applications used for communication (such as host emulators), network programs (such as Web browsers and their plug-ins), and utilities. Although most users don't have many utilities installed on their systems, those utilities should be standardized if the enterprise uses them.

Application Versions

In addition to selecting the applications to include in the standard, you should also consider including the version. Certainly, Microsoft Word changed quite a bit between version 2.0 and Word 97. Trying to support all an application's versions is not feasible. Simply specifying an application without a version is not a good example of standardization. In addition to specifying the application and its version, the standard should cover any patches required by the environment.

Services

Services also must be included in a standard. Although they are a type of software, they are typically overlooked in a standards process. The same basic items are required to form a standard for services as for software: the service's name, the version, and any patches.

Most services are customized in each environment. As a result, these configuration changes should also be noted as part of the standard.

Hot Fixes/Patches

Another significant area that must be standardized is that of OS patches. Service Pack 3 (SP3) for Windows NT 4.0 certainly fixed a number of problems (including several significant bugs in SP2), but its chief problem was that it didn't go far enough. The unprecedented number of hot fixes that had to be produced for systems running SP3 proves this. *Hot fix* is Microsoft's term for a bug fix that corrects a problem, but which usually has not been tested as thoroughly as a service pack. Subsequent service packs include final versions of all hot fixes produced up to that time. To Microsoft's credit, many of the problems the post-SP3 hot fixes corrected were not even discovered until after SP3 had shipped. Nevertheless, tracking all the hot fixes could at times be a full-time job. Several Web sites dedicated pages to explaining what each fix did, and in some cases, which fixes made others obsolete or corrected problems caused by other fixes!

In order to ensure that your systems are protected from known bugs, it is important to standardize which fixes are applied. It's all too common for these fixes to be applied haphazardly, leaving some machines fixed and others not. As with BIOS updates and device drivers, it's best not to apply a hot fix unless it is truly needed. This is not just conventional wisdom; it is Microsoft's stated policy on hot fixes. Unlike Service Packs and some application patches, it's not easy to determine whether a hot fix has been applied to a system. Although the HOTFIX.EXE used to apply each hot fix has the ability to query a system for all of its installed hot fixes, none of the automated inventory programs look for this information. Instead, this data must be discovered manually. As a result, it's critical that the installation of hot fixes be standardized. Furthermore, you should note when a system has a hot fix installed so that such information will be easily accessible if it's ever needed.

In general, try to keep your systems updated with the latest service packs, but always remember to avoid hot fixes unless they are necessary. For example, prior to the arrival of NT 4.0's SP4, it was necessary to install several hot fixes to protect against denial of service attacks. For systems at risk, such as those directly connected to the Internet, these hot fixes were needed. However, after SP4 shipped, the systems could be updated with it, and they no longer required the hot fixes.

Services on Non-Microsoft OSs

The term "service" is Windows 2000 and NT-specific, but the same standardization concept should be applied to NetWare.NLMs, and UNIX daemons. All standards should include name, version, and patches applied, and configuration should be noted to complete the standards document.

Naming Schemes

Aside from the typical hardware and software that must be included in a standard, a number of other items must be standardized. Most enterprises have at least informally standardized the majority of these items, but the process should be formalized. The first of these items is naming schemes. There are three important name types to consider:

- Domain names
- Computer names
- Usernames

Domain Names

The first and likely the easiest naming scheme to standardize is the domain name. Most organizations have a single domain, and its name is already set. Larger organizations that span more than one domain will find this area more important than those with single domains. Hopefully, the domain names are descriptive, which allows for easier administration. Domains called `CHICAGO` and `ATLANTA` or `SALES` and `ACCOUNTING` are much easier to understand than `RED` and `BLUE` or `N1701` and `THE-DOMAIN`. Note that whatever the standard is currently, the best standard allows only DNS-legal characters in the name. This will be discussed in detail in Chapter 7.

Computer Names

Another naming scheme to standardize is computer names. As with domain names, you should strive for DNS-compliant names in the final standard. Many people like to name their computers for science fiction or cartoon characters, but these names do not promote easy administration. Ease of administration is one of the two most important components of a good computer naming scheme. The other is that the names be descriptive. While this may mean to some that certain computers should be called BUGGY or SLUGGISH, that is not the intent of being descriptive.

A descriptive name lets you know if a given computer is functioning as a server or a workstation. In practice, this typically means that server names follow a different format than workstation names. For instance, workstations may be named according to their location, and servers may be named according to their location, primary function, and a number, such as CHICAGO-SQL01. For both servers and workstations, the type of location used in the standard will vary depending on the size of the organization and your DNS naming scheme (see Chapter 7). The location may be as general as a city name (as in the example above) or very specific (specifying a certain building, floor, and desk location, for example).

Usernames

The final naming standard is that of user logon names. This is usually the hardest naming standard to define. As with computer names, the key ingredients of a user logon name standard are that they should be descriptive and easy to administer.

There are a number of ways to name accounts that clearly should *not* be the standard. For example, the standard should not use pet names (such as ACE and W2KGURU), first names, or first name and last initial schemes (such as LAURA or JOSHR). These may work in very small organizations, but they don't scale beyond twenty or fifty users.

Although a number of schemes should *not* be the standard, just as many schemes meet the requirements. Some environments prefer to use random alphanumeric strings like A6GH435 as user account names as a means of increasing security. Most enterprises do not even begin to need a security mechanism this stringent, especially with Windows 2000's support of smartcards as a means of user authentication. Another similar plan uses employee ID numbers. However, this makes administration difficult because administrators will constantly have to look up ID numbers and usernames to perform their duties. The advantage to this solution is that no two users should get the same account name. This is not a huge advantage, however. If the objective is to provide security, the administrator accounts should be protected, not ordinary user accounts. When users are given user names like those just listed, they tend to write down their names and perhaps even their passwords. Of course, this prevents the scheme from achieving its goal of security. It's much better to make usernames easy to remember.

The typical naming scheme is first initial, last name, such as BGATES. The chief difficulty in this is in resolving collisions. A collision occurs when two people's user accounts would have the same name, such as Andrew Smith and Audrey Smith or Pat Hannon Sr. and Pat Hannon Jr. In these cases, each user needs a different user account. One option for resolving collisions is to add the middle initial, such as AJSMITH. However, this does not resolve a Sr/Jr collision. In this case, appending an S or J to the account may be the best means of resolving the collision. Although an alternative solution is to append a number to one or both of the accounts, this can be cumbersome in practice for two reasons. First, it is difficult to select the right user during administration (such as assigning permissions). Second, numbered accounts imply that one user has multiple accounts, which could create additional confusion.

Usernames As Computer Names

It's often tempting to name computers based on their primary user's logon name. However, this idea is flawed for two reasons. First, turnover is inevitable, and after a while, many machines won't match their current user's name. Second, people occasionally change their names, for example, when they go through a marriage or divorce; when the user's name changes, the logon name will also change but the computer name usually will not.

In all likelihood, your organization already has a standard for user logon names. If this is the case, it can be very difficult to switch to a new standard. However, if the existing standard is of poor quality, it still may be worthwhile to visit the issue as part of your standardization process.

Network Protocols

Network protocols must be standardized for communication to occur. Your enterprise probably has an established standard for network communication. However, it may not be optimized. The fewer protocols in use, the better. Windows 2000 and downlevel versions support three primary protocols for networking: NetBEUI, NWLink IPX/SPX, and TCP/IP. They are listed here in order of increasing difficulty to administer.

Several years ago, protocol selection was clear: You used NetBEUI for single-segment Microsoft networks, and you used IPX/SPX for Novell networks. In fact, Windows for Workgroups didn't even originally ship with TCP/IP support. Now, the entire mindset has changed due to a little thing called the Internet. TCP/IP, despite its relative complexity, is now supported by everything from Microsoft to Novell to UNIX and mainframes.

Microsoft's message to those contemplating a Windows 2000 migration is clear: Make TCP/IP your sole network protocol if at all possible. Certainly, IPX/SPX is still required for older versions of Novell NetWare, but the latest NetWare version natively supports TCP/IP and does not require IPX/SPX.

Some people believe that Microsoft's SMB file sharing standard requires NetBEUI to operate and, therefore, install it on all their systems; this is not correct and is not necessary. What is required for SMB is NetBIOS, which is an upper-layer protocol that the lower-layer protocols such as NetBEUI, IPX/SPX, and TCP/IP can encapsulate. In the case of TCP/IP, this NetBIOS encapsulation over TCP/IP is called NBT. (See Chapter 5 for more information on NetBIOS.)

As mentioned before, TCP/IP is more complex than the other two protocols. NetBEUI and, to a certain extent, IPX/SPX configure themselves. However, TCP/IP requires that each client be configured with an IP address and its subnet mask. Although each client can be manually configured, the better option is to use DHCP, which allows the client to be automatically configured by the server. Another required element until the rollout of Windows 2000 is WINS, which allows computers to find one another using NetBIOS on an IP network. While this could be a painful migration to TCP/IP in the near future, the improvements to DHCP, WINS, and DDNS mentioned in Chapter 1 will make for an environment that is significantly easier to configure.

This area does not offer a multitude of choices for the standard. You should standardize solely on TCP/IP if at all possible. Period. Unfortunately, a dwindling number of applications still rely on different protocols for communication. Identifying these and dealing with them will be the subject of Chapter 5.

Certainly, there are a lot of things to consider when moving to TCP/IP. For example, if your network is currently running IPX/SPX exclusively, you need to perform the following steps to migrate to TCP/IP:

1. Set up an IP addressing scheme.

2. Set up your routers for IP.

3. Deploy the TCP/IP software to all machines.

4. Set up DHCP if it will be used.

5. Set up WINS for Windows NT or DDNS for Windows 2000.

6. Assign an IP address to each machine, either via DHCP, which is the preferred method, or by visiting each machine and giving it a static address.

7. Look at the current software to verify that it's not protocol-dependent.

8. Remove IPX/SPX from all machines.

9. Disable IPX/SPX support on your routers.

User Rights and Permissions

Whereas network protocols have one clear standard, the area of user rights and permissions has few. Each organization enforces varying levels of security. You must choose a standard that is appropriate for the data your enterprise works with. Fortunately, you can use the answers to the following questions when forming your standard:

- Are users allowed to change the time on their workstations?

- Do they have individual private network shares, and if so, how are they secured?

- Are there shares that only certain groups can access?

- Are permissions enforced at the share level, file level, or both?

- Are any events being audited?

- Are account lockouts enforced?

- Are permissions set in the Registry?

- Must passwords be difficult or of a certain length?

- Are previous passwords tracked?

- Do users have administrative rights to their workstations?

- How does one qualify for a domain administrator account?

- Do domain administrators have a single, powerful account, or do they have an unprivileged account for everyday work and an admin account for administrative duties?

By answering these questions, you will see what your current security policy allows. They may also bring up points that you haven't considered.

Windows 2000 provides a myriad of settings related to security. With AD, transitive trusts, auditing, and file rights to name a few, it is all too easy to overlook one or more areas. Fortunately, a utility is available from Microsoft to help document the current security status. The Security Configuration Editor (SCE) first debuted with Windows NT 4.0 Service Pack 4 and will be an integral tool in Windows 2000. This tool can answer many of the questions above. Once a standard has been achieved, SCE can be used to apply the standard and to assure that it is maintained. Take care, though, because a policy that is too stringent will cause many applications to fail. Also, user frustration is directly proportional to the level of security enforced.

Step 3: Documenting the Standard

Once the inventory snapshot has been taken, it's time to create the standard. If you include hardware, software, services, security, patches, naming standards, and network protocols, along with any custom information about your environment, in the standard, this could become a massive document. Nevertheless, the standard is worthless unless it is committed to paper.

Document Creation Process

Hammering out a standard will require one or more meetings. These meetings should include the IT department head, you, and representatives of those groups that will be affected. This could be a large group and will likely include server administrators, network administrators, computer security administrators, and endusers. Yes, endusers must be included in this process. One of the functions of IT is to support the endusers. Making a decision about which office suite to support without consulting the endusers will significantly lower IT in the eyes of the endusers. Not everyone is needed at each meeting, but everyone should have a chance to review the full document before it's finalized.

When the standard has been agreed to, the actual document can be crafted. Each item of the standard should be explained in the document, and examples should be given as often as possible, especially in areas of potential confusion. Naming standards definitely should include examples, because they can be difficult to explain otherwise.

Maintaining the Documentation

At last, the final page of the standards document comes out of the printer. While the creation process is complete, the standards process is just beginning. Now that the documentation has been created, it must be maintained.

This process comprises the following steps:

1. Everyone needs to become familiar with the standard so they are following it as they work in the future. Distribute the documentation to your IT staff or, better yet, post it on your intranet.

2. Be receptive to comments regarding the documentation, and evaluate suggested changes.

3. Periodically execute a formal review of the documentation to ensure that it is current. This means ensuring that the environment hasn't diverged from the standard and ensuring that the standard isn't lacking areas relating to new technologies or business needs.

Step 4: Bringing the Environment into Compliance

After you establish a standard, you must bring the environment into compliance with the standard. It may be tempting to apply the standard only to new installations, but this doesn't work well in practice. Unless the current machines are standardized, a surprising number will linger for years in the environment. By implementing a change control system and standardizing existing systems, you follow the most productive path to standardization.

Implementing Change Control

In your organization, there is (hopefully) one person who is notified when certain operations must be performed on a server, such as rebooting it or installing major software. Odds are, there is no formal process to this; it is simply custom to inform this person. Similarly, they probably don't write down the planned operation. This is the very beginning of a change control system, but it must be greatly expanded to ensure a trouble-free environment.

Change control promotes a better operating environment by tracking changes as they are made. When the need to make a change is perceived, you don't immediately implement the change. This invites negative, unintended side effects. Instead, the change consists of these steps:

1. A change request is submitted to the person in charge of the area needing change.

2. This person reviews the request to ensure that it is consistent with relevant standards, that the implementation plan for the change is well thought out, and that the change is likely to produce the desired effect.

3. When the change is approved, it is scheduled at an appropriate time. Depending on the situation and the type of change being made, this might be during off-peak hours, during working hours, or immediately.

4. Users who will be affected by the change are notified, and if circumstances allow, they are given an opportunity to request that the change be implemented at a different time. By doing so, you avoid the possibility of interfering with a business need that has been scheduled without your knowledge.

5. The change is implemented.

6. The change is noted in the change history for the area being changed.

Components of Change Control

There are three key components in implementing a change control system:

- Requiring permission for a change
- Notifying appropriate personnel of the change
- Providing a configuration history

Requiring Permission for a Change

By requiring permission to make a change, you ensure that the change is done in the best way. There are two advantages to this approach. First, technical approaches that are flawed can be prevented from damaging the infrastructure because the most experienced people can review the change before it is performed. Second, if permission is required, the change can be scheduled at an appropriate time.

Although it's appropriate to make some changes during working hours, quite a few should not be attempted during this critical period. Time should be included in the schedule for rigorous testing of the change before pronouncing it complete. Scheduling changes allows the administrator to select the appropriate time for the change. If various parties need multiple changes, they can be scheduled so they don't conflict.

Notifying Appropriate Personnel of Change

Communication is a key part of change management. All parties who might be affected by a scheduled change should be informed. Typically, email is the best mechanism for this, but a different system may be needed if the change will be to the email system! There are three advantages to informing key people prior to the change.

- There might be a business or technical reason for postponing or canceling the change. If you inform the affected parties, they have a chance to voice these concerns before the change is put into effect.

- Someone may make an important contribution to the change process. Had she not been notified, she would not have been able to provide her input. A surprising amount of helpful information can be gained—sometimes from unexpected sources—simply by making everyone aware of changes before they occur.

■ Correlating a problem with its cause will become easier. For example, instead of a user saying that a certain function quit working "sometime last week," he may be able to say that it quit working "after you applied that new patch." This should make problem solving much easier. Toward this end, one of the parties that should always be notified of a planned change is the help desk. They are usually the first to know when users have problems, so notifying them ensures that problems that occur as a result of the change can be resolved more quickly.

Providing Configuration History

A configuration history makes troubleshooting much easier. It's much simpler to determine the cause of a problem when all the system's changes are recorded. For instance, if a particular machine's history indicates that a certain component has been replaced repeatedly, it should be easier to conclude that another defective component is responsible for these repeated failures.

Change Control Scope

So what enterprise components should be included in change control? Troubleshooting would be easier if change control were extended down to the enduser workstation, but the nature of these workstations makes this policy cost-prohibitive. Rather, the standard approach is to enforce change control on the server and network infrastructure. This includes all hardware, software, and configuration information, such as Registry settings. In general, anything that could negatively impact endusers should be included under change control. Other operations on change controlled systems, such as logging in, using applications, and printing, should not require change control in the great majority of environments.

Change Control in Emergencies

These change control procedures may be fine for day-to-day operations, but you should also know how to effectively use change control in a crisis. During an emergency, it's important not to throw change control by the wayside. It is all too easy to simply wade in and start making changes in an attempt to rectify the situation quickly.

If a change-controlled server is down, change control should be an integral part of bringing it back into service. The configuration history should be consulted to see if any recent changes have been implemented. Then, as the troubleshooting process progresses, change control should be utilized as various changes are attempted to fix the machine. However, the scheduling and notification components can usually be bypassed.

What is key here is to note each change made in the course of troubleshooting. This makes it much easier to back out of a change that does not resolve the problem. A good way to implement this is to have one person work on the system while another person notes each change. When the problems have been resolved, the incident and any permanent changes can be committed to the long-term log for the system.

Rolling Out the Standard

Using change control, the standard must be rolled out to those areas of the enterprise that are currently non-compliant. This process will take some time, but should not be nearly as lengthy as the initial inventory or standards-crafting operation.

The first item to consider during this transition period is the speed of change. Although it is easy to make simple changes rapidly, this is not advisable. Changing a setting so that it is compliant should not cause problems, but by moving slowly, you should have ample time to deal with each change individually on the off chance that there is a problem with the standard. It is all too easy to change multiple things at once; if a problem occurs, however, it can be difficult to determine the cause of the problem. (This is where change control makes troubleshooting easier.) Without change control, you'll likely end up backing out of all the changes you make to fix a problem in just one area. If you move slowly and change one thing at a time, you may save more time than if you were to adjust multiple items, back up, and redo the changes.

The second important consideration for the transition is to recognize the impact of each change on the environment. For instance, renaming a key file server can prevent users from accessing critical files if they're not informed in advance of the change. In many cases, administrative tools can be used to mitigate the impact of a change. In this example, changing login scripts to point to the new server name would significantly reduce the impact on endusers. Additionally, the help desk should be a key ally during this process to assist users impacted by any changes.

Violating the Standard

At times, especially when conforming an existing environment to a standard, you will encounter situations in which you're tempted to violate the standard. Theoretically, you should not deviate from the standard even slightly. However, sometimes it is necessary to do so. These situations vary for each organization, so an example that might make sense to some people would not qualify as an exception to others. The simple rule is that the standard should be violated only when the cost of implementing and maintaining the standard outweighs the benefits of implementation.

Standards and Testing Labs

Don't overlook testing labs when deploying the standard. Although a standard sometimes needs to be ignored in a lab environment, this should be avoided if possible. By ensuring that your labs follow the same standards as your production environment, you reduce the chance that something that works fine in the lab doesn't work in production.

When possible, it's best to grant exceptions that are temporary. These temporary violations should include a plan to reach compliance in the long term (again, as defined by the organization). When a permanent violation is required, it should be noted in the standards documentation. Whoever is in charge of this area of the standard should revisit each exception on a regular basis to ensure that the reason for the exception is still valid. For instance, if one department uses a nonstandard word processor and can't pay for the upgrade to the standard version, you may want to grant the department a temporary exception. This could be done with the understanding that the upgrade would be included in the department's next budget. When budget time arrives, the issue should be reviewed to make sure that the budget items are in place.

Because the reasoning for an exception will vary by organization, it's important that these exceptions be minimized as much as possible. Once an area of the standard is violated in more than ten percent of its implementation, the standard begins to lose effectiveness. Many of the cost benefits also are lost, as administrators must always check to see if what they are working on is standardized or not.

If you find that certain standards are routinely being violated, that area of the standard should be closely scrutinized. Perhaps the wrong choice was made in selecting that particular part of the standard. If you find that to be the case, you should not hesitate to select a better alternative for the standard. Of course, you must be sure to mention this in the change control history of the standard.

Step 5: Maintaining and Reviewing the Standard

Without a doubt, a standardization process costs a significant amount of time and money. This type of investment demands long-term dividends. These benefits are possible only if the standard is rigorously defended. This is a two-fold process. First, the standard must be continually applied to the environment, by both reviewing existing systems and standardizing new systems as they join the environment. Second, the standard must be reviewed to guarantee that it continues to provide value.

Maintaining the Standard

After you've crafted a standard and applied it to your environment, feel free to celebrate. This is a major achievement for any organization. Just make sure that you're on the job the next day, because standards tend to disintegrate without proper maintenance. Properly maintaining the standard is much less costly than going through the entire standardization process every year or two and then stopping after the initial standardization.

To ensure that the standard is maintained, repeat the inventory at regular intervals. This should probably be carried out quarterly or perhaps monthly. When you discover exceptions, utilize change control to return them to the standard. This review is also a good time to revisit any known violations to see if they can now be standardized.

Reviewing the Standard

Computing is an extremely dynamic field. In this environment, a static standard will quickly become a wasted investment. Eventually, parts of the standard will become obsolete. New technologies will introduce issues you never thought of during the standard's creation. Because this is inevitable, the standard should be reviewed periodically to ensure that it is still relevant. At least once a year, a new inventory should be performed. This will answer several questions:

- Is the environment remaining compliant? If not, find out why.
- Are there new issues that should be included in the standard?
- Are any areas of the standard no longer required?

With a dynamic environment, a static standard will not work. The standards process is ongoing. Your standard five years from now will likely look very different from what it does today.

4

Assessing Critical Applications

APPLICATIONS ARE THE SOUL OF ANY computer system. The operating system (OS) is simply a means to access the applications and provide services to them. Although OS upgrades such as Windows 2000 provide great enhancements in usability, there is a tradeoff in that some applications may not operate properly in the new environment. Although Microsoft is investing a large amount of time ensuring compatibility, some applications simply won't be able to work with the new OS. Therefore, it's critical to determine which applications will fail and to have alternatives ready by the time your Windows 2000 rollout commences.

Applications fail under Windows 2000 for two reasons:

- Some applications simply don't follow best practices for Windows programming. Even though these specifications are publicly available from Microsoft, some programmers prefer to color outside the lines or are simply unaware of Win32 API best practices.

- Many applications were hard-coded for Windows 9x or specifically for Windows 95. As a result, they do not perform properly in an NT/2000 environment.

  The main cause for incompatibilities among Windows 9x applications is security. When a Windows 9x application is unable to read a file or Registry setting because of security issues, the application typically fails—and not gracefully. An NT- or 2000-aware program would note the error and present an informative dialog box or would do without the information. Another cause for incompatibility among these applications is the difference in the Win32 API between Windows 9x and Windows NT/2000.

The preceding reasons for application failure are based on the traditional definition of "application." However, it's important to realize that this chapter will treat the term with a larger meaning. In this context, an *application* is any software that is not included with the operating system. Certainly, this is a broad definition for applications. Included are not just office suites, Web browsers, and terminal emulators, but also system services, third-party device drivers, and utilities. The wide scope of this definition is required because any of these software components might have trouble with Windows 2000.

Identifying and dealing with critical applications is a multi-step process. Below is the general approach; each step is discussed in detail within the chapter with the exception of step 1, which is covered extensively in Chapter 3.

1. Use the software inventory to determine what software exists in the organization (see Chapter 3 for details).

2. Identify which of these applications are critical in your environment.

3. Determine which applications will have trouble with Windows 2000.

4. Use the inventory to see what the impact will be from the non-compliant applications.

5. Discuss the impact of each non-compliant application with management and users, and then prioritize the order in which problem applications will be resolved.

6. Decide what type of workaround to use for the non-compliant applications. This typically involves upgrading or replacing the application. In some cases, the application may be retired altogether.

Identifying Critical Applications

The first step in assessing your organization's critical applications is determining which applications are critical. There are two reasons for this focus. First, if your rollout is pressed for time, you can focus on testing those applications that are most important. Second, if you are able to test all the applications that will migrate to Windows 2000 (which is the recommended path), you will be able to determine which applications should receive the most rigorous testing.

It's important that you are able to recognize critical applications. The best definition of a *critical application* (termed by some as "mission-critical") is an application that your organization requires to conduct its business. For a simple example of this, think of a Web hosting company. Its Web server software is no doubt a critical application. One group of applications that is usually critical regardless of the type of organization is accounting programs that deal with accounts payable, accounts receivable, and (hopefully) payroll. Although management typically defines which applications are critical, endusers often have an opinion as well.

Endusers within an organization will vary greatly in determining which programs are critical. For example, students at a university probably consider a word processor and Web browser critical. Professors find spreadsheets for grade tracking or perhaps email to be critical. Finally, administrators at the university define the financial aid programs, billing system, and grade reporting system as critical. Although some at all levels may claim that programs such as Solitaire are critical to them, this merely shows that users may have a distorted view of computing priorities. Be sure to confirm that what they define as their critical programs meet legitimate business needs.

Unfortunately, determining your organization's critical applications is not an easy process. Certain applications will clearly be critical; others will obviously not matter as much. Despite this, many may be difficult to classify. The best approach when defining critical applications is to work with management to come up with a definition and then present to them a list of applications that meet the definition. To an extent, this definition will depend on your organization. Whereas the university in the preceding example depended on a range of applications, a stockbrokerage's critical applications might consist solely of a spreadsheet and a transaction tracking system.

Of course, hashing out a list of critical applications may take just as long as testing all the supported applications in your environment. Certainly, it's best to make sure that all applications run instead of testing only the critical ones.

Potential Pitfalls

Whether you only have time to test the most critical applications, or you have the luxury of verifying all your programs, this section shows you the typical problems various types of applications have in transitioning to Windows 2000. To accomplish this, the applications are classified by their OS types. This is because applications written for a given OS typically have similar types of trouble with Windows 2000. For each OS type, different areas are likely to cause trouble.

There are quite a few reasons why applications may fail to work on Windows 2000. The good news is that you will find most applications to be functional under Windows 2000. The larger the vendor and the application's market share, the more likely that the application will work. Large vendors typically have an established technique they follow when creating applications, and a usual part of this methodology is to adhere to Microsoft's guidelines for programming applications. Should such an application have trouble with Windows 2000, odds are good that the vendor will quickly make a fix available.

Of the various OS types, some are more likely to encounter trouble than others. In general, OS/2 applications, followed closely by POSIX applications, will be least compatible. (However, if they run on NT, they should run on Windows 2000.) DOS and Windows 3.1 applications are likely to run, but some will fail. Most Windows 9x applications will transition to Windows 2000 without a problem. Finally, Windows NT applications are very likely to run, although some services and utilities may have difficulty.

OS/2 and POSIX Applications

Although Windows 2000 continues the NT tradition of offering support for certain OS/2 and POSIX applications, this support is quite limited. In both cases, the odds of owning either type of application are quite low. Because neither type of application benefits from the new Windows 2000 features, the only justification for upgrading these applications' OS to Windows 2000 would be to achieve a common operating environment within the organization. However, those few who have such software would find a much happier user experience if they were to migrate to a Win32, Windows 2000-ready application.

DOS Applications

Many DOS applications will run properly under Windows 2000 without modification. A subset of those DOS applications that work in Windows 9x function under Windows 2000. However, five main areas may cause trouble for DOS applications on Windows 2000. The following sections discuss those five problem areas in detail.

Direct Hardware Access

Programs that talk directly to the hardware, instead of going through BIOS or DOS calls, will not work in Windows 2000. This includes any terminate-and-stay resident (TSR) drivers that the application requires. For example, DOS networking tools will not work under Windows 2000. Due to 2000's security model, only kernel-mode software can directly access the hardware. Normal applications, which run in user mode, can only indirectly request for the kernel to interact with the hardware. The only solution for programs with this problem is to upgrade, replace, or retire them.

The FAT File System

In the days of DOS, the FAT file system was the only format in use. As a result, some applications rely on the presence of a FAT file system for their storage. This can cause two types of problems. First, applications requiring FAT will fail on NTFS partitions. This type of application must be upgraded, replaced, or retired. Second, many applications that do not otherwise depend on FAT believe that the DOS FAT maximum partition size of 2GB is the maximum size for any partition and will have trouble on partitions greater than 2GB. Typically this is manifested as a negative value when the application displays the amount of space on the volume.

In some cases, this particular problem can be resolved by decreasing the free space on the partition to less than 2GB, either by using a smaller partition or by filling the free space on a larger partition. While an upgrade is advisable if one is available, this problem is usually not a critical failure. The application can sometimes continue to function.

Year 2000 Issues

Although this is not necessarily a problem with Windows 2000 compliance, it must be considered, depending on your timeframe for Windows 2000 deployment. Many DOS applications that use dates may have problems with the year 2000. If any critical applications are DOS based, they must be tested exhaustively. How to resolve any issues you discover will vary by application. You might be able to correct some problems with the current version, but in some cases, upgrade, replacement, or retirement may be necessary.

Graphics

Programs that display graphics cannot run in a window. Examples of such programs are DOS-based games and graphics programs. Instead of running in a window, they must be displayed in full-screen mode. Typically, this is not a major concern due to the small number of such programs in use today. Should you have such an application, it must be upgraded, replaced, or retired.

Security

DOS programs do not understand the Windows 2000 security model. This includes Active Directory (AD), file and share permissions, and user rights. As a result, a DOS application will not fail gracefully when it tries to do something that's prevented by the current security context. This can cause misleading error messages, program crashes, and possible data loss. Relaxing security may allow the program to run properly.

Windows 3.x Applications

The majority of Windows 3.x (16-bit) applications run accurately on Windows 2000. Many applications designed for Windows 3.1 are still in use in the corporate environment. Windows 2000 supports many of these 16-bit applications. Windows 3.x and DOS applications both have similar trouble spots, but the symptoms and methods for resolution vary somewhat.

Direct Hardware Access

Like DOS applications, 16-bit applications cannot directly access the system's hardware. Instead of using device drivers or TSRs, Windows 3.x applications use virtual device drivers (VXDs). If an application requires a VXD, it will not migrate to Windows 2000. Examples of this type of application are third-party networking systems for Windows 3.x. Upgrade, replacement, and retirement are the only solutions for this type of problem.

The FAT File System

Windows 3.x applications are especially prone to assuming they are running on a FAT partition. Like DOS applications, they may have trouble with partitions greater than 2GB. The most common examples of this are setup programs, which typically check for sufficient free space prior to installing an application. Many times, those that have trouble have interpreted more than 2GB of free space as a negative value. As a result, setup does not allow you to continue because it believes there is insufficient space available.

As with DOS applications with this problem, you can try reducing the amount of free space to less than 2GB, either by using up space or using a smaller partition. If the problem is with the setup program, this limitation can usually be worked around as described here. If the main application is affected, you may need to upgrade, replace, or retire the program, depending on the severity of the problem.

Year 2000 Issues

Like DOS applications, many Windows 3.x applications were not written with the year 2000 in mind and may or may not work as expected. While few programs will fail to run, some will produce bad data or have minor problems. For example, a non-compliant spreadsheet may miscalculate amortizations if they extend beyond 2000. Whether the program can continue to be used depends on the severity of the problem.

Security

Like DOS applications, Windows 3.x programs don't understand Windows 2000's security model. When such a program requests an operation and it is denied due to security, the program may fail in unpredictable ways and give erroneous error messages. Therefore, it may be necessary to relax some areas of system security in order for these applications to function.

Device Drivers

Device drivers, such as for printers, pointers, network cards, and sound cards, are not compatible with Windows 2000. Therefore, any application that depends on a specific Windows 3.x driver will fail. For many devices, Windows 2000 drivers are available from the manufacturer or on the Windows 2000 CD. If no driver is forthcoming, a driver for similar hardware can sometimes be used. Be sure to test this approach thoroughly before implementing it in a production environment. If no driver is forthcoming and there is no similar driver, the hardware will have to be replaced or retired.

CPU Starvation

One of the major changes from Windows 3.x to Windows 2000 is in the area of CPU utilization. Under Windows 3.x, applications were cooperatively multitasked. In other words, each application controlled when it relinquished the CPU to the next application. Poorly written or malicious programs could hog the CPU, starving the other programs by not giving them access. This would typically cause the system to lock up or become unstable, which was an all-too-frequent occurrence. Windows 2000 solves this by taking the opposite approach. Instead of depending on the programs to govern themselves, the system rations CPU time to each application. When an application's time expires, the system takes over and hands the CPU to the next application.

While this is the default for Win32 programs, Win16 applications by default run in a shared memory space (similar to their Windows 3.x environment) in Windows 2000. However, Win16 programs can be made to run in separate memory spaces. As a result, they are then preemptively multitasked instead of cooperatively multitasked. If you have several 16-bit applications that must be migrated and one or more is CPU-intensive, be sure to set up each intensive application so that it runs in a separate memory space. This will ensure fair CPU utilization for all 16-bit applications.

Windows 9x Applications

Most Windows 9x applications run properly under Windows 2000, but they are vulnerable to the same sort of problems DOS and 16-bit applications are. Because they are 32-bit applications, they should have fewer problems with Windows 2000 than applications originally designed for DOS or Windows 3.x.

Device Drivers

Device drivers, such as for video cards, are not compatible with Windows 2000. If an application requires a specific Windows 9x driver, it will fail. There is one exception to this, however. Windows 98 supports the Windows Driver Model (WDM). This specification is designed by Microsoft to end the problem of each new OS requiring completely new device drivers. WDM drivers are compatible with Windows 2000 and should migrate without a problem.

Year 2000 Issues

It is wishful thinking to believe that all modern Win32 applications are Y2K-compliant. Be sure to confirm that any application that will migrate to Windows 2000 is Y2K-compliant.

Long Filenames and Compatibility

DOS and Windows 3.x applications are often perceived as having one incompatibility with Windows 2000 that is typically not an actual problem. This perception involves long filenames. While none of these programs will properly display long filenames, they are able to use the 8.3 names generated automatically by Windows 2000.

However, this is not true if you are using the NTFS file system and have disabled 8.3 compatible naming via the Registry. If short names are disabled, these programs will be unable to access the file system. Although disabling 8.3 name generation speeds up the file system slightly, its use is not recommended.

Security

DOS and Win16 programs are likely to fail when a request is rejected due to security. Windows 9x programs, on the other hand, may be more graceful. Because they are written using the Win32 API, they will receive more descriptive failure codes from the system. However, if a program was written without Windows 2000 and security in mind, it may still fail. As with the other OS types, relaxing permissions may allow the application to operate.

Win32 API

Although Windows 9x and Windows 2000 share the Win32 API, there are differences in the API between the two platforms. As was mentioned earlier, many of the differences lie in the area of security, although other differences also exist. Often, utility programs such as virus scanners and disk defragmenters are affected by these differences. If you encounter such an application, your only options are to upgrade, replace, or retire it.

Registry Problems

Unless separate user profiles are enabled, the HKEY_CURRENT_USER Registry hive is usually the same regardless of who logs in under Windows 9x. For this reason, some programs will use HKEY_CURRENT_USER\Software (which should store user-specific information) to store information that should really reside under HKEY_LOCAL_MACHINE \Software (which should store non user-specific information). This becomes a problem under Windows 2000, in which each user has a separate HKEY_CURRENT_USER hive that is loaded only when he or she logs in locally. Applications with this problem may refuse to run or have strange configuration problems.

Many times, this problem can be solved by copying a working user's HKEY_CURRENT_USER Registry entries for the program to other users' HKEY_CURRENT_USER Registry hives that need to run the program. If a large number of users needs to run the application on a large number of computers, it will be easier to upgrade to a version that uses HKEY_CURRENT_USER properly.

Windows NT Applications

Very few Windows NT applications will have trouble with Windows 2000. Although there are certainly quite a few changes from Windows NT to Windows 2000, they are mainly new features, not changes to the existing functionality. Properly written Windows NT applications should migrate without a problem. However, some Windows NT services and system utilities may have trouble migrating to Windows 2000.

Windows NT Services

Windows NT services will have more trouble with Windows 2000 than other types of NT applications. This is not to say that all NT services will fail to migrate. In fact, most will do so without a problem. However, system services are much more affected by the new Windows 2000 features than applications are.

Services that are most likely to have trouble are those whose functions are also performed by Windows 2000. For example, several third-party applications allow for more granular administration of Windows NT. Because AD is designed to provide this functionality, these services are no longer needed. Therefore, if those services are migrated to Windows 2000, they may or may not function properly. Similar situations exist for file quota software and user authentication, such as smartcards.

If the equivalent Windows 2000 functionality is not utilized, the NT service should continue to function. However, increased functionality will be gained by utilizing services that understand the new features of Windows 2000, such as AD and the new file system permissions.

System Utilities

System utilities, for the most part, should not be migrated to Windows 2000. Two examples of this are disk defragmenters and backup utilities. Defragmenters do not understand NTFS5 and are therefore incompatible with Windows 2000. They should continue to function with FAT and NTFS partitions, but the better route is to move to a Windows 2000 and NTFS5 compatible version. Similarly, backup utilities do not understand AD or the new file permissions. As a result, these programs won't properly back up or restore the new permissions or, more importantly, the AD. This is not an acceptable situation. Upgrade these utilities to versions that support Windows 2000. Essentially, if any utility works directly with file systems or permissions and users, it should be upgraded for best functionality.

Additionally, any utilities that access the Security Accounts Manager (SAM) database should be upgraded to an AD version. Although they will continue to work when used on Windows 2000 domain controllers (DCs) in compatibility mode, one of the goals of your Windows 2000 migration should be to move the DCs to native mode.

Some system utilities are exempt from this rule. The best examples of this are virus scanners. Migrating the existing Windows NT version to Windows 2000 should not be a problem. Of course, this would be a good time to upgrade if the scanning engine needed to be replaced.

Leveraging Inventory

Now that you know how various applications may have trouble with Windows 2000, you can put the software inventory from Chapter 3 to use once again. From this inventory, you gain a list of applications in your environment. When an application turns out to be non-compliant, the inventory shows how widely the application is distributed and which computers will have to be fixed.

For example, if a certain application is incompatible with Windows 2000, you can use the inventory to determine which machines currently are running the application. As a result, you can learn the magnitude of the problem. If just one or two machines run the program, you have greater flexibility in dealing with the problem than if the entire organization uses it. Without an inventory, you won't have a good idea of which machines use the application. In fact, you may not even be aware that the application is being used by the enterprise.

After using your inventory database to produce a list of all the software in use in the enterprise, apply your definition of critical applications to decide which programs pose the greatest potential obstacle for a smooth rollout. You can then proceed to check each application based on its priority.

Discovering Problem Applications

Now that you've used the inventory to prioritize your applications, it's time to see what difficulties your critical applications will have. If you're a veteran of migrating from Windows 3.x or Windows 9x to Windows NT, you're probably good at taking your knowledge of a program and making an educated guess as to whether the program will run under NT. This knowledge will be a great assistance with your Windows 2000 deployment. When you're not sure if an application or service will work, there are two good methods for finding out:

- **Contact the vendor.** Typically, the vendor's Web pages will list any known issues with the current application and Windows 2000. In some cases, a patch may be available that fixes any problems. If there's no information on the Web site, try talking to tech support.

- **Hands-on testing.** Install Windows 2000 in a test lab and see if the application functions as it should. This is the best method for testing applications because it can reveal a large percentage of any troubles. However, testing can't prove that no problems exist. For this reason, an enduser of the application should test its functionality with the goal of duplicating the daily operations. This should expose most bugs that could interfere with the current workflow.

A hybrid approach works best. First, check with the vendor for compatibility information. Then, test this information hands-on. You may find that a problem listed by the vendor doesn't cause a problem in your environment. For example, some bugs occur only intermittently or infrequently. If the bug occurs once a month and has a minor effect, you might continue to use the application without change. Of course, you may find just the opposite. It may be that your organization is the first one to use a certain feature in an application under Windows 2000, and the vendor may be unaware of the problem. In order to avoid these scenarios, this hybrid method is the best approach to take if sufficient time is available.

This was the method used for a Windows NT migration I participated in recently. We migrated 1200 desktops from Windows 3.1 to Windows NT 4.0 Workstation. Because we followed this process, there were very few surprises with the applications. When Windows 3.1 applications had a problem with Windows NT, we were aware of the problem in advance and had an alternative ready. Note that due to the large number of applications in use by the organization, the application testing phase of the project lasted for several months. You should probably plan to spend two weeks with each application to ensure that it will transition properly.

Upgrade, Replace, or Retire?

By this point in the process, you should have discovered what is hopefully a short list of applications that will not survive the transition to Windows 2000. The question then becomes whether to upgrade the application, replace it, or retire its functionality. Sometimes the answer will be clear cut; other times, there may be no easy solution. See Table 4.1 for a quick reference of the pros and cons of each solution.

Table 4.1   **Determining Whether to Upgrade, Replace, or Retire**

Solution	Pros	Cons
Upgrade	Leverage existing data without manually re-creating. Usage and support knowledge about the current application should apply to the upgrade. Usually cheaper than replacement.	Vendor or product may no longer be desirable. Problems with current system may not be solved by the upgrade.
Replace	May gain significant enhancements over current system. New interface may be a great improvement.	Data may need to be converted. New interface may require retraining. Support knowledge from the old application will not transfer. Usually more expensive than upgrading.
Retire	One less application to support. Product may no longer be required. Cheapest of the three solutions.	Functionality is probably still required. Requires extensive planning and management approval.

Upgrading

The primary reason for upgrading an application during rollout is to arrive at a version that is compatible with Windows 2000. A side benefit is that most upgrades also offer additional benefits. These benefits typically include both fixes for bugs and increased functionality. However, some upgrades discontinue various features. Before you roll out an upgrade simply because it is compatible with Windows 2000, test it to ensure that it can still be used for its original function.

As Table 4.1 shows, any worthwhile upgrade allows you to make use of the data entered in the previous version of the application. For instance, word processors always are able to read and write older versions' file formats. Similarly, database products convert existing databases into new storage formats as part of the upgrade process. In other cases, applications have only configuration information, such as terminal emulators. Applications that do not offer the ability to leverage the existing data or configuration negate an important reason for upgrading. You will heartily agree if you find yourself responsible for re-entering thousands of database records!

Likewise, a good amount of the information you know about the current version ought to apply to the new version. Although you are likely to encounter bugs similar to those in the current version if they're not fixed, you likely will be able to use the workarounds you use for the current application on the upgrade. As a result, your help desk will have an easier transition to an upgrade than to a replacement application.

In most situations, another key factor in determining whether to upgrade or replace is the cost. It is typically much cheaper to upgrade to a new version than to replace the application (see Table 4.1). In some cases, the upgrade is free. However, when you factor in the costs of data conversion and retraining that coincide with replacing an application, the cost difference can become even more extreme.

Finally, the current version and an upgrade typically have a similar interface and functionality. This means that the users' familiarity with the current version will reduce the learning curve for the upgrade. Although most applications follow this trend, seminal releases typically have a greatly revised interface, which will lessen the value of this factor.

The Role of Management

Your organization's management will have a large impact on the success of the rollout. The project must be adequately staffed and have a timeline that's not overly optimistic. Additionally, management can be a great help when you need endusers to test an application's functionality. For example, making sure the payroll system works on Windows 2000 requires one or more people from accounting to spend some time using the product under Windows 2000. In some cases, office turf wars can make this process difficult without management assistance.

When management is made aware of the potential pitfalls and the benefits of success, they can make people available to help. This includes both technical staff for the project and endusers for application testing. Only through partnership with management can a project of this scope succeed—whatever the size of the organization.

If you decide an upgrade is the best approach, be sure to test the upgrade extensively. Use a test lab similar to the one you used to test the original application with Windows 2000. Install your current OS and the current application, and then upgrade both. Test to make sure that the application functions properly and that the previous data is still intact. Once the rollout begins, be sure every machine is backed up before any changes are made, even if the application tested flawlessly.

Replacing

While upgrading is usually an attractive option, there are times when the best course of action is to replace the software with a different product. Vendors going out of business and bad experiences with the current software are just two of the many reasons this might be the best option.

As Table 4.1 shows, moving to a new product may provide a great improvement in functionality. In the fast-evolving world of software, yesterday's market leader can be today's also-ran. The industry is littered with companies that established a great product and then grew complacent. Certainly, when you find an application that must be upgraded or replaced, it is worth the effort to do a full, competitive evaluation, comparing the upgrade with its competitors.

Of course, with a new application comes a new interface. This can be positive or negative. On the positive side, the interface may be much easier to use than the old application. On the other hand, it may take some time for the users to become familiar with this new interface. Some applications may have a steep learning curve.

A final good news/bad news point to consider is the disposition of the data entered in the current system. The bad news is that this data must be moved to the new application. Although many applications provide migration utilities that translate competitors' data formats into their own, these do not exist in all cases. Sometimes data must be manually re-entered into the new system, or a custom program must be used for the conversion. In some cases, some or all of the data simply cannot be transferred, and alternatives must be used to provide the information.

Hope for Windows 9x Applications

There is hope for some applications running on Windows 9x. Microsoft is providing an interface so that developers of these applications can provide what is called a *migration.dll*. As part of the Windows 2000 upgrade process, all migration.dlls on the system are run, giving their applications a chance to correct whatever problems they would otherwise have. This procedure will only work on Windows 9x and is for applications that do not properly upgrade. Typically, these upgrade failures result from the differences in Registry structure and in the Win32 API between Windows 9x and Windows 2000.

Retiring

In some cases, the best approach to take with a non-compliant application is to retire it. Don't confuse this with replacement; if the functionality has been taken over by another program, you are replacing the application. Only if the functionality is discontinued is the application retired. For example, retiring a modem pool in favor of remote access via the Internet is replacement. Discontinuing remote access altogether is retirement.

Retiring an application has its advantages. As you can see in Table 4.1, a retired application means one less program that requires support. Additionally, this option is very cheap, usually having no cost. However, functionality is very rarely retired. It's much more likely that a new application provides the capability, serving as a replacement.

A great deal of planning must go into retiring an application. You must confirm that the users can do without its capabilities. Management usually has to sign off on a change of this magnitude. No doubt, several meetings will be required before the retirement is approved.

It's rare to retire functionality. However, in the case of retiring NetBIOS (as discussed in Chapter 5), you can gain significant advantages.

Don't Forget the Endusers

It is all too easy to forget that IT exists to make information accessible to the users. To change to new applications without regard to their usability flies in the face of most IT departments' mission statements. Additionally, it will invite the wrath of the endusers. To alleviate this problem, try to include users of the product in the evaluation process.

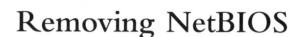

5

Removing NetBIOS

WHEN DESIGNING A NETWORK, ADMINISTRATORS ARE faced with a major question: What protocol(s) should be used? The more protocols supported, the greater the likelihood that two devices will be able to communicate without any intervention. For example, in order for a Windows 2000 workstation to reach a UNIX FTP server and a Novell NetWare 4.11 server, the workstation must be configured with both TCP/IP and IPX/SPX (or Microsoft's IPX implementation, called NWLink). While this interoperability has its advantages, each additional protocol a device supports has an impact in terms of performance. This is due to the additional memory and processing required to multiplex protocols. An additional factor enters the picture if multiple subnets will be connected. Routers and some switches must be configured for each protocol that will be routed.

Rather than configuring devices with multiple protocols, you can have every device use the same protocol. That way, the same broad connectivity can be achieved without the burden of supporting multiple protocols. This is the direction that the industry is heading toward. This movement is made possible by the phenomenal growth of the Internet and its underlying protocol, TCP/IP. Even Novell recently made its NetWare OS capable of native IP communication, ending its former reliance on IPX/SPX.

In a similar vein, Microsoft no longer requires NetBIOS to communicate with other Microsoft network clients. As a result, you can remove the protocol from the network by following the plan outlined by this chapter.

NetBIOS Overview

Although in the earlier example the Windows 2000 workstation simply requires TCP/IP and IPX/SPX, earlier versions of the Microsoft network client required that additional protocols be loaded. Prior to Windows 2000, all Microsoft networks required NetBIOS support over each transport protocol (usually TCP/IP, IPX/SPX, and NetBEUI). This was required to enable the Microsoft clients to communicate with one another, even if this support was not required. (Examples in which this functionality was not required include machines functioning purely as Internet clients or servers and Novell NetWare clients.) This section explores the distinguishing traits of NetBIOS, its naming standard, its name registration and resolution, routing, and the advantages of removing it from a network.

General Characteristics

Unlike familiar protocols, such as TCP/IP and IPX/SPX, NetBIOS is not actually a protocol you will see if you analyze your network's packets. This is because NetBIOS is a Session layer protocol, rather than a Network or Transport layer protocol. NetBIOS specifies the interface for programs to communicate with it, and then relies on lower level protocols such as IP, IPX, and NetBEUI to actually transport the NetBIOS information between machines. This process is called *encapsulation*. What you will see in packets is NetBIOS encapsulated within the transport protocols. For instance, NetBIOS via IP is called NBT or NetBT. Over IPX, it's known as NBIPX. Finally, NetBIOS can be transmitted via NetBEUI, which is common on small networks and older Microsoft networks such as Windows for Workgroups 3.11.

NetBIOS Names

An easily recognized characteristic of NetBIOS is its naming scheme. As an administrator, you've no doubt seen network names such as `ADMINISTRATOR<03>`, whether in WINS or network traces. This is a typical example of a NetBIOS name. These names convey three important properties:

- Naming Conventions
- The type of service
- The scope of the name

"Standard" NetBIOS

Although many vendors have implemented NetBIOS, no official standards exist for the protocol. This chapter will focus on Microsoft's implementation, which is used by all of its operating systems.

Naming Conventions

NetBIOS machines identify one another using friendly text names. These names can include the letters A-Z (which are always uppercase), numbers 0-9, and the special characters ! @ # $ % ^ & ( ) - _ ' { } . ~. Although NetBIOS names are 16 characters in length, the computer or service name is limited to the first 15 characters.

NetBIOS names are dynamic. This means that names can be registered and released as needed. For instance, when a NetBIOS machine boots, it registers its `<00>` and `<03>` type computername. However, the username for the `<03>` Messenger service is only registered as the users log in. When they log out, the `<03>` registrations are released. Under NBT, you can force Windows 2000 to re-register all of its current names by running `NBTSTAT -RR`.

For computers running NBT, you can see what names the computer has registered by running `NBTSTAT -n`. Following is the output from a machine running Windows 2000:

```
Local Area Connection:
Node IpAddress: [10.1.1.1] Scope Id: []
                NetBIOS Local Name Table

      Name                Type         Status
   _ _ _ _ _ _ _ _ _ _ _ _ _ _ _ _ _ _ _ _ _ _ _ _ _ _ _ .

      MYCOMPUTER    <00>  UNIQUE    Registered
      MYCOMPUTER    <03>  UNIQUE    Registered
      WORKGROUP     <00>  GROUP     Registered
      MYCOMPUTER    <20>  UNIQUE    Registered
      ADMINISTRATOR <03>  UNIQUE    Registered
      WORKGROUP     <1E>  GROUP     Registered
      WORKGROUP     <1D>  UNIQUE    Registered
      .._MSBROWSE_.<01>   GROUP     Registered
```

Third-Party Network Stacks

Although recent Microsoft operating systems have shipped with Microsoft network stacks, do not confuse an OS with its network provider. Third parties supply network stacks for NetWare, LANtastic, and TCP/IP, which do not require any Microsoft components and as such do not require the NetBIOS support in each transport protocol. Usually, these stacks were used with Windows 3.1, which had no built-in network functionality. Although these third-party stacks are not as prevalent today, they are still in use. While unlikely, it's possible that your organization is in this situation. This is most common when using a non-Microsoft server, such as LINUX or NetWare, or in a peer-to-peer system, such as LANtastic.

There are few reasons to use a third-party network stack on Windows 2000. It's best to use the built-in stack, as it provides a great deal of functionality.

Type of Service

Unlike the DNS naming scheme of IP, which only identifies computers, Microsoft's NetBIOS names combine both a name and the type of service into the NetBIOS name. To do this, they reserve the sixteenth character for a special identifier to show what type of service the name represents, such as Master Browser, User, or Server. In order to make more identifiers available, they ignore the character limitations of the previous section and instead allow the full values of 00-FF (hex). The two most frequently used service types are COMPUTERNAME<00>, which specifies a computer, and USERNAME<03>, which is used by the Messenger service.

Because some services may be provided on more than one computer, names can either be unique names (registered to only one machine), or group names (registered to multiple machines). For example, only one COMPUTERNAME<00> or USERNAME<03> may be registered on the network. On the other hand, all domain controllers can register the DOMAIN<1C> name.

Name Scope

The NetBIOS namespace is flat. That is, all NetBIOS names on a network must be unique. Although a group name can be registered to multiple machines, two groups cannot share the same NetBIOS name. NetBIOS supports a Scope ID, which many administrators initially believe is similar to the hierarchical host naming used by DNS. However, this is not the case; although the Scope ID is used to segment NetBIOS name spaces, different Scope IDs cannot communicate with one another. For this reason, the Scope ID is virtually always left blank.

Layered Networks

The layers mentioned in the section "General Characteristics" refer to the OSI Reference Model for networking (See Figure 5.1). The OSI model is a fundamental concept for understanding network operations. Rather than describe specific means for communication, it is a method for abstracting the function of various network components.

The model consists of seven layers, with each layer communicating with its equivalent layer on remote network devices (See Figure 5.2). To achieve this, data is passed down to layer 1 on the sender, crosses the network, and is passed back up to the sending layer on the receiver. The bottom two layers are implemented in hardware (the network card), the middle four layers in network software (the protocol stack), and the top layer in the network application. Protocols such as IP and IPX are Network or layer 3 protocols, and provide relatively basic network services. Transport is layer 4, and TCP and SPX are examples of layer 4 implementations. The Session layer, which is layer 5, is where NetBIOS resides.

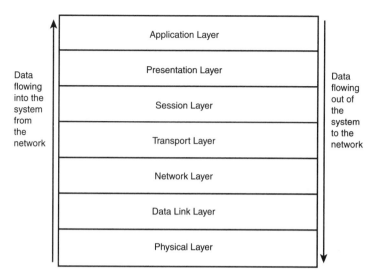

Figure 5.1 This is the OSI model for a machine's network interface. Each layer communicates with its neighbors to pass information between the computer and the network.

Routing

NetBIOS has a very simple naming scheme. Notably absent is a subnet identifier. For a protocol to be routed between subnets, it must support a method of identifying different subnets. NetBIOS has no identifier because it has no concept of subnets. There are two reasons for this:

- NetBIOS is a Session layer protocol. The Session layer is not concerned with routing. It is the duty of the Network layer to ensure that any routing takes place.

- At the time NetBIOS was created, most PC networks consisted of small, one-subnet LANs. It is likely that the explosive growth of networking and subsequent need for network segmentation were never considered in NetBIOS design.

NetBIOS Service Types
Microsoft maintains a list of more than 30 service types and their hex identifiers in Knowledge Base article Q163409. It's available on the web at

http://support.microsoft.com/support/kb/articles/q163/4/09.asp.

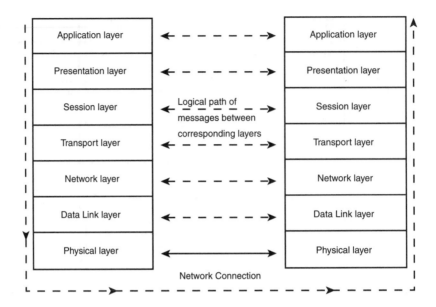

Physical path of data between machines

Figure 5.2 Although the OSI model physically sends messages between computers at the Physical layer, each layer logically communicates with its matching layer on the other machine.

Because NetBIOS depends on other protocols to enable routing, you must examine these other protocols' implementations of NetBIOS to learn how each handles routing.

NetBEUI

NetBEUI stands for NetBIOS Extended User Interface. It is a protocol that was purpose-built to transport NetBIOS across a network. Like NetBIOS, NetBEUI is unaware of subnets.

The use of NetBEUI is impractical aside from single-subnet networks or when two devices will always be on the same subnet. One example of this is NetBEUI used as a means of adding security to a SQL server connected to a Web server on the Internet. The Web server would use IP for Web traffic, of course, but would communicate with the SQL server using NetBEUI. The SQL server would have NetBEUI as its only network protocol. By doing this, it becomes much harder for someone to directly attack the SQL server from the Internet.

NBIPX and NBT

Both IPX and IP support routing. As a result, it's natural that NBIPX and NBT both can be routed. For NBIPX to work across subnets, routers must be configured to forward NBIPX broadcasts (used for name resolution) across subnets. In contrast to local broadcasts, which don't propagate beyond the local subnet, these global broadcasts are forwarded to all connected IPX networks. This means that every IPX device must process the packet, regardless of whether it is participating in a Microsoft network. On busy networks, all available bandwidth on the network could be consumed by machines broadcasting their NetBIOS names, leading to a broadcast storm.

Under NBT, routing of traffic is supported, but global broadcasts are not. The chief impact of this is twofold. First, broadcast storms are not as likely to occur, because name resolution broadcasts are locally broadcast only. Second, in order for cross-subnet name resolution to occur, the machines must use either LMHOSTS, DNS, or (preferably) WINS.

Name Registration and Resolution

As it does with routing, NetBIOS depends on the underlying protocols to perform name registration and resolution. *Name registration* reserves a NetBIOS name for use by the registering machine. This prevents other machines from using the name, which would cause problems. While only one machine can register a name if it's one of the unique types, multiple machines can register a group name.

Name resolution is the process of transforming sixteen-character NetBIOS names into the network addresses used by underlying protocols. For instance, NetBIOS name resolution in NBT consists of transforming the NetBIOS name into an IP address. Because each protocol performs name resolution differently, each one—NetBEUI, NBIPX, and NBT—will be examined separately.

Broadcast Storms

When a broadcast is sent on a network, all machines must look at the message to determine if it's of importance to them. Even if it's not, this consumes a small amount of memory and processing power for each broadcast. More important is the impact on the network, because the machines can process packets much more quickly than the network can produce them. As a result, it is possible for networks to become swamped by broadcast packets. Multiple machines would try to broadcast, and due to the amount of traffic, they would have limited success. The number of machines wishing to transmit would grow, which would result in a broadcast storm.

NetBEUI

Because of the single-subnet mentality of NetBEUI, the task of resolving friendly text names, such as SERVER or COMPUTER1, into network hardware addresses is accomplished by broadcasting to the network. Essentially, the broadcasting computer sends a single packet to the attention of all computers on the network segment, requesting the hardware address of the desired host. If a computer has registered the requested name, it responds to the querying computer, and communication could then be established between the two machines using directed (non-broadcast) packets between the two hardware addresses. In the same way, each time a machine boots, it broadcasts its own registered name(s) to the network to see if another device has registered them. This prevents two machines from having the same name, which would cause problems.

NBIPX

Name resolution under NBIPX is similar to that of NetBEUI. Broadcasts are used for name registration and resolution. However, IPX networks can encompass multiple subnets. In order for NBIPX to work across subnets, the routers must be configured to forward NBIPX broadcasts.

Although NBIPX allows NetBIOS to function in multiple subnet networks, its reliance on broadcasts for name resolution makes it a bad choice for implementation. Note that if your systems use NWLink for connectivity, they are also using NBIPX— whether it is desired or not. Because routers do not forward NBIPX broadcasts by default, the impact from NBIPX broadcasts is limited to their local subnet. On active subnets, though, this can still waste a surprising amount of bandwidth. When routers forward NBIPX broadcasts, broadcast traffic can grow quickly.

NBT

Both NetBEUI and NBIPX use broadcasts for name resolution. For multi-subnet networks, this is not efficient. Seven methods are available for NBT to perform name resolution, depending on the machine's configuration:

- **Host name.** The machine will look to see if the requested name matches its own name. This is the fastest resolution method.

- **Local cache.** Recently resolved names are maintained in a local NetBIOS name cache. The machine always checks this cache for a name prior to using the network for name resolution. To ensure that the cache stays up-to-date with changes on the network, entries in the cache expire after ten minutes by default. This method is only slightly slower than checking the host name. To see the contents of a machine's NBT name cache, run NBTSTAT -c. To force a machine to reload its cache, run NBTSTAT -R. This can fix problems if a cached address is no longer correct.

- **NetBIOS Name Server (NBNS).** This is a centralized system for resolving NetBIOS names into IP addresses, similar in function to DNS. By far, the most common NBNS is Microsoft's implementation, called WINS. Despite a number of bugs, it is a key part of downlevel Microsoft IP-based networks. Systems configured to use WINS register their names with WINS and query WINS for name resolution. Because the clients are given the WINS server address, no broadcasts are required, making WINS much more efficient than broadcast-based resolution. The speed of this method depends on the bandwidth and load of the network and the load on the WINS server.

- **Broadcasting.** This method uses network broadcasts to register and resolve NetBIOS names. Since these broadcasts are not forwarded to other subnets, this method is successful only if both machines are on the same subnet. Note that by default, machines will make three broadcasts for each name resolution. By default, if no machine replies to a broadcast within 750 milliseconds, the next broadcast is sent. As a result, this method will take 2,250 milliseconds or 2.25 seconds if there is no matching name on the network. Although this method may be just as fast as using WINS for successful queries, the inefficiency of using broadcasts makes this a less-attractive solution, even on single-subnet networks. Additionally, broadcasting is much slower than WINS when the requested name has not been registered.

- **LMHOSTS file.** Similar to the HOSTS file used for normal IP name resolution, the LMHOSTS file is a text file used on clients to map NetBIOS names to IP addresses. It is normally used to enable machines to communicate with one another across subnets when there is no NBNS. Clients usually have servers or domain controllers listed. The replying machine does not need an LMHOSTS entry for communication to occur, although the replying machine would be unable to initiate connections if that were the case. This method is faster than WINS or broadcasting, but slower than the host name check or cache due to the overhead involved in file operations.

- **HOSTS file.** If the machine is configured to use standard IP name resolution for NetBIOS name resolution, it can check its HOSTS file for a host name matching the requested NetBIOS name. Since a machine's NetBIOS name and IP host name are the same by default, this method may work in some situations. This method is roughly as fast as the LMHOSTS method.

- **DNS.** As with the HOSTS method, a machine configured to augment its NetBIOS name resolution with standard IP name resolution can check with DNS for the requested NetBIOS name. Since a machine's NetBIOS name and IP host name are the same by default, this method may work in some situations. For example, when performing a drive mapping, this method works if the server is listed in DNS. However, when performing a NETSEND to a user, using this method doesn't work because usernames are not registered by DNS. This method is roughly as fast as a WINS query.

RFCs 1001 and 1002 define three types of NBT name resolution, using a mix of broadcasting and NBNS/WINS. There is also a fourth type, called the H-node or hybrid. All four are shown by Table 5.1.

B-Nodes

Computers running NBT default to B-nodes. Since they have no WINS information, this is the only mode they can use. Microsoft uses the cache and LMHOSTS file in its B-node implementation. The order used is cache, broadcast, and LMHOSTS, respectively. If one method fails, the next is tried until the name is resolved or no more resolution methods remain.

P-Nodes

To minimize broadcast traffic, systems can be configured as P-nodes. They must be given the address of at least one name server. If the name server is unavailable, the machine will be unable to resolve remote machine names unless they're already cached. Even if the remote machine is on the same subnet, the name can't be resolved because a P-node will never broadcast.

P-nodes are rarely used in practice, since it's best to try to use broadcasts as a backup if the name server is down or cannot be reached.

M-Nodes

An M-node will broadcast for a name first, and if unsuccessful, it will try using a name server. M-nodes are typically used when most of the traffic will be on the local subnet and the name server is on the other side of a WAN link. For example, in a small regional office of a larger corporation, this scenario is more efficient than contacting the WINS server over a slow link for a machine that is on the local subnet.

H-Nodes

If a system is configured with a WINS address, it will become an H-node by default. This node type offers the best mix of name server and broadcasts for a multisubnet LAN.

Table 5.1 **NBT Name Resolution Types**

Node Type	First Method	Second Method
B-node (Broadcast)	Broadcast	None
P-node (Peer-to-Peer)	Name Server	None
M-node (Mixed)	Broadcast	Name Server
H-node (Hybrid)	Name Server	Broadcast

In the course of a name resolution, all seven of the methods listed may be tried. The listing is the order used by H-nodes for resolution. Note that methods are sometimes skipped; for instance, if the LMHOSTS or HOSTS file is not present, or no DNS server is configured, that method will be skipped.

Advantages of Removing NetBIOS

If there are no downlevel Microsoft clients remaining after your Windows 2000 deployment, you can gain several advantages by removing NetBIOS from your network:

- **End to your reliance on WINS.** WINS, which has always had its share of troubles, is no longer needed once NetBIOS is retired. Clients will use DDNS for name registration and resolution.

- **A single method of name resolution.** Previously, clients would try to perform name resolution via both NetBIOS and the regular method supported by each underlying transport protocol (such as DNS for IP). This made name resolution unnecessarily complex because some scenarios required clients to try seven different methods of name resolution. Moving to a single name resolution method cuts this number in half.

- **Easier network support.** Since fewer protocols must be supported, it becomes easier to support the network.

- **Increased network performance.** Without NetBIOS and the multiple methods of name resolution, your network will perform better, due to the reduced traffic.

- **Increased performance connecting to multihomed servers.** Under NetBIOS, connection requests are made on all transports available at the client. If multiple connections succeed, all but one is canceled, which is inefficient. Using standard IP with DNS name resolution allows for simpler selection of the proper connection to the server.

- **Enhanced security.** Several methods of attacking Windows computers involve NetBIOS. By removing NetBIOS from your systems, especially those directly connected to the Internet, you gain an additional level of security.

Windows 2000 and NetBIOS

Microsoft decided to end Windows' reliance on NetBIOS in Windows 2000. NetBIOS is no longer required only on TCP/IP. Windows 2000 fails to separate NetBIOS from NWLink and NetBEUI, encouraging users to switch to TCP/IP instead. With the current direction of networking, this transition to TCP/IP is only natural. Whereas previously vendors tried to support every major protocol, everyone is now standardizing on TCP/IP. As you learned at the beginning of the chapter, this "one protocol everywhere" approach is more efficient than the older "every protocol everywhere" approach.

Windows 2000 also provides new features that make the switch to TCP/IP advantageous for the user. These include IPSec, QoS, and DDNS, which are discussed in Chapters 7 and 8.

NetBEUI and NWLink

Windows 2000 continues the Microsoft tradition of supporting NetBEUI. Very small networks, such as those with one subnet, can gain advantages from NetBEUI's simplicity of setup and operation. While it may continue to be a good choice for small networks, TCP/IP is commonly the choice for other networks. (By default, it's the only protocol installed on Windows NT 4.0 and Windows 2000.) Even small networks should use IP if they will be accessing the Internet.

Since NetBEUI was purpose-built for NetBIOS, there's no way to remove NetBIOS and its limitations from NetBEUI. To gain the benefits of removing NetBIOS, you have to move to TCP/IP.

Just as with NetBEUI, NBIPX can't be removed from NWLink. In order to remove NetBIOS, you'll need to migrate to TCP/IP. However, most organizations are using IPX for connectivity to other devices, such as Novell's NetWare. If your network is in this situation, you'll need to choose from among several options: You can live with NBIPX, upgrade to NetWare 5 and remove IPX; or migrate from NetWare to Windows 2000 and remove IPX.

TCP/IP

Like its predecessor, Windows NT 4.0, Windows 2000 makes TCP/IP the default choice when installing networking. IP is the only protocol to undergo significant changes from the previous version. As with most of Windows 2000, the majority of these changes entail greater functionality, rather than changes to the way the features operate. First take a look at WINS and then at its successor, DDNS.

WINS

In a pure Windows 2000 environment with no NetBIOS dependencies, WINS is not needed. However, WINS has still been updated. The reason for this is twofold. First, all networks will go through a transition period from the current OS to Windows 2000. WINS is needed during this transition time. Second, some networks will be unable to remove one or more NetBIOS applications.

WINS on Windows 2000

If your WINS server is running Windows 2000, don't disable NBT! Doing so will cause WINS to fail.

DDNS

In Windows NT, WINS provided an important service of dynamically registering computer names and services on the network. WINS was required for two reasons:

- **The need for centralized name resolution across subnets.** As was discussed previously, NetBIOS encounters problems when used with multiple subnets. For NBT, an NBNS (usually in the form of WINS) provides a centralized location for name resolution within the network. By configuring the NBT clients to be H-nodes, they automatically query the NBNS for name resolution before sending out any broadcasts.

- **To make up for the static nature of DNS.** IP addresses can be assigned statically (where each machine is individually assigned a permanent address) or dynamically (where the machine gets a new address each time it boots). Static addresses require that each address manually be assigned and tracked, leading to overhead. Additionally, changing the address scheme can be very difficult, since each machine must be visited. Dynamic addressing in the form of a DHCP server offers a much more attractive solution. Until now, the tradeoff has been that WINS is required because DNS is not designed for the dynamic updates required when DHCP is used to register clients.

Microsoft designed Dynamic DNS (DDNS) to overcome both of these problems, allowing WINS to be retired. Since DNS has always provided centralized name resolution, no changes were required to address this portion of WINS functionality. As the name implies, the main difference between DNS and DDNS is that DDNS is dynamic in nature. Essentially, the dynamic capabilities of WINS have been integrated into DNS, forming DDNS. The main difference between DDNS and WINS is that WINS translates NetBIOS names to IP addresses, while DDNS translates host names to IP addresses. Of course, this means that any remaining NetBIOS applications will no longer have a means of resolving NetBIOS names. For more information on DDNS, see Chapter 7.

Transitioning Away from NetBIOS and WINS

In order to transition away from NetBIOS and WINS, you need a way to determine which machines and applications use NetBIOS, and plan a transition to eliminate these items from your network. This process is much the same as the one used in the previous chapter, Chapter 4, "Assessing Critical Applications."

Direct Hosting

The successor to NetBIOS-based connectivity is called *direct hosting*. By default, Windows 2000 computers attempt to use both NetBIOS and direct hosting to make network connections. While NBT uses ports 137, 138, and 139, direct hosting uses only port 445.

1. Find out which applications and machines use NetBIOS.

2. Determine the impact changing these items will have on the network.

3. Decide whether to upgrade, replace, or retire the services offered by NetBIOS applications and machines.

4. Fully implement a DDNS system for the network.

5. Migrate to Windows 2000 and implement the needed changes for applications in order to remove NetBIOS.

6. Decommission WINS.

7. Test applications, services, and machines.

It's important to note that the following conditions must be met before you plan NetBIOS removal. If either condition is not true, NetBIOS must remain active on the network.

- All current operating systems that use NetBIOS (such as Windows for Workgroups 3.x, Windows 9x, Windows NT 3.x and 4.x) must be upgraded to Windows 2000.

- All applications that use NetBIOS (such as Microsoft SMS's Remote Control application) must be upgraded, replaced, or retired.

Step 1: Finding Out Where NetBIOS Is Currently Used

Two areas must be examined to create a list of NetBIOS applications and machines. The best place to look is the WINS servers. The other sources are the client machines.

Assessing the WINS Environment

By examining the entries in your WINS database, you can learn a great deal about NetBIOS in your environment. Assuming that you will be upgrading all your systems to Windows 2000, you can take your WINS database and eliminate the following entries:

- `COMPUTERNAME<00>`

- `DOMAIN<00>`

- `COMPUTERNAME<01>`

- `\\—__MSBROWSE__<01>`

- `COMPUTERNAME<03>`

- `USERNAME<03>`

- `COMPUTERNAME<06>`

- `DOMAIN<1B>`

- `DOMAIN<1C>`

- DOMAIN<1D>

- DOMAIN<1E>

- COMPUTERNAME<1F>

- COMPUTERNAME<20>

- COMPUTERNAME<21>

- COMPUTERNAME<BE>

- COMPUTERNAME<BF>

These entries are OS-specific. After you upgrade to Windows 2000 and disable NetBIOS on a machine, none of these entries will be required. Any remaining entries need to be investigated. You'll have to find out what system or application requires those entries and then decide how you will provide a non–NetBIOS alternative.

Client Computers

For machines that don't register their NetBIOS names with WINS, you will need to look at each machine individually before you can safely remove NetBIOS. NBTSTAT is capable of querying remote machines for their registered names. You can use NBTSTAT -a <computername> if you know the remote machine's name, or NBTSTAT -A <address> if you know the machine's IP address. In lieu of visiting each machine, you might try using the -A method against each valid IP address in your network. (Use a batch file and redirect the output to a file in order to speed up the process.)

Although the preceding method may work for operating systems and services that are constantly running, it may not give you information on applications which use NetBIOS. For this, you need to know which applications use the network. Most applications can access remote files through the network redirector, but the focus here is on applications that directly access the network. If you have any such applications and aren't sure if they use NetBIOS, NBTSTAT once again is the answer. Run NBTSTAT -s 1, which will display current activity for NBT once per second. Then run the application and create network activity. By analyzing the NBTSTAT output, you can determine whether the application is using NetBIOS. The following is a sample of this type of output:

```
Local Area Connection:
Node IpAddress: [10.1.1.1] Scope Id: []


                  NetBIOS Connection Table

Local Name            State      In/Out  Remote Host  Input  Output
— — — — — — — — — — — — — — — — — — — — — — — — — — — — — — — —
MYCOMPUTER    <00>    Connected  Out     WIN98 <20>   398B   748B
MYCOMPUTER    <03>    Listening
ADMINISTRATOR <03>    Listening
```

Alternatively, you can use a network sniffer or packet analyzer, such as Microsoft's Network Monitor. Although this may not tell you what application caused the NetBIOS traffic, it will find all such traffic on the network. The best way to use this is after you believe you've found all the NetBIOS traffic generators. Then use an analyzer, filtering only for NetBIOS traffic. Let it run for a day or more, and you may find new sources of NetBIOS traffic.

Step 2: Determining the Impact of Removing NetBIOS

Once you've discovered where NetBIOS is used on your network, you can determine the consequences of removing it. Will doing so cause a critical application to fail? In a best-case scenario, you will find that only your operating systems use NetBIOS. In that case, you can proceed quickly with the transition. In a worst-case scenario, a critical application relies on NetBIOS, and there is no alternative available for the long term. In this situation, NetBIOS will have to remain active on the network, although it will likely play a reduced role. There is little reason to develop a removal plan if you reach this point.

Most likely, you will find your network somewhere between the best and worst cases. Although applications depend on NetBIOS, alternative solutions are usually available. While careful planning is required, you should be able to engineer the removal of NetBIOS.

Step 3: Deciding What to Do with the NetBIOS Applications and Machines

Assuming that the impact of removing NetBIOS is not severe, you can plan how to migrate from NetBIOS applications. There are three options:

- Upgrade to a newer version of the application that doesn't require NetBIOS.
- Replace the application with a competitor that doesn't rely on NetBIOS.
- Retire the application without replacing its services.

Faster Client Searches

Microsoft's SMS provides two methods for speeding up the search on clients for NetBIOS. First, you can configure it to collect clients' LMHOST files, if they exist. Second, it can be used to distribute and run a batch file that could perform an NBTSTAT -n, redirect the output to a text file, and analyze file for any unknown entries (beyond the standard computer name and username entries).

Additionally, it includes an enhanced version of Network Monitor that can analyze all the traffic on the network, not just packets addressed to the machine running Network Monitor (as is the case for the version with Windows 2000).

These options are discussed in-depth at the end of Chapter 4, "Assessing Critical Applications." Review that material, and use it to determine the best course of action.

Step 4: Fully Implementing DDNS

Before you can migrate away from NetBIOS, you must have the replacement system prepared. DDNS replaces the functionality of WINS, and as a result, it must be ready for operation before any Windows 2000 clients are deployed. DDNS deployment is an entire process in its own right, and Chapter 7 covers how to best develop your DNS structure. Before moving along with NetBIOS removal, make sure that at least one DDNS server is operational.

Step 5: Migrating to Windows 2000 and Implementing a NetBIOS Removal Plan

Once DDNS is in place, you can begin the Windows 2000 deployment process. As this occurs, you should replace the NetBIOS applications on downlevel systems with their successors, as you determined in step 3. During this time, both DDNS and WINS will play roles in name registration and resolution on the network. To ensure that connectivity is not impaired, make sure that Windows 2000 and downlevel systems query both WINS and DDNS for name resolution.

Step 6: Decommissioning WINS

After the final downlevel machine has been shut down, you can begin the process of removing WINS from the network. Microsoft calls this process decommissioning. Step 6 involves four steps:

6.1 Set up DDNS for all clients.

6.2 Configure clients not to use WINS.

6.3 Decommission individual WINS servers.

6.4 Configure clients to disable NBT.

Step 6.1: Setting Up DDNS for All Clients

If your network uses DHCP for address assignment, this step is easy. For each DHCP scope, ensure that one or more DDNS servers are listed under the DNS option. For those machines which are assigned static addresses, verify that the TCP/IP properties window lists a DNS server. DHCP servers, and usually most other servers, have static addresses.

Step 6.2: Configuring Clients Not to Use WINS

Merely configuring each machine for DNS will not cause any WINS traffic to subside. When Windows 2000 is configured with both types of name servers, it attempts to resolve names and perform connections in parallel. This adds to the inefficiency on the network in the short term.

To continue to remove NetBIOS, you must now configure clients not to use WINS. Note that this step cannot be performed on any client that is continuing to use NetBIOS connectivity. As with DDNS, this change is easy for DHCP clients; simply delete the NBNS/WINS option from each scope. For machines with static addresses you will have to mutually remove the WINS server addresses from the machine's TCP/IP properties window.

When this process is complete, WINS traffic should drop to zero. If certain applications are still in the migration process, traffic levels will be reduced, but not eliminated. Although WINS traffic will be discontinued, clients will revert to B-nodes, and the parallel connection attempts will continue using broadcasts.

Step 6.3: Decommissioning Individual WINS Servers

As WINS traffic is reduced, fewer WINS servers will be required. Each WINS server can be retired individually as circumstances dictate. Be aware that records needing to be tombstoned must be tombstoned on the record's owner, or the tombstoning will fail. In order to avoid this, don't shut down a WINS server immediately after removing its address from the clients. Instead, leave it in its replication group, and tombstone all of the records it owns. Let it continue to run until all of the records are tombstoned across the replication group, and then shut down the server.

Step 6.4: Configuring Clients to Disable NBT

When the last WINS server is decommissioned, the clients can now disable their NetBIOS capability. Once this is done, the parallel connection attempts will end, and only direct hosting will be used. This completes the removal of NetBIOS from your network.

Step 7: Testing Applications, Services, and Computers

At this point, you should have a pure Windows 2000 network, and NetBIOS is disabled on all computers. You now need to confirm your results from Step 2. Any problems associated with NetBIOS removal should appear at this stage. Should you encounter problems, you'll need to decide how to resolve them. If the problems are serious enough, you may want to enable NetBIOS on problem machines and continue to live with NetBIOS and its inefficiencies.

II

Designing Windows
2000 Networks

6

Designing the Active Directory

THE QUALITY AND STABILITY OF YOUR Active Directory design will define the success or failure of your company's Windows 2000 implementation. The underlying design principals for NT 3.x–4.0 networks and Windows 2000 networks are radically different. In response to these differences, you must change your fundamental approach if your objective is to continue to design high-quality, useful, and architecturally stable Microsoft networks. This chapter offers an in-depth view of the most important Active Directory design concepts. In the sections that follow, the core building blocks of Active Directory are explored in detail. Each section advocates an architectural approach that is focused on stability, usefulness, and—perhaps most importantly—the requirements of endusers and administrators. The areas to consider in your Active Directory design follow:

- Planning a domain structure
- Planning an OU structure
- Planning a site structure

Planning a Domain Structure

The basic design process for Windows 2000 domains is very different from the design process for NT 3.x–4.0 domains. In NT 3.x–4.0 networks, your domain structure is reflected in the relationship between master user domains and resource domains. You generally choose from one of several domain models to form these relationships. Typical NT 3.x–4.0 domain models include the following:

- The single domain model
- The single master domain model
- The multiple master domain model
- The complete trust domain model

Selecting an NT 3.x–4.0 domain model to suit your requirements is relatively simple. In fact, you are often forced into a particular domain model to comply with limits of the SAM or to delegate administrative tasks. All these constraints are unique to NT 3.x–4.0. In Windows 2000, limitations such as these no longer exist. As a result, basic NT 3.x–4.0 domain design principals are rarely valid in Windows 2000. Your existing NT 3.x–4.0 domain model should definitely not be the basis for Windows 2000 domains you're creating. Instead, you should consider your company's physical and operational structure, as well as the requirements of your network administrators. To form a design strategy for your Windows 2000 domains, you must take the following actions:

1. Assess your current environment.
2. Determine when to create a Windows 2000 domain.
3. Organize your domains into Trees or Forests.

Assessing Your Current Environment

To evaluate guidelines for creating Windows 2000 domains with any effectiveness, you must first assess your current environment (see "Determining When to Create a Domain" for details). You can establish your domain design strategy by first understanding how your company is organized—operationally, physically, and administratively. An appraisal of your company's operational environment will give you a better understanding of how it conducts its day-to-day business. You must also understand the characteristics of your company's physical environment. The way in which your company is physically organized will help you define various technical requirements for your design. Your company's administrative needs must also be considered. How your company plans to manage its resources will influence your design as well.

Examining Your Operational Environment

Your company's operational environment defines how it distributes and manages its resources. The size of a company usually has a significant influence on its operational structure. Therefore, one of your first tasks will be to classify your company by size. Most companies can be classified as operating locally, regionally, nationally, or internationally.

The region(s) in which your company does business helps define its operational structure. For example, an international company is more likely to run its business by physical geography than a local company is. Figure 6.1 shows the regional and operational divisions for Long Haul Trucking, a national heavy equipment carrier. As a growing freight carrier based in the U.S., Long Haul Trucking has offices in Los Angeles, Yakima, Houston, and Chicago. Functionally, Long Haul Trucking operates as four business units: Administration, Receiving, Shipping, and Sales.

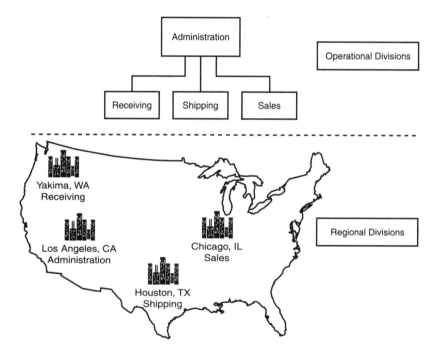

Figure 6.1 The operational structure of a company can usually be determined by examining its functional boundaries.

Exploring Your Physical Environment

Exploring the physical characteristics of your company will help you establish your technical requirements. Determining the locations in which your company operates is only a basic step. To fully define your company's physical environment, you must also examine its user community and network topology. When you review the company's user base, gather the following information:

- The number of employees working in each location
- The number of employees in each division or business unit[1]
- The company's average growth rate and its plans for expansion

Next, you should review all your company's local and remote networks. You should collect the following data as part of your network assessment:

- The speed of each local network link
- The TCP/IP subnets in use at each location
- The organization of links between locations
- The speed of each remote network link
- The utilization of each local and remote link during normal business hours

The physical environment of Long Haul Trucking is shown in Figure 6.2. Most of the company's 86,000 employees are based in the Houston shipping office. Over the next three to five years, conservative estimates call for a two percent growth rate across the board. Each location runs 10MB switched Ethernet to the desktop, collapsed into a 100MB fiber backbone. The Houston shipping office is the central hub of the company's wide area network. Local bandwidth utilization in each of the offices is negligible. However, abnormally high utilization is often reported for the Yakima-Houston link.

With a keen understanding of how your company is physically organized, you move one step closer to forming your domain design strategy.

Identifying Your Administrative Requirements

Identifying your company's administrative requirements will help you plan for managing its resources. Most companies manage their network resources using a centralized, decentralized, or hybrid administrative model. The fine points of these administrative models are outlined here:

- **Centralized administrative model.** This model is commonly used in small companies with few locations. These smaller organizations often rely on a single administrative team for all their network services.

---

1. If your company operates internationally, you may also need to determine the number of multilingual users in each division or business unit.

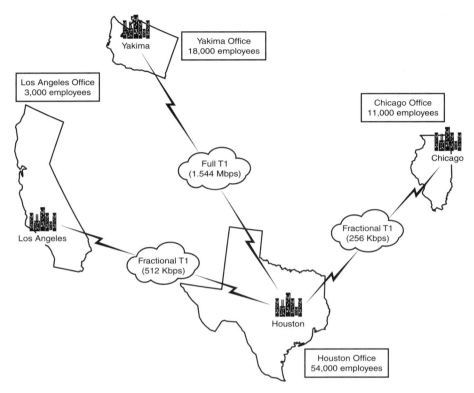

Figure 6.2 Several fractional and full T1 links are used to connect Yakima, Los Angeles, and Chicago to the Houston core.

- **Decentralized administrative model.** In this model, a number of administrators are responsible for managing the company's network resources. These teams are often divided by location, division, or business unit.

- **Hybrid administrative model.** Businesses that use this model decentralize the administration of some resources while centralizing others. For example, a company may centralize the management of its most important services and decentralize routine tasks, such as adding, deleting, and managing user accounts.

Long Haul Trucking uses a decentralized administrative model. Each of its four locations is large enough to necessitate local administration. Figure 6.3 shows how the administrative operations of Long Haul Trucking might look under different circumstances.

You should now have a good understanding of how your company is organized. You've gathered information on the organization's operational, physical, and administrative structures. With this information in hand, you are well prepared to determine when it is appropriate to create a domain.

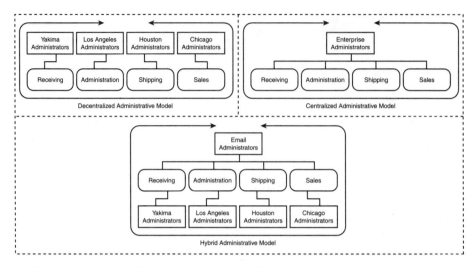

Figure 6.3   It is valuable to analyze how Long Haul Trucking might function using the centralized or hybrid administrative model.

Determining When to Create a Domain

The guidelines for creating Windows 2000 domains and NT 3.x–4.0 domains are fundamentally different. Therefore, using your NT 3.x–4.0 domain model as the basis for your Windows 2000 domain design is *not* recommended.

Instead, you should build a solid foundation for Windows 2000 by examining your company's operational, physical, and administrative characteristics. To put Windows 2000 into service, your company will require a minimum of one domain. You may need more than one Windows 2000 domain under the following conditions:

- To support decentralized administration
- To isolate domain replication traffic
- To balance domain replication traffic
- To support multiple domain policies
- To address international differences
- To comply with internal political pressures

The reasons for creating multiple Windows 2000 domains are further detailed in the sections that follow.

To Support Decentralized Administration

One major reason to use multiple Windows 2000 domains is to support decentralized administration. Your company's regional offices may not accept a domain design that gives them limited administrative control. Instead, they may want complete and total control over their local resources.

To Isolate Domain Replication Traffic

More than one domain will also be required to isolate domain replication traffic. For a Windows 2000 domain to stay synchronized, each of its domain controllers periodically replicates changes with domain controllers in the same domain. When you create a new domain, you isolate it from the existing domain replication traffic. The only replication traffic in the new domain is from the domain itself and from synchronization of the global catalog.

To Balance Domain Replication Traffic

The traffic generated by periodic domain replication can become an issue if you have a large user population, giving you yet another reason to create multiple domains. If a domain will contain more than one million objects, you should create multiple domains to balance the load. This will speed up searches in Active Directory and optimize domain replication traffic.

To Support Multiple Domain Policies

Another reason to create more than one domain is to support multiple domain policies. Domain policy is different from a normal Group Policy in several ways. Windows 2000 domain policy affects every user in the same domain. In a single Windows 2000 domain you have no way, for example, of giving one group of users a Minimum Password Age setting that is different from another. If you need to support several different domain policies, you have no option but to create multiple domains.

To Address International Differences

You will also need multiple domains to address international differences. If your company operates abroad, you should create domains to reflect its geographical differences—in language, currency, and day-to-day business practices. The network resources of an international company are always separated by physical geography. As a result, nearly all businesses that operate abroad require separate domains to support decentralized administration.

To Comply with Internal Political Pressures

The final reason you might need to create more than one domain is to comply with internal political pressures. Executives or other personnel may ask you to create additional domains for a level of privacy or autonomy. You should do your best to deny these requests. These additional domains will only complicate your Windows 2000 design. If you are faced with such a request, your best approach is to argue that an organizational unit (OU) is more appropriate. This gives the OU administrator control over the OUs' resources without compromising your design (see "Strategies for Delegating OU Administration" for more details).

Organizing Domains in Trees and Forests

After you establish the number of domains that is appropriate for your company, you must consider how to organize them into a useful hierarchy. As one of your essential Windows 2000 design tasks, you need to decide whether to arrange your company's domains into a Tree or a Forest. The sections that follow compare Trees and Forests and offer recommendations for naming your Windows 2000 domains.

Comparing Trees and Forests

Some companies need a single Tree to support their enterprises, while others need a Forest of Trees. Trees and Forests both form a structure in which every domain shares the same configuration, global catalog, and schema. When one of your domains is joined to this hierarchy, it establishes a two-way transitive Kerberos trust relationship with its immediate parent. Therefore, all domains forming a Tree or Forest can share their resources globally.

There are more differences than similarities between Trees and Forests, however. To decide whether to organize your company's Windows 2000 domains into a Tree or Forest, consider the differences listed in Table 6.1.

Figure 6.4 shows a company that is more suited to using a Tree than a Forest to organize its domains. The Tree of domains in Figure 6.4 is used by Fit Rite Retail, a U.S.–based consumer clothing chain. Each of the company's 50 clothing stores is managed regionally. The network administrators in Fit Rite's major regions require their own domains to support decentralized administration and unique domain policy requirements. The Tree created for Fit Rite Retail by its corporate administrators is made of four separate domains: `fitrite.com`, `east.fitrite.com`, `central.fitrite.com`, and `west.fitrite.com`.

Table 6.1   **Distinctions Between Trees and Forests That Affect the Organization of Company Domains**

Trees	Forests
Form a single contiguous namespace.	Made of several disjointed namespaces.
Useful for companies that operate as a single entity.	Useful for companies that operate as several entities, such as partnerships, holding companies, conglomerates, and joint ventures.
Simpler for users and administrators to navigate and understand.	More difficult for users and administrators to navigate and understand.
LDAP searches in a Tree can always be resolved by LDAP referrals. (LDAP referrals are only valid in the Tree from which a search is initiated.)	LDAP searches in a Forest will not always be resolved. Forest searches are limited to replicated attributes in the global catalog and objects in the Tree from which a search is initiated.

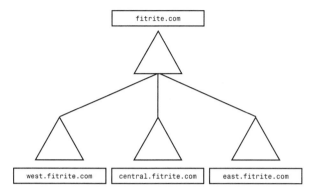

Figure 6.4   Fit Rite Retail uses a Tree instead of Forest because it operates as a single entity.

In contrast, to support its two independent consulting service lines—Vanguard Technology Consulting and Vanguard Business Consulting—the Vanguard Consulting Group requires the Forest of Trees shown in Figure 6.5. The first Tree in this Forest supports domains for Vanguard Technology Consulting. Vanguard Technology Consulting is divided into several different areas separated by international boundaries. To support its international differences and to decentralize administration, Vanguard Technology Consulting needs individual domains to represent its presence in the United States, Europe, and Asia.

The second Tree in Vanguard's Forest supports Vanguard Business Consulting. Like its sister company, Vanguard Business Consulting (`vbc.com`) also has an international presence. However, its domains are named for its various functional divisions. Vanguard Business Consulting requires five separate domains to support unique domain policies in its assorted divisions.

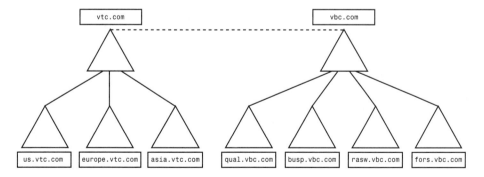

Figure 6.5   The Forest of domains used by the Vanguard Consulting Group
supports two distinct entities.

For the most part, Vanguard Technology Consulting and Vanguard Business Consulting operate independently. However, the two self-sufficient consulting companies are joined in a Forest to share certain resources. The sister companies communicate on a regular basis to disclose valuable business intelligence gained in the field. Because they belong to a Forest, all of Vanguard's domains can share their resources worldwide.

To decide between creating a Tree and creating a Forest, you must consider your company's organizational structure. In short, let the way your company operates drive the design.

Once you've decided whether your company's operation requires a Tree or Forest, your next objective is to create stable naming standards for your company's domains. Methods for forming these standards are detailed in the following section.

Naming Domains in Trees and Forests

How you name the domains in Trees and Forests is very important, and usually more difficult than it sounds. Windows 2000 uses the location services of Dynamic DNS (DDNS) to resolve domain names to IP addresses. As you form your company's naming standards, you must remember that Windows 2000 domain names are DDNS names (see Chapter 7, "Planning a Dynamic DNS Structure," for details).

Picking a suitable name for your internal root domain is the most critical step. This domain will form the root domain in your company's Tree. Your internal root domain is also the uppermost domain in DDNS. Altering this domain name at a later date will be almost impossible. Selecting suitable names for your subdomains will also help you avoid any would-be problems. If you stick to the guidelines offered in the following sections, you should be able to form stable, meaningful, and intuitive naming standards for your Windows 2000 domains.

Naming Your Company's Root Domain

Your first Windows 2000 domain forms the root domain in Active Directory. This domain name should be representative of your corporate identity. For example, Long Haul Trucking might use `lhtrucking.com` as its root domain name. Most companies with an Internet presence will use internal and external root domain names that are different. For instance, Long Haul Trucking might use `longhaul.com` as its external domain name and `lhtrucking.com` for its internal domain name[2]. There are many advantages to using separate internal and external root domain names. For more in-depth information on this topic, see Chapter 7. The section titled "Planning Your DDNS Namespace" can help you decide whether to present your namespace differently on the Internet than you do internally.

---

2. After you choose your internal root domain name, you should formally register it on the Internet. You can register your domain name using the InterNIC's registration forms. You can download these forms from `www.internic.net`.

The most important rule for naming your internal root domain is to make sure it represents a name that will remain static. If your company has plans to merge with another entity or to make significant organizational changes, you must take this into consideration. Table 6.2 lists the most important guidelines for naming your root domain. Listed with each design principle are both good and bad examples.

Table 6.2 **Suggested Guidelines for Naming Root Domain**

Guideline	Good Example	Bad Example
When you name your root domain, you should keep it simple, short, and representative of your corporate identity.	`lhtrucking.com`	`eighteenwheeler.com`
Use a root domain name that will remain relatively static. Avoid using a name with a potentially short life span.	`yourcompanyname.com`	`somedepartment.com` (Departments are notorious for renaming themselves.)
Follow DNS naming standards when naming your root domain. The allowed characters include A–Z, a–z, 0–9, and the hyphen.	`mycompany.com`	`@home.com`
Before choosing a root domain name, verify that it is not registered by someone else.	You choose a name that is not registered by verifying its availability with the InterNIC.	Instead of checking with the InterNIC, you whimsically select a root domain name that is already registered.
If you have an Internet presence, you should use different internal and external root domain names.	Your external root domain name is `mycompany.com` and your internal root domain name is `corp.com`.	Your external and internal root domain names are the same.

Naming Your Company's Subdomains

There is no simple procedure you can follow for naming your subdomains, but you can follow a few general guidelines. These design principles are listed in Table 6.3. Good and bad examples are offered for each suggested rule.

Table 6.3 **Recommended Guidelines for Naming Subdomains**

Guideline	Good Example	Bad Example
Name your company's subdomains based on geopolitical boundaries.	`namerica.corp.com`	`win2000dom.corp.com`
Never name your subdomains after business units or departments.	`euro.corp.com`	`it-quality.corp.com`
Do not use existing top-level domain names or registered domain names for your subdomains.	`asiapac.corp.com`	`com.equipment.com`
Keep your subdomain names as friendly as possible.	`yakima.longhaul.com`	`sa-chi-na.lhaul.com`

If you form static, easily recognizable, and intuitive naming standards for your root domain and your subdomains, you will be able to avoid problems later on. You shouldn't be of the last-minute mindset when forming your company's domain naming standards.

The following case study illustrates how Long Haul Trucking uses the following information to form its domain design strategy:

- The assessment of its current operational, physical, and administrative environment
- Guidelines for creating Windows 2000 domains
- The company's evaluation of whether to form a Tree or Forest
- Guidelines for naming Windows 2000 domains and subdomains

Case Study: Long Haul Trucking

This case study should give you a better feel for how the Windows 2000 domain design process works. You've been reading about this example company's structure throughout this section; that should provide you with a framework for the case study's recommendations for a real-world setting.

To recap, Long Haul Trucking is a national freight carrier with 86,000 employees spread across several locations (Los Angeles, Yakima, Houston, and Chicago). Functionally, Long Haul Trucking operates as four distinct business units: Administration, Receiving, Shipping, and Sales. The sections that follow detail the information that was collected at various stages in the design process and the decisions that were made based on these findings.

Operational Environment

The operational environment of Long Haul Trucking defines how it distributes and manages its resources. As you can see in the following table, its nationally based resources are divided across the central and western United States. It manages these resources in its four major divisions. Following are the results of assessing the operational environment:

Design Criteria	Details
Operational size	Functions as a national company with locations in Los Angeles, Yakima, Houston, and Chicago
Operational structure	Separated into four divisions: Administration, Receiving, Shipping, and Sales

Physical Environment

Gaining a better understanding of its physical environment helps Long Haul Trucking establish technical requirements for its domain design. The critical information listed in Table 6.4 was gathered by examining its user community and network topology.

Administrative Requirements

Following is an evaluation of the company's administrative requirements. By identifying these requirements, Long Haul Trucking can better plan for managing its network resources.

Design Model	Long Haul Details
Centralized administrative model	Does not qualify as a small company or as a company that manages its resources using one team.
Decentralized model	Requires a decentralized administrative model because each of its divisions is large enough to demand local administration.
Hybrid administrative model	Does not require the hybrid model. Each of its divisions administers local resources autonomously.

Requirement for Multiple Domains

Table 6.5 lists how Long Haul Trucking used the results of its thorough assessment to evaluate the guidelines for creating Windows 2000 domains.

Table 6.4 **Assessment of the Physical Environment**

Design Criteria	Details
Number of employees in each location	3,000 users in Los Angeles, CA 18,000 users in Yakima, WA 54,000 users in Houston, TX 11,000 users in Chicago, IL
Anticipated growth rate	Expects to grow two percent across the board in the next 3–5 years
Speed of local network links	All locations are 10MB switched to the desktop, collapsed into a 100MB fiber backbone
Speed of remote network links	512Mbps Houston–Los Angeles 1.544Mbps Houston–Yakima 256Mbps Houston–Chicago
TCP/IP subnets by location	172.20.0.0 Los Angeles 172.21.0.0 Yakima 172.22.0.0 Houston 172.23.0.0 Chicago
Organization of remote links	All locations joined at the Houston network core
Utilization of local and remote links	Local network utilization is negligible; Remote network utilization is sufficient except for the Houston–Yakima link, which is 70 percent utilized

Table 6.5 **Assessment Results and Guidelines**

Design Requirement	Details
Need to isolate domain replication traffic	Domain replication traffic must be minimized on the overworked Houston–Yakima link.
Need to balance domain replication traffic	With 86,000 users, the number of objects in a single domain will be somewhat excessive.
Requirement for multiple domain policies	More stringent domain policy must be enforced in Los Angeles.
International considerations	There are none.
Political factors	One of the vice presidents of sales is lobbying for a private domain to support her executives.

Decision to Create a Tree or Forest

Long Haul Trucking is not a conglomerate, partnership, or holding company, and it is not involved in any joint ventures. Therefore, its organizational structure mirrors a Tree of domains, not a Forest of Trees.

Selection of Domain Naming Standards

Tables 6.6 and 6.7 show how Long Haul Trucking formed naming standards for its root domain and subdomains.

Table 6.6 **Root Domain Naming Standard for Long Haul Trucking**

Design Criteria	Details
Should be simple, short, and representative of the company's corporate identity.	`longhaul.com` and `freight.com` were up for consideration.
Must have a name that will remain relatively static.	`longhaul.com` and `freight.com` both pass this test.
Should follow DNS naming standards for naming the root domain.	Both `longhaul.com` and `freight.com` follow DNS naming standards.
Should verify that root domain name is not already registered by someone else.	After contacting the InterNIC, Long Haul dropped `freight.com` from consideration because it was already registered.
Should use different internal and external root domain names if there is an Internet presence.	`longhaul.com` is used for the company's external Internet resources. Instead of using `longhaul.com` for internal resources, the company will use `lhtrucking.com`[3].

---

3. If `lhtrucking.com` were an established DNS namespace that would not be upgraded to support SRV records or dynamic update, Long Haul Trucking could create a delegated subdomain. This would allow the company to form a subdomain such as `namerica.lhtrucking.com` to support its Windows 2000 resources. For more information on delegated subdomains see Chapter 7, "Planning a Dynamic DNS Structure."

Table 6.7 **Subdomain Naming Standard for Long Haul Trucking**

Design Criteria	Details
Should name subdomains based on geopolitical boundaries.	Regionally-based subdomains such as `west.lhtrucking.com` and `central.lhtrucking.com`, as well as state-based subdomains such as `cali.lhtrucking.com`, `wash.lhtrucking.com`, `texa.lhtrucking.com`, and `illi.lhtrucking.com` were up for consideration.
Should never name subdomains after business units or departments.	Subdomains such as `admin.lhtrucking.com` and `sales.lhtrucking.com` were not considered.
Should not use existing top-level domain names or registered domain names for subdomains.	None of the subdomains that were considered conflicted with registered domain names.
Should keep subdomain names as friendly as possible.	The state-based subdomains were not too friendly. Instead, subdomains were named based on cities: `losangeles.lhtrucking.com`, `yakima.lhtrucking.com`, `houston.lhtrucking.com`, & `chicago.lhtrucking.com`.

Final Domain Structure Design

By considering all of these related criteria, Long Haul Trucking was able to finalize its domain design strategy. The most significant influences on the company's final design decisions follow:

- The characteristics of its organizational structure caused Long Haul Trucking to select a Tree instead of a Forest.

- The requirement for decentralized administration prompted Long Haul Trucking to create a separate subdomain for each location.

- The need to support a different domain policy in Los Angeles underscored the justification for separate geographically-based subdomains.

- The number of personnel employed by the company would overload a single domain, slowing its searches and congesting the company's LAN and WAN with replication traffic.

- The speed of the Houston-Yakima network link was inadequate to support intra-domain replication traffic. Forming multiple domains will decrease replication traffic across the Houston-Yakima link.

- The need to support separate internal and external root domain names prompted the company to select `lhtrucking.com` as its internal root domain name.

- The requirement to give its subdomains friendly names encouraged the company to use city names instead of abbreviated state names for its subdomains.

Together, these factors formed the foundation on which Long Haul Trucking made its design decisions. To meet the company's functional and technical requirements, Long Haul Trucking created a subdomain for each of its locations. Figure 6.6 shows a Tree that consists of the company's internal root domain and each of its subdomains.

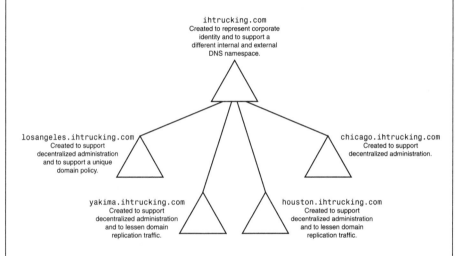

Figure 6.6 Listed next to each domain in the Tree are some of the factors that prompted its creation.

Planning an OU Structure

After solidifying your domain design strategy, you must determine how your company will arrange its organizational units (OUs). Your company can use OUs to organize its resources in a more meaningful hierarchy. An OU is a simple container object. Like a Windows 2000 domain, an OU can contain other objects, such as users, groups, and printers. OUs are most useful when they are used to delegate administrative tasks. For example, you can delegate a user the ability to manage all the objects in a particular OU. You have quite a bit of flexibility in Windows 2000 when delegating administrative tasks. See "Strategies for Delegating OU Administration" for more details.

To plan a useful OU structure, you must examine your company's organizational structure and its administrative requirements.[4] Before you form your company's OU structure, however, you must understand when it is appropriate to create an OU.

Determining When to Create an OU

There are very different reasons for creating OUs and creating domains. The various domains in your organization represent large groups of resources that are often managed by a team of administrators. OUs are used to logically organize and more granularly manage these resources. The following are valid reasons for creating OUs:

- **To delegate administrative tasks.** Your company's OUs can take the place of its former resource domains. You can group various objects, such as users, computers, and groups, into an OU so that a sub-administrator can manage them. This lets you define distinct areas of administrative control within a domain. (See "Strategies for Delegating OU Administration" for more details.)

- **To divide users with unlike policy requirements.** Windows 2000 Group Policy can be assigned to users and computers that reside in the same site, domain, or OU (see Chapter 11, "Simplifying Administration," for details). A good way to separate groups of users and computers with unlike Group Policy requirements is to place them in different OUs.

- **To simplify resource administration.** Just like the various folders in your file system, OUs in your Windows 2000 domains are container objects. Files inherit permissions from the folders in which they are stored. Objects in Windows 2000 domains, such as printers, other OUs, and file shares, inherit permissions from the OU they reside in (see Chapter 10, "Creating a Security Plan," for more information). By assigning permissions at the container level instead of to each object, you can greatly simplify day-to-day resource administration.

Securing an OU and Its Contents

To control which users can view and access the contents of an OU for security reasons, first remove the OU-level Read permission from the Authenticated Users group. Then assign appropriate OU-level permissions to the users or groups that require access to the OU's contents. To take advantage of inheritance, you should set these permissions when you create the OU. If the OU already contains other objects, apply your new permissions to "this object and all subobjects."

4. Enterprise-level organizational and administrative characteristics are considered to form your company's domain design strategy. To form a meaningful OU structure, you must now examine domain-level organizational structure and administrative requirements.

■ **To scope the visibility of objects.** There are several reasons for controlling how your domain objects can be viewed. For example, to give your users an easy way to find printer objects, you might group your company's printers in a PRINTERS OU. There may also be cases in which particular domain objects should be visible only to certain users. Under these circumstances, you can use OU-level permissions to control which users can view the OU's contents. Most likely, you will want to scope object visibility to make working in a large domain more personal. For example, the employees in your human resources department will appreciate finding their resources grouped logically in a single OU instead of scattered throughout the entire domain.

To make OUs useful, you must form a strategy for organizing them so they are meaningful to users. The following section contains general guidelines, as well as several common ways of intuitively arranging OUs.

Forming a Meaningful OU Hierarchy

OUs form a meaningful structure for the various objects in a domain. Your primary goal in forming this structure is to make your OUs useful for users and administrators. There are literally hundreds of ways to organize your company's OUs. To build a meaningful OU hierarchy, you must consider your company's domain level organizational structure and its administrative requirements. You must also adhere to some general guidelines.

General Guidelines for OU Structures

By following a few general guidelines, you can create an OU structure that is both useful and meaningful. One of these guidelines addresses the recommended number of OU levels in a particular domain. You are not bound by any technical limitations when nesting your OUs; your OU hierarchy can be made of countless levels. In spite of this, OU designs with fewer levels will return better performance[5]. LDAP searches will be slower in domains with deep OU structures. Consequently, when you design the levels in your OU structure, consider the performance tradeoff for forming deep hierarchies.

Another guideline to follow when creating your OU structure is perhaps even more important. No matter why they are formed, all of your company's OUs should represent structures that will remain relatively static. For example, the `losangeles.lhtrucking.com` domain may form an OU for each of its business units: MARKETING, ACCOUNTING, and SERVICES. These OUs are suitable for the `losangeles.lhtrucking.com` domain because they represent the division's core business units, which are not likely to change.

---

5.   It is recommended that you limit your company to a maximum of 10 OU levels. LDAP search performance will begin to degrade noticeably at around 5 OU levels.

OUs that represent the geopolitical boundaries of a company, such as NAMERICA, EUROPE, and ASIA, are also appropriate. Similar to a company's core business units, its geopolitical boundaries are not likely to change.

Poor OU designs are those that group objects for a certain project or to support seasonal employees. The problem with creating an OU of this type occurs when the OU is no longer required. When an OU no longer serves its original purpose, you will be forced to reorganize its contents. To avoid this predicament, adhere to a strict OU creation policy: Create OUs that are not likely to change.

Assessing Your Organizational Structure

Your OU structure should reflect how the divisions of your company are organized and managed. The organizational structure of each division, practice, or location should identify how its employees work. This structure can be simply defined as the physical or functional divisions within a domain. Assessing your company's domain level organizational structure helps you define stable names for potential OUs.

Figure 6.7 shows the organizational structure of the Houston-based shipping division of Long Haul Trucking. To run its day-to-day operations, the shipping division is divided into four areas. These four areas represent functional structures that will remain relatively static. Depending on the division's administrative requirements, each of these areas may be represented as separate OUs within the domain.

Gathering Your Administrative Requirements

Gathering the administrative requirements in each division, practice, or location that forms a domain will help you create an OU structure that is useful to administrators and users alike. The divisions of a company often manage their resources using a centralized, decentralized, or hybrid administrative model.

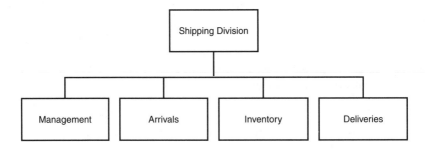

Figure 6.7   The structure of the company's shipping division helps its administrators define prospective OUs.

You must closely examine the administrative model that is used to manage the physical or functional divisions within a domain. For example, Figure 6.8 shows the OUs that are used in the `houston.lhtrucking.com` domain. The Houston-based shipping division manages its network resources using a hybrid administrative model. It forms an OU for each of its four main areas. The most significant influences on the shipping division's OU design strategy include the following:

- A separate OU is required for each division in the `houston.lhtrucking.com` domain to facilitate delegating administrative tasks.

- Naming its OUs after core operational areas helps to prevent future restructuring; these areas represent divisions within the domain that will remain relatively static.

- Dividing its resources into four OUs also gives users and administrators a more personalized view of the `houston.lhtrucking.com` domain.

Organizing Your OUs by Location

Companies that use single domains to group different physical offices can organize their OUs by location. Figure 6.9 shows the OU structure for Progressive Communications, a U.S.–based telecommunications provider. The first level of OUs for Progressive Communications represents the company's regional boundaries. Because they have a presence in the western, eastern, and central United States, they created three top-level OUs: WEST, CENTRAL, and EAST. The second level of OUs in this hierarchy corresponds to the locations of the company's physical offices.

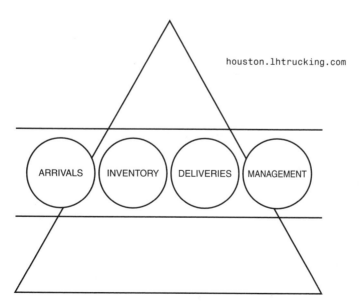

Figure 6.8 The OUs in the Houston domain mirror its four main areas.

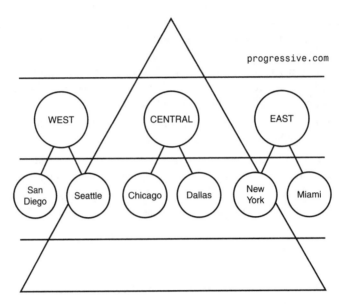

Figure 6.9 When Progressive Communications opens a new office in one of its regions, it adds an OU for that office beneath an existing top-level OU.

Organizing Your OUs by Function

Companies that rely on single domains to organize separate divisions, practices, or business units can arrange their OUs by function. The OU hierarchy for Lucid Cryptography is shown in Figure 6.10. The first level of OUs in the company's domain represents how it functionally operates. The company fashioned three OUs in its topmost level: ADMIN, RESEARCH, and PROJECTS. The second level in this structure matches sub-practices in each of the company's functional divisions. Lucid Cryptography adds an OU beneath each functional division every time it forms a permanent sub-practice, such as its new triple DES over HAM radio practice (3DES/HAM)!

Organizing Your OUs by Location and Function

When single domains are used to organize resources by both function and location, companies can build a hybrid OU structure. Figure 6.11 shows the OU structure for Rapid Delivery, a shipping company with offices abroad. Its top-level OUs are location based. Because the company has offices in the United States, Europe, and Asia, it created three OUs at the first level: UNITED STATES, EUROPE, and ASIA. The second-level OUs represent the functional divisions within the company.

Before you decide how to organize OUs in your individual domains, take the time to explore your company's distinctive traits and requirements. All your up-front design work will help you avoid rebuilding OUs at a later time. OUs in a particular domain are most useful when they are used to delegate administrative tasks. Recommendations for delegating these tasks are covered in the section that follows.

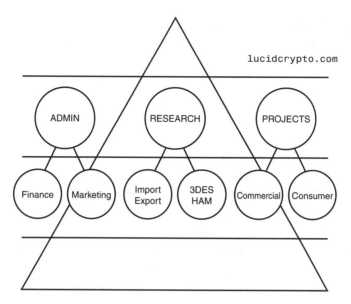

Figure 6.10 `lucidcrypto.com` has a function-based OU structure.

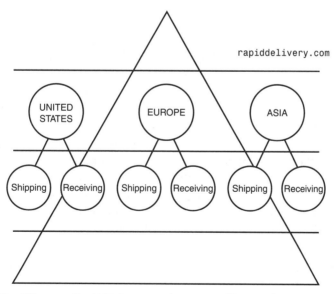

Figure 6.11 Whenever Rapid Delivery acquires a new office, its administrators create and manage that office's resources in an existing second-level OU.

Strategies for Delegating OU Administration

The security architecture of Windows 2000 allows you to delegate users and groups a custom-defined set of administrative abilities. This newfound capability represents quite a difference from the "all or nothing" administrative model in NT 3.x–4.0. To form a useful plan for delegating tasks in each of your OUs, you must understand your company's administrative requirements in detail[6]. Before you create this plan, you must be familiar with all your options.

To form an effective plan for delegating tasks at the OU level, you must first understand your capabilities. Table 6.8 lists your alternatives when delegating administrative tasks.

These alternatives should give you a good idea of different ways you can delegate administrative tasks. The following section details how to form a strategy for delegating these tasks in all your company's OUs.

Forming an Effective OU Delegation Plan

To form your delegation strategy, you must understand your company's administrative requirements at the OU level. To do this, you should consider the administrative tasks allowed in an OU and whether or not you will delegate these tasks to a particular user or group. The most common OU-level administrative tasks are listed in Table 6.9. You can use the columns in Table 6.9 to define the users and groups to whom you will delegate these tasks.

Table 6.8   **Options for Delegating Administrative Tasks**

Alternative	Description
Delegate complete administrative control over an OU and its contents to a user.	This gives a user the ability to change properties on the OU itself and to create, delete, or modify any objects in the OU.
Delegate administrative control over objects of a specific type in an OU to a user.	This allows a user to manage only specific objects in a particular OU, such as group, printer, or file share objects.
Delegate the ability to create and/or delete objects in a particular OU to a user.	This gives a user the ability to create and/or delete every object in a particular OU, including users, groups, printers, and so on.
Delegate the ability to create and/or delete objects of a certain type in an OU to a user.	This allows a user to create and/or delete only specific objects in a particular OU, such as user or printer objects.
Delegate administrative control over certain properties of objects in an OU to a user.	This gives a user the ability to manage certain properties of objects in an OU, such as the password property of user objects.

6. Domain-level administrative requirements are evaluated to create useful OU structures. To create a plan for delegating administrative tasks, you must now consider your OU-level administrative requirements.

Table 6.9 contains only the most common OU-level administrative tasks. Because you can delegate administration down to the "per-user per-property" level, listing every possibility in this table would fill hundreds of pages. For example, a user object has more than 300 individual properties. Each property is secured by an access mask, which defines who can read or write to it. This means that there are more than 600 possible permissions for each user object (300 properties × 2 permissions for each property).

In this section, you examined the valid reasons for creating OUs, how to organize OUs into a meaningful hierarchy, and some of the common ways to use OUs to delegate administrative tasks. In the section that follows, you will learn how to plan a site structure in Active Directory.

Planning a Site Structure

The logical structure of an NT 3.x–4.0 network almost always mirrors its physical structure. In Windows 2000, however, the logical and physical structure of your network does not have to match. The Tree or Forest forming your company's domain namespace represents your network's logical structure. To define the physical structure of your network, you must configure one or more site objects in Active Directory. The sections that follow further detail the role of sites in Windows 2000 and introduce guidelines for developing a useful and effective site topology.

Understanding the Role of Sites

Your company's site objects are used to define areas of good network connectivity. To configure a site object in Active Directory, you associate it with one or more TCP/IP subnets. Each TCP/IP subnet that you define for a site should share a high bandwidth link (512Kbps or greater). In general, you will create a site object for each area of your network that is separated by low bandwidth.

The site objects you create for your company can be used for any of the following reasons:

- To throttle replication traffic
- To isolate workstation logon traffic
- To identify resources by proximity

These reasons are discussed more fully in the sections that follow.

Creating Naming Standards for Objects

Each of your company's OUs is used to store objects such as users, groups, and printers. Chapter 3, "Implementing Standards," heavily stressed the importance of standardization. You should create naming standards for every object type in Active Directory. This will help you avoid naming conflicts and simplify how users and administrators view shared resources. As with other friendly names, you should use a naming convention that is useful, stable, and intuitive.

Table 6.9 **Common OU-Level Administrative Tasks**

Administrative Task	Domain Admins	Particular Group	Individual User
Ability to completely control the OU and all of its contents	❑	❑	❑
Ability to create all child objects in the OU	❑	❑	❑
Ability to delete all child objects in the OU	❑	❑	❑
Ability to create user objects in the OU	❑	❑	❑
Ability to delete user objects in the OU	❑	❑	❑
Ability to modify group membership for user objects	❑	❑	❑
Ability to reset passwords for user objects	❑	❑	❑
Ability to create group objects	❑	❑	❑
Ability to delete group objects	❑	❑	❑
Ability to modify member list for group objects	❑	❑	❑
Ability to create printer objects	❑	❑	❑
Ability to delete printer objects	❑	❑	❑
Ability to modify keywords for printer objects	❑	❑	❑
Ability to modify locations for printer objects	❑	❑	❑
Ability to create shared folder objects	❑	❑	❑
Ability to delete shared folder objects	❑	❑	❑
Ability to modify keywords for shared folder objects	❑	❑	❑
Ability to modify UNC name for shared folder objects	❑	❑	❑
Ability to create computer objects	❑	❑	❑
Ability to delete computer objects	❑	❑	❑
Ability to modify member list for computer objects	❑	❑	❑

To Throttle Replication Traffic

Each of the domains in your company's Tree or Forest forms a separate partition in
Active Directory. This partition holds the values for every object in the domain
and each of its properties. To synchronize each change to an object or property,
every domain controller in the same domain replicates this partition. This replication
relationship is shown in Figure 6.12. To synchronize updates in the mycompany.com
domain, Active Directory uses multi master replication.

Two replication methods are used to synchronize partitions in Active Directory:
intra-site replication and inter-site replication.

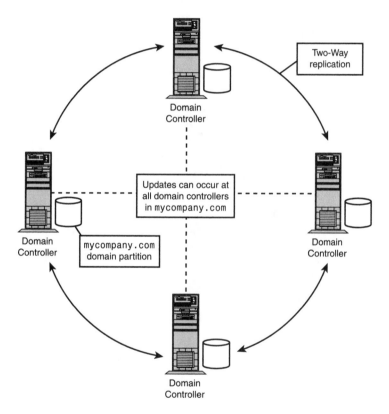

Figure 6.12   Every domain controller in mycompany.com is a master in this relationship; each has
Read/Write copy of the mycompany.com partition.

To build an effective site topology, you must understand how replication works in both situations. Intra-site replication is used within a site. The replication topology for domain controllers within a site is configured automatically by a server process known as the *knowledge consistency checker*. This automatically generated topology is shown in Figure 6.13. The knowledge consistency checker defines a ring topology with a minimum of two replication paths among domain controllers for added redundancy. This allows replication among domain controllers to continue even if a single domain controller becomes temporarily unavailable.

Inter-site replication is used to synchronize domain controllers in separate sites. The replication topology for domain controllers in separate sites must be manually configured. To preserve valuable bandwidth, the replication that occurs between sites is always compressed. The inter-site replication topology for mycompany.com is shown in Figure 6.14. The replication between Chicago and Houston is scheduled to occur during off-peak hours.

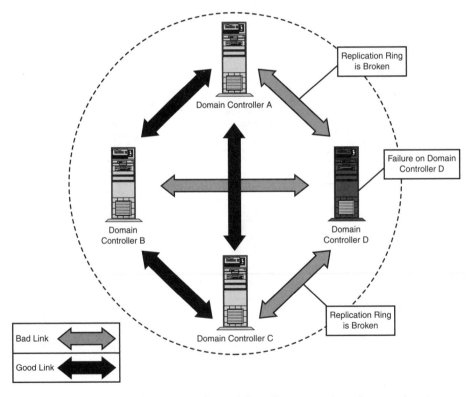

Figure 6.13 When domain controller D fails, replication continues between domain controllers A, B, and C because there are two replication paths from each domain controller.

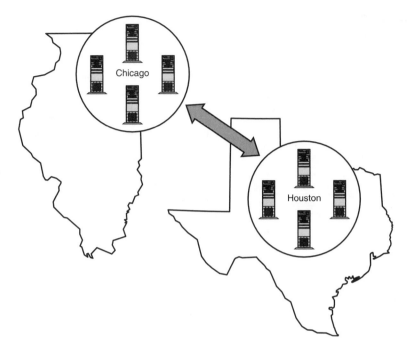

Figure 6.14 This inter-site replication topology preserves the modest bandwidth that is available between the two sites during the workday.

To Isolate Logon Traffic

You can also define site objects to isolate logon traffic. During the logon process, a workstation interrogates the site objects in Active Directory to find a domain controller in its local site. By defining different sites in the same physical location, you can more closely control the logon process. This would be especially helpful in universities and other campus area networks that resemble the topology shown in Figure 6.15. The west campus administrators would like to completely isolate the west campus from the east campus logon requests. To meet this requirement, two sites—East Campus and West Campus—are configured for `campusnet.com`. When users in the East Campus site log on, their workstations look to Active Directory to find a local domain controller.

To Identify Resources by Proximity

Sites are also used to find a variety of other resources within close proximity. For example, in certain LDAP searches, a workstation uses site information to find a nearby global catalog server. The distributed file system (DFS) is another resource that offers site-enabled location services. When attaching to a DFS Tree, a workstation examines the site objects stored in Active Directory to find a DFS child node in close proximity. Giving the operating system knowledge of good network connectivity is extremely useful. Accordingly, Microsoft is planning to use the concept of sites in many of its core BackOffice products—including the next version of Exchange (code-named Platinum). It is also expected that a variety of third-party applications will leverage sites as well.

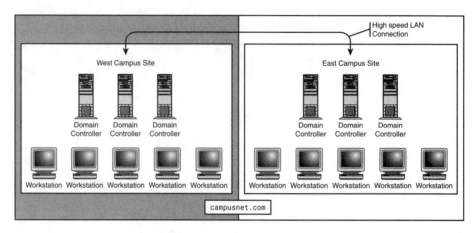

Figure 6.15 Because this domain contains two separate sites, the west campus is isolated from east campus logon requests.

Forming an Efficient Site Topology

Forming an efficient site structure for a company that is relatively small will be quite simple. If an organization wires its workplace using LAN technologies, it will most likely function as a single site. Forming a site structure becomes increasingly complex when a company is divided into several different locations.

The following steps present a site structure design strategy you can use to consider the needs of an organization with multiple physical locations:

1. Review your company's physical environment to gather information for your site design.

2. Examine the physical locations in your company that form a single domain.

3. Define the areas of your network that will be created as individual sites.

4. Identify the physical network links between your sites to define your company's site link objects.

5. Assign a cost and replication schedule to each site link object.

6. Configure a site link bridge for added redundancy over your secondary physical links (optional).

Step 1: Reviewing Your Company's Physical Environment

To form your domain design, you should explore your company's physical characteristics. As a result, you should already have most of the information you need to create a well-organized site structure. In your review of the current environment, you must examine your company's physical locations and network topology. To build your company's site structure, you need the following information:

- The locations in which your company has offices
- The speed of the local networks in each office

- The TCP/IP subnets in each office
- The organization of links between offices
- The speed of your company's remote links
- The utilization of local and remote links during normal business hours

With this information in hand, you can begin to more closely examine your company's physical locations.

Step 2: Examining Physical Locations Forming Your Domains

Once you've reviewed your environment, check out the physical locations forming your company's domains. Figure 6.16 shows the physical locations for Lincoln Medical Group, a health maintenance organization operating in the Midwest. Lincoln Medical Group has a single domain that is shared by four locations: Chicago, Indianapolis, Green Bay, and Saint Paul. Each of the company's offices is configured with 10MB switched Ethernet running to the desktop collapsed into a 100MB backbone. Several frame relay and fractional T1 links connect Indianapolis, Green Bay, and Saint Paul to the center of operations in Chicago. Local bandwidth is not a problem, and most of the company's wide area links are well-utilized.

The physical characteristics of Lincoln Medical Group are further detailed in Table 6.10.

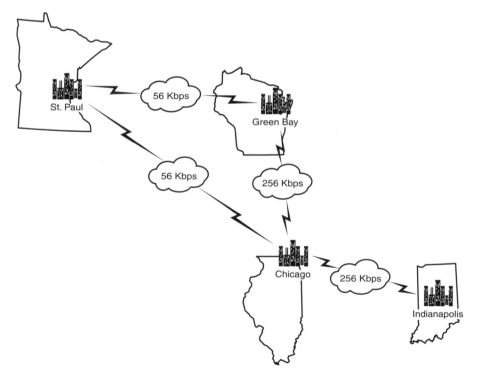

Figure 6.16   The Chicago office is the headquarters for Lincoln Medical Group and the main hub of the company's wide area network.

Step 3: Defining the Network Areas to be Created As Sites

The next task you must undertake is to define the areas of your network that will be individual sites[7]. To determine whether a network area should be defined as a site, consider the following questions:

- Does the area of your company's network require scheduled replication?

- Does the area of your company's network require control over the logon process?

- Does the area of your company's network require the identification of resources by proximity?

The sites and associated TCP/IP subnets for Lincoln Medical Group are shown in Figure 6.17. Lincoln Medical Group requires a site for each of its locations to better control replication and logon traffic and to identify local resources. Each site object is named for the physical location it represents. The site objects created for Lincoln Medical Group include Chicago, Indianapolis, Green Bay, and Saint Paul.

Step 4: Identifying Physical Links to Define As Site Links

You must identify the physical network links between sites to define your company's site link objects. Defining your site link objects should be a relatively simple task. If one of your sites is connected to another with two network links, classify each link as either primary or secondary[8]. Your primary links are the network links between sites with the highest available bandwidth. If just one network link connects two of your sites, classify that link as a primary link as well.

Table 6.10 **Physical Topology for Lincoln Medical Group**

Characteristic	Chicago	Indianapolis	Green Bay	St. Paul
TCP/IP subnets	10.10.x.x	10.20.x.x	10.30.x.x 10.31.x.x	10.40.x.x 10.41.x.x
Remote links	(see links to Chicago)	Main link: 256Kbps to Chicago Backup link: 56Kbps to St. Paul	Main link: 256Kbps to Chicago	Main link: 56Kbps to Chicago
Remote link utilization	(see links to Chicago)	70% on main	65% on main 5% on backup	90% on main

Figure 6.18 shows the primary and secondary links for Lincoln Medical Group. Each

---

7. If an area of your network has no domain controllers, you will not need to consider replication traffic. This may be the case in a company connected by high bandwidth links (greater than 512Kbps).

8. Here, you are classifying physical network links as primary or secondary to simplify the site structure design process; you cannot define a link as primary or secondary in Active Directory.

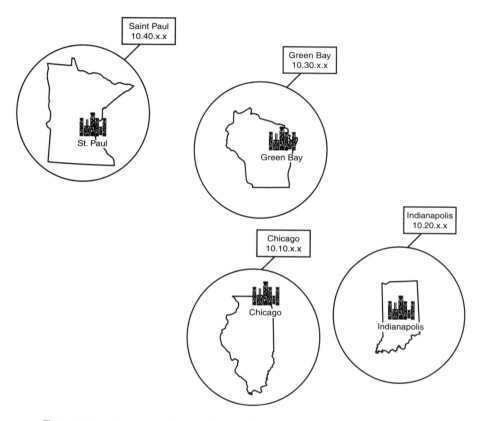

Figure 6.17   The areas defined as sites for Lincoln Medical Group represent areas of good network connectivity.

primary link is defined as a site link object in Active Directory. The following site links for Lincoln Medical Group are named for the physical connections they represent[9]:

- Indianapolis-Chicago
- Green Bay-Chicago
- Saint Paul-Chicago

9. You might also want to consider using a name such as Indianapolis-Chicago 100 Primary 256K to be more descriptive [Site Link Name¦Cost¦Primary\Secondary¦Link Speed].

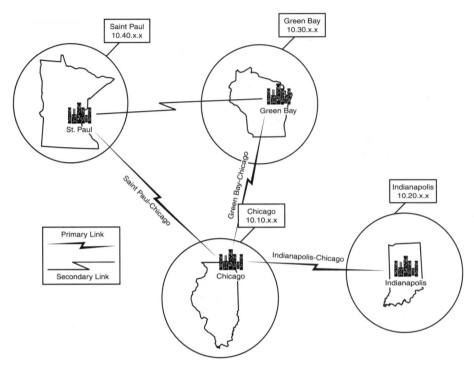

Figure 6.18 The primary physical links in the Lincoln Medical Group network are defined as site link objects in Active Directory.

Step 5: Assigning a Cost and Schedule to Site Link Objects

Your next task is to assign a cost and replication schedule to each site link object. The default cost of a site link object is 100 (the lower the cost, the higher the priority). When multiple site link objects connect two separate sites, replication occurs over the lowest cost link. This is extremely important when you define a site link bridge over a physical secondary link. See the section "Configuring One or More Site Link Bridges (Optional)" for more details.

The default replication between sites occurs once every 3 hours, 24 hours a day, 7 days a week. In all but a very few cases, you should use the default replication schedule. However, keep the following things in mind when making your decision:

- You may need to replicate updates more frequently if an application or user depends on having the latest changes to directory data.

- Less frequent updates might be required if a dial-up link that connects two sites is configured to be unavailable during certain time periods.

- If the physical link between sites is over utilized during business hours, you may define a less frequent replication schedule.

The default cost (100) and replication schedule (3★24★7) is assigned to site link objects in the Lincoln Medical Group network.

Step 6: Configuring One or More Site Link Bridges (Optional)

Your final task—which is optional—is to configure a site link bridge over your secondary physical links to provide redundancy for replication traffic. Figure 6.19 shows the primary and secondary physical links in the Lincoln Medical Group wide area network. Three site link objects are defined for the primary links connecting Indianapolis, Green Bay, and Saint Paul to Chicago. The company would like to use its connection between Green Bay and Saint Paul as a backup link for replication traffic. If the primary physical link between Green Bay and Chicago or Saint Paul and Chicago fails, replication traffic should travel over the secondary physical link. Therefore, the following statements describe the company's desired behavior under the two failure scenarios:

- If the primary physical link between Green Bay and Chicago fails, replication traffic must travel from Green Bay to Saint Paul and then from Saint Paul to Chicago.

- If the primary physical link between Saint Paul and Chicago fails, replication traffic must travel from Saint Paul to Green Bay and then from Green Bay to Chicago.

Lincoln Medical Group can provide fault tolerance for replication between Green Bay, Saint Paul, and Chicago by creating a site link bridge. This is accomplished with the following steps:

1. The company must define the physical backup link between Green Bay and Saint Paul as a site link object.

2. The company's administrators must create a site link bridge object representing the physical secondary replication path (Green Bay-Saint Paul).

3. The company then adds the Saint Paul-Chicago, Green Bay-Chicago and Green Bay-Saint Paul site link objects to the site link bridge.

Figure 6.20 shows this fault tolerant configuration in more detail. The site link bridge object can use the physical connection between Green Bay and Saint Paul as a backup path for replication. The replication cost of the site link bridge object is the sum of the Saint Paul-Chicago, Green Bay-Chicago, and Green Bay-Saint Paul site links (100 + 100 + 110 = 310). Recall that when multiple pathways connect two separate sites, replication always occurs over the lowest cost link (the lower the cost, the higher the priority). This ensures that the backup replication path, defined by the site link bridge, is used only when a failure occurs on a primary physical link.

If you take the time to consider your company's requirements, you can define sites, site links, and site link bridges to build a useful, effective, and fault-tolerant site topology. Your domains, organizational units, and sites form the foundation for your company's Active Directory. Taking the necessary steps to understand each of these design tasks will be well worth the time and effort.

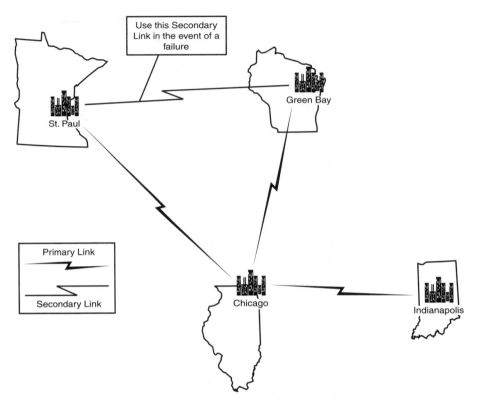

Figure 6.19 The redundancy plan for Lincoln Medical Group allows replication to occur in the event of a primary physical link failure.

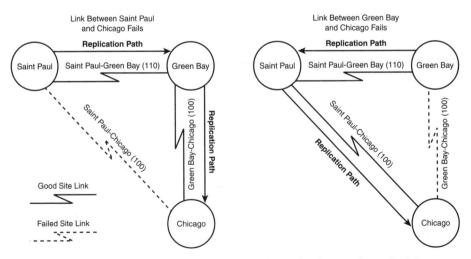

Figure 6.20 This is the detailed replication redundancy plan for Lincoln Medical Group.

7

Planning a Dynamic DNS Structure

THE WINDOWS 2000 DYNAMIC DOMAIN NAME SYSTEM (DDNS) is an update to a long-standing name resolution standard. The well-known name resolution standard, of course, is the Domain Name System (DNS), an open Internet standard defined in several Request for Comments (RFCs). Dynamic DNS (DDNS), a replacement for WINS in Windows 2000, is now the preferred name resolution service.

To completely understand DDNS, you must first be familiar with its roots. Many design standards that are true for DNS are valid for DDNS as well. To gain a better understanding of DNS, you should think about several key areas, which are covered in the following sections:

- History of DNS and the Internet
- Problems with LMHOSTS.TXT
- The Introduction of DNS
- DNS in Microsoft Networks

After you learn the basic functionality and history of DNS, you'll move on to the details of how DNS works, followed by the role of Dynamic DNS in Windows 2000. After that, you'll focus on designing a Dynamic DNS structure, integration of WINS and DDNS, and planning for DHCP services.

History of DNS and the Internet

Before you attempt to design DDNS for Windows 2000, you should understand the history of DNS. Whenever you use the Internet, you also use DNS. DNS is the service that gives you the ability to resolve host names to IP addresses. When you search for a host by its friendly name—for example, www.microsoft.com—a DNS server returns that host's IP address to you. Without DNS, you would have to remember each actual address yourself; the friendly names would be useless. This is a daunting task when you consider the number of hosts you talk to on a daily basis. Imagine having to remember the IP address of each Web server you visited yesterday. With DNS, memorizing these addresses is not your concern.

In the Internet's infancy, DNS was not used for name resolution as it is now. The Internet, initially known as the ARPAnet, used a simple flat text file named HOSTS.TXT to resolve host names to IP addresses. There was no immediate need to find a substitute for HOSTS.TXT in the '60s, when the ARPAnet was formed, because the ARPAnet's host file contained only a small number of entries. These entries were for the hosts shared by research staff in the Defense Advanced Research Projects Agency (known as ARPA or DARPA). Each time a host was added to the ARPAnet, an entry was made in the central host file, which was maintained by the Stanford Research Institute's Network Information Center (known as the NIC). But with the rapid growth of the ARPAnet, the NIC soon became overwhelmed with managing changes to HOSTS.TXT.

Problems with HOSTS.TXT

One of the problems with HOSTS.TXT was that one central host, SRI-NIC, was responsible for distributing it to each host on the ARPAnet. Each time a change or addition was made to HOSTS.TXT, every host on the ARPAnet had to contact SRI-NIC for the latest version. As the ARPAnet grew, the load on SRI-NIC grew proportionally. Eventually, this increasing load caused performance problems.

Another problem the NIC faced was related to managing the host file. Administrators of networks that were connected to the ARPAnet had no way to administer sections of HOSTS.TXT themselves. This meant that all changes and additions were centrally administered by the NIC by default. It was impossible for the NIC to delegate the tasks of adding or deleting entries in the host file.

A further problem was apparent with HOSTS.TXT. By design, the host file was flat. This made it difficult to determine the location of a given host in the ARPAnet namespace.

DNS Request for Comments

To gain a better understanding of the Domain Name System (DNS), you should review several Request for Comments (RFCs). Core RFCs, such as 1034 and 1035, define the inner workings of DNS. Dynamic DNS (DDNS) is defined in a more recent submission: RFC 2136. This RFC describes *dynamic update*, a series of rules that allows DNS to update its entries dynamically.

The Introduction of DNS

As demand on the ARPAnet grew, the problems with HOSTS.TXT became clear. Some of these problems included the growing burden on SRI-NIC, the inability to decentralize host file management, and the lack of an intuitive namespace. These problems led Paul Mockapetris to design a new name resolution standard with the following improvements:

- The new name resolution standard would be more scalable than HOSTS.TXT.
- The new name resolution standard would allow distributed administration of hosts.
- The new name resolution standard would arrange all hosts in an intuitive hierarchy.

Windows 2000 and HOSTS.TXT

Although HOSTS.TXT is less flexible than DNS, you can still use it as a viable name resolution alternative. On Windows 2000 systems, HOSTS.TXT is found in the %SystemRoot%\system32\drivers\etc folder. This flat host file is arranged in the following format:

```
# Copyright (c) 1993-1995 Microsoft Corp.
#
# This is a sample HOSTS file used by Microsoft TCP/IP for Windows NT.
#
# This file contains the mappings of IP addresses to host names. Each
# entry should be kept on an individual line. The IP address should
# be placed in the first column followed by the corresponding host name.
# The IP address and the host name should be separated by at least one
# space.
#
# Additionally, comments (such as these) may be inserted on individual
# lines or following the machine name denoted by a '#' symbol.
#
# For example:
#
#      102.54.94.97     rhino.acme.com          # source server
#      38.25.63.10      x.acme.com              # x client host

127.0.0.1    localhost
```

This new name resolution standard, of course, was DNS. The original DNS specification was submitted by Paul Mockapetris in RFCs 882 and 883. Today, almost 15 years later, the current DNS specifications reflect Mockapetris's original goals. To address scalability issues, DNS was designed as a distributed database. DNS servers on separate networks, for example, can be configured to contain only a subset of host records. Hosts that reside in other portions of the namespace can be resolved using *forwarders*, pointers to other DNS servers that are listed in the local DNS database. This allows for segmentation of DNS without the loss of global name resolution services. This design improves scalability by breaking the namespace into smaller units. Each server is not required to have a copy of the entire DNS database.

Distributing the database gives you another advantage. Each portion of the DNS namespace can be managed by a separate entity (see the secion "The DNS Namespace" for more information). Work that was once performed solely by the NIC can be delegated to one or more local administrators.

Determining the location of hosts is also simplified. Each host can easily be identified by its unique position in the DNS hierarchy.

DNS in Microsoft Networks

DNS is currently the preferred name resolution standard in mainstream heterogeneous networks, such as the Internet. Instead of using DNS names, however, Microsoft networks have traditionally relied on NetBIOS names. To resolve a NetBIOS name to an IP address, you can use broadcasts, LMHOSTS files, and WINS. WINS is the preferred name resolution service in NT 3.x–4.0. Networks that are built with NT 3.x–4.0 use WINS instead of traditional DNS for a simple reason: to support clients that use dynamically assigned IP addresses. When a WINS client, for example, receives a new IP lease from DHCP, its IP address is updated in WINS. This type of update operation is known as a *dynamic update*.

Until recently, dynamic update was supported only by WINS. Windows 2000 is the first Microsoft release to include a Dynamic DNS (DDNS) server. Because DNS is not required in NT 3.x–4.0, few Microsoft environments have an established DNS namespace. Most companies that do use DNS often use it only on a limited basis. For example, it's common to bring up a DNS server in a Microsoft environment to support an Intranet or a few UNIX hosts. Implementations like these represent partially developed namespaces. As with mature UNIX networks, Windows 2000 requires fully developed global DNS services. If your DNS services are only partially developed, you must create your DNS namespace from scratch.

How the Domain Name System Works

To form a solid DDNS design, you need to understand what makes DNS work. First you need to understand some of the core components of DNS, including domains, subdomains, and hosts. Then you'll get into the inner workings of this critical enterprise service. To introduce you to the basic components of DNS and to explain how DNS works, this section is broken into several topics:

- The DNS namespace
- Delegation of domains
- Name resolution

The DNS Namespace

Let's first take a look at the general makeup of DNS: the hierarchical structure that represents domains, subdomains, and hosts. This hierarchy forms an inverted Tree known as the *domain namespace*. Figure 7.1 shows this Tree-like structure. Each domain in this Tree is assigned a name referred to as a label, which signifies its position in the hierarchy. This label can be up to 63 characters in length. The top-most node in this inverted Tree is called the *root*. From the root domain, the DNS Tree can branch in any number of ways, having as many as 127 branches. The root domain can contain both subdomains and hosts. These subdomains, in turn, can contain subdomains and hosts of their own.

The domains that reside just below the root domain are called top-level domains. To get a better understanding of this, consider the domain namespace of the Internet. The uppermost Internet domains, including .com, .edu, and .mil are all top-level domains. Domains that sit just below top-level domains are known as second-level domains. The Internet namespace consists of numerous second-level domains, which represent large and small entities alike. Domains positioned beneath second-level domains, such as www.mycompany.com, are called *subdomains*. In fact, any domain that sits below the root domain is technically a subdomain. After all, every DNS domain is a subdomain of its immediate parent.

Additional Sources for DNS Information

To gain more comprehensive knowledge, you should pick up a good DNS book. No administrator should be without a copy of *DNS and BIND,* the timeless classic written by Paul Albitz and Cricket Liu (O'Reilly, 1998). Another very useful book recently published by New Riders is *Windows NT DNS* by Michael Masterson, Herman Knief, Scott Vinick, and Eric Roul (1998). *Windows NT DNS* includes more than 250 pages dedicated solely to this essential topic. DNS is a critical enterprise service. You should take some steps to familiarize yourself with it.

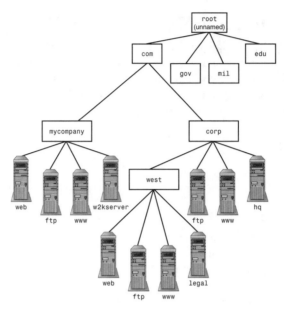

Figure 7.1 Because DNS is a hierarchical and intuitive structure, it's relatively simple to determine a host's position in the namespace and easy to delegate administrative responsibility for domain and subdomain management.

Each host in the domain namespace is identified by its *Fully Qualified Domain Name (FQDN)*, which is the concatenation of its name and the name of its parent. Consider w2kserver, a host shown in Figure 7.1. Because it sits beneath .mycompany, which sits beneath .com, its FQDN is w2kserver.mycompany.com.

Delegation of Domains

If the DNS namespace is segmented into one or more subdomains, it can be managed by several different authorities. The smallest portion of the DNS namespace that can be managed by a separate authority is called a *zone*. Simply put, the DNS namespace represents the logical organization of network resources, whereas DNS zones represent the physical storage area for those resources. When a DNS server boots, it loads a complete set of the names in a domain from a zone—not from the domain itself. A DNS zone can contain a single domain or a domain with several subdomains. Since zones provide storage for domain and host information, they are essential for host name resolution. The distinction between zones and domains is an important one.

DNS and Resource Records

The records that are contained in DNS domains are known as resource records. There can be many types of resource records in a given domain. Each of these records is used for a different purpose. For example, an MX record is used to support mail, and an NS record is reserved for name servers. You can find a complete listing of the allowed record types in RFCs 1035 and 1183.

Consider the position of domains and zones in Figure 7.2. The `mycompany.com` domain has been separated into several zones by delegation. The delegated subdomains in `mycompany.com` include `.us`, `.jp`, and `.uk`. Each delegated subdomain is housed in an independent zone. However, the `.west` subdomain, which is positioned below the `.us` domain, shares a zone with its parent. There are plenty of good reasons to place several domains in a single zone. Perhaps the `.us` administrative team doesn't trust `.west` to manage its portion of the namespace. Instead of breaking `.west` into its own zone, `.west` and `.us` are managed together. This lets the `.us` administration team manage a single zone containing both domains. When the `.west` administrative team is ready to manage its subdomain and all of its resources, the `.us` administrative team can break the current zone into smaller pieces.

Host Name Resolution

Perhaps the most important function in DNS is host name resolution itself. In its most basic form, host name resolution is the process that resolves a host name to an IP address. To communicate with another system on a TCP/IP network, a host must first obtain that system's IP address. This IP address, naturally, can be found by querying DNS.

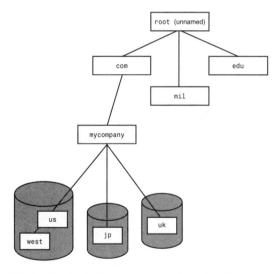

Figure 7.2 Notice that both the `.us` and `.west` subdomains are in a single zone.

Any client that queries DNS for information is known as a *resolver*. To resolve a host name to an IP address, a resolver sends a query for that host name to a DNS server. If the DNS server is authoritative for the zone containing that host name, it answers the resolver directly. If it is not authoritative for that zone, the DNS server responds in one of two ways—recursive or iterative—depending on the type of query that is sent by the resolver. To build effective DNS services, you should understand the type of queries your resolvers will send. DNS servers that answer recursive queries will be more heavily taxed than those that answer iterative queries. These differences are detailed in the following sections.

Recursive Queries

Recursive queries force the DNS server to answer the resolver directly. If the DNS server is not authoritative for the zone queried, it will attempt to locate a server that is. The DNS server will then query this server, acting as resolver, and return the results of its query to the client resolver. When you use recursive queries, the bulk of the name resolution workload resides on the DNS server.

Iterative Queries

An iterative query works differently. When a DNS server receives an iterative query, it simply returns its best answer by interrogating the zones it is authoritative for. If the query cannot be resolved from a local zone, the DNS server will return information to the resolver that will help it find an answer. The resolver must then follow this information trail itself. With iterative queries, the bulk of the work involved is placed squarely on the client.

Role of Dynamic DNS in Windows 2000

As you've learned, the majority of NT 3.x–4.0 networks have little use for DNS. In most downlevel networks, DNS is primarily used to support services provided by Intranets or UNIX hosts. Further, the preferred locator service in NT 3.x–4.0 is WINS, not DNS. WINS provides downlevel networks with core name resolution services.

For example, to find an NT 3.x–4.0 PDC or BDC, a downlevel client must send a query to WINS (broadcasts and LMHOSTS files can also be used). The role of WINS, however, changes dramatically in Windows 2000. Dynamic DNS (DDNS) replaces WINS in Windows 2000 as the preferred locator service. To resolve the name of a Windows 2000 domain controller to an IP address, you must query DDNS.

Using Dynamic DNS names for computers and services instead of NetBIOS names is a fundamental change in Microsoft networks. This change elevates the priority of DNS to the Microsoft administrator. Reliance upon Microsoft's new Dynamic DNS server for name resolution services will eventually become commonplace. However, dependence on DDNS is a relatively recent addition to the Microsoft framework. As such, it's essential that you understand its role. Each section that follows further details the role of Dynamic DNS in Windows 2000.

LDAP and Dynamic DNS

Windows 2000 is a Lightweight Directory Access Protocol (LDAP) server. LDAP is a lightweight version of Directory Access Protocol (DAP), an X.500 directory access protocol. Instead of simply providing basic compatibility with LDAP, Microsoft built Windows 2000 as an LDAP server from the ground up. In Windows 2000, LDAP is used to read and write to the Active Directory.

To locate a Windows 2000 server that can service an LDAP request, a client must send a query to DDNS. The Windows 2000 DDNS server contains a service (SRV) resource record for each LDAP service. A listing of the common LDAP SRV records that can be found on a Windows 2000 DDNS server follows:

```
ldap.tcp.<DnsDomainName>
ldap.tcp.<SiteName>.sites.<DnsDomainName>
ldap.tcp.pdc.ms-dcs.<DnsDomainName>
ldap.tcp.gc.ms-dcs.<DnsTreeName>
ldap.tcp.<SiteName>.sites.gc.ms-dcs.<DnsTreeName>
ldap.tcp.<DomainGuid>.domains.ms-dcs.<DnsTreeName>
ldap.tcp.writable.ms-dcs.<DnsDomainName>
ldap.tcp.<SiteName>.sites.writable.ms-dcs.<DnsDomainName>
```

These SRV records show that the LDAP service can be used via the TCP protocol to locate a particular resource. For example, to find a domain controller in the `mycompany.com` domain, a client needs to query DDNS to resolve `ldap.tcp.mycompany.com` to an IP address.[1]

Domain Names and Dynamic DNS Names

In NT 3.x–4.0 networks, a company's DNS namespace rarely mirrors its NT domain namespace. For example, a client in an NT domain named `corp` is usually configured with a DNS name such as `client.mycompany.com`. Essentially, this client is a member of two separate domains: the `corp` domain, which hosts the company's NT resources, and the DNS domain `mycompany.com`. Each of these domains, however, serves a different purpose. The `corp` domain is an NT domain that stores accounts and resources. The `mycompany.com` domain is a DNS domain. The primary role of a DNS domain is to resolve host names to IP addresses.

In Windows 2000 networks, on the other hand, a company's Active Directory domain namespace mirrors its DDNS namespace (DDNS names *are* Active Directory domain names). This is a major shift from the use of DNS in NT 3.x–4.0. Each domain represented in the Active Directory appears as a domain in DDNS. When you form your company's DDNS structure, you must consider how domains and subdomains will be used in the Active Directory. Your Active Directory design will have a significant influence on your DDNS design. (For more information, see Chapter 6, "Designing the Active Directory.").

---

1. The LDAP specification was developed at the University of Michigan. It is further defined in RFC 1777.

The level of integration that is required between DDNS and Active Directory will cause problems in certain networks. Consider a network that already has an established DNS namespace. An example of a network like this is shown in Figure 7.3. This particular company has a DNS namespace that differs from its proposed Active Directory namespace. Further, the existing DNS namespace for this company is well established: It has been in place for several years to support long-standing UNIX resources. As you can imagine, it will be difficult to implement an Active Directory namespace that differs from an existing DNS namespace. To move forward with your implementation, you will be forced to make a change to either your Active Directory design or your company's existing DNS structure. Deciding which route to take in this circumstance can be difficult. If you are faced with this difficult decision, reference the section "Implementing Windows 2000 in an Established DNS Environment." That section provides detailed coverage of each option you need for implementing Windows 2000 in a network with an established DNS namespace.

The Role of Dynamic Update

Although WINS was once the only Microsoft name server to support dynamic update, it is now supported in Windows 2000 by Dynamic DNS. Supporting dynamic update is essential in today's medium and large-sized TCP/IP networks. Most of these networks rely on Dynamic Host Configuration Protocol (DHCP) to allocate their client's IP addresses. DDNS has several advantages over traditional DNS. One of these advantages, for example, allows a Windows 2000 domain controller to update its entry in DDNS itself. In NT 3.x–4.0 networks, updating an entry in DNS is a manual operation.

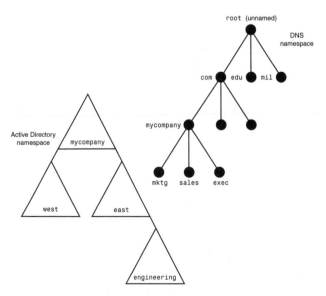

Figure 7.3 The proposed Active Directory namespace and this company's existing DNS namespace differ.

Although support for DNS dynamic update is strongly recommended in Windows 2000, it is not strictly required. Instead, support for SRV records is the minimum requirement. For example, after Service Pack 4 (SP4) is installed, an NT 4.0 DNS server can support SRV records. After SP4 is applied, an NT 4.0 DNS server will not, however, support dynamic update. In a Windows 2000 network of any size, it is impractical to implement DNS without dynamic update.[2] If you do not support dynamic update, you will be forced to update SRV records in DNS manually. Every time an IP address changes on your network, you and your non-dynamic DNS server will share more time.

Instead of wasting your time updating DNS records, you should focus on properly deploying DDNS. DDNS gives you the best of both WINS and traditional DNS. It merges the dynamic capabilities of WINS with the robustness and stability of traditional DNS.

Downlevel Name Registration

In the coming months and even years, you should expect WINS and DDNS to coexist. WINS will be around as long as you need to support downlevel clients and NetBIOS-dependant applications. If you need to make a full transition to DDNS and eliminate WINS as part of your Windows 2000 upgrade, you can. To make this transition, you should reference Chapter 5, "Removing NetBIOS."

Downlevel clients have no awareness of DDNS or Active Directory. You might think that to find a downlevel client, a Windows 2000 client has no option but to query WINS. After all, the WINS database should contain the client's NetBIOS name-to-IP address mapping. Choosing the WINS server as a way to resolve this client's name is technically a correct answer, but configuring your Windows 2000 clients to query DDNS *and* WINS may not be desired; keeping WINS around means supporting NetBIOS.

One of your Windows 2000 transition goals is probably to get rid of as much NetBIOS traffic as possible. If that's so, instead of supporting WINS, your Windows 2000 clients should rely solely on DDNS. Your downlevel clients will generate NetBIOS traffic as long as they remain downlevel clients. After you upgrade them to Windows 2000 (or another DDNS-enabled client), they will be free from their dependence on WINS and will rely solely on DDNS.

To resolve the NetBIOS name of a downlevel client to an IP address by querying DDNS only, you need to implement Windows 2000 DHCP servers. When a Windows 2000 DHCP server leases a downlevel client an IP address, the DHCP server will update the client's entry in the DDNS database. This update process, which essentially enters the NetBIOS name of a downlevel client as an A record in DDNS, is called *downlevel registration*. Downlevel registration simplifies your transition to Windows 2000. As long as you implement Windows 2000 DHCP servers, your DDNS-enabled clients will be able to resolve downlevel NetBIOS names through DDNS without any help from WINS.

2. For more information on dynamic update, see RFC 2136. It outlines the rules that allow DNS servers to support dynamic update.

Designing a Dynamic DNS Structure

DDNS design and Active Directory design are closely related. As with Active Directory design, forming your DDNS design right the first time is critical. If you rush this process or fail to consider all of its implications, you'll be forced to redesign DDNS. Recreating your DDNS namespace will be extremely painful. This redesign process could involve reworking your plans for both DDNS *and* Active Directory. Going back to the drawing board on one of these is difficult to swallow. Tackling two will be much worse. Take the design process slowly. Base your DDNS design on well-proven, solid standards. Each section that follows will serve as your guide.

Active Directory and DDNS

When you form an Active Directory domain, it is a domain in your Active Directory namespace as well as your DDNS namespace. An Active Directory domain, such as mycompany.com, exists as a physical partition in Active Directory and as a zone in DDNS. When authenticating to the network, a client must validate its logon based on account information stored in Active Directory. This same client must also dynamically register its host name in a DDNS zone. For example, a client that logs on to Active Directory using a distinguished name, such as client@mycompany.com will update DDNS with its current host name and IP address. After DDNS has been dynamically updated, an A record exists in DDNS for client.mycompany.com that can be queried for and resolved to an IP address by other members of the mycompany.com domain. Notice that a member of an Active Directory domain stores its host record in a DDNS domain with the same domain name.

When you first begin to design DDNS, you must consider your design for Active Directory. Chapter 6, "Designing the Active Directory," covered some of the common reasons to create separate Active Directory domains. You must consider these criteria when planning your DDNS domains. You will need to create separate domains in DDNS for the same reasons you create separate domains in Active Directory:

- To support decentralized administration
- To support multiple domain policies
- To address multilingual, currency, and time stamp formats.
- To isolate replication traffic
- To comply with internal political pressures

Your Active Directory namespace and DDNS namespace should be identical. If separate domains are needed to meet the goals of Active Directory, DDNS should mirror this structure. As you've learned, your Active Directory design has the most significant influence of any factor on your DDNS design.

Planning Your DDNS Namespace

In the ideal case, your design goals for DDNS and Active Directory will be identical. This is seldom true, however, and somewhere along the way you will be forced to compromise. Since this book hasn't covered any DDNS design standards, you aren't prepared to do this yet. Given that DDNS is an evolution of it predecessor, DNS, you have many existing design standards to consider. These design standards can help you define your DDNS namespace. Some of the common DNS design standards follow:

- Your top-most domain should remain static. This domain will usually be the name of your company, for example, `mycompany.com`.

- Companies that have a national or international presence will often divide the DNS namespace into subdomains to delegate administrative tasks.

- When a single domain will be extremely large, you should consider breaking it into several subdomains. This will ease your administration of the large domain and reduce the load on your DNS servers.

- You can create subdomains based on a number of factors. Common subdomains often represent geopolitical boundaries, distinct administrative lines, or business units.

- Some companies create subdomains to mirror their IT support structure.

Given the number of alternatives and the flexibility of DDNS, determining how to divide your namespace based on proven DNS design standards can be difficult. Then again, there is probably a natural division of some sort in your organization. As an example, let's put some of these standards into practice. Suppose your company, Acme Incorporated, has five branch offices. Because each of these offices is geographically separate, you might create five subdomains. Given that the name of the company is not likely to change, you name the corporate domain `acme.com`. This may very well be the beginning of an appropriate namespace design.

To be sure, you must weigh two related factors. First, consider your division of subdomains. You should not force your company into an awkward domain structure. For example, if you place fifteen business units into five subdomains to simplify administration, you may do so at the expense of confusing your users. Business units that act autonomously require separate domains.

Next, consider whether these five subdomains match your plans for Active Directory domains. If they do not, you must compromise somewhere. Usually the reasons for forming Active Directory domains outweigh those for forming DDNS domains. You shouldn't give up an Active Directory domain that must be created to support a unique domain policy, for example, just because is doesn't fit perfectly into your DDNS namespace design. Carefully weigh the pros and cons of each decision you make. Your compromise will be unique, and it will take some time to develop. If your company has an Internet presence, you have further considerations. You need to decide whether your namespace will be presented on the Internet differently than it is presented internally. The next two sections will help you understand the implications of one option versus another.

Same Internal and External Namespace

For the sake of consistency, some companies present a single DNS namespace to internal and external users. In this scenario, a single DDNS domain, such as `mycompany.com`, represents a context in which resources can be resolved to IP addresses both inside and outside the firewall. This implementation is shown in Figure 7.4.

Maintaining a single namespace for internal and external users presents some challenges. For instance, you don't want to expose your internal host records to every Internet user. Offering up all your internal IP addresses to the Internet community is like publishing your credit card number in the yellow pages. At the same time, you need to provide internal users with the means to resolve both internal and external resources to IP addresses.

One way to maintain a sound level of security without giving up the ability to resolve both internal and external names to IP addresses is shown in Figure 7.4. Two DDNS zones are shown for the `mycompany.com` domain. To hide the IP addresses of internal resources from external users, no replication is configured between the internal and external zones. Essentially, even though they share the same domain name, each zone acts independently: They are both primary zones that reside on different DDNS servers. The external `mycompany.com` zone contains resource records for hosts such as `www.mycompany.com` and `ftp.mycompany.com`. It does not, however, contain resource records for internal hosts. To get the IP address of an internal host, such as `server01.mycompany.com` or `web.mycompany.com`, you must query the internal DDNS server.

Storing internal and external resource records in separate zones is certainly secure. But how will internal users access external resources in the `mycompany.com` domain? If these internal users, for example, attempt to access `www.mycompany.com`, what will happen? After all, the internal and external DDNS servers are separate. The internal DDNS server has no entry in its zone for the `www.mycompany.com` host.

One popular way to ensure that internal users have access to external resources is to mirror those resources inside the firewall. You can then configure your proxy to interpret names that end in `*.mycompany.com` as internal names. Your users will then resolve these names to mirrors of external resources that you've listed in your internal DDNS zone.

Keep in mind that using the same namespace for internal and external resources is more difficult than using two namespaces that are different.

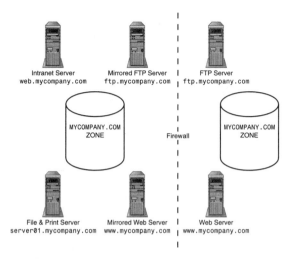

Figure 7.4 In this company with the same internal and external namespace, the external Web
and FTP servers are mirrored inside the firewall.

Different Internal and External Namespace

It is far more common for a company with an Internet presence to have separate
internal and external domain names. The company in Figure 7.5 uses `mycompany.com`
outside the firewall and `corp.com` inside the firewall. By using different internal and
external namespaces, this company provides privacy for its internal resources while
simplifying the name resolution process. There is no need to mirror external servers
inside the firewall or to configure proxies to differentiate between external servers and
mirrored servers.

This implementation is quite simple. Two DDNS zones are shown in Figure 7.5.
The first DDNS zone is set up outside the firewall. Its job is to provide name resolution services for the `mycompany.com` domain. The second DDNS zone is placed inside
the firewall. It resolves all names in the `corp.com` domain. This company's user community is able to differentiate between internal and external resources based on their
Fully Qualified Domain Names (FQDNs).

This DDNS design makes it necessary for you to implement two namespaces:
`mycompany.com` and `corp.com`. Each domain name must be registered on the Internet
separately. Even though `corp.com` is only used internally, it should be formally registered nonetheless. This prevents it from being used by someone else at a later time. If
you don't reserve this domain name and someone else does, your users will be unable
to differentiate between internal and external resources. It will be quite a shock for
your CEO to see a different company's corporate Web site when she points her
browser to `www.corp.com`. The cost of registering your internal domain name is
insignificant considering this ill-fated alternative.

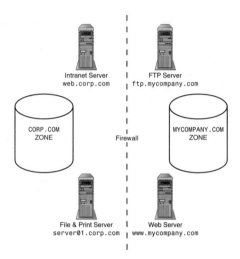

Figure 7.5 In this company with different internal and external namespaces, the corp.com zone contains the resource records for all corp.com resources, and the mycompany.com zone contains resource records for all mycompany.com resources.

Weigh all of these factors when forming your DDNS design. If your organization decides to support a single namespace, your DDNS design will be more complex. Different internal and external namespaces are much easier to implement. In your final analysis, you should find a solution that best serves your company's needs.

You have more decisions to make if you plan to implement Windows 2000 in an established DNS environment.

Implementing Windows 2000 in an Established DNS Environment

Introducing Windows 2000 DDNS servers into an environment with an established DNS namespace can be difficult. You may have no control over this existing namespace. This will often be the case in networks that require DNS for non-Microsoft operating systems. Even if you do have control of the established namespace, you might choose to keep it intact. Recreating your company's DNS namespace from scratch may be extremely difficult. For example, consider the process of recreating the namespace for an international corporation.

Most established DNS environments will be built with UNIX servers running BIND, the Berkeley Internet Name Domain (a popular implementation of DNS).[3]

---

3. BIND was originally developed at U.C. Berkeley under a grant from the U.S. Government. Versions released since then have been sponsored by several organizations including, Digital, Vixie Enterprises, and most recently, the Internet Software Consortium. For the latest information on BIND visit the Internet Software Consortium at www.isc.org.

BIND version 8.1.2 or later meets the DNS requirements of Active Directory. If your organization is already running this version of BIND or later, your job is relatively easy. You just need to audit the existing BIND environment to verify its stability. More often than not, however, existing BIND implementations will be based on BIND version 4.x. BIND version 4.x is by far the most popular. To meet the DNS requirements of Active Directory, you must upgrade your BIND 4.x environment to BIND 8.1.2 or later. Another alternative is to migrate your BIND servers to Windows 2000.

The minimum DNS requirement for Active Directory is support for service resource records (SRV RRs). Without SRV RRs, you can't provide basic DNS support for Active Directory, such as support for LDAP service records. Support for dynamic update is also recommended, but not specifically required. However, you should not implement Windows 2000 without DNS servers that support dynamic update. Keeping your DNS servers up-to-date by manually updating their SRV RRs will be next to impossible.

If your company will not upgrade or migrate its DNS servers to a platform that supports SRV RRs and dynamic update, you have a few alternatives (see Table 7.1). One of your options is to create a separate namespace based on Windows 2000 DDNS servers. This new DDNS namespace will have the sole function of servicing Windows 2000 clients. For example, if the second-level domain in your established DNS namespace is `bigcorp.com`, you can create a new domain, such as `win2000.com`, to meet the DNS requirements of Active Directory. This solution, however, is not desirable. Its primary drawback is that your company will be forced into creating and managing two separate namespaces. This DNS configuration is not uniform and is difficult to manage.

If you are in this situation, the best solution is to create a delegated subdomain. A delegated subdomain is simply a Windows 2000 DDNS subdomain in the established DNS namespace. It's noteworthy to add that any domain you create below your second-level domain does not need to be registered on the Internet. Only second-level domains need registration. This configuration meets your DNS requirements for Active Directory and offers all the advantages of keeping your existing namespace.

Table 7.1 **Alternatives for Implementing Windows 2000 in an Established DNS Environment**

DNS Environment	Alternative 1	Alternative 2
BIND 4.x	Upgrade to BIND 8.1.2 or later	Migrate to Windows 2000 DDNS
BIND 8.1.2 or later	Run Windows 2000 with BIND 8.1.2	Migrate BIND 8.1.2 to Windows 2000
NT 4.0 DNS	Upgrade to SP4 and manage SRVs by hand	Migrate to Windows 2000 DDNS or BIND 8.1.2 or later
Third-party DNS supporting SRV RRs and dynamic update	Run Windows 2000 with third-party DNS	Migrate to Windows 2000 DDNS

In this setup, the established DNS environment remains untouched. The only changes are to delegation entries in the established DNS zone files. These DNS servers will show that your Windows 2000 DDNS server is authoritative for the new delegated subdomain. With a Windows 2000 DDNS server in place, you will be free to build as many sub-domains in your portion of the namespace as needed. Every additional subdomain can be placed in the DDNS hierarchy directly beneath your delegated subdomain. For example, if your delegated subdomain is `win2000.wontmovefrombind4.com`, valid sub-domains such as `namerica.win2000.wontmovefrombind4.com` and `europe.win2000.wontmovefrombind4.com` can easily be added.

Although implementing Windows 2000 in an established DNS environment can be difficult, it is far from impossible. As long as you closely examine your options, you should be able to overcome each roadblock along the way.

Creating DDNS Naming Standards

Choosing a name for your DDNS domains and subdomains sounds simple, but it usually isn't. This chapter has already introduced some useful guidelines. However, it hasn't gone into much detail. Selecting an appropriate name for your second-level domain is most critical. This domain name will form the root of your company's Active Directory Tree or Forest. It is also, of course, the top-most domain name in DDNS. Changing this name at a later date will be difficult. Determining appropriate names for your DDNS subdomains can also help you avoid a lot of hassle later on. If you follow some simple guidelines, you should be able to create naming standards for domains and subdomains that will stand the test of time.

Naming Your Second-Level Domain

Most companies will choose a second-level domain name that is representative of their corporate identity. For example, John Doe & Associates might choose a name such as `johndoe.com`. This may not always be appropriate. For example, if the name of your corporation happens to violate DNS naming standards, you must choose something else. These standards are further defined in RFC 1123 and dictate that domain names be formed using any of the 52 alphanumeric characters—uppercase A–Z, lowercase a–z, the hyphen (-), and any number 0–9. It should be noted that Windows 2000 DDNS servers support UNICODE by default. For compatibility with non-Microsoft DNS servers such as those running BIND, UNICODE should be disabled.

Once you've selected a second-level domain name, you should register it on the Internet. You can register a second-level domain name through the InterNIC. To start this process, download the complete set of registration forms from `www.internic.net`.

The most important rule to follow when forming your second-level domain is to ensure that it remains static. If your company will shortly undergo a merger or any other organizational change, take this into account.

Naming Your Subdomains

There is no fail-proof method for naming your subdomains. However, you should follow several guidelines:

- Consider naming your subdomains based on geopolitical boundaries. Such names are often more stable than those based on business units.

  Geopolitical naming does have some flaws. For example, all your administrators may understand that Marketing is in Chicago, but to outside observers, Chicago is just a city. For all they know, Marketing could be in Dallas or Baltimore. Still, considering the alternatives, geopolitical naming is your best option.

- Do not name your subdomains after a business unit. In today's companies, business units are constantly changing, so choosing to name your subdomains by business unit can be catastrophic. In a given month, business units may merge, change names, or disappear entirely.

- Never use existing top-level domain names or registered domain names for your subdomains. Doing this can encumber your name resolution capabilities.

- Keep your domain and subdomain names as friendly as possible. Cryptic naming conventions are more difficult to understand. They make the namespace less intuitive.

If you take the time to form standards for your second-level domain name and all your subdomains now, you can avoid many problems later. You don't want to take an "I'll cross that bridge when I come to it" attitude with DNS naming standards.

Forming Zone Replication Strategies

After you've standardized your company's domain names, you should form a strategy for replicating your zone data. Replicating your zones to a number of DDNS servers offers several benefits:

- Distribution of the name resolution workload between multiple DDNS servers.

- Fault-tolerance for your zone data. If one DDNS server goes down, you still have a copy of its replicated zones.

- Ability to provide very efficient, bandwidth-friendly name resolution services. You can replicate zone data to geographically separate locations. This is especially important for DDNS servers in locations on the other side of slow WAN links.

Windows 2000 supports two methods for replicating zone data. It is strongly recommended that you use the Active Directory for zone replication. Although it is not suggested, standard zone replication is also supported. Both replication methods are covered in the sections that follow.

Standard Zone Replication

Using standard zone replication consists of organizing primary, secondary, and caching-only DDNS servers in a hierarchy. The goal of this zone replication hierarchy is to provide highly available, bandwidth-efficient global name resolution services.

Consider the zone replication hierarchy shown in Figure 7.6. The primary DDNS server for mycompany.com is positioned at the top of this hierarchy. To provide fault-tolerance for the zone data and to provide local users with more responsive name resolution services, a secondary DDNS server is installed on each IP subnet. This company has also considered name resolution services for its remote user population. Caching-only DDNS servers are placed in every remote location that is separated from the network backbone by a slow WAN link.

This replication hierarchy follows a single-master update model. The master in this replication relationship is the primary DDNS server. It has the only Read/Write copy of the mycompany.com zone. Because the primary DDNS server is the single master, it handles all dynamic updates. The secondary servers store Read-Only copies of the mycompany.com zone. They receive regular updates to their zone data through zone transfers from the primary. Secondary servers offload query traffic from the primary in areas of the network where the mycompany.com zone is most heavily taxed. Caching-only DDNS servers do not have a local copy of the mycompany.com zone. Instead, they provide query services by caching the names they learn while performing recursive queries. After a caching-only server has been in use for a period of time, its cache is populated with a number of resource records. These resource records can be retrieved from the server's cache when answering subsequent queries.

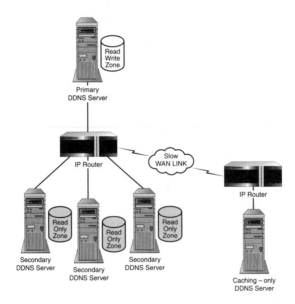

Figure 7.6 As you can see, in a standard zone replication hierarchy, losing the primary DDNS server would cut off support for DNS dynamic updates.

In the standard zone replication hierarchy, the primary DDNS server represents a single point of failure. If the primary DDNS server goes down, dynamic updates cannot be processed for the domain. This makes standard zone replication much less attractive than using the Active Directory for zone replication.

Active Directory Zone Replication

When you use the Active Directory for zone replication, each domain controller is the equivalent of a standard primary DDNS server. Storing your primary zones in the Active Directory is strongly recommended.

Using Active Directory for zone replication gives you the following advantages over standard replication:

- Replication planning for DDNS zone data is greatly simplified. Your DDNS zone data is replicated based on your Active Directory replication topology.

- The replication model for directory-integrated zone data is multi-master. Manual and dynamic updates to zones are allowed at every DDNS server.

- Active Directory zone replication is more efficient than standard replication is. Replication in Active Directory is processed at the property level. This generates less replication traffic than does standard replication.

- You can delegate administration for directory-integrated zone data at a granular level (per user per resource record).

An example of a directory-integrated zone replication hierarchy is shown in Figure 7.7. Each DDNS server for mycompany.com is a peer in this hierarchy. The mycompany.com domain controllers and member servers are strategically positioned in the enterprise to give the company's users responsive file, print, and application services. The site topology for mycompany.com is designed for rapid convergence of Active Directory updates across all IP subnets. Replication to remote locations occurs on a less frequent schedule. The mycompany.com administrators have put a great deal of thought into their Active Directory replication strategy. To leverage this well-planned replication strategy, the mycompany.com DDNS zone is stored in Active Directory.

The benefits of replicating your DDNS zones in Active Directory are hard to ignore. Perhaps the most important benefit is in simplifying replication itself. This benefit makes choosing standard zone replication difficult to justify. Nonetheless, you should consider both forms of zone replication to choose a method that suits your requirements best.

If you will continue to support NetBIOS and WINS, you have additional design considerations for DDNS. These are each covered in the following section.

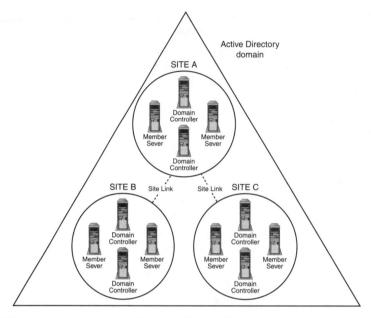

Figure 7.7 In a directory-integrated zone replication hierarchy, you are not dependent on a single DDNS server.

WINS and DDNS Integration

There are more reasons to integrate WINS and DNS in NT 3.x–4.0 networks than in Windows 2000 networks. Nonetheless, integrating WINS and DDNS in Windows 2000 can help you in the following situations:

- It can prove valuable if you need to support downlevel clients during your Windows 2000 transition. If you are unable to implement Windows 2000 DHCP servers, for example, you should definitely consider integrating WINS and DDNS.

- A Windows 2000 DHCP server can update DDNS with the IP addresses of your downlevel clients. In this configuration, a downlevel client can be found by querying both DDNS *and* WINS.

- If Windows 2000 is not used for the downlevel client's DHCP server, you should configure DDNS for WINS lookup. This will allow you to query DDNS to resolve downlevel names to IP addresses.

Inside WINS Lookup

Enabling WINS lookup allows DDNS to use WINS to look up names that cannot be found in the DDNS server's database. In NT 3.x–4.0 networks, WINS lookup was often used to help users of non-Microsoft operating systems find WINS clients (Microsoft clients). In Windows 2000, this is still a valid reason to implement WINS lookup.

For example, with WINS lookup enabled, a UNIX client can query DDNS to resolve a downlevel server's dynamic IP address. If you have any downlevel Microsoft clients or servers that can't talk to DDNS, you should use WINS lookup to resolve their names to IP addresses. This is required, as an example, for a Windows 2000 client to map a downlevel share, or printer. To provide these resolution services, a DDNS server requires an entry in its database known as a WINS record. An example of a WINS record follows:

```
<DnsDomainName>    IN WINS       <IP address of WINS server>
```

DDNS servers can have multiple WINS records listed in their IP databases. This simply provides you with a level of fault tolerance for DDNS and WINS integration.

WINS lookup is always configured on a per-zone basis. If a host sends DDNS two queries, for example, one for `client.mycompany.com` and another for `client.us.mycompany.com`, each query will be forwarded to a different WINS server (assuming the queries fail in DDNS).

You must consider another issue when configuring DDNS for WINS lookup. Suppose your company has an established DNS namespace. Each of your internal domains, for example, runs on a legacy DNS server, without support for WINS records. Let's say that the legacy DNS domains are `corp.com` and `mycompany.com`. The basic problem is that neither DNS domain can support WINS lookup. If you have no way to replace these DNS servers, you must find a workable solution. Possible solutions to this problem include the following:

- You can implement a second DNS namespace. This solution, however, is not often desired. Adding another DNS namespace complicates and adds to your administrative payload.

- You can create a subdomain with Windows 2000 DDNS servers that sits beneath the existing domain. As an example, you can create a subdomain, such as `namerica.corp.com`, within `corp.com`. Because this subdomain is built with Windows 2000 DDNS servers, it can easily support WINS lookup. This is the best way to tackle the problem.

Enabling WINS lookup can be extremely helpful in a mixed environment. It can also simplify your transition from downlevel clients to Windows 2000. Remember, however, that one of your goals in implementing Windows 2000 is to eliminate NetBIOS traffic, and ultimately WINS. Use WINS lookup on a temporary basis. Make whatever changes are necessary to move from WINS a priority.

Inside Reverse WINS Lookup

Reverse WINS lookup is possible in Windows 2000; however, it is not robust or efficient. Reverse lookup is the process of obtaining a host name when given an IP address. WINS reverse lookup involves forwarding a reverse lookup query from DDNS to WINS. More accurately, the DDNS server sends a NetBIOS node adapter status to the IP address that is being reverse-mapped. Microsoft WINS servers were not designed to provide reverse lookup capabilities. This functionality is only allowed through DDNS (or downlevel Microsoft DNS) and WINS integration. In order for reverse WINS lookup to work, a DDNS server must be configured with a WINS-R record in its local database. The WINS-R record has the following format:

```
<DnsDomainName>    IN WINS-R    <domain name to add to returned NetBIOS
➥name>
```

The hurdle to overcome with WINS reverse lookup is related to WINS itself. WINS is a flat database. DDNS is hierarchical. WINS reverse lookups need to associate a host name with a DDNS domain name. However, because WINS is flat, this can often be difficult. Suppose you have two DDNS domains: mycompany.com and yourcompany.com. In each domain you've created a WINS-R record. These records appear in their respective DDNS databases as the following:

```
@        IN WINS-R       mycompany.com
@        IN WINS-R       yourcompany.com
```

When a reverse lookup is sent to a mycompany.com DDNS server, the DDNS server sends a NetBIOS node adapter status to the IP address specified in the lookup. It then returns the results of the adapter status to the DDNS client. To do this, it appends the returned NetBIOS name to its DDNS domain name, mycompany.com. Nothing guarantees that the DDNS domain name in the WINS-R record is accurate. The reverse lookup process includes no verification of the client's DDNS domain membership.

In our example, the DDNS client might receive **host.mycompany.com** as the answer to its reverse lookup. This host, however, might actually be a member of yourcompany.com. To overcome this limitation, you should place your dynamic WINS clients in a single DDNS zone. This will guarantee that reverse WINS lookups work. Remember that, as with normal WINS lookup, reverse WINS lookup should be enabled temporarily. One of your priorities should be to eliminate all NetBIOS traffic.

Planning DHCP Services

If you're not using DHCP now, plan to implement it as part of your Windows 2000 upgrade. DHCP has become an integral element in efficient network design. One of the reasons that Microsoft DNS (now Dynamic DNS or DDNS) supports dynamic update is for tighter integration with DHCP. Windows 2000 DHCP servers support several new functions. For example, they can now store their static IP entries in Active Directory. A Windows 2000 DHCP server can also run on a Microsoft cluster, and it supports both user and vendor classes. Each of these improvements makes implementing Windows 2000 DHCP difficult to pass up.

The goal of the following section is to clearly outline the role of DHCP and to then provide proven guidelines for designing effective DHCP services.[4]

---

4. The most recent DHCP specification is defined in RFC 2131. This RFC outlines a standard set of rules for obtaining IP addresses dynamically.

The Role of DHCP

Before DHCP became popular, network administrators were forced to use static IP addresses. As we've indicated, DHCP lets you assign IP addresses dynamically. If you use DHCP, your clients will acquire IP addresses from a central authority. This is accomplished in several steps:

1. The DHCP client sends a broadcast packet called a DHCPDISCOVER packet to the network. The DHCP client's physical address is included in the packet.

2. If a DHCP server is found, it replies with a broadcast packet called a DHCPOFFER packet. Included in the packet are the DHCP client's physical address, the IP address that is offered, and options for the IP lease (such as default gateway, lease time, WINS server address and so on).

3. Upon receiving the DHCPOFFER packet, the DHCP client responds to the DHCPOFFER by sending another broadcast packet called a DHCPREQUEST packet. The packet is identified as a request, which tells the DHCP server that the client is requesting the offered address.

4. Finally, the DHCP server responds to the DHCPREQUEST by sending the DHCP client a DHCPACK packet. This acknowledgment completes the DHCP initialization process.

The advantages to using DHCP over static IP addressing are many. For example, administrators who manage static IP addresses often complain that it is difficult to prevent duplicate address allocations. Additionally, human error is always a factor: IP addresses and options are often mistyped. Further, more administrative overhead is associated with managing a static address pool. DHCP provides you a solution that is both more accurate and less troublesome. DHCP services are a must in Windows 2000 networks.

Designing DHCP Services

To ensure a proper DHCP deployment, take the following actions:

1. Determine how many DHCP servers you should use.

2. Define and configure DHCP scopes, as well as superscopes.

3. Define and configure reservations.

Number of DHCP Servers

A single DHCP server can support many clients. However, it is very common to provide fault tolerance for DHCP services by implementing backup servers for one or more scopes (pools of IP addresses). Implementing duplicate DHCP scopes on separate servers provides added redundancy. If one of your DHCP servers becomes unavailable, you can enable its scopes on your redundant backup server. This allows the backup server to service the range of IP addresses that is defined in the redundant scope.

In Windows 2000, your DHCP servers can be configured for an even higher level of redundancy. Windows 2000 DHCP servers are cluster-aware. This means that DHCP scopes can be instantiated on one cluster member if the other becomes unavailable. It is not practical to implement a Microsoft cluster to solely support DHCP. However, if you are already planning to implement a cluster, you should strongly consider running your DHCP services in the cluster. Clustered DHCP services are by far the most fault tolerant.

When deciding on the number of DHCP servers you should implement, you should also consider the location of your IP routers and whether you want to place DHCP servers on each IP subnet. The link speed between network segments on which DHCP services will be provided should be considered as well. Slower WAN links such as dial-up links require DHCP servers on both sides. This allows you to provide responsive DHCP services to remote users; the users will not need to traverse your WAN link for an IP lease.

Scopes

DHCP scopes represent groups of addresses that are available to DHCP on a particular subnet. You usually create a scope for each of your IP subnets. These scopes can then be used to define unique settings for the users that will receive their IP addresses from DHCP. Your scopes should be designed based on the needs of endusers. For example, one of your user groups may require a lease duration that is longer than another. The parameters that can be defined for a DHCP scope include the following:

- The pool of IP addresses to include in the scope
- The pool of addresses to exclude from the scope
- The subnet mask that is associated with the scope
- Options such as user class or vendor class (available only on Windows 2000 DHCP servers)
- Other options such as default gateway, lease time, WINS server address, and so on
- The scope name
- The duration of the IP lease

Superscopes

Like regular scopes, superscopes are containers that group IP addresses. Superscopes are required when two logical IP subnets exist on one physical segment. This type of con-figuration is becoming more popular. It is often called a *multi-net*. If you place two regular scopes on a multi-net, they will not function properly. With regular scopes configured on a multi-net, nothing ties a client who is seeking an IP lease to a partic-ular DHCP scope. A client can potentially obtain an IP lease on a subnet on which it does not reside. Superscopes solve this problem, and they are supported on Microsoft's DHCP servers as of NT 4.0 Service Pack 2.

To configure DHCP on a multi-net, you must add two individual scopes to a superscope. This will ensure proper operation of DHCP services.

Reservations

When designing your DHCP services, you must also consider reservations. Reservations ensure that your DHCP server does not try to lease an IP address that is statically allocated. Static addresses are still common for WINS servers, Dynamic DNS servers, print servers, and UNIX hosts. You need to survey your static IP addresses before enabling DHCP. This will prevent you from duplicating any existing assignments.

If you weigh each of these factors when designing DHCP, you'll be on the right track. DHCP will simplify the management of your company's IP addresses. This should free you up a little to tackle more serious issues—such as meeting the needs of endusers and administrators.

8

Forming TCP/IP Standards

TCP/IP-BASED NETWORKS HAVE BECOME AN INTEGRAL part of enterprise connectivity. In order to derive the benefits from a TCP/IP environment, you must establish standards and a well-thought-out strategy for implementing some of the newer, more advanced features. This chapter will provide a brief overview of the standards that serve as a framework for TCP/IP implementations, as well as some of the newer features that are innate to Windows 2000.

When designing your Active Directory model, it is important that you mirror or correlate the design of your site topology with that of your IP addressing scheme. (For help designing your site topology in Active Directory, see Chapter 6.) Having a hierarchical IP addressing scheme also enables you to do the following:

- Improve performance (robustness)
- Ease troubleshooting
- Gain greater administrative control
- Facilitate establishing a security model

This chapter covers each of these areas, along with the IP standards-based technology Microsoft has included that will improve administration and provide greater performance, including Quality of Service, IPSec, IEEE 802.1p, and Cisco Networking Services for Active Directory.

IP Addressing Overview

An *IP address* is 32 bits in length and has two components: the network number and the host number. Each 32 bit address is divided into four octets.[1] By translating each octet into its decimal equivalent, you can identify any device by its dotted-decimal address[2].

Every TCP/IP address has a classification associated with it. These allocations have been divided into several "class" types. Essentially, the *class* of an IP address is the mechanism that is used to delineate the separation between the network and host portion of an IP address. This section first discusses Class A, B, C, D, and E determinations. Then it covers two other crucial aspects of IP addressing: subnetting and the use of RFCs with TCP/IP.

Class Determination

When designing your network, you must know and understand the size of your environment. The size or quantity of your devices will directly correlate to the IP addressing scheme you will implement. Your IP addressing scheme will be determined by the number of networks you will need and the number of hosts that will reside within each network.

When you're determining IP classes and/or addresses, the most significant bit is always the leftmost bit. Similarly, the leftmost octet is the most important in an IP address. To determine the class of an address, use the following simple rule:

- If the leftmost bit is 0, it's a Class A address.
- If the leftmost bit is 1 and the second leftmost bit is 0, it's a Class B address.
- If the first and second leftmost bits are 1s and the third leftmost bit is 0, it's a Class C address.
- If the first, second, and third leftmost bits are 1s and the fourth leftmost is 0, it's a Class D address.

Class A Addresses

Class A addresses lie within the range from 0.0.0.0 to 127.255.255.255. Essentially, there are 128 Class A addresses. However, certain special cases restrict the total number of networks and hosts that are available for use. Specifically, address 0 is reserved for "the local network," and 127 is reserved as the loopback address. Therefore, it is generally accepted that 126 networks exist within the Class A address space.

---

1. An octet is equivalent to eight bits and is more commonly referred to as one byte.
2. i.e. 174.16.204

Each Class A address can have 2^{24} or 16,778,216 unique hosts. The class of an IP dictates a minimum number of addresses allocated for the network portion. A Class A address reserves the entire first octet for use as the network portion. The value of the first byte of an address determines the class of an address. Notice, as in Figure 8.1, that the leftmost bit of any Class A address is always 0; none of the other bits matter.

Class B Addresses

Class B addresses lie within the range from 128.0.0.0 to 191.255.255.255. Essentially, there are 16,384 Class B addresses. Each Class B address can have 2^{16} or 65,536 unique hosts. A Class B address reserves the entire first two (2) octets for use as the network portion. Notice in Figure 8.2 that while the two leftmost bits are considered, all other bits are insignificant.

Class C Addresses

Each Class C address lies within the range from 192.0.0.0 to 223.255.255.255. Essentially, there are 2,097,152 Class C addresses. Each Class C address can have 2^{8} or 256 unique hosts. Notice that in Figure 8.3, the three leftmost bits are considered.

Scientific	2^7	2^6	2^5	2^4	2^3	2^2	2^1	2^0
Decimal	128	64	32	16	8	4	2	1
IP address reservation	0	x	x	x	x	x	x	x

Figure 8.1 Having the bit designation can help you determine how many bits are in an address's network portion.

Sources on TCP/IP and Windows 2000

The intention of this chapter is not to provide a technical overview of TCP/IP and all the services contained within the IPv4 standard. For that, you should refer to a more complete reference on TCP/IP, such as Karanjit Siyan's *Windows NT TCP/IP*. For specific RFCs on TCP/IP, see the Internet Engineering Task Force (IETF) Web site at www.ietf.org.

IP Class Reflects Size of Company

Remember that you should base your IP addressing scheme on the number of networks and hosts your environment will need to support. This directly correlates to the size of your company. Class A addressing schemes provide the greatest amount of segmentation and control. Larger organizations that do not have publicly registered Class A addresses can use NAT and RFP 1918 to reap the same benefits as a registered Class A address. Class address and company size should correlate with the following listing:

Class	Address Range	Available Networks	Available Hosts Per Network
A	1–126	126	16,777,214
B	128–191	16,384	65,534
C	192–223	2,097,152	254

Scientific	2^7	2^6	2^5	2^4	2^3	2^2	2^1	2^0
Decimal	128	64	32	16	8	4	2	1
IP address reservation	1	0	0	0	0	0	0	0

Figure 8.2   When the two leftmost bits equal 1 and 0 respectively, the address falls in the range between 128 and 191.

Class D and E Addresses

Similar to Class A through C addresses, D & E addresses reserve octets that uniquely distinguish the class of the address. Class D addresses are reserved for multicast group usage. There is no relevance to the network and host address portions in multicast operations or applications.

In multicast operations or applications, one or more hosts can belong to a group—either by assignment or by joining—and can share data with all members of the group through the use of a single Class D address. For example, multicast applications are used for streaming video education services to multiple desktops or for use in providing video conferencing capabilities to multiple users within any workgroup. As a result of grouping and sending various requests through various sets of Class D IP addresses, an exponential number of possibilities exist for unique multicast addresses. Specifically, there is the potential for having approximately 268,000,000 unique multicast groups.

Class E addresses are reserved for future use and, as of this writing, are designated for experimental use only.

Subnetting

Subnetting enables an organization to granulize the host address within an IP addressing standard. Organizations decide to subnet as a method of overcoming organizational or topological problems. Subnetting facilitates distinguishing the dividing line between the network and host address bits. As a result, additional networks are created, but the maximum number of hosts is reduced. The newly defined network bits designate a *subnet*, a network within a larger network.

With subnets, the use of network addresses is more efficient. There is no change in how the outside world views the network. However, within the organization, layering or structure is added.

Scientific	2^7	2^6	2^5	2^4	2^3	2^2	2^1	2^0
Decimal	128	64	32	16	8	4	2	1
IP address reservation	1	1	0	x	x	x	x	x

Figure 8.3   A Class C address reserves the three leftmost bits for the network portion of the address.

From an addressing standpoint, subnets are an extension of the network. Network architects should decide the size of subnets based on your organization's current and future growth needs.

A subnet is defined by applying a bit mask. It is more commonly referred to as the subnet mask to the assigned IP address. If a bit is designated as "on" in the mask, the equivalent bit is interpreted as a network bit. If the bit is designated as "off," the bit belongs to the host portion of the IP address. The subnet is known only within the local IP address environment.

For example, an IP address of 192.178.16.66 with a subnet mask of 255.255.255.192 identifies host number 2 within subnet 192.178.16.66. A subnet mask of 255.255.255.192 essentially creates four subnets within the Class C address of 192.178.16.0, as you can see in Figure 8.4.

It is generally accepted that subnets and hosts containing all zeros or all ones are excluded as viable subnets or hosts. However, some manufacturers' (Cisco, Nortel Networks, Hewlett Packard) software feature sets do allow for the use of either instance or both.

RFCs and TCP/IP

Many Requests for Comments (RFCs) define or standardize the use of TCP/IP. *RFCs* are essentially an evolving series of reports, proposals for protocols, and protocol standards that describe the functions within the TCP/IP standard. However, not all RFCs are standards. Standards must be followed in order to ensure interoperability between components of an IP-based network environment. There is a process in place by which all proposed standards submitted to the Internet Engineering Task Force (IETF) will be reviewed. The five assignments are listed in Table 8.1.

Table 8.1 **Proposed RFC Assignments Reviewed by the IETF**

Status	Description
Required	Must be supported by all TCP/IP networks and hosts; always implemented.
Recommended	Should be supported by all TCP/IP networks and hosts; usually implemented.
Elective	Support is optional for all TCP/IP networks and hosts; not widely implemented.
Limited Use	Not intended for general use by most TCP/IP networks and hosts; rarely implemented.
Not Recommended	Not recommended for implementation.

Subnet 1	192.178.16.0-63
Subnet 2	192.178.16.64-127
Subnet 3	192.178.16.128-191
Subnet 4	192.178.16.192-255

Figure 8.4   The four subnets created by the 192.178.16.0 subnet Class C address are of equal size.

Each RFC is classified as one of the following: approved Internet standard, proposed Internet standard, Internet best practices, or for your information (FYI). A list of the RFCs that define IP usage are described in Table 8.2.

The TCP/IP-based RFCs listed in Table 8.2 are but a few of the documents that define the accepted uses for TCP/IP addressing standards. Further review of RFCs can be obtained at `www.ietf.org`. Mainly, you want to focus on RFC 1918, which defines the guidelines for creating a privately managed IP addressing scheme. When you consider the development of your Active Directory scheme, it will be important to have alignment with your IP addressing scheme. The next section of this chapter will discuss the specific importance of RFC 1918 and why you should align your design with the Active Directory hierarchy.

IP Addressing Design

Now that you've learned some of the basics regarding IP addressing, you're ready to turn to the issue of properly aligning your site topology in the Active Directory structure with your TCP/IP-based network environment. Having a hierarchical IP addressing scheme is important because it will improve performance (robustness), simplify troubleshooting, ease administration, and facilitate establishing a security model. Similarly, having an Active Directory design that is aligned with your IP addressing scheme will provide the same benefits within a Windows 2000 environment.

Table 8.2   **RFCs Needed to Establish TCP/IP Standards**

RFC	Description	Status
950	Internet Standard Subnetting Procedures	Internet Standard
1112	Host extensions for IP multicasting	Internet Standard
1597	Address Allocation for Private Internets	Informational – FYI
1883	Internet Protocol, Version 6 (IPv6) Specification	Proposed Standard
1918	Address Allocation for Private Internets	Best Current Practices

Improving Performance

Providing the most optimized IP design for your routed or switched network environment is paramount for most network administrators. RFC 1918 provides the guidelines for establishing a privately managed IP network, commonly referred to as a 10.0.0.0 network. For large sites that do not have the luxury of owning a Class A address, there are a couple of alternatives. Either you can use several Class B addresses, or you can use RFC 1918 combined with Network Address Translation (NAT) and an assigned Class B or C address.

For example, let's assume you have 100 sites, and you want to establish a privately administered IP addressing environment. By using a 10.0.0.0 network with a 255.0.0.0 subnet mask, you have 256 Class B addresses available to allocate amongst all sites. Within each Class B address, 256 Class C addresses can be distributed to certain departments or other logically defined designations. You will use your Internet-assigned Class B addresses along with your 10.0.0.0 addresses and NAT for such devices as servers, routers, and other devices that need to be recognized by your internal resources through the Internet. This effectively enables you to translate the internal addresses to a table of registered addresses that have been allocated for communication with the rest of the Internet.

Your goal is to create a numerical hierarchy scheme that isolates different geographical areas, companies, regions, sites, or departments. The key to establishing a proper IP addressing scheme is to allocate a numerical standard that logically distinguishes physical or virtual locations. Properly planning your IP addressing scheme will maximize router performance and network performance. This planning and design process ensures that local network traffic will remain local, and traffic that must traverse other networks will arrive at its destination using the fewest possible routes.

Easing Troubleshooting

The next issue you should address when aligning your IP addressing scheme with your Active Directory design involves facilitating troubleshooting. Correlating your Active Directory addressing design with the IP addressing scheme should enable you to identify problems or issues quickly. Being able to quickly determine the root of your issue will rely on the quality of the core model of your network or Active Directory representation, of course. The more hierarchical and standards-based your model is, the easier it will be to hone down your issues.

Remember that troubleshooting is a systematic approach to solving your problems. Begin by identifying the specific symptoms, then identify all the potential problems that may be causing the symptoms, and then systematically eliminate each potential problem until all the problematic symptoms have disappeared. You should prioritize the potential problems and eliminate them moving from most likely to least likely.

It is always easier to recover from an issue or problem if you are proactive or prepared ahead of time. Perhaps the most important requirement in any IP or Active Directory environment is to have current and accurate information available for support personnel. At a minimum, you should have the following information available:

- A logical and physical map of the Active Directory structure and the IP addressing scheme.

- Physical locations of all devices with their corresponding IP addresses and Active Directory names—including an accurate representation of all IP addresses, subnet masks, DNS names, and parts of the Active Directory hierarchy (sites, names, location, parents, child, and siblings).

- List of all Active Directory configuration variables and IP address protocols.

- Pertinent telephone numbers for key personnel or service providers.

The idea is to have as much as possible of the configuration information for both the Active Directory and IP environment readily available and updated.

Gaining Greater Network Administrative Control

Another function greatly affected and assisted by aligning the Active Directory structure and IP addressing scheme is systems and network administration, especially when you consider the new and advanced capabilities inherent to Windows 2000. The Windows 2000 Active Directory is the start for enabling policy-based networking via Group Policy (see Chapter 11, "Simplifying Administration," for more information on Group Policy).

Conceptually, *policy-based networking* refers to a set of client-defined rules that determines how various network services are performed. If these functions are defined within a distributed model along with network-based rules and services, an administrator has the necessary tools to perform centralized policy management.

Imagine being able to give priority access to a set of users, such as executives or senior managers, for a specific set of application(s). Another example enables an administrator to set bandwidth priorities for the finance division users when they are performing month-end closing functions. Windows 2000 Active Directory and its inherent Quality of Service Admissions Control Service (QoS-ACS) can make the aforementioned examples possible. However, if the QoS or policy-based networking services are not properly aligned with the IP addressing scheme, neither will work.

In addition, Microsoft's QoS-ACS allows policies to be created either on a subnetwork or enterprise basis. Consequently, having your IP addressing scheme mirror the Active Directory will enable quicker and tighter control when you're configuring a policy. For example, having a VLAN[3] in place that defines users based on their type of job function will facilitate those same users having either a guaranteed level of service delivery or a best effort. If the subnetting is appropriately configured, you can successfully configure any of the corresponding policies by simply looking at your subnet address.

---

3. A virtual LAN is a group of users identified logically instead of by physical proximity.

Facilitating a Secure Environment

Lastly, having your Active Directory structure aligned with your IP addressing scheme enables you to provide information that can be securely accessed by the largest number of users. Maybe you do not want to use policy-based security controls. In every security plan, there must be a method or process for user authentication, authorization, and accountability. Through policy-based networking, you can tie your security policy to specific IP addresses. If they have an Active Directory structure that mirrors the IP scheme, administrators should be able to define, deploy, and enforce security policies without having to work one-by-one across many different devices. For more details on security in Windows 2000, see Chapter 10, "Creating a Security Plan."

If properly designed, policy-based networking will allow network administrators to define relationships between organizational structure (Active Directory) and network infrastructure (IP addressing) in order to achieve maximum efficiency from network and server resources.

New IP Services

Some of the new IP services that are standards-based must be considered in any Windows 2000 environment. The idea is to use the services that are available inherently within Windows 2000 to gain greater network and OS efficiency and to decrease the administrative burden. When it is appropriate for your environment, you can use the standards outlined here to add significant value to any Windows 2000 implementation.

Traditional QoS Services

Simply stated, QoS enables an administrator to allocate bandwidth based on applications for any specifically defined set of users. Thus, if you define a service level, transmission and delivery of data should be guaranteed throughout a network environment. Several mechanisms deliver or establish QoS guarantees. RFC 2212 defined the QoS standard as accepted by the IEEE.

From a network perspective, Asynchronous Transfer Mode offers the lowest level and most true end-to-end QoS environment. ATM offers three mechanisms from which QoS can be delivered:

- Available Bit Rate (ABR)
- Constant Bit Rate (CBR)
- Variable Bit Rate (VBR)

These mechanisms allow a network administrator to specify various levels of guaranteed service delivery. For a network topology that involves Ethernet, IEEE standard 802.1q and 802.1p, the Resource Reservation Protocol (RSVP), the Real-Time Protocol (RTP), and other protocols enable QoS-like functionality. Natively, Ethernet does not support QoS.

Windows 2000 QoS Services

Microsoft's implementation of QoS involves the following:

- A QoS ACS, which is used to perform priority bandwidth management and control on a specified subnet.

- An integrated version of RSVP for transmitting and receiving communication devices. This version enables a traffic highway reserved for QoS services to be formed.

- Management tools that permit controlling services to prioritize and schedule traffic.

Message Service

QoS implementations require that a server and client have additional services enabled within each environment. These services, which Microsoft has included as additional services, must be explicitly enabled. Microsoft has also included its own version of RSVP (an IETF standard defined in RFC 2205) to be implemented across all servers and clients. In this context, RSVP is used as a message service for prioritizing bandwidth requests. In the purest sense, it is a protocol for allowing an application to dynamically reserve network bandwidth.

RSVP essentially creates a path between end-stations which then creates the required bandwidth reservation along a path predetermined by a network protocol. It is important to note that if all the devices along the path do not support RSVP or are not RSVP compliant, a bandwidth reservation cannot be made. If all the network devices along the path do not support RSVP, a best-case delivery will be assumed.

Traffic Control

Microsoft also includes QoS services that provide traffic control. Specifically, *traffic control* is a mechanism that reduces delay and latency while transmitting network traffic. Traffic control works in combination with QoS ACS and RSVP to ensure that service level and priorities are established in line with bandwidth management. More importantly, it controls data flow through devices that are not RSVP compliant. The traffic controls DLL shapes and prioritizes traffic using a process automatically installed on any Windows 2000 computer. Basically, traffic control is enabled through a process of packet classification and scheduling. The packet classifier identifies the class to which any packet belongs. The packet scheduler determines the delivery schedule and handles competition between queued packets that need access to network resources.

Several service levels are also configured for each QoS ACS policy and are an integral part of the traffic shaping properties. Appropriate service levels are determined by grouping traffic patterns into two groups: elastic or real-time. *Elastic traffic* adapts easily to change; *real-time traffic* is generated by applications that require dedicated traffic. Microsoft supports three service levels: best effort, controlled load, and guaranteed service.

Best efforts is supported only by elastic traffic, and the other two levels are supported for real-time traffic flows.

Through this implementation of QoS, Windows 2000 combines IP standards-based protocols to provide network users guaranteed service levels.

IP Security (IPSec)

IPSec is a framework of open standards that ensures secure communications over public networks like the Internet.[4] IPSec is one of the key components of standards-based, flexible solutions for deploying enterprise-wide security policies. Its interoperability ensures that compliant devices or systems will be able to exchange keys and encrypted communications with other IPSec products.

Four components make up the IPSec standard: encryption and encapsulation, authentication and anti-replay, key management and digital signatures, and support for unique digital certificates.

Encryption and Encapsulation

The IPSec Internet Protocol Encapsulated Security Protocol uses either 40/56 bit DES or 112/168 DES to encrypt the IP address of a sender along with the entire IP datagram or payload. The encrypted original IP datagram is encapsulated in a new IP packet, using the receiving device's IP address as the new destination of the packet. This mode provides the highest level of security between devices because the packet information and the original IP header are encrypted and encapsulated. This provides protection against the most sophisticated attacks, in which packets are grabbed in transit between devices, and the hacker uses the source or destination IP address to mount attacks against an organization or enterprise.

Authentication and Anti-Replay

The secure hash Algorithm (SHA-1 or MD-5 (RSA)) guarantees that the data stream is not changed or modified in transit. IPSec anti-replay service ensures that rogue packets are not inserted into the data stream. With anti-replay service, each IP datagram passing within the secure association is tagged with a sequence number. On the receiving end, each packet's sequence number is checked to verify whether it falls within the range. If an IP packet tag number does not fall within the range, the packet is blocked and discarded.

Key Management and Digital Signatures

ISAKMP/Oakley key management using Internet Security Association Key Management Protocol (ISAKMP) version 8 is the key management protocol that enables the use of a single standard architecture to secure transactions with different vendor products that are fully IPSec compliant. Manual keying is also a feature of the

---

4. Both QoS and IPSec must be implemented through an entire environment's infrastructure. If not, only partial benefits will be derived.

IPSec standard that allows for "hardwired" interoperability between certain IPSec compliant device manufactures. The Digital Signature Standard (DSS) and RSA provide proof of authorship for signatures on digital certificates.

Support for Unique Digital Certificates

IPSec compliance allows for the import of an organization's uniquely signed x.509 v.3 digital certificate into an IPSec manufacturer's hardware and software client. This allows organizations to integrate IPSec into their Public Key Infrastructures (PKI) applications for additional levels of user authentication and even stronger network security.

Microsoft has integrated IPSec functionality and compliance as a feature set within Windows 2000. Microsoft may use terms like "tunneling" to describe encapsulation. All IPSec services within Windows 2000 are delivered through policy-based administration.

802.1p

Ethernet environments that support IEEE 802.1p prioritization can queue packets according to their priority. IP Precedence or 802.1p provides signals for differentiated QoS, while RSVP provides signaling for guaranteed QoS. 802.1p utilizes three bits in the IPv4 header Type of Service (ToS) field to specify class of service (CoS) priority levels for each IP packet. You can partition traffic in up to six class of service (CoS) designations using IP Precedence.

IEEE 802.1p and IP Precedence bits are *class-of-service* (CoS) schemes. CoS is a way to group common applications or users with similar service requirements into one of several broad service or priority classes. For example, all voice could travel first-class (top priority), financial applications second class (second priority), and the rest coach (third priority). Combined with any of the popular network queuing methods, packets can then be appropriately expedited. When used in a policy-enabled network, 802.1p priorities can also be set in the host or network client. 802.1p enables service classes to be established using existing queuing mechanisms with no changes to existing applications or other network devices. Third-party tools would be needed to enable 802.1p-based policies within the Active Directory.

Cisco Networking Services for Active Directory (CNS/AD)

Though it is not an IP standard, CNS/AD is based on a newly adopted industry standard known as *DEN*, or *Directory Enabled Networking*. Whenever policy-based networking is discussed, directory technology must not be far away. CNS/AD is a middleware tool that enables users to obtain personalized network performance, develop "network aware" applications, and propagate directory-based events that replicate dynamic data critical to policy-based networking. CNS/AD offers an easier way to deliver Cisco IOS services through the Active Directory model. This is important because all the QoS and IPSec standards mentioned previously can be controlled or set for network-based services through the CNS/AD application.

Remember that for end-to-end QoS and security to be effective, all devices—both network and systems—must be protocol compliant. Eventually, you will see that setting your systems and networking policies will be configured through the Active Directory service. Essentially, CNS/AD is a set of extensions to Microsoft's Active Directory that will provide the critical foundation and functionality to implement policy-based networking applications.

CNS/AD provides a fully functional directory service that supports dynamic and event service components that facilitate policy-based networking and personalized services.

9

Estimating Hardware Needs

I F APPLICATIONS FUNCTION AS THE HEART of a system and the OS acts as the brain, hardware plays the part of the legs. The most efficient software can only go so fast on slow hardware. On properly sized servers, response time will be excellent, yet the system will lack an exceptionally large price tag. As you consider the upgrade to Windows 2000, one of the most important considerations is whether your current systems are powerful enough to continue to perform acceptably under Windows 2000. Hopefully, your current servers are properly sized for their present OS. If they have power to spare, you should be able to upgrade to Windows 2000 without any hardware changes. However, if your systems are only adequate or underpowered, you'll definitely need to make hardware changes in conjunction with your Windows 2000 rollout. Of course, if hardware changes are needed, you face the familiar upgrade or replace question. This will be discussed in the latter half of the chapter.

Analyzing Current Systems

Your current servers may be powerful enough that they don't require additional hardware to run Windows 2000 well. However, some servers that performed satisfactorily for Windows NT will be too slow running Windows 2000. This section looks at why resource requirements have changed so drastically and then shows you how to determine if your systems will make the grade with Windows 2000.

Increased Resource Requirements

Windows NT 4.0 required a 486 CPU with 16MB of RAM as the minimum hardware. In reality, acceptable performance wasn't achieved with anything less than a Pentium CPU and 64MB of RAM. By contrast, Windows 2000 has a minimum requirement of a Pentium 166MHz CPU and 64MB of RAM, with 128MB required for acceptable performance. Just as with NT, performance will be poor on the minimum hardware. While any adequately funded enterprise will have no problems meeting the CPU requirement, the most common problem will no doubt be having enough RAM.

For some, the drastic increase in required RAM is a surprise. Why did the requirement increase so much? In short, Windows 2000 has greatly increased hardware requirements because it offers so many new features. As a simple example, install Windows NT 4.0 and Windows 2000 as standalone servers on two computers. Then examine the list of services running on each. You'll see that Windows 2000 has nearly double the number of services running. Each of these new services contributes to the increased resource requirements.

By far, Active Directory (AD) is the biggest new feature. AD places greater demands on hardware than NT domain controllers (DCs) did. Additionally, as long as Windows 2000 DCs provide downlevel compatibility, they'll have to support AD and SAM-style authentication simultaneously.

Besides the new features, many features present in Windows NT have changed—some substantially. NTFS offers encryption, mount points, and dynamic resizing in its new version, NTFS5. DDNS (the new version of DNS) now supports dynamic updates and replaces WINS (see Chapter 7 for more information on DDNS). Windows 2000's TCP/IP implementation ends Microsoft networks' reliance on NetBIOS and offers QoS, IPSec, and IGMP2.

Any of these features, taken individually, would have had a small incremental impact on system resources. However, because they are all present in Windows 2000, hardware that was workable for Windows NT may not be suitable for Windows 2000.

Examining Current Systems

With the increased hardware requirements of Windows 2000, it's important to see if your hardware will be adequate. Windows 2000 depends on four system components to ensure satisfactory performance. Any of these can throttle the others by causing a bottleneck.

- CPU(s)
- Memory
- Mass storage
- Network connectivity

You're going to examine each of the four critical areas on each server—CPU, memory, mass storage, and network connectivity—to see if they will do well after the transition. This is another time when the inventory you (hopefully) collected in Chapter 3 comes in handy. It will point out all of the servers so that none are overlooked, and it will tell you what sort of hardware components they currently have.

CPU(s)

The first critical area to examine is the CPU. If your system is performing well with its current CPU, odds are good that it will continue to do so with Windows 2000. However, if the server will be offering new functionality, you may want to go with a faster CPU. Current systems with multiple CPUs should be fine with Windows 2000 unless they are heavily utilized currently.

Memory

The most important area to examine for Windows 2000 performance is that of memory. By far, the majority of server performance problems can be traced to a lack of memory. Any system with less than 128MB is not likely to perform well under Windows 2000. When insufficient memory is available, the system tries to compensate by using virtual memory on the hard drive in the form of the pagefile. Since hard drives are much slower than RAM, system performance will suffer greatly.

The new features in Windows 2000 require 20–32MB more memory than NT 4.0 did. Imagine that all of your systems today have 32MB less RAM than they actually do. If they still perform well, you should have no memory troubles under Windows 2000.

System Monitor

By far, the best way to find performance information and detect bottlenecks is by using System Monitor. For the best information on how to make use of System Monitor, check the Windows 2000 Resource Kit. Additionally, a number of articles are available on Microsoft's TechNet, along with article Q146005 in the Microsoft KnowledgeBase at http://support.microsoft.com.

If you're looking for performance information on Windows NT systems, note that System Monitor was called Performance Monitor prior to Windows 2000. Aside from the interface, there are few differences between the two.

Because NT's Performance Monitor and Windows 2000's System Monitor measure the same metrics, results from the two programs can be meaningfully compared. Use Performance Monitor on current systems to produce a baseline of performance. Then create an identical system running Windows 2000 and run the same baseline with System Monitor. Odds are, Windows 2000 performance will be somewhat slower. You can then use that data to determine how to best restore that performance.

Mass Storage

Windows 2000 requires more space for the OS than Windows NT did. Additionally, because many systems may need more RAM, they will require a larger paging file. Aside from these increased space requirements, Windows 2000 will have roughly the same performance with disk systems as Windows NT did.

Network Connectivity

While Windows 2000 will be just as efficient with the network as was Windows NT, a good number of Windows 2000 servers will require more bandwidth due to AD and other network services, such as Kerberos. If there is plenty of bandwidth to spare, both at the server and the clients, this should be no problem.

Non-Essential Components

Servers perform best when they are not used as workstations in addition to their server duties. Users should log on locally only to perform administrative work on the server. If this advice is followed, several system components have a very limited impact on system performance:

- Video card and monitor
- Keyboard and mouse
- CD-ROM/DVD-ROM
- Sound card

Upgrading Components or Replacing Machines

If you've determined that the current machine won't make the cut when you move to Windows 2000, you need to decide whether the component should be upgraded or the machine should be replaced. Each method has its advantages.

Simulating Reduced Memory

To get real-world performance data on your systems with 32MB less RAM, you can use the /MAXMEM switch in the BOOT.INI file. Note that this only works for x86 systems, and not on RISC systems such as the Alpha. Copy the right side of the equals sign on the DEFAULT= line to a new line under the [OPERATING SYSTEMS] section. Add ="Windows NT Version X W2K RAM Test" /MAXMEM=z to the new line, where z equals the current amount of RAM in MB minus 32. Reboot into this boot option and see if performance is acceptable. Don't forget to reboot back into the normal configuration when you're finished!

There are two main reasons for upgrading:

- **Cost.** Cost is often the largest factor in determining an upgrade versus replace question. Upgrading one or more components is almost always cheaper than replacing the entire machine.

- **State of the current system.** If the current system is nearly perfect except for one or two areas, an upgrade is best. The best examples of this are systems with insufficient memory or storage. If they have a fast CPU and network connection, more RAM or hard drives are all that is required.

The decision whether to upgrade or replace also depends on the component causing the bottleneck. The type of component will determine whether you're able to upgrade. When you know the feasibility of an upgrade, the cost involved and the state of the current system determine whether the upgrade is worthwhile.

In the realm of hardware, replacement can often be more attractive than piecemeal upgrades. There are several reasons for this:

- **New technology.** When one component needs an upgrade, it's often a good time to upgrade other components to their latest technologies. The hardware industry moves so quickly that what was leading-edge six months ago has usually been dethroned by something even better. Due to this speed, it's likely that if one component needs a boost, all the other components could be faster or better as well.

- **Support.** Warranties on replacement parts typically last from a month to a year. While that may be fine for the upgraded component, the other part of the server may no longer be covered. By replacing everything at once, you can usually get a complete three-year warranty as part of the purchase.

- **A spare machine.** By replacing a current server wholesale, you free the original server for other tasks. Perhaps it's needed in your testing lab or will make a great desktop machine. Maybe you will keep it as a hot spare for the new machine. At the very least, you can donate it to charity.

Now that you know the advantage of each strategy, take a look at the four key system components that have been discussed throughout the chapter. This shows you specific considerations for each component type.

Monitors

A monitor has zero impact on system performance. Unless you're often at the system console, this is a good place to save some dollars by going with a cheap, 14" VGA screen. Alternatively, you may use a console switch to use one keyboard, mouse, and monitor to control several servers. If so, go with a nicer monitor because it'll likely be used more often. By using the switch, you still save some money.

CPU(s)

If the component causing the bottleneck is the CPU, it's often better to replace the system than to upgrade it. Unless you're simply moving to a higher speed within the same family, you typically need a new motherboard, which might dictate new RAM and expansion cards.

In a similar manner, if you have a multiprocessor system and decide to add another CPU, replacement may be the best option. Typically, the CPUs must not only be of the same family and speed, but must be nearly the same revision within a speed. Unless the server manufacturer has such a CPU available, it may be difficult to find a matching processor.

The only time an upgraded CPU makes sense is if you're going from near the bottom speed of a family to nearly the top speed of the family. In this case, it may be worthwhile. However, sometimes the current motherboard can't handle a faster CPU of the same family, in which case replacement is required. While some high-end servers offer the option of being able to switch CPU families by replacing a CPU daughtercard, these upgrades can be costly in comparison to outright replacement.

Memory

While it may be better to replace a CPU bottlenecked system, this is not the case for systems needing RAM. Upgrading is by far the method employed most often to deal with a RAM shortage. Usually, one or more memory slots are available for more RAM to be added. Even if all the slots are full, you can usually consolidate two or more of the old modules into a single larger module, freeing a slot for adding more.

When you add RAM, make sure that the hard drives have enough space for a larger paging file. For most servers, adding more RAM will require enlarging the paging file. Note that once you have a page file of 250–500MB, there's little benefit to increasing it further. While there may be enough space for the increased page file, be sure to also leave room for temporary files, such as for the print spooler. Additionally, the Server service will typically complain if any one drive has less than ten percent free space.

Finally, make sure that the CPU has sufficient L2 cache available. For example, if you take a system from 128MB to 1GB, you'll definitely want additional cache. For smaller increases, this is not as necessary.

There are only two minor reasons to consider replacing a machine due to memory. First, if the current machine uses a memory type that's no longer available, replacement is necessary. Second, if you want to move from standard parity checking memory to the more error-resistant ECC RAM, your current system may not support ECC, which would require replacement.

Benchmarking Upgrades

It's important that you not simply install an upgrade and think your performance problem is solved. It is essential that the system be benchmarked, both before and after any upgrades, to ensure that the upgrade has fixed the performance problem. Use System Monitor for these benchmarks and compare the results. You may be surprised and find that fixing one bottleneck only makes a different bottleneck apparent.

Mass Storage

Just as with RAM, it's more common to upgrade hard drives than to replace the entire system. Hard drives usually have even more options for expandability than RAM. Even if the number of drives you need won't fit in the server's case, external storage units can be used to accomplish the upgrade without completely replacing the system.

As with memory, the only time replacement is required is if spare parts are no longer available. While you're rarely forced into replacing a machine, it is often beneficial to replace the entire drive system simultaneously. For instance, you might upgrade from a standard SCSI-II system of several 1–2GB drives to a SCSI-II Ultra/Wide hardware RAID controller with an array of 9GB drives. This would increase storage capacity, access speed, and reliability, leaving the remainder of the machine intact.

Network Connectivity

The network connection is another component people are more likely to upgrade than replace. Because most network cards are expansion cards, it's a simple matter to swap them out and replace their driver. As with CPUs, make sure that the other components can handle the increased capacity without causing a different bottleneck.

As with most components, the only time an upgrade is required is if the system can't accommodate an upgrade. For instance, a 486 EISA server won't be able to use PCI network cards, which are widespread today. This precludes it from participating in faster networks such as 100MB and 1GB Ethernet, FDDI, and ATM.

Ideal Systems

If you determine that you need to replace a machine or simply purchase a new machine, you might find youself asking the common question, "What type of hardware should I buy?" Every year, *PC Magazine* publishes its concept of the "perfect server." However, because they focus on specific hardware recommendations, their machine is no longer the greatest after several months.

This section will attempt to answer this "ideal server" question, but in a different manner. While some specifics will be used, the objective here is to remain general enough that the information provided will continue to be valuable to you despite the fast-changing pace of hardware.

Backups
Be sure that the backup system can handle any increase in mass storage capacity. If not, you'll have to decide whether to upgrade or replace it.

System Roles

One of the key selling points of Windows 2000 is its versatility as a server. It is able to fulfill several very different roles. You can't create a single configuration and call it an ideal server, because different roles have different requirements. Each system component has a different level of importance, depending on the system's role. Rough rankings of each component's importance to each role are listed in Table 9.1.

Table 9.1 **Component Importance for System Roles**

System Role	CPU	Memory	Mass Storage	Network
Domain controller	2	1	3	1
File/print	3	2	1	2
Database	2	2	1	2
Web/FTP	3★	2	3	1
Number cruncher	1	2	3	3

1=critical, 2=important, 3=unimportant

★=If a Web server processes pages prior to transmission (as with .ASP files), the CPU will be important, and in some cases, critical.

Domain Controllers

Domain Controllers are tasked with a number of responsibilities: to maintain the Active Directory; authenticate users; provide access to the Global Catalog; and service client requests for DHCP, WINS, DDNS, Kerberos, and LDAP. Due to their network-oriented nature, a fast network connection is critical, as indicated in Table 9.1. Also highly important is the system's memory, which will need to cache a large amount of information. The CPU is not nearly as important, but domain controllers perform a fair amount of processing. The storage system is relatively unimportant so long as it is large and fast enough.

File/Print Servers

Obviously, mass storage is the most important component of a file or print server. Very fast, large disk arrays are best for these servers. Plenty of extra space should be available on these drives. A faster network will speed responsiveness, as will the increased cache available from a large memory, but these are secondary considerations. The CPU is not critical on these systems, but they shouldn't be underpowered.

Database Servers

As the name suggests, database servers are primarily concerned with data. This means that the storage system must be of top quality. Databases can take a massive amount of space, and they often require a great deal of free space for future growth or repair operations.

The CPU, memory, and network components are all equally important. Database work requires a fair amount of server processing, and multiple CPUs may be helpful. The results of a request need to be sent to the client over the network. Finally, databases are always memory-hungry.

Note that several types of systems are databases at heart and, therefore, fall into this category of server. For example, most email systems are simply databases with special client software.

Web/FTP Servers

Internet or Intranet servers are concerned with a single task: receiving client requests and responding to them. As a result, their network connection is critically important. All of the other components are of secondary concern so long as they can process network requests and responses quickly enough. As with most system roles, memory is important due to its ability to cache data, which will speed response times.

Number Crunchers

Systems doing full-time graphics rendering or encryption work are obviously dependent on the CPU. Multiple CPUs are highly recommended in such cases. The only other important component is memory—again, for its ability to cache data. Neither the mass storage nor the network components are critical to performance.

CPU(s)

Most system roles do not depend on an extremely fast CPU. Nevertheless, a slow CPU can hobble an otherwise powerful system. You should consider the following when evaluating the value of a CPU as you create an ideal system:

- CPU type
- Speed
- Cache
- Number of CPUs

Certainly, a very busy SQL database will require more and faster CPUs than a domain controller on a fifty-workstation network. Unfortunately, Microsoft doesn't provide a simple table (similar to Table 9.1) that cross references the services offered on a server with the number of users in order to arrive at a certain "best" CPU configuration. Servers offering file sharing, DDNS, WINS, DHCP, or domain controllers can effectively utilize smaller CPUs. Servers that do a lot of processing (such as database, Web, and firewall servers) require much more CPU horsepower.

CPU Type

Once you determine you want to buy a CPU, you need to choose from the different processor types Windows 2000 runs on. The choice of processor family will limit your choices in the other three factors for CPU performance. The main architectures are Intel's x86 and Compaq's Alpha. Within the x86 architecture, quite a few families are available for use. These include Pentium, Celeron, Pentium Pro, Pentium II, Pentium II Xeon, Pentium III, and Pentium III Xeon. On the far horizon is a 64-bit processor code-named Merced. Alpha CPUs also have several families, each faster than the last. This section covers which types are the best for your needs.

For an ideal system, a few CPU families can be eliminated immediately. The Pentium line is the minimum requirement for Windows 2000 and is rarely available today. It should not be seriously considered for server use. Additionally, the Celeron line of CPUs gets its cheap cost from a small (nonexistent on some models) L2 cache. This would significantly impair the performance of a server. Finally, although there are several x86 clone makers, such as AMD and Cyrix, none of them has tried to establish a presence in the server market. While they may make good, cheap desktop CPUs, they shouldn't be considered for servers.

All the remaining CPU families make good server CPUs. Systems with roles that are not CPU-intensive can use any of these CPUs. Most server roles call for Xeon or faster processors. Systems that are highly CPU-dependent should use Xeon or Alpha CPUs. For systems needing maximum CPU horsepower, an Alpha CPU offers the fastest speed. However, not many programs are available in native Alpha code. While Compaq's FX!32 program can emulate an x86, performance can be an issue, and not all programs work under emulation.

Speed

Within a processor family, speed differences are not that great. In order for an average user to notice a difference in system performance, the difference (whether faster or slower) has to be at least ten percent. As a result, someone used to the performance of a 333MHz Pentium II would probably not notice the speed difference on a 350MHz Pentium II if all other components were the same. An additional factor to consider is that toward the top of a family's speed range, the price rises much faster in proportion to speed. As a result, for new purchases, you may want to look for a price/performance sweet spot at about seventy-five percent of the current top of the line for the CPU family of interest. Only spend the extra money for the fastest processors if the system role is very CPU intensive.

What's an Alpha?

For more information on the Alpha CPU, read "Life in the Alpha Family" by Aaron Sakovich in the January, 1999, edition of *Windows NT Magazine*. You might also check out the AlphaNT Source Web site at www.alphant.com.

Cache

The cache for a CPU can be responsible for ten to thirty percent of a CPU's speed. As a result, it's an important consideration for creating an ideal system. This section addresses how cache works and offers suggestions for an ideal system's cache.

Cache, which is a type of memory, works at or near the CPU's speed. In comparison, main memory is typically an order of slower magnitude. As data is accessed in main memory, it is added to the cache, replacing data that hasn't been used recently. If data needed by the CPU isn't in the cache, the CPU sits idle while waiting for the data to be retrieved from main memory. (This is not as true for CPUs with multiple instruction pipelines; some are capable of doing other work while they wait.) Obviously, if the CPU could get all the data it needed from cache instead of main memory, the CPU could be more productive.

In order to maximize CPU performance, most systems have two caches. L1 cache runs at the speed of the processor, which means that data in the L1 cache is immediately available to the CPU. Due to its high cost, L1 is usually small, in the tens of KB. L2 cache runs more slowly but is still much faster than main memory. Because it is less expensive, typical L2 cache may range in size from 512KB to 2MB. Large systems may have an L3 cache, which is usually several MB. Although slower than L2, L3 cache is still faster than main memory.

In general, the more cache, the faster the system will run. However, this is tempered by the substantially increased cost of CPUs with more cache. If the server in question will be very busy, it may be worthwhile to invest in a larger cache. For servers with less utilization, cheaper cost will likely outweigh the benefits of a larger cache.

Number of CPUs

One of Windows 2000's most interesting hardware capabilities is its support of multiple CPUs. For CPU-intensive applications such as graphics rendering and certain database operations, this capability can be very important. Before you decide to purchase a multiple CPU system, consider the following:

- If you have only a single CPU-intensive program, make sure it's multi-threaded. If it's a professional-quality 32-bit server application, odds are good that it supports multiple threads. If the application were single-threaded (as 16-bit programs are), it would be unable to use more than one CPU at a time.

- Make sure that you're not bottlenecking your CPUs with other system components that can't keep up. A 32-CPU system with Arcnet and a single IDE hard drive will never approach its full potential for throughput.

Mammoth Servers

For a 1GB RAM system to achieve the same average L2 cache hit ratio as a 512MB RAM system with 512KB of L2 cache, the larger system needs twice the cache. As these very large systems become technically feasible and affordable, cache size should be considered carefully. If the system will have more than 256MB of RAM, you should upgrade to the largest cache available.

Note that increasing the number of CPUs provides diminishing returns. A two-CPU system will not be twice as fast as an otherwise identical single-CPU system. The more CPUs, the smaller the performance gain from each. Another similar issue to consider is that multiple CPU systems may push you toward an all-your-eggs-in-one-basket setup. Be sure you remember to provide for fault tolerance when considering multiple CPU systems. It's usually better to have two 8-CPU systems that share an application than to have a single 16-CPU system. If the 16-CPU system fails, no one can access the application; however, if one of the 8-CPU systems goes down, the other can continue to service requests.

Memory

If you have extra money to spend on a system and you're not sure where to use it, get extra memory. Whether it's for a new system or an upgrade, additional memory nearly always offers the biggest performance gain for the money. There are three factors to consider when evaluating a system's memory:

- Size
- Speed
- Fault tolerance

Size

The most important factor in memory's performance is the amount of RAM the system has. The minimum memory requirement for Windows 2000 Server is 64MB. You should consider 128MB to be the minimum for adequate performance. This gives 2000 enough room to load itself and have a decent amount of space left for a few applications and a file cache. Most servers, regardless of their roles, should have 192 to 256MB of RAM in order to function efficiently. Heavily utilized servers will benefit from additional RAM; memory sizes of several GB are not unheard of.

Speed

For x86 servers, the CPU's bus speed to memory varies. Pentium and early Pentium II CPUs talked to memory at 66MHz. 350MHz and faster Pentium IIs, along with newer CPUs, can access memory at 100MHz, and 133MHz is expected in the near future. Obviously, the faster the CPU's interface with memory, the faster the system will be overall. For this reason, your servers should include a 100MHz or faster Front Side Bus (FSB), with memory certified to run at that speed.

Fault Tolerance

Standard RAM uses parity for error checking. Each byte has an extra bit dedicated to ensuring that the other eight bits are accurate. However, parity can reliably detect only certain errors; other errors can fool it into thinking there's no problem. Additionally, detecting an error leads to a system halt with a "memory parity error" message. If a system is mission critical, use memory with better error capabilities than standard RAM.

Many server class machines increase reliability by using a different type of error correction called Error Correcting Code (ECC). The increased number of bits used for error checking renders it much less likely to be fooled. Additionally, ECC can correct some errors, enabling the server to continue functioning until the memory can be replaced. However, these extra bits cost more money. ECC costs are increased further because they have a much smaller sales volume than does standard RAM. Nevertheless, ECC is a must for mission critical servers. For less important machines, you'll need to determine if ECC's benefits fit into your budget.

Mass Storage

Although memory is a type of storage, it is erased if power is lost. This section looks at permanent storage, which usually takes the form of hard drives. You need to consider three factors when designing the storage system on an ideal server:

- Speed
- Interface
- Fault tolerance
- Storage layout

Speed

Whereas RAM response times are measured in nanoseconds, hard drive response times are measured in milliseconds. Since many CPU cycles can be wasted waiting for hard drives to fulfill requests, shaving even a single millisecond from a drive's access time can be a performance gain. Systems that rely heavily on their storage systems should look for an ideal system whose drives are as fast as possible. Short of using very large RAM drives for permanent storage, you can use several techniques for making hard drive access faster:

- **Drive speed.** The faster a hard drive's RPM, the faster it will respond. Most of today's drives run at 5400RPM, but some go as fast as 10,000RPM. While these drives are fast, they are also loud and tend to operate at higher temperatures than other hard drives, requiring extra cooling fans. Of course, this is not a critical concern for most servers because they are typically isolated in climate-controlled rooms. Busy servers should have 7200 or 10,000RPM drives for best performance.

- **Number of drives.** By having more drives in a system, you distribute the load between them. There's a greater chance that a needed drive will be idle when a request is made.

- **Caching**. Satisfying a request from RAM rather than a hard drive is much faster. As a result, storage data is cached in several locations, including the hard drive itself, the controller, and the OS. Look for hard drives with large caches. Also, use controllers that allow caching on the controller. Finally, make sure that the OS has enough RAM to allocate an adequately sized file cache.

- **Intelligent controllers.** Controllers can enhance performance by offloading disk processing from the CPU. This allows the CPU to do other work while waiting for the data to arrive. Also, controllers can reorder disk requests based on the data's location on the disk in order to reduce access times.

Interface

When you're selecting the hard drives for an optimal system, the interface to use is an important decision. Fortunately, the choice is currently straightforward. There are three major types of hard drive interfaces today: IDE, SCSI, and Fibre Channel. IDE is not suitable for any but the smallest servers. SCSI is used by the great majority of servers and offers a balance of performance and cost. The SCSI interface continues to evolve and has a number of variants. For this reason, make sure that all the server's SCSI components can interoperate with one another. Fibre Channel is just beginning to appear on servers. With its advantages over SCSI, however, it may eventually replace SCSI as the storage interface of choice on servers. At present, though, only busy servers will see a performance benefit when compared with the cost.

Fault Tolerance

Fault-tolerant storage systems are a must for a server. Usually, the OS is mirrored using RAID 1, and data files are stored on stripe sets with parity using RAID 5. While the extra drives add cost to a system, the ability to run even if a drive fails is an important ability for a server. All but the smallest servers should use hardware RAID for performance and fault tolerance.

Storage Layout

Although storage layout is not a part of the hardware, storing various files in the proper locations will have an impact on the system. By placing different file types on different drives, you can increase performance. Additional performance can be gained by using multiple disk controllers, so that there are fewer disks on each controller channel. Generally, the following types of files should all reside on separate disk systems for best performance:

- System pagefile(s)
- Operating system
- Programs
- User data

- Database data files
- Database log files

It's always a good idea, but partitioning a system's data as described earlier is most important on systems where performance is heavily impacted by the storage system. An easy standard to follow for single-purpose servers is to use the first drive for the OS and pagefile and then use a second and third drive for two other data types (such as programs on one and user data on the other).

Network

Most servers are worthless without a network. However, this component is all too often overlooked in planning a system. A frequent mistake is to simply plug the server into an open connection on a hub shared with clients—typically 10Mb Ethernet. Remember that all client requests have to funnel down the server's network connection. As a result, the server should be connected by a faster or more efficient medium than the clients in most cases. The following components make or break the network's speed:

- **Server connection speed.** Nearly all client networks run on 10Mb Ethernet. Most network technologies run faster than this. Possibilities for connecting a server include 100Mb or 1Gb Ethernet, ATM, and FDDI. Of these, 100Mb Ethernet, ATM, and FDDI are the most widely used for servers.

- **Network efficiency.** In order to make the network connection more efficient, look at how the networks handle data transmission. Ethernet simply allows any machine to send data if it believes the wire is clear. This can cause collisions. As a result, Ethernet is only thirty percent efficient. For example, 10MB Ethernet's maximum throughput is typically only 300–400KB. By contrast, ATM and FDDI are much more efficient, and their true throughput is much closer to their theoretical throughput.

- **Client connection speed.** Fina3lly, remember that a server with a fast connection may still have slow response times to a client if the client's subnet is very busy. The client network should also be evaluated to determine if it's a factor in causing a bottleneck.

Logical and Physical Drives

In the storage layout sense, a drive is a physical hard drive or a RAID array. There is little performance advantage to separating data onto different logical drives (partitions) on the same physical hard drive.

10

Creating a Security Plan

CREATING A SECURITY PLAN IS THE ESSENTIAL practice of establishing standards that protect your resources and data. This includes the information that resides on your storage devices, as well as the data in transmission on your LAN, WAN, and dialup links. With Windows 2000, the ability to create a key line of defense for your systems against unauthorized actions is greatly enhanced. You should examine each aspect of Windows 2000 security and make it your priority to create an effective and useful security plan.

You must consider every element of Windows 2000 security to create an effective security plan. Your security plan will be only as good as its weakest link. If you only establish a few policies or guidelines and disregard key areas of security, you dilute your plan's overall value. This chapter covers the details of Windows 2000 security from top to bottom. Each section that follows is dedicated to a unique aspect of system security. These sections cover the following topics:

- Providing secure authentication services
- Protecting the file system
- Understanding user rights
- Securing Active Directory
- Leveraging certificate services
- Windows 2000 default security configurations

The goal of this chapter is to impart an in-depth understanding of Microsoft's security architecture, and to provide effective guidelines for securing Windows 2000 networks.

Providing Secure Authentication Services

Perhaps the most fundamental aspect of Windows 2000 security is authentication itself. In its most basic form, *authentication* is the process that confirms the identity of a security principal (user, group, or special identity). This confirmation process includes two basic steps.

Authentication to a Windows 2000 system starts with a process known as interactive logon. During *interactive logon*, the identity of a security principal is confirmed to a domain account or to the local computer.

After interactive logon is completed, a security principal is free to access network resources. When attempting to access a resource, such as a shared folder, a second authentication process is invoked transparently. This process is known as network authentication. *Network authentication* is the process that confirms a security principal's identity to a network service.

Implementing secure authentication services is not always as simple as relying on Microsoft's core authentication protocols. For example, in 1998, a popular security group produced a network-sniffing tool with the ability to decipher NT passwords presumably secured by interactive logon and network authentication. Consequently, to provide robust authentication services, you must also consider the appropriate level of security for the everyday traffic on your LAN and WAN. To provide secure authentication services you must therefore create two sets of standards: one for using Microsoft's core authentication protocols and another for optional security protocols and devices, such as smart cards and IP Security. This section discusses these protocols and devices and then details the specifics required to establish secure authentication standards.

Core Authentication Protocols

The default installation of Windows 2000 supports three core authentication protocols. In addition to offering authentication services, these core protocols provide message integrity and privacy to distributed applications. These protocols include the following:

- NT LAN Manager (NTLM)
- Kerberos V5
- Secure Sockets Layer/Transport Layer Security (SSL/TLS)

NT LAN Manager (NTLM)

For the most part, Windows 2000 uses the NTLM protocol only to authenticate to and from downlevel clients or servers (such as NT 3.x–4.0 Workstation/Server). NTLM is the default authentication protocol for NT 3.x–4.0. In Windows 2000, however, NTLM is replaced by Kerberos. As a result, your standards for Microsoft's core authentication protocols should address whether or not to continue supporting NTLM. The guidelines listed in Table 10.1 can help you make this decision[1].

Kerberos V5

Unlike NT 3.x–4.0 networks that rely solely on NTLM, Windows 2000 supports both NTLM and Kerberos. As was mentioned earlier, Kerberos replaces NTLM in Windows 2000 as the default authentication protocol. *Kerberos* is an industry standard, platform-independent security protocol developed at the Massachusetts Institute of Technology (MIT). It offers several advantages over NTLM, including faster session establishment, the ability to create transitive trusts, and support for delegation of authentication.

Table 10.1 **When to Support NTLM Authentication**

Condition	Action
Your network consists of many downlevel clients and/or servers.	You must support NTLM until all downlevel clients and servers upgrade to Windows 2000.
You have several UNIX clients that currently use your NT 3.x–4.0/2000 servers. These clients are not configured for the Kerberos protocol.	You may need to support NTLM if your UNIX clients are using an SMB (server message block) client to connect to NT/2000. If your UNIX clients are using standard TCP/IP protocols, such as FTP and Telnet, you can eliminate NTLM.
You have several UNIX clients configured to use the Kerberos protocol. These clients currently use an SMB client to connect to your Windows NT/2000 servers.	To eliminate NTLM, you can configure your UNIX clients to authenticate to Windows 2000 using Kerberos. (See the Windows 2000 Resource Kit utilities KTPASS.EXE and KSETUP.EXE for details.)
Your current NT/2000 clients connect to a UNIX server running an SMB daemon.	If you continue to use the SMB daemon, you most likely cannot get rid of NTLM. To eliminate NTLM, you can use an NFS client on your NT/2000 systems instead. Microsoft provides an NFS (network file system) client as part of its Services for UNIX package.

1. It should be noted that the conditions and actions listed in this table are based on mainstream SMB clients and servers that are available as of Q1 1999. It is very likely that an SMB client and/or server that natively supports Microsoft's implementation of Kerberos will be developed in the future.

The central component of Kerberos security is the *Key Distribution Center (KDC)*. The KDC runs on each Windows 2000 domain controller as a part of Active Directory, which stores passwords and other sensitive account information. Every KDC issues tickets. Kerberos clients use these tickets during authentication and to access network resources. Your Windows 2000 KDCs issue two types of tickets: user tickets and service tickets. The Kerberos authentication process consists of several steps. These steps follow.

You must first obtain a user ticket during interactive logon. Your KDC issues you this user ticket only after you've authenticated using your encrypted password. After you've received a user ticket from your KDC, you can request a service ticket. You will need a service ticket to access any network service. At the time you access a network service, your Kerberos run time will first look in your local ticket cache to see if you already have a valid service ticket. If no service ticket is found, you must send your user ticket in a service request to the KDC. After the KDC receives your request and determines that you're authorized to access this particular network service, it will send you a valid service ticket. Finally, after receiving the service ticket, you encrypt it and add it to your ticket cache.

Every attempt you make to access this network service in the future will require the service ticket issued by your KDC. Instead of re-initiating the authentication process, you will reuse the service ticket stored in your ticket cache. This lessens the KDC's authentication workload, and accelerates your network service access time.

Your standards for Microsoft's core authentication protocols should definitely include Kerberos. Specifically, you should define standards for each of the Kerberos protocol's adjustable parameters. By adjusting the parameters listed in Table 10.2, you can change the behavior of Kerberos.

If you set any of these parameters lower than their defaults, the level of Kerberos security in your network is heightened. Consider the maximum service ticket lifetime. If you set this for 45 minutes rather than 60 minutes, your clients must re-authenticate to network services more frequently. In an average eight-hour day, a 60-minute maximum causes service tickets to expire 8 times a day. Using a 45-minute maximum increases the re-authentication frequency to roughly 10 times a day.

Secure Sockets Layer/Transport Layer Security (SSL/TLS)

The final core security protocol that is supported by Windows 2000 is the *Secure Sockets Layer/Transport Layer Security (SSL/TLS)* protocol. Windows 2000 uses the SSL/TLS protocol and X.509 certificates to authenticate smart card users and to protect connections on unsecured networks. The SSL/TLS protocol can be used to secure Internet/intranet traffic, mail traffic, and client side transactions, such as those invoked from a browser. Some of Microsoft's core products, including IIS and Exchange, have long supported the SSL/TLS protocol. Smart card use, however, is only supported in Windows 2000.

Table 10.2 **Settings That Control How the Kerberos Protocol Operates**

Parameter	Default Setting
Maximum lifetime that a user ticket can be renewed	7 days
Maximum service ticket lifetime	60 minutes
Maximum tolerance for synchronization of computer clocks	5 minutes
Maximum user ticket lifetime	10 hours

Smart Card Authentication

Smart cards are credit card-sized devices that provide a secure storage area for user credentials, passwords, and other sensitive information. You can use smart cards in Windows 2000 to support certificate-based authentication. Smart cards isolate sensitive security-related tasks involving every aspect of the authentication process. Because smart cards are relatively small, they are also extremely portable. This level of portability provides smart card users with secure storage at work, home, or on the road.

The SSL/TLS protocol is used in the smart card authentication process. This authentication process consists of the following steps:

1. To initiate authentication, smart card users enter their cards into an ISO-compliant reader. The insertion of the smart card starts the Secure Attention Sequence. This has the same effect as pressing Ctrl+Alt+Del, except that instead of entering a username and password, a smart card user must enter a valid PIN.

2. SSL/TLS requests the user's certificate. This certificate is retrieved from the smart card's secure storage area and is subsequently passed to SSL/TLS.

3. The certificate's expiration date and the issuing Certificate Authority's (CAs) digital signature are both verified.

4. SSL/TLS requests the CAs certificate. After receiving this certificate, SSL/TLS validates this certificate's integrity by checking its digital signature.

5. The SSL/TLS protocol then checks to see if the user's certificate is in the CA's revocation list.

6. If the certificate is valid, SSL/TLS queries Active Directory for a domain account corresponding to the subject name in the user's certificate.

7. If a valid domain account is found, SSL/TLS generates the user's authorization identity. This is the identity of the domain account associated with the subject name in the user's certificate. Subsequent access to resources in the domain is permitted based on the rights and permissions associated with this account.

When used properly, smart cards offer exceptionally strong authentication services. If you decide to use these services, your security standards should define guidelines for smart card use and management. Table 10.3 can help you form these standards.

Table 10.3   **Smart Card Usage and Management Standards**

Options	Recommended Standard
Using smart cards in every department or just in areas that regularly handle sensitive information	Unless everyone in your company works with highly sensitive data, consider implementing smart cards only where they're needed most. Good examples would include your server room and in your legal and human resources departments.
Optional or mandatory use of smart cards for every logon	You must decide whether or not to block traditional logon for smart card users. The downside of this is poor usability. If users don't have their cards, they can't log on. The upside of this is tighter security. Absolutely no one except the holder of the smart card can authenticate with the user's identity. In highly secure environments, make smart card use mandatory.
Frequency of PIN code changes	You can form this standard the same way that you form your maximum password age policy. Of course, there is no way to secure the authentication process if smart cards and PIN codes are left sitting on users' desks.
Certificate revocation frequency	This standard is somewhat like your maximum password age policy. However, to form your certificate revocation standards, you should consider all your certificates, not just those used by smart card users. See the "Standardizing Certificate Services" section for details. Form this standard only after you understand the full scope of your certificate needs.
Single or multiple smart card vendors	It's always best to use one vendor for hardware-based security services. Choose a well-known, established smart card vendor and stick with it.

Smart cards will provide you with rock-solid authentication services. Protecting your LAN and WAN traffic from prying eyes, however, is the job of IP Security.

IP Security

We've already pointed out that your authentication standard should address the level of security for traffic that flows on your LAN and WAN. In Windows 2000, you can address this requirement by implementing IP Security. *IP Security* provides a cryptographic defense to keep internal and external communications private. Microsoft's implementation of IP Security is based on the standards developed by the Internet Engineering Task Force (IETF) IP Security working group.

IP Security works closely with Active Directory to obtain its policy information. An IP Security policy is made of rules, filter lists, and negotiation policies. Retrieval of this policy information from Active Directory occurs when a system starts. On Windows 2000 Professional and Windows 2000 Server, IP Security is disabled by default. To begin using IP Security, you can create your own security polices, or use one of the predefined policies supplied by Microsoft. The predefined IP Security policies available in Windows 2000 follow:

- **Secure Responder.** Normally communicates without using IP Security. Uses the Default Response rule to negotiate security only with hosts that request IP Security. Only the requested protocol and port traffic with the host are secured.

- **Secure Initiator.** Normally communicates securely. Accepts unsecured communication, but always responds using IP Security. Allows unsecured communication with non-IP Security-aware hosts after a 40-second negotiation attempt.

- **Lockdown.** Always communicates securely. You can implement one of these policies or define your own to provide end-to-end security for your LAN and WAN traffic. IP Security provides you with a packet-level line of defense against data interception, modification, and access by unauthorized entities. Some of the common uses for IP Security follow:

- Securing departmental traffic, such as the sensitive communications in financial and legal environments

- Protecting client-server communications on an application-by-application basis

- Safeguarding the data that is transmitted on unsecured networks between multiple hosts forming a virtual private network

- Shielding WAN communications between sites in an enterprise network

If you plan to use IP Security for any of these reasons, establish standards for IP Security configuration and management. To establish these standards, though, you need a more detailed understanding of IP Security's inner workings. IP Security is covered in more detail in Chapter 8, "Forming TCP/IP Standards."

Security Policy Standards

There are a number of policies that affect authentication. The way you choose to configure these policies defines a system's security behavior. As a result, your authentication standard should define default settings in each of the following areas:

- Password policy
- Account lockout policy
- User account properties
- Security options

Password Policy

Password policy regulates how your users must establish and manage their passwords. This includes password complexity requirements, how often passwords must change, and so on. The recommended settings in Table 10.4 lists each configurable parameter, its description, and suggested values for low, average, and high security implementations.

Table 10.4 **Password Policy Settings**

Setting	Description	Low	Avg.	High
Enforce password uniqueness by remembering last	Setting this parameter higher prevents users from switching between their favorite passwords.	1–8 passwords	9–16 passwords	17–24 passwords
Maximum password age	This is the time period that the user is given to use a new password.	91–999 days	31–90 days	8–30 days
Minimum password age	Setting this parameter higher prevents users from reverting back to their previous passwords for *x* number of days.	1–30 days	31–90 days	91–180 days
Minimum password length	This is a critical setting, since shorter passwords are more susceptible to dictionary attacks.	4 characters	5 or 6 characters	7–14 characters
Passwords must meet complexity requirements of installed password filter	Installing a password filter allows you to define more complex password requirements. For example, you can install a password filter that requires users to make passwords that consist of lower case, upper case, and numeric characters.	No	Yes	Yes
User must log on to change password	Enabling this forces users to log on to change their passwords when they expire.	Disabled	Not Applicable	Enabled

Account Lockout Policy

Account lockout policy dictates the behavior for locking and unlocking user accounts. This includes the account lockout count, how long to lock accounts, and so forth. The recommended settings in Table 10.5 list each configurable parameter, its description, and suggested values in low, average, and high security environments.

User Account Properties

There are several *user account properties* that control privileges for user accounts. These privileges define how a user account can be used. This includes allowed logon hours, whether a smart card is required to log on, the account expiration date, and so on. The recommended settings in Table 10.6 list each configurable parameter, and suggested values for a stricter level of security.

Table 10.5   **Account Lockout Policy Settings**

Setting	Description	Low	Avg.	High
Account lockout count	This value determines how many times users can attempt to log on before their accounts are locked.	5 attempts	3 or 4 attempts	1 or 2 attempts
Lockout account for	This parameter controls how long an account is locked after triggering the account lockout count.	1–15 minutes	30–60 minutes	61–480 minutes
Reset account after	This parameter is a counter for unsuccessful logon attempts which increments for *x* number of minutes before returning its value to zero.	1–15 minutes	30–60 minutes	61–480 minutes

Table 10.6   **User Account Properties**

User Account Property	Recommendation
Logon hours	For a higher level of security, deny logon during non-business hours.
Logon To…	In high security environments, associate your accounts with one or more workstations.
User must logon using a smart card	Enforce smart card logon to establish a higher level of security for interactive logon.
Account expires	Set expiration dates on user accounts that will have a temporary lifetime, such as an account for a consultant, contractor, or temp.

Security Options

Security options control a wide range of security behavior for the operating system itself. This includes whether or not to display a legal notice at logon, whether the Administrator account name will be renamed, and so on. Table 10.7 lists recommendations for the more useful security options.

The quality of your authentication standard is critical. This standard literally guards the front door to your network. The following section looks at standards to protect files, folders, and shares.

Table 10.7   **Suggested Values for Security Options**

Option	Recommendation
Allow system to shutdown without having to log on	Set this to disabled to require a valid logon before shutdown.
Change Administrator account name to	Since the Administrator account is a common target, you should change its name to something less obvious.
Do not display last username in logon screen	This should be enabled to hide the name of the last user's logon name from a would-be intruder.
Forcibly logoff when logon hours expire	By default, users will stay connected if they have a session that is open when logon hours expire. Set this to enabled to enforce your logon hours.
Message text for users attempting to log on	You should consider entering a legal notice that will be displayed to all users attempting to access your network.
Shutdown system immediately if unable to log security audits	Take caution when evaluating whether or not to enable an immediate shutdown in the event the system is no longer able to log security audits. This may be an excellent security policy, but shutting the system down during business hours may not be acceptable.

Protecting the File System

The goal of this section is to establish standards that safeguard the file system. The default NTFS permissions that are assigned to files, folders, and shared folders at installation time favor usability over system security. For example, as part of the installation process, the special identity Everyone is assigned `Full Control` permissions to `%SystemDrive%`. Subsequently, every folder created below the root installation drive inherits these permissions. If you aren't careful, you can end up sharing a folder beneath `%SystemDrive%` with more people than you bargained for. To avoid making mistakes like this one, you should standardize the file, folder, and shared folder permissions on all your systems.

Windows 2000 supports three well-known file systems: FAT, FAT32, and NTFS. FAT and FAT32 are unsecured file systems. They are only appropriate for desktop operating systems, such as Windows 3.x, Windows 95, and Windows 98. NTFS, on the other hand, is highly secure. NTFS is the de facto standard in most Microsoft networks. Accordingly, the subsections that follow assume you've formatted your volumes with NTFS.

Folder Permissions

You can assign *folder permissions* to restrict the level of access that users have to folders, such as `%SystemRoot%`, `%SystemRoot%\Repair`, and `%SystemRoot%\System32`. Folder permissions also control the level of access that users have to the files and subfolders contained within them. Table 10.8 lists the standard folder permissions, and the level of access that each permission offers.

File Permissions

File permissions restrict the level of access that users have to files, such as NTLDR, BOOT.INI, and NTDETECT.COM. The standard file permissions and the level of access they allow are listed in Table 10.9.

Table 10.8 **Folder Permissions**

Permission	Description
List Folder Contents	Allows a user to view the folder's contents.
Read	Allows a user to view the folder's contents, permissions, ownership, and attributes.
Read & Execute	Allows a user to traverse folders. Also permits the actions allowed by the List Folder Contents and Read permissions.
Modify	Allows a user to delete the folder. Also permits the actions allowed by the Read & Execute and Write permissions.
Write	Allows a user to create files and subfolders, change folder attributes, and view the folder's permissions and ownership attributes.
Full Control	Allows a user to change folder ownership and to delete files and subfolders. Also permits the actions allowed by all other folder permissions.

Special File and Folder Permissions

The standard file and folder permissions are usually sufficient to secure your resources. These standard permissions, however, are actually sets of special permissions. You can choose from a total of fourteen special permissions to give users, groups, or special identities a more granular level of access to files and folders.

Table 10.9 **File Permissions**

Permission	Description
Read	Allows a user to read the file and list its permissions, ownership, and attributes.
Read & Execute	Allows a user to execute the file. Also permits the actions allowed by the Read permission.
Write	Allows a user to overwrite the file, list its permissions and ownership, and change its attributes.
Modify	Allows a user to modify and delete the file. Also permits the actions allowed by the Read & Execute and Write permissions.
Full Control	Allows a user to change file ownership. Also permits the actions allowed by all other file permissions.

File Permissions

The available file permissions are Full Control, Modify, Read & Execute, Read, and Write. Each of these is made of a grouping of special permissions. Table 10.10 lists each of the file permissions and the set of special permissions that form them.

Table 10.10 **Special File Permissions**

Special Permissions	Full Control	Modify	Read & Execute	Read	Write
Change Permissions	x				
Create Files/Write Data	x	x			x
Create Folders/Append Data	x	x			x
Delete	x	x			
Delete Subfolders and Files	x				
List Folder/Read Data	x	x	x	x	
Read Attributes	x	x	x	x	
Read Extended Attributes	x	x	x	x	
Read Permissions	x	x	x	x	x
Synchronize	x	x	x	x	x
Take Ownership	x				
Traverse Folder/Execute File	x	x	x		
Write Attributes	x	x			x
Write Extended Attributes	x	x			x

Folder Permissions

The available folder permissions include Full Control, Modify, Read & Execute, List Folder Contents, Read, and Write. Like file permissions, each folder permission is made of a set of special permissions. Table 10.11 lists each of the folder permissions and specifies the grouping of special permissions that form them. Note that the List/Folder Contents permission is inherited only by folders, not by files. The Read/Execute permission is inherited by both folders and files.

Shared Folder Permissions

Shared folder permissions apply to folders only, not to individual files. Shared folders are commonly referred to simply as *shares*, or *file shares*. You can use file shares to give users, groups, and special identities access to network resources. Table 10.12 lists each of the shared folder permissions, and specifies what each permission allows.

Table 10.11 **Special Folder Permissions**

Special Permissions	Full Control	Modify	Read & Execute	List Folder Contents	Read	Write
Change Permissions	x					
Create Files/Write Data	x	x				x
Create Folders/Append Data	x	x				x
Delete	x	x				
Delete Subfolders and Files	x					
List Folder/Read Data	x	x	x	x	x	
Read Attributes	x	x	x	x	x	
Read Extended Attributes	x	x	x	x	x	
Read Permissions	x	x	x	x	x	x
Synchronize	x	x	x	x	x	x
Take Ownership	x					
Traverse Folder/Execute File	x	x	x	x		
Write Attributes	x	x				x
Write Extended Attributes	x	x				x

Table 10.12   **Share Permissions**

Permission	Description
Read	Allows a user to display folder names, file names, file data, and attributes; run program files; and change folders within the shared folder.
Change	Allows a user to create folders, add files to folders, change data in files, append data to files, change file attributes, and delete folders and files. Also permits the actions allowed by the Read permission.
Full Control	Allows a user to change file permissions and take ownership of files. Also permits all tasks allowed by the Change permission.

Calculating Permissions

The central mechanism used by Windows 2000 to provide protection for its file system, as well as for its other resources, is object-based access control. Every resource in Windows 2000 is defined as an object. This includes folders, files, shared folders, and groups, as well as services, devices, threads, and windows (there are many more). To implement access control for its objects, Windows 2000 uses *Access Control Lists (ACLs)*. The ACL of an object defines its security properties, which include its permissions, as well as its auditing, ownership, and inheritance behavior. Listed in every object's ACL are one or more *Access Control Entries (ACEs)*. These entries define the access rights to an object for each user, group, or special identity.

The ACL of an object, such as a folder, can contain multiple ACEs. These ACEs can each define different permissions for the same user. For example, a user may be granted the Read permission to a folder directly and the Modify permission through membership in a group. To determine users' effective access rights, you must under-stand the rules for combining NTFS permissions. There are several rules to determine how individual NTFS permissions combine to produce effective permissions. These rules, as well additional rules for calculating NTFS permissions, follow:

- Multiple individual permissions
- Deny and allow permissions
- Folder and file permissions
- Inheritance of permissions
- Shared folder and standard permissions
- Permissions on copied or moved files

Multiple Individual Permissions

When the ACL of a file contains multiple entries for the same user, the user's effective permissions are calculated by combining each individual permission. For example, if the user is granted the Read permission directly and the Write permission through membership in a group, the user's effective permissions are both Read and Write.

Deny and Allow Permissions

Another rule for calculating permissions defines how deny and allow permissions combine. When you deny a permission for a file, folder, or share, it overrides every instance in which that permission is allowed. Consider a user belonging to two groups. If one group the user is a member of has `Full Control` to a folder, and another group is denied `Full Control`, that user has no effective permissions. The `Deny Full Control` permission overrides the `Allow Full Control` permission.

Deny permissions should not be used regularly as a means of restricting access to files, folders, or shares. Instead, deny permissions have a specific role. Deny permissions should only be used to exclude an individual from a group that is given access to a file, folder, or share. This capability allows you to deny access to an individual for a resource without completely removing them from the group.

Folder and File Permissions

Additionally, permissions that are assigned to files override permissions that are assigned to folders. As an example, you can assign a user the `Modify` permission for a file, without specifying any permission for the file's containing folder. Access to the containing folder is not required to access the file.

Inheritance of Permissions

NTFS permissions can also be inherited. Permissions that are assigned to folders are, by default, inherited by files and subfolders below them. Despite this default behavior, you can prevent permissions inheritance. You can always block inheritance from a folder by setting new permissions on any subfolder. Every file and folder that is contained by this subfolder will then inherit its permissions. You can also control the behavior of inheritance at the time you assign permissions. For example, when you set permissions on a folder, you are given several options that affect inheritance. You can apply this folder's permissions to the following:

- This folder and subfolders
- This folder and files
- Subfolders and files only
- Subfolders only
- Files only

These options give you plenty of flexibility. Whenever you set folder permissions, you can simply choose inheritance behavior that meets your requirements.

Shared Folder and Standard Permissions

There are added rules that define how shared folder permissions combine with standard permissions. When accessing secured files contained within a shared folder, the most restrictive permissions always apply. If you assign a user the `Read` permission to a shared folder and the `Read & Execute` permission to a file contained in the shared folder, that user's effective permissions are `Read`. The `Read` permission is the most restrictive.

Permissions on Copied or Moved Files

The final rule you must understand to calculate permissions defines how permissions for files and folders are affected when they are copied or moved. Whenever you *copy* a file or folder within an NTFS volume or between volumes, the file or folder inherits its permissions from its new containing folder. When you *move* a file or folder, however, its permissions may persist. Files and folders that move *within* NTFS volumes retain their original permissions. A file or folder that moves *between* NTFS volumes, on the other hand, will inherit its permissions from its new containing folder.

Establishing Access Control Standards

This section can help you form access control standards. To create these standards, you must have a solid grasp of NTFS permissions. You should understand exactly how to calculate permissions to properly secure your files, folders, and shares. It's all right if you haven't memorized how the fourteen special permissions combine to form each standard permission. You can reference those details when you need them (refer to Tables 10.10 and 10.11). More often than not, you'll use standard permissions to secure your resources, anyhow. This section will help you establish your access control standards.

Permissions Usage Standards

You should set a few standards for using permissions to simplify the management of access control. Perhaps the most important standard to establish is related to the organization of files and folders on your NTFS volumes. You should group together files and folders that have similar permissions requirements. This allows you to leverage inheritance when assigning folder permissions at the highest level. Every subfolder and file contained below this high-level folder will inherit its permissions from a folder above. Create a standard set of folders on each of your volumes with specific roles. Some of these folders, for example, can secure your business applications, whereas other folders can be used to protect departmental data, such as documents, spreadsheets, and so on.

You should also establish standards for how permissions are assigned. Instead of assigning permissions to individual users, you should create groups of multiple users with similar access requirements. This allows you to assign and modify permissions for several users at once. After you've created several groups, managing access to their data and applications is much easier. Providing new employees with IT services is also simplified. You can configure new users with the permissions they require by simply adding them to the appropriate groups. Standardize on the groups you need to provide access to files, folders, and file shares.

DFS Permissions

You can use the *Distributed File System (DFS)* to organize distributed resources in a logical hierarchy. DFS organizes shared folders that can exist on several different computers into one easy-to-navigate Tree. DFS does not restrict or broaden the permissions assigned to shared folders that are contained in its hierarchy. Users can gain access to shared folders in DFS only if they have sufficient permissions.

Further, standardize how you will use shared folders. For example, it's poor form to assign permissions at the share level to restrict access to files and folders beneath them. This will always create more issues than it supposedly solves. Instead, it is best to give the Everyone identity `Full Control` permissions. Files and folders beneath the share should subsequently be secured by standard NTFS permissions. If you assign Everyone a restrictive permission such as `Read`, you've effectively limited your options. You will never be able to assign permissions to that share that are more liberal than `Read`. Remember, when share permissions combine with standard NTFS permissions, the most restrictive permission applies. In this case, the most restrictive permission is `Read`.

If you establish some simple permissions usage standards, managing access to your files and folders will be a whole lot easier. You'll also benefit if you establish a standard set of file system permissions. This is the sole focus of the next section.

File System Permissions Standards

To protect the data that resides on your servers and workstations, you should standardize their NTFS permissions. During installation, Windows 2000 configures its ACLs to offer a high level of compatibility for applications. The default permissions on a Windows 2000 system are not insecure; however, in high security environments there remains room for improvement. Understanding this, Microsoft provides *Security Configuration Editor (SCE)* and *Security Configuration Manager (SCM)*—together referred to as *Security Configuration and Analysis*. By themselves, SCE and SCM are extremely valuable. They help you automate the often painstaking task of analyzing, configuring, and auditing a system's security settings. Further, their functionality is not limited to just the file system. Instead, you can use SCE and SCM to analyze, configure, and audit just about every aspect of system security. This tool set can help you establish default security standards in the following areas:

- Account policies
- Local policies
- Event log
- Restricted groups
- System services
- Registry
- File system
- Active Directory objects

Classifying Existing Servers and Workstations

To establish a default set of standard NTFS permissions for your systems, you will work exclusively in the File System area. Your first step in establishing these standards, however, will be to classify your existing servers and workstations. This may be as simple as grouping your servers and workstations by their general roles. For example, you might create three system classes: domain controllers, member servers, and workstations. However, in most environments this definition will be too general. Servers and workstations you group together by class must share the same permissions standards. In larger companies, it may be more appropriate to classify systems by the services they provide. For instance, you might create several classes, including file servers, application servers, print servers, low security workstations, high security workstations, and so on.

Creating a Standard Set of NTFS Permissions

Once you've defined your system classes, you can use Security Configuration and Analysis to establish NTFS permissions standards for each. To do this, you must first identify the standard set of NTFS permissions for their files and folders. For example, you might standardize your file servers by defining permissions for a set of ten different data folders. After that, you can develop permissions standards for every other system class, including application servers, print servers, and so on. After establishing standard NTFS permissions for each class, you can use Security Configuration and Analysis to store them permanently in several templates.

Creating these templates gives you quite a few benefits. When you install a new file server or application server, for example, you can use your template to automatically configure it with your default permissions standard. This same template can also be used as a baseline for auditing permissions. As an example, you can audit the NTFS permissions on each of your servers to check for unauthorized changes. In addition, if in your audit you find that changes were made to security, you can use your template to reapply your standard.

Securing Operating System–Specific Files and Folders

Deciding which NTFS permissions are best to secure your company's applications and data will be straightforward. With a solid understanding of how permissions work, and an awareness of some key usage standards, you should be able to secure files, folders, and shares at will. However, securing operating system-specific files and folders, such as NTDETECT.COM, NTLDR, and %SystemRoot%, will prove challenging.

Fortunately, Microsoft includes some standard templates with Windows 2000 to help. In a normal installation of Windows 2000 Server and Professional, these templates are stored in the %SystemRoot%\Security\Templates directory. Each template that Microsoft predefines includes configuration settings for every aspect of system security. This includes parameters for Account Policies, Local Policies, File System, and so on. Additionally, there are several templates for you to choose from. Each template provides a unique level of security. A listing of Microsoft's standard templates follow:

- Typical Workstation Settings
- Compatible Workstation Settings
- Secure Workstation Settings
- High Security Workstation Settings
- Typical Server Settings
- Compatible Server Settings

- Typical Domain Controller Settings
- Secure Domain Controller Settings
- Highly Secure Domain Controller Settings

The level of security that each template provides is reflected in its name, as follows:

- **Typical template.** Contains Microsoft's default security settings, which are applied to a system at installation time. It provides the maximum compatibility for applications.

- **Compatible template.** Initializes the system's ACLs to favor application compatibility when making a tradeoff between functionality and system security. It is a little more aggressive than the Typical template.

- **Secure template.** Initializes the system's ACLs to favor security when making a tradeoff between functionality and system security. It's the opposite of the Compatible template.

- **Highly Secure template.** Implements the most stringent of security settings. No tradeoff is made to security to maximize application compatibility. As a result, applications on a system that is configured with Microsoft's Highly Secure template may not function.

Take caution when enforcing strict NTFS permissions standards. You need to be aware of every potential tradeoff to application compatibility. Before you decide on the appropriate level of security for your systems, rigorously test each of your applications and services. Make sure that they function on a system configured for high security as they always have. Taking this necessary precaution will help you uncover issues beforehand, limiting a potentially damaging effect to productivity. After your compatibility testing, you should walk away understanding which Microsoft template works best in your environment.

Finalizing Your NTFS Permissions Standards

After choosing a template that suits your requirements best, you can finalize your NTFS permissions standards. To complete this undertaking, combine the template you created to secure your applications and data with one of Microsoft's templates. Make sure that you copy only those settings from Microsoft's template that pertain to the file system. Exclude configuration parameters that define behavior for Account Policies, System Services, the Registry and so on. After combining the two templates, your work is through. The single template that you've created now stores your NTFS permissions standards.

Creating standards for NTFS permissions yields a good return on investment. Using the new Encrypting File System, discussed in the next section, has similar advantages.

Encrypting File System

You should also decide whether or not to use the *Encrypting File System (EFS)* when establishing your file system standards. EFS offers an added level of protection for files that are susceptible to theft, such as those on laptops. Unlike other cryptographic solutions, Microsoft's EFS works in the background, encrypting and decrypting files during everyday read and write operations. When you're using EFS, you see no difference between files that are encrypted and those that aren't. EFS works by encrypting and decrypting files using standard Public Key cryptography. The common element in all forms of Public Key cryptography is the use of a key pair. One of these keys is usually kept private, whereas the other can be made public. When you use EFS, you have several options for using key pairs. Table 10.13 lists all of your options, as well as the pros and cons for each.

Before you standardize on whether or not to use EFS, you should determine which of these options suits your requirements. Companies that plan to use certificate services for other needs already have an investment in a Public Key Infrastructure (PKI). Adding certificate-based services to this existing infrastructure, such as EFS, does not represent a significant cost. Before you finalize your standards for any certificate dependent services, read the later section "Leveraging Certificate Services." It focuses on the fine points of Microsoft's new Certificate Server.

Table 10.13   **Encrypting File System Key Pair Options**

Key Pair Option	Pro	Con
Using EFS with only a user key pair	A single user key pair is simple to configure.	If users lose their key pairs, their encrypted files will be lost.
Using EFS with a user key pair stored on a smart card	This offers an added level of protection for the users' files.	Like a standard key pair, a key pair stored on a smart card can be lost. If users lose their smart cards, all their encrypted files will be lost.
Using EFS with a user key pair and a recovery key pair	This gives you the ability to recover encrypted files.	Every sensitive cryptographic computation runs on the Windows 2000 operating system.
Using EFS with a user key pair and recovery key pair stored on a smart card	You have the ability to recover encrypted files, as well as the added protection inherent in smart card storage.	All sensitive cryptographic computations are completed by the smart card, and you can recover any encrypted files. If there is one downside, it will be cost of administration

Microsoft's EFS can enhance file system security by storing files using standard Public Key cryptography. Coupling EFS with a dependable file, folder, and share permissions standard is even more potent. Standardizing the user rights on your servers and workstations can be equally rewarding.

Understanding User Rights

In general, access to Windows 2000 objects such as files, folders, and shares is regulated by standard permissions. User rights, on the other hand, permit other activities, which are not always associated with a particular object. There are two classes of user rights: Privileges and Logon Rights. After detailing these particular user rights, you'll learn how to establish standards for each.

Privileges

Table 10.14 lists each privilege and the level of activity it permits.

Table 10.14 **Privileges**

Privilege	Description
Act as part of the operating system	Allows a process to act as a trusted part of the operating system. Certain protected subsystems of Windows 2000 have this right.
Add workstations to domain	Allows a user to add a new computer to that domain.
Back up files and directories	Allows a user to circumvent file and directory permissions for the purpose of backing up the system.
Bypass traverse checking	Allows a user navigating an NTFS directory Tree to pass through directories without permissions to access them.
Change the system time	Allows a user to set the time for the internal clock of the computer.
Create a pagefile	Allows a user to create and change the size of a pagefile.
Create a token object	Allows a process to create access tokens.
Create permanent shared objects	Allows a process to create special shared resources, such as system devices used within Windows 2000.
Debug programs	Allows a user to do low-level debugging of system code running on Windows 2000.
Enable computer and user accounts to be trusted for delegation	Allows a user to set the trusted for delegation setting on a user or computer object. A process that is running on a computer that is trusted for delegation or in the security context of a user that is trusted for delegation can access resources using the client's delegated credentials.

continues

Table 10.14   **Continued**

Privilege	Description
Force shutdown of a remote system	Allows a user to shut down a computer from a remote location on the network.
Generate security audits	Allows a process to make entries in security audit logs.
Increase quotas	Allows a user to increase the processor quota assigned to a process.
Increase scheduling priority	Allows a user to increase the execution priority given to a thread.
Load and unload device drivers	Allows a user to load and unload device drivers from memory.
Lock pages in memory	Allows a process to keep data in physical memory, preventing the system from paging the data to virtual memory on disk.
Manage auditing and security log	Allows a user to specify what types of resource access are to be audited.
Modify firmware environment values	Allows a user to modify system environment variables.
Profile a single process	Allows a user to use Windows 2000 performance-monitoring tools to monitor the performance of a process.
Profile system performance	Allows a user to monitor the performance of the entire system.
Remove computer from docking station	Allows a user to undock a laptop through the Windows 2000 interface.
Replace a process-level token	Allows a user to modify another process's access token.
Restore files and directories	Allows a user to restore backed-up files and directories.
Shut down the system	Allows a user to shut down the local computer.
Take ownership of files or other objects	Allows a user to take ownership of any securable object in the system including files, directories, printers, Registry keys, processes, and threads.

Automated Security Configuration and Analysis

Microsoft's Security Configuration Editor and Security Configuration Manager form *Security Configuration & Analysis*—a set of tools for analyzing and configuring system security. You can use Security Configuration & Analysis to create and enforce all of your security standards. This includes standards such as those for authentication, the file system, user rights, Active Directory, and certificate services. As you establish these standards, you can store them in one or more security templates. This will help you simplify applying and monitoring a comprehensive security configuration.

To automate the application of a default security configuration to a large number of computers, such as hundreds of Windows 2000 Professional workstations, you should import the settings in your security template to a Group Policy object. This will allow you to apply a default security configuration to a number of machines at once using Active Directory as the delivery mechanism. For more information on using Group Policy, see Chapter 11, "Simplifying Administration."

Logon Rights

Table 10.15 lists the level of activity each logon right permits.

Setting Standards for User Rights

Setting standards for user rights is by no means as elaborate as standardizing the file system, certificate services, or network authentication. There are a handful of guidelines for user rights, nonetheless, that you should always adhere to. To simplify everyday account administration, you should heed the following recommendations:

- Assign user rights to groups instead of to users. This lets you assign the necessary user rights to a small number of groups, instead of assigning them to individual users.

- Monitor and audit user rights on an ongoing basis. This is yet another reason to assign user rights at the group level. Keeping track of assignments that are set for groups is much easier than tracking user rights for each user.

You should not take the task of creating standards for user rights on your systems lightly. Misusing or improperly configuring user rights in a Microsoft network can lead to serious security problems. The method you choose to protect the objects in Active Directory is also important.

Table 10.15 **Logon Rights**

Logon Right	Description
Access this computer from network	Allows a user to connect to the computer over the network.
Deny access to this computer from network	Denies a user the right to connect to the computer over the network.
Deny log on locally	Denies a user the right to log on at the computer's keyboard.
Deny log on as a batch job	Denies a user the right to log on to the system using a batch queue facility.
Deny log on as a service	Denies a service the right to log on under a user account.
Log on as a batch job	Allows a user to log on using a batch queue facility.
Log on as a service	Allows a user to log on as a service, as a way of establishing a security context.
Log on locally	Allows a user to log on at the computer's keyboard

Securing Active Directory

To safeguard objects such as users, groups, and printers from unauthorized access, you must create robust security standards that protect Active Directory. This necessary element of defense is perhaps the most important one in your overall security plan. The objects in Active Directory are secured much like files in the file system. Just like a normal everyday file, an object in Active Directory has an Access Control List (ACL). The purpose of an object's ACL is to protect it from unwelcome access.

Many different types of objects are supported by Active Directory, including users, groups, printers, and so on. Each of these objects has a unique ACL, which lists all of its valid permissions. The ACL of a domain object, for example, lists valid permissions such as `Manage Replication Topology` and `Add/Remove Replica in Domain`. These permissions are valid for domain objects, but not for user objects. Some of the valid permissions for user objects include `Modify Group Membership` and `Change Password`.

This section first explains the security model of Active Directory. This explanation includes topics such as object and property permissions, standard and special permissions, delegating access control, and calculating permissions. This section then details the aspects of Active Directory you should consider to establish your security standard. Establishing a standard for the use and management of Active Directory should be high on your list of priorities.

Object and Property Permissions

When you set permissions for an object, such as the `Change Password` permission, an entry is made in the object's ACL. This entry defines who can access and/or manage the object, and is known as an Access Control Entry (ACE).

Every type of object in Active Directory supports what is known as *granular access control*. This fine-grained level of control lets you define permissions on a per object and per property basis. Any permission that is assigned at the object level will also apply to the object's properties. Assigning the object level `Write` permission, for example, also lets a user write to any of the object's properties. If this were a group object, the user could write to properties such as the group's display name, description, Web page address, and so forth. Property level permissions, on the other hand, allow you to assign access rights that are more restrictive. For example, you can assign a user the `Read` permission for one of an object's properties, such as the email address property of a user object. By supporting granular access control at a per object per property level, Active Directory helps you meet just about any requirement.

Standard and Special Permissions

As you've learned, the valid permissions for one object can be different from those of another object. For example, you can assign the `Modify Group Membership` permission for a user object but not for a domain object. Furthermore, each type of object has standard and special permissions. Standard permissions are those that are used most frequently. Like standard NTFS permissions for files and folders, an object's standard permissions are actually a set of special permissions. For example, the standard `Read` permission is a grouping of four special permissions: `Read All Properties`, `Read Permissions`, `List Contents`, and `List Object`. Although permissions can differ from one object to another, several standard permissions are common. These include the following:

- `Read`
- `Write`
- `Create All Child Objects`
- `Delete All Child Objects`
- `Full Control`

In general, you'll use an object's standard permissions to control its management and access. However, any time you need to, you can define a custom level of access to an object using its special permissions.

Delegating Access Control

Active Directory also supports delegating administrative tasks. In its simplest form, this means that an administrative task, such as the ability to reset the password of a user object, can be delegated to another user or group. Delegating administrative tasks at the object level, however, is inefficient and often unmanageable. Typically, administrative tasks should be delegated at the container level. The most common container to delegate administrative tasks in is an *organizational unit (OU)*. Delegating routine tasks at the OU level lets you form an administrative model that is both efficient and easy to manage.

You have several options when delegating tasks at the OU level. One of your options is to delegate complete administrative control of an OU. For example, you can give a user `Full Control` permissions for an OU, which allows the user to create, delete, and manage the OU and any of its subobjects. This is by far the most sweeping level of administrative control to delegate. A more conservative option is to delegate administrative control of objects only of a specific type. As an example, you can delegate `Full Control` permissions in a particular OU for the user objects it contains. You can also delegate more restrictive access, such as the ability to change passwords, group memberships, or account restrictions. Alternatively, you can delegate the ability to create and or delete objects in a specific OU. This level of administrative control can be delegated for all object types, or for just objects of a particular type, such as printer objects. When you set permissions at container level objects, such as OUs, you have several ways to apply them:

- **This object only.** This restricts the permissions you set to the object itself—subobjects are not affected.
- **This object and all subobjects.** This causes permissions to be valid for the OU itself, for all of the OU's subobjects, and for the subobjects of subobjects—until reaching the end of the OU hierarchy.

- **Apply to objects and/or containers within this container only.** This limits the scope of permissions to normal objects and container objects (such as other OUs) within the OU itself.

- **To subobjects only.** This confines the application of permissions to only the subobjects of an OU—the OU itself is not affected.

You have a great deal of flexibility when delegating administrative tasks. The rules for calculating permissions in Active Directory, however, are not flexible at all.

Calculating Permissions

Just like files and folders, objects in Active Directory are secured by ACLs. An object's ACL can contain several entries, or ACEs, that each define different permissions, possibly for the same user. As with effective NTFS permissions, effective object permissions are cumulative. All users' effective permissions can be calculated by combining each of their individual permissions. For example, if a user is assigned the `Create All Child Objects` permission directly, and assigned the `Delete All Child Objects` permission through a group membership, the user's effective permissions are both `Create All Child Objects` and `Delete All Child Objects`.

If you deny a permission for an object, it reverses every instance in which that permission is allowed. For example, if a user is given the `Reset Password` permission directly, but denied the `Reset Password` permission through membership in a group, that user's effective permissions are nothing. The `Allow Reset Password` permission is superseded by the `Deny Reset Password` permission.

When you move an object from one OU to another, its permissions may or may not persist. When you move an object that inherits its permissions from an OU above, it loses its original permissions. It will inherit a different set of permissions from its new parent OU. However, when you move an object that is configured with explicit permissions, its original permissions will persist.

Much like files inherit their permissions from folders, subobjects can inherit their permissions from objects above. By default, every object in Active Directory is configured to *allow inheritable permissions from parent to propagate to this object*. This permits permissions that are set on a parent object, such as an OU or domain, to be inherited by child objects. Despite this setting, any object can be configured to prevent inheritance. If you choose to block inheritance from objects above, the only valid permissions will be those that are assigned explicitly.

You can always find out whether an object's permissions are explicitly assigned or inherited from above. Inherited permissions have a dimmed check box next to them in the ACL Editor's user interface—explicit permissions do not.

Security Standards for Active Directory

You have a high degree of flexibility when securing Active Directory. There are many ways to delegate administrative tasks, apply object permissions, and control inheritance behavior. Because there are so many alternatives, establishing a unified security standard that safeguards Active Directory is essential.

You should establish standards for assigning permissions. For instance, you should avoid assigning permissions at the object or property level whenever possible. Tracking permissions assigned at this level will be particularly challenging. To avoid this unnecessary challenge, define inheritable permissions at the OU or domain level instead. This allows you to simplify the management and assignment of permissions by leveraging Active Directory's built-in inheritance model.

Where you choose to assign inheritable permissions will depend largely on your administrative needs. Defining inheritable permissions at the domain level, for example, is the best way to enforce global security standards. To enforce decentralized security standards, however, assign inheritable permissions at the OU level instead.

To simplify everyday administration, you should assign permissions to groups instead of to individual users. Permissions that are assigned at the user level are difficult to track and manage. Tracking and managing permissions assigned to groups is much easier.

Use the Deny permission for objects in Active Directory sparingly. The only valid reason to use the Deny permission is to exclude an individual from a group that has access to an object. For example, you can use the Deny permission to deny users access to an object in Active Directory without removing the users from a group.

Although you should take measures to secure every account in Windows 2000, pay special attention to accounts with sweeping control over Active Directory. There should be a select set of staff with this level of administrative control. You should periodically check each of these accounts for vulnerabilities, such as password complexity. Auditing the actions performed by administrators holding these accounts is also useful.

Finally, at regular intervals, track your permissions assignments. Keep tabs on the permissions that are assigned to container objects, such as OUs and domains. One change to the inheritable permissions at the OU or domain level can cause significant problems.

It's worthwhile to establish standards that protect Active Directory. Creating a plan to leverage Microsoft's new Public Key certificate services is also worth the effort.

Leveraging Certificate Services

Employing state-of-the-art certificate services for use with standard Public Key technologies once meant turning to a third party, such as VeriSign, Entrust, or Netscape. With the release of Windows 2000, however, you can issue and manage your own certificates using Microsoft's Certificate Services. Certificate Services forms the core of your Public Key security infrastructure, protecting data and communications through authentication, privacy, encryption, and non-repudiation. In the sections that follow, you'll learn about the certificate services available in Windows 2000. After that, you'll examine the details to create standards for certificate use and management.

Certificate Authorities

To make use of a Public Key certificate, you must first trust its issuer. The issuer of a Public Key certificate is known as a *certificate authority (CA)*. When you trust a CA, you imply that you have faith in its authentication policies. Simply put, you trust that the CA is able to discern between unauthorized and authorized certificate requests. You can create four types of CAs with Microsoft's Certificate Services:

- Enterprise Root Certificate Authorities
- Enterprise Subordinate Certificate Authorities
- Standalone Root Certificate Authorities
- Standalone Subordinate Certificate Authorities

Enterprise Root Certificate Authorities

An *Enterprise Root CA* is typically the top-level CA in your Public Key Infrastructure (PKI). It requires the services of Active Directory in order to verify a certificate requestor's identity. Because the Enterprise Root CA is usually the top-level CA, it signs its own CA certificate. It then publishes that certificate to the Trusted Root Certification Authorities store on every server and workstation in the Windows 2000 domain.

An Enterprise Root CA uses certificate types that are based on predefined certificate templates. These templates simplify the process of issuing and requesting certificates for common purposes, including code signing, smart card logon, IP Security, and so on. When using certificate templates, the Enterprise Root CA can verify user credentials during certificate enrollment. Each template is secured by an Access Control List (ACL). This ACL is evaluated to determine whether or not the user requesting the certificate is authorized to receive it.

Enterprise Subordinate Certificate Authorities

Although an Enterprise Root CA can be used to issue certificates directly to users, it generally is used to authenticate one or more Enterprise Subordinate CAs. An *Enterprise Subordinate CA* usually issues certificates directly to users. These certificates are then used to support services such as smart card logon, IP Security, encrypting file system, and so on. Because an Enterprise Subordinate CA also uses certificate templates, the process of issuing and requesting certificates is simplified. Unlike an Enterprise Root CA that self-signs its own certificate, an Enterprise Subordinate CA must obtain its certificate from another CA.

Standalone Root Certificate Authorities

Like an Enterprise Root CA, a *Standalone Root CA* is usually the top-level CA in your PKI, but it doesn't require Active Directory or membership in a Windows 2000 domain. For a Standalone Root CA to be trusted, an administrator must explicitly publish its certificate to a domain member's Trusted Root Certification Authorities store. Any subsequent certificate requests that are sent to the Standalone Root CA are automatically set to a pending status. To fulfill a certificate request, an administrator must intervene to verify the identity of the requesting entity. A Standalone Root CA has no way to verify a requester's credentials itself. Additionally, a Standalone Root CA doesn't support certificate templates.

Standalone Subordinate Certificate Authorities

Although a Standalone Root CA is capable of issuing certificates directly to users, more often than not, it is used to authenticate one or more Standalone Subordinate CAs. Similar to an Enterprise Subordinate CA, a *Standalone Subordinate CA* typically is configured to issue certificates directly to users. To issue these certificates, however, it doesn't need to be a member of a Windows 2000 domain, or have access to Active Directory. Like an Enterprise Subordinate CA, a Standalone Subordinate CA must also obtain its CA certificate from another CA. Certificate templates, which simplify the certificate enrollment process, are not supported.

Certificate Authority Hierarchies

The relationship between root and subordinate certificate authorities (CAs) forms an inverted Tree most often referred to as a *CA hierarchy*. In this natural hierarchy, the root CA is the most trusted entity—every subordinate CA must be certified by the root CA. In addition, by establishing a path of authority between every subordinate CA and the root CA, each certificate that is issued in the enterprise is verified. Subordinate CAs are usually deployed in locations that require the ability to set policies and issue certificates themselves.

   The benefit of establishing a CA hierarchy is a single point of enterprise level control and management. For example, if a subordinate CA is compromised, the root CA can revoke its certificate. Revoking the subordinate CAs certificate voids each certificate issued by the subordinate CA. Every other certificate in the enterprise is unaffected.

Standardizing Certificate Services

If you employ Microsoft Certificate Services, you should establish comprehensive standards for Public Key certificate use and management. You should first define which type of root CA suits your requirements best. Due to its tight integration with Active Directory, an Enterprise Root CA can help simplify certificate issuance and revocation. Its support for certificate templates is especially useful. However, if you administer a heterogeneous environment, a Standalone Root CA can provide comparable services without any dependence on Windows 2000 domains, or Active Directory.

To support one or more different locations that require the ability to set policies and issue certificates themselves, you need the services of subordinate CAs. If this is the case, you must select the type of CA to use in a subordinate role. This will usually be less difficult than selecting your root CA type. In fact, your subordinate CAs will almost always be of the same type as your root CA. The requirements that drive you to choose a particular type of CA at the root are usually just as valid in your other locations.

After you decide whether to use Enterprise or Standalone CAs, you should define each CA's function and role. This should include the primary role of the CA, the type of certificates that the CA can issue, and the individuals who can receive each certificate type. In small or mid-size organizations, a root-level CA may serve every function and role in the enterprise. Large organizations that require a number of certificate functions, conversely, will usually have defined functions and roles for each CA. One CA might be responsible for smart card logon, while another CA might handle IP Security, Code Signing, or another common service. The Public Key certificate services your organization requires will help you define your needs.

You should then establish standards for certificate revocation and renewal. Your certificate revocation standard must define procedures to revoke certificates that are inappropriately used, or that are not needed anymore. This includes establishing your *certificate revocation list (CRL)* and CRL publishing standards. Your standards for certificate renewal, on the other hand, should cover whether or not to renew certificates at all, and if you will renew them, which certificate types are suitable for renewal. Finally, you should define when it is appropriate to renew each type of certificate.

If you take the time to establish standards and operating policies for Microsoft's Certificate Services, you can safely enjoy the benefits of Public Key technology.

Windows 2000 Default Security Configurations

This last section can be used as a reference to the default security settings of Windows 2000 Professional and Windows 2000 Server. Some of these default settings are appropriate in environments where security is not of a great concern. As indicated in each prior section, you should change any default settings to mirror your security requirements.

Windows 2000 Professional

Each section that follows details the configuration that is automatically set when the Windows 2000 Professional operating system initializes the following:

- File and folder permissions
- User rights
- Password policy

- Account lockout policy
- User account properties
- Security options
- Users and groups

File and Folder Permissions

Table 10.16 lists the permissions assigned to files and folders on Windows 2000 Professional systems at installation time. These settings favor application compatibility over system security.

Table 10.16 **Windows 2000 Professional File and Folder Permissions (Assumes `%SystemDrive%` is `C:\`)**[2]

Files & Folders	Permissions
`C:\`	Everyone (ALL):(ALL)
`C:\BOOT.INI`	Everyone (ALL)
`C:\NTDETECT.COM`	Power Users (RX)
	Administrators (ALL)
	SYSTEM (ALL)
`C:\NTLDR`	Power Users (RX)
	Administrators (ALL)
	SYSTEM (ALL)
`C:\Documents and Settings\`	SYSTEM (ALL):(ALL)
	Administrators (ALL):(ALL)
	Authenticated Users (RX):(RX)
`C:\Program Files\`	Authenticated Users (RX):(RX)
	Power Users (RWXD):(RWXD)
	Administrators (ALL):(ALL)
	SYSTEM (ALL):(ALL)
	CREATOR OWNER (ALL)
`C:\WINNT\`	Authenticated Users (RX):(RX)
	Power Users (RWXD):(RWXD)
	Administrators (ALL):(ALL)
	SYSTEM (ALL):(ALL)
	CREATOR OWNER (ALL)

continues

2. Note that the permissions shown in Table 10.16 (and later in Table 10.21) do not list inheritable permissions, such as permissions set for *This Folder and Subfolders* or *This Folder Only.*

Table 10.16 **Continued**

Files & Folders	Permissions
C:\WINNT\Config\	Authenticated Users (RX):(RX) Power Users (RWXD):(RWXD) Administrators (ALL):(ALL) SYSTEM (ALL):(ALL) CREATOR OWNER (ALL)
C:\WINNT\CSC\	Administrators (ALL)
C:\WINNT\Driver Cache\	Authenticated Users (RX):(RX) Power Users (RWXD):(RWXD) Administrators (ALL):(ALL) SYSTEM (ALL):(ALL) CREATOR OWNER (ALL)
C:\WINNT\inf\	Authenticated Users (RX):(RX) Power Users (RWXD):(RWXD) Administrators (ALL):(ALL) SYSTEM (ALL):(ALL) CREATOR OWNER (ALL)
C:\WINNT\Installer\	SYSTEM (ALL):(ALL) Everyone (RX):(RX)
C:\WINNT\repair\	Authenticated Users (RX) Power Users (RWXD):(RWXD) Administrators (ALL):(ALL) SYSTEM (ALL):(ALL) CREATOR OWNER (ALL)
C:\WINNT\security\	Authenticated Users (RX):(RX) Administrators (ALL):(ALL) SYSTEM (ALL):(ALL) CREATOR OWNER (ALL)
C:\WINNT\system\	Authenticated Users (RX):(RX) Power Users (RWXD):(RWXD) Administrators (ALL):(ALL) SYSTEM (ALL):(ALL) CREATOR OWNER (ALL)
C:\WINNT\system32\	Authenticated Users (RX):(RX) Power Users (RWXD):(RWXD) Administrators (ALL):(ALL) SYSTEM (ALL):(ALL) CREATOR OWNER (ALL)

Files & Folders	Permissions
C:\WINNT\system32\config\	Authenticated Users (RX) Administrators (ALL):(ALL) SYSTEM (ALL):(ALL) CREATOR OWNER (ALL)
C:\WINNT\system32\drivers\	Authenticated Users (RX):(RX) Administrators (ALL):(ALL) SYSTEM (ALL):(ALL) CREATOR OWNER (ALL)
C:\WINNT\system32\ GroupPolicy\	SYSTEM (ALL):(ALL) Administrators (ALL):(ALL) Authenticated Users (RX):(RX)
C:\WINNT\system32\Repl\	Authenticated Users (RX):(RX) Power Users (RWXD):(RWXD) Administrators (ALL):(ALL) SYSTEM (ALL):(ALL) CREATOR OWNER (ALL)
C:\WINNT\system32\spool\	Authenticated Users (RX):(RX) Power Users (RWXD):(RWXD) Administrators (ALL):(ALL) SYSTEM (ALL):(ALL) CREATOR OWNER (ALL)
C:\WINNT\system32\wbem\	Authenticated Users (RX):(RX) Power Users (RWXD) Administrators (ALL):(ALL) SYSTEM (ALL):(ALL) CREATOR OWNER (ALL)
C:\WINNT\Tasks\	Everyone (RWX):(RWX) Administrators (ALL):(ALL)

User Rights

The default user rights for a Windows 2000 Professional system are listed in Tables 10.17 and 10.18. You should define and configure these rights to suit your environment as part of your security standard.

Table 10.17 **Windows 2000 Professional Default Privileges**

Privilege	Assigned to...
Act as part of the operating system	No one
Add workstations to domain	No one
Back up files and directories	Backup Operators and Administrators
Bypass traverse checking	Authenticated Users
Change the system time	Power Users and Administrators
Create a pagefile	Administrators
Create a token object	No one
Create permanent shared objects	No one
Debug programs	Administrators
Enable computer and user accounts to	No one be trusted for delegation
Force shutdown of a remote system	Administrators
Generate security audits	No one
Increase quotas	Administrators
Increase scheduling priority	Administrators
Load and unload device drivers	Administrators
Lock pages in memory	No one
Manage auditing and security log	Administrators
Modify firmware environment values	Administrators
Profile a single process	Power Users and Administrators
Profile system performance	Administrators
Remove computer from docking station	Administrators
Replace a process-level token	No one
Restore files and directories	Backup Operators and Administrators
Shut down the system	Users, Power Users, Backup Operators, Authenticated Users, and Administrators
Take ownership of files or other	Administrators

Table 10.18   **Windows 2000 Professional Default Logon Rights**

Logon Right	Assigned to...
Access this computer from network	Power Users, Authenticated Users, and Administrators
Deny access to this computer	No one from network
Deny log on locally	No one
Deny log on as a batch job	No one
Deny log on as a service	No one
Log on as a batch job	No one
Log on as a service	No one
Log on locally	Users, Power Users, Authenticated Users, Backup Operators, and Administrators

Password Policy

Table 10.19 lists the default password policy for a newly installed Windows 2000 Professional system. These settings are especially important for laptop users because they will often authenticate locally while on the road.

Account Lockout Policy

The account lockout policy for a Windows 2000 Professional system that is set at install time is shown in the following table. Like password policy, account lockout policy is also particularly important for mobile users[3].

Policy	Default Setting
Account lockout count	0 Invalid logon attempts
Lockout account for	Not Defined
Reset account after	Not Defined

Security Options

Table 10.20 lists the default security options for Windows 2000 Professional. These settings define a number of operating system level security behaviors.

3. You should not ignore the importance of password and account lockout policy simply because you don't support mobile users. Anyone can walk up to an unattended Windows 2000 Professional system and attempt to log on locally.

Table 10.19 **Windows 2000 Professional Default Password Policy**

Policy	Default Setting
Enforce password uniqueness by remembering last	1 Passwords
Maximum password age	42 Days
Minimum password age	0 Days
Minimum password length	0 Characters
Passwords must meet complexity requirements of installed password filter	Disabled
User must logon to change password	Disabled

Table 10.20 **Windows 2000 Professional Default Security Options**

Option	Setting
Allow Server Operators to schedule tasks	Not Defined
Allow system to shutdown without having to log on	Enabled
Audit access to internal system objects	Disabled
AutoDisconnect: Allow sessions to be disconected when they are idle	Enabled
AutoDisconnect: Amount of idle time required before disconnecting session	15
Change Administrator account name to	Not Defined
Change Guest account name to	Not Defined
Clear virtual memory pagefile when system shuts down	Disabled
Digitally sign client-side communications always	Disabled
Digitally sign client-side communication when possible	Enabled
Digitally sign server-side communication always	Disabled
Disable Ctrl+Alt+Del requirement for logon	Not Defined
Disallow enumeration of account names and shares by anonymous users	Disabled
Do not display last username in logon screen	Disabled
Encrypt data in client side cache	Disabled
Message text for users attempting to log on	Not Defined
Message title for users attempting to log on	Not Defined
Number of previous logons to cache in case domain controller is not available	10

Option	Setting
Prevent users from installing print drivers	Disabled
Prompt user to change passwords this many days in advance	14
Restrict CD-ROM access to locally logged on user only	Disabled
Restrict Floppy access to locally logged on user only	Disabled
Restrict management of shared resources such as COM1	Disabled
Secure Channel: Digitally encrypt or sign secure channel data always	Disabled
Secure Channel: Digitally encrypt secure channel data always when possible	Enabled
Secure Channel: Digitally sign secure channel when possible	Enabled
Send downlevel LanMan compatible password	Always
Send unencrypted password in order to connect to 3rd Party SMB servers	Disabled
Shutdown system immediately ifunable to log security audits	Disabled

Users and Groups

Several accounts are created during the installation of Windows 2000 Professional. These accounts are known as *built-in* accounts.

The following are built-in user accounts on Windows 2000 Professional:

User Account	Description
Administrator	Built-in account for administering the computer/domain
Guest	Built-in account for guest access to the computer/domain

The following are built-in local groups on Windows 2000 Professional:

Local Group	Description
Administrators	Members can fully administer the computer/domain
Backup Operators	Members can bypass file security to back up files
Guests	Users granted guest access to the computer/domain
Power Users	Members can share directories and printers
Replicator	Supports file replication in a domain
Users	Ordinary users

Windows 2000 Server

Each section that follows details the security configuration of a newly installed Windows 2000 Server built as a domain controller:

- File and folder permissions
- User rights
- Password policy
- Account lockout policy
- User account properties
- Security options
- Users and groups

File and Folder Permissions

The permissions assigned to files and folders on Windows 2000 Server at installation time are listed in Table 10.21. Before moving a Windows 2000 server into production, you should always consider the level of file and folder security it requires.

Table 10.21 **Windows 2000 Server File and Folder Permissions (Assumes `%SystemDrive%` is `C:\`)**[2]

Files and Folders	Permissions
`C:\`	Everyone (ALL):(ALL)
`C:\BOOT.INI`	Server Operators (RX)
	Administrators (ALL)
	SYSTEM (ALL)
`C:\NTDETECT.COM`	Server Operators (RX)
	Administrators (ALL)
	SYSTEM (ALL)
`C:\NTLDR`	Server Operators (RX)
	Administrators (ALL)
	SYSTEM (ALL)
`C:\Documents and Settings\`	SYSTEM (ALL):(ALL)
	Domain\Administrators (ALL):(ALL)
	Authenticated Users (RX):(RX)
`C:\Program Files\`	Authenticated Users (RWXD):(RX)
	Domain\Administrators (ALL):(ALL)
	SYSTEM (ALL):(ALL)
	Domain\Server Operators (RWXD):(RWXD)
	CREATOR OWNER (ALL)

2. Note that the permissions shown in Table 10.16 (and later in Table 10.21) do not list inheritable permissions, such as permissions set for *This Folder and Subfolders* or *This Folder Only*.

Files and Folders	Permissions
C:\WINNT\	Authenticated Users (RWXD):(RX) Domain\Administrators (ALL):(ALL) SYSTEM (ALL):(ALL) CREATOR OWNER (ALL) Domain\Server Operators (RWXD):(RWXD)
C:\WINNT\Config\	Authenticated Users (RWXD):(RX) Domain\Administrators (ALL):(ALL) SYSTEM (ALL):(ALL) CREATOR OWNER (ALL) Domain\Server Operators (RWXD):(RWXD)
C:\WINNT\Driver Cache\	Authenticated Users (RWXD):(RX) Domain\Administrators (ALL):(ALL) SYSTEM (ALL):(ALL) CREATOR OWNER (ALL) Domain\Server Operators (RWXD):(RWXD)
C:\WINNT\inf\	Authenticated Users (RWXD):(RX) Domain\Administrators (ALL):(ALL) SYSTEM (ALL):(ALL) CREATOR OWNER (ALL) Domain\Server Operators (RWXD):(RWXD)
C:\WINNT\Installer\	SYSTEM (ALL):(ALL) Everyone (RX):(RX)
C:\WINNT\NTDS\	SYSTEM (ALL):(ALL) Domain\Administrators (ALL):(ALL)
C:\WINNT\ntfrs\	Authenticated Users (RWXD):(RX) Domain\Administrators (ALL):(ALL) SYSTEM (ALL):(ALL) CREATOR OWNER (ALL) Domain\Server Operators (RWXD):(RWXD)
C:\WINNT\repair\	Authenticated Users (RX) Domain\Administrators (ALL):(ALL) SYSTEM (ALL):(ALL) CREATOR OWNER (ALL) Domain\Server Operators (RWXD):(RWXD)
C:\WINNT\security\	Authenticated Users (RX):(RX) Domain\Administrators (ALL):(ALL) SYSTEM (ALL):(ALL)

continues

Table 10.21 **Continued**

Files and Folders	Permissions
C:\WINNT\system\	Authenticated Users (RWXD):(RX) Domain\Administrators (ALL):(ALL) SYSTEM (ALL):(ALL) CREATOR OWNER (ALL) Domain\Server Operators (RWXD):(RWXD)
C:\WINNT\system32\	Authenticated Users (RWXD):(RX) Domain\Administrators (ALL):(ALL) SYSTEM (ALL):(ALL) CREATOR OWNER (ALL) Domain\Server Operators (RWXD):(RWXD)
C:\WINNT\system32\config\	Authenticated Users (RX) Domain\Administrators (ALL):(ALL) SYSTEM (ALL):(ALL)
C:\WINNT\system32\dhcp\	Authenticated Users (RX):(RX) Domain\Administrators (ALL):(ALL) SYSTEM (ALL):(ALL)
C:\WINNT\system32\dns\	Authenticated Users (RWXD):(RX) Domain\Administrators (ALL):(ALL) SYSTEM (ALL):(ALL) CREATOR OWNER (ALL) Domain\Server Operators (RWXD):(RWXD)
C:\WINNT\system32\drivers\	Authenticated Users (RX):(RX) Domain\Administrators (ALL):(ALL) SYSTEM (ALL):(ALL) Domain\Server Operators (RWXD):(RWXD)
C:\WINNT\system32\GroupPolicy\	Authenticated Users (RX):(RX) Domain\Administrators (ALL):(ALL) SYSTEM (ALL):(ALL)
C:\WINNT\system32\Microsoft\	Authenticated Users (RWXD):(RX) Domain\Administrators (ALL):(ALL) SYSTEM (ALL):(ALL) CREATOR OWNER (ALL) Domain\Server Operators (RWXD):(RWXD)
C:\WINNT\system32\Microsoft\Crypto\	Authenticated Users (RWXD):(RX) Domain\Administrators (ALL):(ALL) SYSTEM (ALL):(ALL) CREATOR OWNER (ALL) Domain\Server Operators (RWXD):(RWXD)

Files and Folders	Permissions
C:\WINNT\system32\Microsoft\ Protect\	Authenticated Users (RWXD):(RX) Domain\Administrators (ALL):(ALL) SYSTEM (ALL):(ALL) CREATOR OWNER (ALL) Domain\Server Operators (RWXD):(RWXD)
C:\WINNT\system32\ras\	Authenticated Users (RWXD):(RX) Domain\Administrators (ALL):(ALL) SYSTEM (ALL):(ALL) CREATOR OWNER (ALL) Domain\Server Operators (RWXD):(RWXD)
C:\WINNT\system32\Repl\	Authenticated Users (RX):(RX) Domain\Administrators (ALL):(ALL) SYSTEM (ALL):(ALL) Domain\Server Operators (RWXD):(RWXD)
C:\WINNT\system32\spool\	Authenticated Users (RX):(RX) Domain\Administrators (ALL):(ALL) SYSTEM (ALL):(ALL) CREATOR OWNER (ALL) Domain\Server Operators (RWXD):(RWXD) Domain\Print Operators (ALL):(ALL)
C:\WINNT\system32\wbem\	Authenticated Users (RWXD):(RX) Domain\Administrators (ALL):(ALL) SYSTEM (ALL):(ALL) CREATOR OWNER (ALL) Domain\Server Operators (RWXD):(RWXD)
C:\WINNT\system32\wins\	Authenticated Users (RWXD):(RX) Domain\Administrators (ALL):(ALL) SYSTEM (ALL):(ALL) CREATOR OWNER (ALL) Domain\Server Operators (RWXD):(RWXD)
	C:\WINNT\SYSVOL\ Authenticated Users (RX):(RX) Domain\Administrators (ALL):(ALL) SYSTEM (ALL):(ALL) CREATOR OWNER (ALL)
C:\WINNT\Tasks\	Everyone (RWX):(RWX)
C:\WINNT\Tasks\	Domain\Administrators (ALL):(ALL)
C:\WINNT\Tasks\	SYSTEM (ALL):(ALL)

User Rights

Tables 10.22 and 10.23 list the default user rights for Windows 2000 Server. These rights should be monitored regularly.

Table 10.22 **Windows 2000 Server Default Privileges**

Privilege	Assigned to
Act as part of the operating system	No one
Add workstations to domain	No one
Back up files and directories	Server Operators, Backup Operators, and Administrators
Bypass traverse checking	Authenticated Users
Change the system time	Server Operators and Administrators
Create a pagefile	Administrators
Create a token object	No one
Create permanent shared objects	No one
Debug programs	Administrators
Enable computer and user accounts to be trusted for delegation	Domain Admins
Force shutdown of a remote system	Server Operators and Administrators
Generate security audits	No one
Increase quotas	Administrators
Increase scheduling priority	Administrators
Load and unload device drivers	Administrators
Lock pages in memory	No one
Manage auditing and security log	Administrators
Modify firmware environment values	Administrators
Profile a single process	Administrators
Profile system performance	Administrators
Remove computer from docking station	No one
Replace a process-level token	No one
Restore files and directories	Server Operators, Backup Operators, and Administrators
Shut down the system	Print Operators, Server Operators, Account Operators, Backup Operators, and Administrators
Take ownership of files or other objects	Administrators

Table 10.23   **Windows 2000 Server Default Logon Rights**

Logon Right	Assigned to...
Access this computer from network	Authenticated Users and Administrators
Deny access to this computer from network	No one
Deny log on locally	No one
Deny log on as a batch job	No one
Deny log on as a service	No one
Log on as a batch job	No one
Log on as a service	No one
Log on locally	Account Operators, Server Operators, Print Operators, Backup Operators, and Administrators

Password Policy

The default password policy shown in Table 10.24 is for a Windows 2000 server installed as a domain controller. This password policy is for all domain controllers in a given domain.

Table 10.24   **Windows 2000 Server Default Password Policy**

Policy	Default Setting
Enforce password uniqueness by remembering last	1 Passwords
Maximum password age	42 Days
Minimum password age	0 Days
Minimum password length	0 Characters
Passwords must meet complexity requirements of installed password filter	Disabled
User must log on to change password	Disabled

Account Lockout Policy

The default account lockout policy for a Windows 2000 server installed as a domain controller is listed in Table 10.25. Like password policy, account lockout policy on a domain controller is valid for all domain conrollers in a particular domain.

Table 10.25   **Windows 2000 Server Default Account Lockout Policy**

Policy	Default Setting
Account lockout count	0 Invalid logon attempts
Lockout account for	Not Defined
Reset account after	Not Defined

User Account Properties

When a new user is created in a Windows 2000 domain, that user is configured with the settings shown in Table 10.26. It is often worthwhile to establish settings for different classes of users (such as normal, temporary, and secure users).

Table 10.26   **Windows 2000 Server Default User Account Properties**

Property	Default Setting
Logon hours	Not Defined
Logon To...	Not Defined
User must logon using a smart card	Disabled
Account expires	Never

Security Options

The default security options for a Windows 2000 server are listed in Table 10.27. These settings control several important aspects of operating system level security.

Table 10.27   **Windows 2000 Server Default Security Options**

Option	Setting
Allow Server Operators to schedule tasks	Not Defined
Allow system to shutdown without having to log on	Enabled
Audit access to internal system objects	Disabled
AutoDisconnect: Allow sessions to be disconected when they are idle	Enabled
AutoDisconnect: Amount of idle time required before disconnecting session	15
Change Administrator account name to	Not Defined
Change Guest account name to	Not Defined
Clear virtual memory pagefile when system shuts down	Disabled
Digitally sign client-side communications always	Disabled

Option	Setting
Digitally sign client-side communication when possible	Enabled
Digitally sign server-side communication always	Disabled
Disable Ctrl+Alt+Del requirement for logon	Not Defined
Disallow enumeration of account names and shares by anonymous users	Disabled
Do not display last username in logon screen	Disabled
Encrypt data in client side cache	Disabled
Message text for users attempting to log on	Not Defined
Message title for users attempting to log on	Not Defined
Number of previous logons to cache in case domain controller is not available	10
Prevent users from installing print drivers	Disabled
Prompt user to change passwords this many days in advance	14
Restrict CD-ROM access to locally logged on user only	Disabled
Restrict Floppy access to locally logged on user only	Disabled
Restrict management of shared resources such as COM1	Disabled
Secure Channel: Digitally encrypt or sign secure channel data always	Disabled
Secure Channel: Digitally encrypt secure channel data always when possible	Enabled
Secure Channel: Digitally sign secure channel when possible	Enabled
Send downlevel LanMan compatible password	Always
Send unencrypted password in order to connect to 3rd Party SMB servers	Disabled
Shutdown system immediately if unable to log security audits	Disabled

Users and Groups

When a Windows 2000 server is installed as a domain controller, the user and group accounts are automatically created. The built-in user accounts on Windows 2000 Server are as follows:

User Account	Description
Administrator	Built-in account for administering the computer/domain
Guest	Built-in account for guest access to the computer/domain

The built-in domain local groups on Windows 2000 Server are as follows:

Domain Local Group	Description
Account Operators	Members can administer domain user and group accounts
Administrators	Members can fully administer the computer/domain
Backup Operators	Members can bypass file security to back up files
Guests	Users granted guest access to the computer/domain
Print Operators	Members can administer domain printers
Replicator	Supports file replication in a domain
Server Operators	Members can administer domain servers
Users	Ordinary users

Finally, the following are the built-in global groups on Windows 2000 Server:

Global Group	Description
Domain Admins	Designated administrators of the domain
Domain Guests	All domain guests
Domain Users	All domain users
Enterprise Admins	Designated administrators of the enterprise

Windows 2000 Datacenter Server

Windows 2000 Datacenter Server will support sixteen-way SMP, up to 64GB of physical RAM, clustering, and load balancing. Because Windows 2000 Datacenter Server is not yet shipping, its default security configuration is not listed here.

Additional Security Resources

To manage security effectively, you need to have the latest news and information as well as an understanding of the industry's tools and utilities. There are a number of resources you can tap into to stay current. Several Web sites you should take a look include the following:

Web Site	Address
Microsoft Security Advisor	www.microsoft.com/security
NTSecurity.net	www.ntsecurity.net
NTBugTraq	www.ntbugtraq.com
LOpht Heavy Industries	www.l0pht.com

Some list servers you should check out include the following:

List Server Name	Subscription Information
Microsoft Security	Subscribe to the service at Notification Service www.microsoft.com/security
NT Security Digest	Subscribe by sending an email message to NTSD-sample@ntsecurity.net
NTBugTraq Mailing List	Subscribe by sending an email to listserv.ntbugtraq.com with subscribe ntbugtraq in the message body

You should also look into the following tools and utilities:

Tool/Utility	Web Site	Description
SuperCACLS by Trusted Systems Services, Inc.	www.trustedsystems.com	Lets you view and manage NT/2000 ACLs on files, directories, and Registry keys
NTSpectre Scope by Palo Verde Software	www.ntspectre.com	Takes a snapshot of the systems configuration to produce a security report
DumpACL by Somarsoft	www.somarsoft.com	Dumps the Access Control List on an NT/2000 system to a file
The Scanner line of products by Internet Security Systems	www.iss.net	Automated security assessment

11

Simplifying Administration

MANY OF THE NEW FEATURES and technologies in Windows 2000 simplify administration. Microsoft has made advances in quite a few areas, from change and configuration management at the desktop to improved scripting capabilities and more robust policy-based administration. You can use these new features and technologies to make day-to-day administration of Microsoft networks a little easier. This chapter introduces several of the new resources you can use to simplify everyday administration:

- Group Policy
- IntelliMirror
- The Distributed File System
- Automatic System Recovery
- Windows Scripting Host
- Auditing
- Resource Kit utilities
- Operating system features

Group Policy

Perhaps the best way to simplify administration in Windows 2000 is with Group Policy. A *Group Policy* is an object you can use to manage the configuration of your users' desktops. This allows you to create and manage desktop configurations to standardize your users' operating environment. For example, using Group Policy, you can set a local disk quota limit, restrict which items can be added to the desktop, or redirect a user's My Documents folder to the network. Table 11.1 lists all the areas you can manage using Group Policy.

Table 11.1   **Core Areas of Group Policy**

Area	Description
Control Panel	Allows you to regulate which items in the Control Panel a user can display and access
Desktop	Allows you to control what is shown on the desktop and what can be added or deleted on the desktop
Folder Redirection	Allows you to redirect the folders containing a user's profile to a location on the network
Network	Allows you to define parameters for offline files, hidden shares, DNS, and SNMP
Printers	Allows you to control printer settings such as scheduler priority and logging behavior
Scripts	Allows you to define logon and logoff scripts, as well as startup and shutdown scripts
Security Settings	Allows you to control security settings such as account policies, local policies, public key policies, and event log policies[1]
Software Installation	Allows you to assign, publish, repair, and remove applications
Start Menu & Taskbar	Allows you to control settings such as those for removing Windows Update from the Start menu or disabling the context menu on the taskbar
System	Allows you to regulate settings such as disk quotas and whether logon/logoff or startup/shutdown scripts are hidden when they run
Windows Components	Allows you to define behavior for offline file management and the common dialog box and to customize from where users load their Start menu, Programs folder, desktop, and Startup folder

1. The security settings you can define in Group Policy objects are quite comprehensive. You can control security settings for: account policies, local policies, the event log, restricted groups, system services, the Registry, the file system, power management, the remote installation service, IP security, public key security, and objects in Active Directory.

By using Group Policy objects to enforce and maintain these configuration settings, you can simplify the management of your computers and lower their total cost of ownership (TCO).

Overview of Group Policy

Policy-based administration in Windows 2000 is extremely powerful. As you can see in Table 11.1, you can use Group Policy to establish and maintain a wide range of configuration settings. To define these settings, you must create one or more Group Policy objects. Settings are stored inside Group Policy objects in two main areas: the user configuration area and the computer configuration area. *User configuration settings* include policies such as those that define desktop, display, and Start menu behavior; *computer configuration settings* consist of policies that control other areas, such as settings for the Registry, the file system, and the event log. User configuration settings are applied at logon time, whereas computer configuration settings are applied when the operating system initializes.

You can use a Group Policy object to apply any of these settings to users and computers in a site, domain, or organizational unit. The settings applied to users and computers that come from Group Policy objects are inherited and cumulative. Group Policy is processed hierarchically, starting with policy in the highest-level container in Active Directory. Users and computers inherit Group Policy from the site and domain they belong to, as well as from the organizational unit in which they reside. When two inherited policy settings conflict, the settings defined in the policy object closest to a user or computer always apply. However, the default behavior for how Group Policy is inherited can be changed in several ways:

- By blocking Group Policy from higher level containers
- By overriding Group Policy in lower level containers
- By setting permissions on Group Policy objects in any container

For instance, an organizational unit level administrator can block all Group Policy that is defined at the site and domain levels. Administrators that control higher level containers, such as sites and domains, can similarly override Group Policy that is defined in organizational units. The default behavior for Group Policy processing can also be controlled with permissions. Users and computers cannot apply a Group Policy object without the Read permission for that object. When the override Group Policy setting and the block Group Policy setting combine, the override Group Policy setting always applies. This allows administrators that control higher level containers in Active Directory to enforce Group Policies in lower level containers.

To create a Group Policy object, you must use the Group Policy Editor. The Group Policy Editor is a snap-in to MMC that can be launched from the property page of a site, domain, or organizational unit. When you create a Group Policy object in Active Directory, several folders are added to the SYSVOL share of the domain controller you are connected to. The top-most folder in this structure is named for the *GUID*, or globally unique identifier, of the Group Policy object. The remaining folders in this structure store the policy object's user and computer settings. This information is stored in the SYSVOL share so that it can be replicated to all domain controllers in the same domain.

Enforcing Group Policy

You can enforce your own user and computer settings to make your environment more manageable. An environment that is more manageable is always simpler to administer. When you create these configuration settings, determine whether different groups of users and computers will require different policies. In some companies, a single Group Policy object will suffice. This will usually be the case in smaller organizations with very few users. In large and mid-size companies, a number of Group Policy objects will more often be required. These organizations will be more likely to have different groups that require different user and computer settings. To support groups that require different Group Policy settings, you can arrange Group Policy objects using either of the following approaches:

- Place a single Group Policy object in a site, domain, or organizational unit. Then put users and computers that require different policy settings in *different* sites, domains, or organizational units.

- Place multiple Group Policy objects in the *same* site, domain, or organizational unit. Then use permissions to control which users and computers can apply a particular Group Policy object.

The latter approach is the recommended method for supporting different groups with different Group Policy requirements. By simply controlling which users and computers have the Read permission for a Group Policy object, you can define different policy settings for different groups that exist in the same site, domain, or organizational unit. This way, you aren't forced to create a structure in Active Directory to support your company's Group Policy requirements.

Several key chapters in this book have stressed the importance of standardization. For example, in Chapter 3, you learned that you must create, document, and maintain standards to lower the Total Cost of Ownership and to simplify your environment. The essential practice of creating, documenting, and maintaining high-quality standards for your systems is the key to manageability. To maintain these valuable standards—which often require quite a bit of planning and hard work to create—you should use Group Policy. If you have a standard for Kerberos, for example, that defines a maximum user ticket lifetime of three hours, you should use Group Policy to enforce and maintain it. The same is true for the other standards you create.[2]

Group Policy Management

When you create your company's Group Policy objects, you should also create a plan to manage them. The way in which each company chooses to administer their Group Policy objects will be somewhat unique. The way you manage your Group Policy objects will most likely mirror how you manage other objects in your domains. For instance, if you currently decentralize the administration of users, groups, and other resources in organizational units, you most likely will manage Group Policy using a similar model. This section offers several different examples of methods for managing Group Policy:

- The centralized model
- The decentralized model
- The task-based model

The Centralized Model

The goal of the centralized management model is to consolidate administrative control of policy. In this model, a single team of administrators is responsible for managing all of a company's Group Policy objects, regardless of their location. This model is the logical choice for companies that plan to centralize the administration of other objects and resources in Active Directory. It can also be useful for companies that need to decentralize the administration of certain resources while centralizing the administration of Group Policy. Figure 11.1 shows this model in more detail.

Notice that the company's second-level administrators do not have the ability to manage any Group Policy objects in organizational units. This is accomplished by modifying permissions on the company's Group Policy objects as described here:

- The top-level administrators are given Full Control permissions to all Group Policy objects, regardless of their location.
- Each second-level administrator is given only the Read permission to each Group Policy object.

---

2. You can use Group Policy to enforce and maintain just about every security standard defined in Chapter 10.

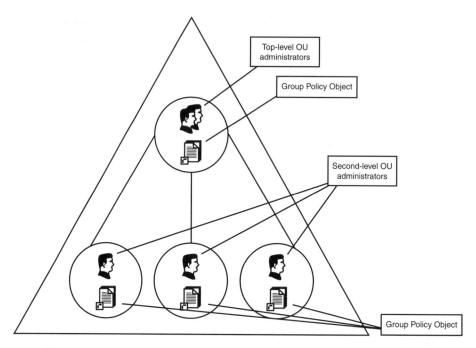

Figure 11.1 You can manage Group Policy centrally even if you decentralize the management of other resources.

The centralized administrative model is useful in companies that need to consolidate the administration of policy, regardless of how they manage other resources.

The Decentralized Model

The decentralized Group Policy model will be useful in organizations that rely heavily on delegated levels of administration. The goal of this model is to decentralize the management of Group Policy objects, distributing the workload to a number of different administrators. The decentralized model is shown in Figure 11.2.

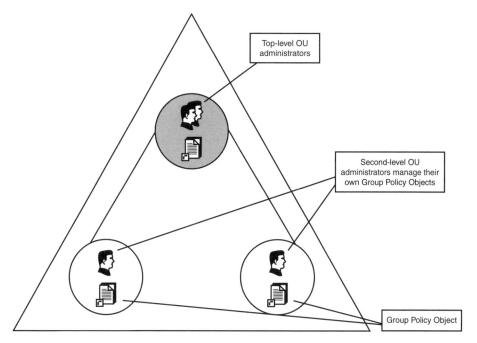

Figure 11.2   The decentralized administrative model places control of policy in the hands of administrators who are closest to users.

Each of the company's second-level administrators is given `Full Control` permissions for their Group Policy objects. This allows them to change Group Policy for users and computers in the organizational unit as they see fit. Top-level administrators are not responsible for all Group Policy objects in the domain.

The Task-Based Model

The goal of the task-based Group Policy administration model is to divide up the management of policy objects by certain tasks. This model is shown in Figure 11.3. The set of administrators that handle security-related tasks are responsible for managing all policy objects that affect security. The second set of administrators ordinarily deploy the company's business applications. They are responsible for all policy objects that affect application installation and maintenance. This model is useful in environments where administrative lines are drawn functionally.

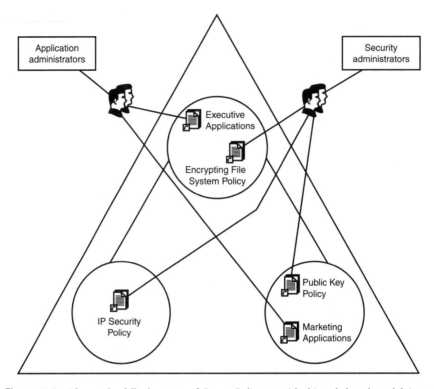

Figure 11.3   If you take full advantage of Group Policy, as with this task-based model, it can help you simplify quite a few routine tasks.

IntelliMirror

Another feature of Windows 2000 that is aimed at simplifying administration is *IntelliMirror*. IntelliMirror is a set of technologies that are built into Windows 2000 for change and configuration management at the desktop. IntelliMirror enables a user's data, applications, and desktop settings to follow them on the network. IntelliMirror is not a single technology that you can install and configure. You can't go down to your local computer store and buy a box of IntelliMirror with Windows 2000. Instead, several different technologies fit beneath the IntelliMirror umbrella:

- Software installation
- User settings management
- User document management

With the software installation feature of IntelliMirror, you can centrally install and maintain applications. The user settings management portion of IntelliMirror gives your users true roaming capabilities: Your users can use any Windows 2000 computer on the network and have access to their applications, desktop preferences, and data. User document management, on the other hand, is aimed at the needs of mobile users. The client-side caching feature of IntelliMirror allows them to continue working on network files even when they are disconnected. When they get back online, their files can be synchronized with copies on the network. The following sections explain more about these three aspects of IntelliMirror.

Software Installation

Software installation works with Group Policy to help you deploy, maintain, and manage your company's applications. You can create a Group Policy object that defines the applications a user can use, regardless of which computer on the network that user accesses.

With software installation, you can either assign or publish applications. When you *assign* an application to a user, its icons are automatically placed in that user's Start menu. When the user selects the icon you've assigned him, the application it is associated with can be installed transparently. *Published applications* work differently. They are not automatically installed in any way or placed in a user's Start menu. Instead, they are listed in Add/Remove Programs as optional applications for users to install. Automatic installation is another interesting feature supported by software installation. It allows you to configure an application to automatically be installed on a user's desktop when that user activates a specific file type, such as a .PDF, .ZIP, or .HTM file.

User Settings Management

You can use the user settings management feature of IntelliMirror to control the desktop configuration of your users' Windows 2000 computers. This lets you centrally define and manage the behavior for each setting you examined earlier in the "Group Policy" section. This allows you to control various desktop settings such as logon and logoff scripts, account policies, and networking parameters. Furthermore, with the roaming profile technology in Windows 2000, your users' data and configuration settings can be stored on the network. This means your users can log on to any Windows 2000 computer, and their configuration settings, data, and applications will follow them. Storing these settings on the network gives you another advantage. If a user's computer becomes inoperable, an administrator can swap it for a new one without losing everything (the user's configuration, data, and applications are all a part of his roaming profile).

User Document Management

The user document management technology that is a part of IntelliMirror is equally helpful in simplifying administration. It allows your users' network files to be available whether or not they are connected to the network. If a user loses her connection or voluntarily takes her computer off of the network, she can continue to navigate her files and folders as if she were still connected. When she connects again, any files she has modified while working offline can be synchronized with network copies. An administrator can set up user document management so that it works automatically when a user is disconnected from a particular file or folder. Offline access to files and folders can also be enabled by users themselves. This makes user document management extremely flexible.

The three core technologies that form IntelliMirror—software installation, user settings management, and user document management—are extremely powerful. Each can go a long way toward helping you simplify administration in Windows 2000 networks.

The Distributed File System (DFS)

Like IntelliMirror, DFS is a feature with which you can simplify administration of Windows 2000. In the case of DFS, simplification is achieved through file share aggregation and fault tolerance. With normal file shares, the server sharing the files must handle the entire burden associated with the share. Additionally, if the server is unavailable, the share and its files are similarly inaccessible. Finally, users must remember the location of all shares they need to use in their daily routines. Large organizations can have quite a few shares, making this a difficult task.

Microsoft created the Distributed File System in an effort to correct these problems. DFS allows shares to be replicated, which allows load balancing and redundancy. Additionally, multiple server shares can be condensed into one or more DFS shares, allowing clients to find their information more easily. By implementing DFS, you can create a logical, centralized structure for files, yet the information can actually be located on many servers.

Overview of DFS Capabilities

DFS shares are actually a hierarchy of server shares. As users access different file folders, they are transparently redirected to one of the servers holding that folder. The only limit to the DFS hierarchy is Windows 2000's limit of 260 characters for a path.

Multiple servers can maintain replicas of a share. When a client requests a DFS address from DNS, DNS returns all the addresses for the share. The client then selects the closest one based on site topology information. Different replicas are tried until a successful connection is made. Each replica has a cache timeout associated with it, and when this timeout expires, the client checks with the server for updated information.

Aside from replicas, different DFS nodes typically hold different types of data. For example, one node may hold individual users' data, while another node might be responsible for data belonging to one or more departments. If you give each node a specific purpose, it becomes easier for you to administrate DFS and the underlying shares.

DFS shares rely on standard NTFS security. One caveat with this is that if a user has access rights to a share, she will continue to have the same level of access all the way down the DFS Tree, unless it's restricted by NTFS permissions. For this reason, you need to give careful thought to the layout of files and directories in DFS, along with their permissions.

Leveraging DFS

Although DFS shares initially require extra work to set up, they will simplify long term administration in a number of ways:

- Users will need to use fewer shares to get their network data.
- Data can be replicated close to the users' locations.
- Servers in a fault-tolerant DFS share can be down, whether due to failure or for maintenance, without inconveniencing the users.

In addition to reducing the number of shares needed by clients, DFS shares can be published to AD as volume objects, which makes them visible to AD browsers. This makes it even easier for clients to find their data.

Fault Tolerance

In order to implement full fault tolerance for a DFS share, the root must be hosted on a Windows 2000 domain member. This is the only way the root node can be replicated. Root nodes use AD to replicate configuration information, which is how fault tolerance is achieved. Although downlevel DFS clients such as Windows NT 4.0 are unable to use the fault tolerance features of a DFS root, they can still access the share by referencing a DFS root server instead of the domain name in the UNC used to map the drive.

Fault-Tolerant Root Nodes

The decision to make a root node fault tolerant must be made when the node is created. If a standalone root is chosen and then needs to become a fault-tolerant root, the DFS share must be deleted and re-created. When this occurs, the DFS hierarchy is also deleted, meaning that the re-creation process could be time consuming. Make sure you select the proper node type when you create the share.

Even if the root is not capable of fault tolerance, (because it's not a Windows 2000 domain member), the child nodes can be replicated. This is accomplished via the DFS Administrator and can be implemented at any time. Replication of data between nodes can be automated or performed manually.

DFS Best Practices

When implementing DFS, you should not overlook these recommended practices:

- Replicas must be located near their clients for effective load balancing.

- You should publish the DFS share in AD as a volume object for easy access.

- For dynamic content, shorten the cache timeout so that clients refresh often enough. Static content can utilize a longer timeout value.

- Periodically run the `Check Status` command on the share structure to ensure that all the replicas are working properly.

- Reference DFS shares by their DFS names rather than their server UNCs. Otherwise, AD will not be queried.

Automatic System Recovery (ASR)

Another way to simplify administration of Windows 2000 is with Automatic System Recovery (ASR). You can use ASR to quickly restore a Windows 2000 computer if it is unable to boot or to function normally. Routine backup of your Windows 2000 computers can help you prevent data loss or damage due to physical component failures and other unforeseen events. ASR is a key component of the improved Windows 2000 backup utility that you can use to make it easier to restore a computer to its original state.

You can use ASR to create a backup copy of a computer's configuration and operating system files. This allows you to restore the computer to an operational state in the event it is catastrophically damaged. To tap into the recovery features of ASR, you must first use the ASR Preparation Wizard. This wizard takes a snapshot of your configuration settings and system files, which can be used at a later time to recover the computer. In the sections that follow, you'll learn how to generate an ASR Saveset, and you'll examine both the text mode and the GUI mode phases of ASR.

Generating an ASR Saveset

When you run the ASR Preparation Wizard from the Windows 2000 backup utility, it creates an image known as an *ASR Saveset*. An ASR Saveset is composed of a computer's data, configuration, and system files. The ASR Saveset also includes a floppy disk, known as an ASR disk, that stores partition information, computer configuration settings, and the location of driver files that must be available to the restore process.

Text Mode Phase of ASR

You must take several steps to restore a computer to its original state using ASR. After you run the ASR Preparation Wizard, you should have a 1.44MB ASR floppy disk and some form of backup media containing your data, configuration, and system files. With a recent copy of your ASR floppy and a backup of your system, you can start the text mode phase of ASR. This phase requires the following steps:

1. Replace or repair any components of your system that are physically damaged.

2. Start the computer as if you were installing Windows 2000 for the first time using the first setup disk or the CD-ROM.

3. When you're asked whether to install a new version of Windows 2000 or repair or recover an existing installation, select the recovery option.

4. Insert the ASR floppy disk, which contains the setup information file.

During the text mode phase of ASR, your hard disk will be repartitioned and formatted if necessary, and Windows 2000 will be reinstalled. The setup information file from your ASR floppy will then be copied to `%systemroot%\system32`. Finally, the Registry will be modified to automatically start your backup application in the GUI mode phase of ASR.

GUI Mode Phase of ASR

The GUI mode phase of ASR begins after you restart the system you are recovering. It consists of the following steps:

1. The backup application that was specified in your setup information file launches automatically after you restart the computer.

2. The configuration information that was specified in your setup information file is restored from backup.

3. After the original configuration and system files are restored, you can restart the computer.

4. Once the computer cycles back up, the GUI mode phase of ASR is complete.

The computer will then be restored to the state it was in the last time you ran the ASR Preparation Wizard. The ASR component of Windows 2000 backup represents a landmark improvement over the traditional backup and restores facilities provided natively with Windows NT.

Windows Scripting Host (WSH)

Yet another way to simplify the administration of Windows 2000 is by scripting. WSH is to Windows 2000 what Visual Basic for Applications is to Microsoft Office. It offers powerful programming capabilities without the overhead of having to write a complete application. A major advantage of WSH over the more traditional batch files is that WSH is object oriented and can use any ActiveX server on the system.

For an administrator who has not programmed before, WSH scripts may appear daunting. However, it's not that difficult to learn how to create new scripts. Because WSH can automate a variety of tasks with just a few lines of code, there is a strong incentive to learn this skill. With their simple, powerful nature, scripts are likely to become more pervasive within the Windows environment.

Overview of Windows Scripting Host

A complete explanation of the Windows Scripting Host could easily fill a book by itself. In this mere section of a chapter, you'll get an overview of WSH and see some of the tasks you can accomplish.

WSH is one of three Microsoft-provided hosts for scripts. The other two are Internet Explorer and Internet Information Server (IIS). WSH is built into Windows 2000 and Windows 98. Both Windows 95 and Windows NT can also run WSH, making the scripts easily portable across the Windows family. Scripts can run under WSH through two programs: WSCRIPT.EXE and CSCRIPT.EXE. WSCRIPT runs in the background, while CSCRIPT runs via the command prompt. Both execute WSH scripts equally well; the main difference between the two is that CSCRIPT supports error levels, which may be useful if the script is part of a larger batch file.

WSH supports multiple languages. It ships with support for VBScript (a subset of Visual Basic) and Jscript (similar to Java), and third parties will offer add-ons for REXX, Perl, and other languages. WSH determines the script's language by its file extension (.VBS for VBScript and .JS for Jscript).

To run a script from the command line enter CSCRIPT *scriptname* [options]. To specify options to the WSH executable (called the host), use "//". For script options, use "/". Although script options vary by script, host options can be displayed by running CSCRIPT //?.

Using Windows 2000 Backup to Recover a Domain Controller

At some point, you may need to recover a failed Windows 2000 domain controller. This can be tricky because domain controllers replicate Active Directory and the SYSVOL share using multi master replication. To restore the Active Directory and SYSVOL share on a domain controller, you need to first start it in directory services restore mode. However, if you use a simple restore process after this, the server's domain partition will be overwritten by more recent copies of the partition that exist on other domain controllers in the domain.

To bring the domain partition back to the state in which it existed when you created your backup, you must use what is known as an *authoritative restore*. To authoritatively restore Active Directory and the SYSVOL share, you need to use the NTDSUTIL utility. After restoring Active Directory and the SYSVOL share from backup, run NTDSUTIL to mark Active Directory objects for authoritative restore. This changes update sequence numbers in the local partition that are higher than other update sequence numbers in the multi master replication topology.

One unique feature of WSH scripts is that they can be limited to a certain amount of time to run. After their time expires, the script is aborted. For example, a script might have a five-minute timeout. If a bug causes an infinite loop or the script isn't complete at the end of five minutes, WSH terminates the script. This feature prevents bugs or poor programming from monopolizing the CPU. The best way to enable this feature is to use a .WSH file. This INI-style file functions much like a .PIF file for DOS applications and stores options for a specific script. Adjusting the values on the Script tab of a script's Properties dialog box will create the .WSH file.

The Windows Scripting Host Object Model

WSH is an object-oriented environment. An object in the context of WSH is any ActiveX server. WSH allows scripts to create connections to objects and uses these objects by requesting them to perform operations or report data. In a sense, the script is the boss, and the objects are subordinates. Virtually all lines of a script will involve interactions with objects. WSH provides four important objects within itself:

- **WScript.** This is the only object that is always available to a script. The main purpose of this object is to allow the script to connect to and disconnect from other objects.

- **WshShell.** This object provides functions that are related to the system shell. These include information about the environment, user input and output, shortcut creation, Registry access, and external program execution.

- **WshNetwork.** As the name suggests, this object is oriented toward networking functionality. It allows for network drive and printer mappings and provides basic information about the network.

- **FileSystemObject.** The FileSystemObject allows WSH to access the file system. All common operations are supported, including directory and file creation, deletion, and searching. Also supported are basic text I/O operations.

All other objects on the system can also be accessed, such as a Microsoft Word document or the Active Directory Services Interface (ADSI). Because WSH has the ability to interact with objects beyond itself, scripts can be quite powerful.

Basic Properties and Methods

All objects have properties and methods, which is how an object interfaces with other objects (such as WSH scripts). *Methods* are similar to functions in a programming sense. To request an object to take an action, you would use a method. For example, if your boss were an object, you could request a raise using the `Boss.PayRaise` method. Methods return values. In the boss example, the value would be Yes or No. Some methods accept or require additional information, called *arguments*. To request a meeting with my boss, I could use `Boss.RequestMeeting`, or I could request a certain time by using `Boss.RequestMeeting("7/11/2000", "9:00PM")`.

Whereas methods request an object to perform a function, properties request that the object report data, usually about itself. Requesting a method from an object may require the object to perform a great deal of work. On the other hand, requesting a property involves little or no work on the part of the object. In a programming context, a property functions like a variable. Sometimes a property can't be modified. However, most properties can be adjusted by the script. Real-world examples of properties are `Car.Color` and `Car.Model`.

Because methods and properties appear similar when viewed in a script, they're easily confused. The best way to prevent this is to remember that a method requests an action (such as `Car.Start`) while a property requests data (such as `Car.Color`).

Common Uses for WSH

WSH can be used to simplify or automate quite a few tasks. From an administrator's standpoint, you might find WSH useful for two things: logon/logoff scripts and user account creation and maintenance.

Creating Logon and Logoff Scripts

Batch files are heavily used for logon scripts. However, WSH offers advantages over batch files because it is able to do much more without relying on external utilities. Below is the listing for a common WSH logon script. You can see what each section does based on the comment line preceding it, which always begins with a " ' ". As you can see, this script performs several functions that a batch file can't without additional utilities, such as reading from the Registry and creating informational windows:

```
'Declare variables
Dim WSHNetwork
Dim WSHShell
Dim Ver

'Setup options
Set WSHNetwork = WScript.CreateObject("WScript.Network")
Set WSHShell = WScript.CreateObject("WScript.Shell")

'Map the standard user drive
WSHNetwork.MapNetworkDrive "Z:", "\\Server\Share"

'Map the admin's drive if they're logging on.
If WSHNetwork.UserName = "Administrator" Then
   WSHNetwork.MapNetworkDrive "F:", "\\Server\Admin$"
   WSHShell.Popup "Hello, Administrator!", 10, "Welcome"
End If

'Check registry for the latest version of FooSoft
'Script may fail here if this key doesn't exist
Ver = WSHShell.RegRead("HKLM\Software\FooSoft\Version")
If Ver < "4.7.1" Then WSHShell.Run "F:\Install\FooSoft\Setup.EXE"
```

Creating User Accounts

One of WSH's most important features is its ability to manage user accounts. This is accomplished through the Active Directory Services Interface (ADSI). Connections to AD under ADSI are accomplished via LDAP. Beyond its AD capabilities, ADSI can also manage downlevel NT domains and Novell NetWare NDS and bindery accounts. The following is an example script that uses ADSI to create users in a top-level OU of the current domain:

```
' Create variables
Dim RootDSE
Dim ouHO
Dim sFirstName, sLastName, sUserName, sPrompt
Dim iInput
Dim user

wscript.echo "This script will create users in the Home Office OU."

' Determine the LDAP path for your domain
Set RootDSE = GetObject("LDAP://RootDSE")

' Connect to Home Office OU of current domain
' Script will fail here if there is no such OU.
Set ouHO = GetObject("LDAP://OU=Home Office, " &
➥RootDSE.Get("DefaultNamingContext"))

Do
    sFirstName = InputBox("What is the user's first name?", "First Name")
    sLastName = InputBox("What is the user's last name?", "Last Name")

    ' Script will fail here if either name is blank.
    sUserName = LCase(Left(sFirstName, 1) & sLastName)

    sPrompt = "Create a user named " & sFirstName & " " & sLastName &
➥Chr(10) & "with a user name of " & sUserName & "?"
    iInput = MsgBox(sPrompt, vbYesNo, "Verify User Information")
    if iInput = vbYes then
        Set user = ouHO.Create("user", "CN=" & sFirstName & " " &
➥sLastName)
        user.Put "samAccountName", sUserName
        user.Put "givenName", sFirstName
        user.Put "sn", sLastName
        user.Put "userPrincipalName", sUserName
        user.SetInfo
        user.SetPassword "password"
        wscript.echo "User Created."
    else
```

```
        wscript.echo "User Creation Cancelled."
    end if
Loop While MsgBox("Create another user?", vbYesNo, "Question") = vbYes

wscript.echo "This will terminate the script." & Chr(10) & "Click OK to
⮑exit."
```

Auditing Events

Another way to simplify administration in Windows 2000 is by auditing the events on your systems. With auditing, you can track user and operating system events to more closely monitor certain computers. The events that you choose to audit are then recorded to the computer's security event log for your review.[3] Each entry that is made in the computer's event log contains the following details:

- Whether the event was a success or failure
- The date and time the event occurred
- The source, category, and event ID
- The user that triggered the event
- The computer the event occurred on

Auditing is useful for tracking the success or failure of a particular action, such as opening a file or modifying permissions on an object in Active Directory. You usually track the success of certain actions to establish usage trends. This can be helpful, for example, to determine how often a file is accessed or an object is read in Active Directory. You can also use auditing to track the failure of an action. This is often done for security reasons. To define what is audited for a particular object, you must modify that object's properties. These properties are listed with the security attributes of the object. Table 11.2 lists the events you can audit in Windows 2000.

The remaining sections explain how to audit certain events to simplify administration.

---

3. For auditing to be effective, you must regularly review your event logs.

Table 11.2 **Events You Can Record and Audit in Windows 2000**

Event	Description
Account Logon	Triggered when a logon request is received by a domain controller
Account Management	Triggered when a user or group account is created or modified
Directory Service Access	Triggered when an object in Active Directory is accessed[4]
Logon	Triggered when a user logs on or off a computer
Object Access	Triggered when an object such as a file, directory, or printer is accessed
Policy Change	Triggered when security options, user rights, or audit policies are altered
Privilege Use	Triggered when a user right is used to perform an action
Process Tracking	Triggered when an application performs an action that is purposefully being tracked by a programmer
System Events	Triggered when an event occurs that affects security, or when a user restarts or shuts down a computer

Auditing Active Directory

Auditing access to objects in Active Directory can be useful for establishing usage trends or tracking access to certain objects for security reasons. Before you can audit any objects in Active Directory, you must first enable auditing of the Directory Service Access event. To do so, you must set the event to "on" status by using the Group Policy Editor. You can then audit any of the Directory Service Access events[5] listed in Table 11.3.

Tracking how the resources in Active Directory are being used is quite simple with auditing. For example, you can audit the Read all Properties event to track how a shared folder object is used. This might be used to tell you how often users are reading the keywords you've assigned to a share.

Auditing is also very useful for logging security-related events associated with objects in Active Directory. For example, you can use auditing to trigger an event each time permissions are modified on an object or when an object in a particular container is deleted.

4. This must be further defined at the object level.

5. These are the most common Directory Service Access events. You can specify different events depending on the object being audited.

Table 11.3 **Events You Can Audit in Active Directory**

Event	Description
`Full Control`	Triggered when any level of access is made to the object
`List Contents`	Triggered when the contents of the object are listed
`List Object`	Triggered when the object is viewed
`Read all Properties`	Triggered when any of the object's properties are read
`Write all Properties`	Triggered when any of the object's properties are written to
`Create all Child Objects`	Triggered when any child object is created
`Delete all Child Objects`	Triggered when any child object is deleted
`Read Permissions`	Triggered when the object's permissions are read
`Modify Permissions`	Triggered when the object's permissions are modified
`Modify Owner`	Triggered when the owner of the object is changed

Auditing the File System

Like auditing object-related events in Active Directory, auditing file system events can also simplify administration. To audit these events, you must first enable auditing of the Object Access event. You can set this event to "on" status using the Group Policy Editor. After enabling auditing for the Object Access event, you can audit the events listed in Table 11.4 to closely track usage trends or to monitor access to files and folders for security purposes.

WSH Resources

For more information on WSH, check out Microsoft's scripting pages at.
`http://msdn.microsoft.com/scripting`. Another good source for information is Glazier Systems' Web site, `http://wsh.glazier.co.nz`.

Creating WSH Scripts

Creating WSH scripts, especially those involving ADSI, can be difficult for those new to WSH scripting. For instance, the user creation example in the section "To Create User Accounts" took me several hours, even though I'm familiar with Visual Basic.

There are two reasons for this difficulty. First, existing documentation for ADSI is highly technical and not written with WSH specifically in mind. Second, debugging support for WSH is very limited. All but the most basic errors simply load the Script Debugger program, sometimes with the offending line highlighted. Usually, no error message is displayed; execution simply halts. This makes the debugging process much more difficult.

Fortunately, both of these problems are likely to be reduced with increased WSH usage. Many third-party resources will become available to assist you with your scripting needs. Also, just as with many things, the more you work with WSH, the better you become at creating scripts.

Table 11.4 **Auditing File System Events**

Event	Description
Traverse Folder / Execute File	Triggered when a folder is traversed or an application is run
List Folder / Read Data	Triggered when a file or folder is listed
Read Attributes	Triggered when the attributes of a file or folder are read
Read Extended Attributes	Triggered when extended attributes of a file or folder are read
Create Files / Write Data	Triggered when a file is modified or created
Create Folders / Append Data	Triggered when a folder is modified or created
Write Attributes	Triggered when an attribute is modified
Write Extended Attributes	Triggered when an extended attribute is modified
Delete Subfolders and Files	Triggered when a file or subfolder in a folder is deleted
Delete	Triggered when a specific file or folder is deleted
Read Permissions	Triggered when the permissions of a file or folder are read
Change Permissions	Triggered when the permissions of a file or folder are modified
Take Ownership	Triggered when a user takes ownership of a file or folder
Synchronize	Triggered when a file or folder is synchronized with an offline copy

To audit a particular file system event, you must enable it at the file or folder level. For example, you can track how the client-side caching features of IntelliMirror are being used by auditing offline folders for the Synchronize event. Quite often, file system auditing will be used for security purposes. You can audit when permissions or attributes are altered on a particular file or folder, for example, to create an enhanced level of security.

Resource Kit Utilities

So far, many of the techniques for simplifying administration discussed in this chapter have to be implemented at design time (usually when you're designing your Active Directory) in order to be beneficial. This section focuses on tools available in the Windows 2000 Resource Kit that can be used at any time.

Everyone knows how to perform daily tasks, such as managing user accounts and adjusting file permissions, but you will occasionally find yourself needing to perform a task you think will require a great deal of manual labor. For example, perhaps you need to apply a special set of permissions to various directories on all of your workstations. Maybe every machine needs to place user-specific data in its Registry. All administrators find themselves in this position eventually. After you read this section, you may be able to simplify the task by automating it.

Although they're not officially supported by Microsoft, the Resource Kit utilities are an excellent set of tools. About half are general utilities; the other half are useful for troubleshooting specific problems. Not all the utilities will be discussed in this section. Rather, the focus is on those you will find most helpful for simplifying administration.

These handy utilities are often worth their weight in gold, because they usually provide capabilities not otherwise available in Windows 2000. If you know and take advantage of the function of each utility, you can simplify your administrative duties and often save a great deal of time.

NETAFX.EXE

NETAFX.EXE is a command line utility that deals with the networking components installed on a machine. It has two functions. First, it is capable of installing new components via the command line, rather than through the standard Windows interface. This makes it useful in batch files for automating the installation of networking components. Second, it provides a very complete list of the networking components currently installed on the machine. While this could be used to provide a crude inventory, a better use is to confirm the presence or absence of a component in conjunction with other operations. For instance, a script might only install an updated network card driver if the older driver for the network card is already installed.

NETDIAG.EXE

Network connectivity can suffer a variety of problems, from server problems to client misconfiguration. As a result, determining the cause of a problem can sometimes be difficult. NETDIAG.EXE attempts to ease the burden of troubleshooting by automating basic functionality tests. NETDIAG is a new addition to the Windows 2000 Resource Kit. One of its best features is that it will run on Windows 9*x*, NT, or 2000. As a result, any modern Microsoft OS can use this troubleshooting tool. In general, an automated test can only do so much troubleshooting; however, with NETDIAG.EXE, an impressive list of functionality is tested:

- Network card
- WAN
- Bindings

- Winsock
- TCP/IP
- DHCP
- NETBT
- DNS Server
- WINS Server
- IPX and NetWare
- Routing
- Distributed Functions: RPC, domains, trusts, Kerberos, LDAP, and IPSEC

LOGEVENT.EXE

Although batch files report their results in various ways, they can't write to the event log. LOGEVENT.EXE provides this functionality. LOGEVENT is best used to report the results from Scheduler service jobs, batch files, and other automated processes. In addition to the fact that it supports writing to the local event log, it can send its events to other machines. Therefore, you can use one machine for centralized reporting, which is very beneficial if the machines creating events are over a WAN link.

NLTESTRK.EXE

NLTESTRK.EXE is a diagnostic utility used to check the secure channels between machines. These channels are mainly used for domain trusts. Another use of secure channels is for the connection between workstations and domain controllers (DCs). Finally, secure channels are used for user logon. NLTESTRK is able to test all this functionality. Additionally, it can test the status of replication between DCs. Although it's called NLTESTRK in Windows 2000, it was available in the Windows NT Resource Kit as NLTEST.

Using NLTESTRK can be a bit daunting due to its large number of options (for a full list, run `NLTESTRK /?`) and cryptic output. Nevertheless, it can be an excellent diagnostic tool if you are having user or machine authentication problems or if domain trusts are failing.

> **Towards Guruhood**
>
> Any administrator can perform day-to-day administrative tasks. However, a thorough knowledge of these tools and the ability to use them is one of the differences between a Windows 2000 administrator and a Windows 2000 guru.

REG.EXE

If you need to change the Registry from the command line (with a batch file, for instance), REG.EXE is the utility you need. It is capable of adding, changing, deleting, or querying Registry entries. It can also be used to back up and restore Registry hives. Beyond these abilities, it can also load and unload hives, such as from a second, inactive copy of Windows 2000 on a system. Originally created for the Windows NT 4.0 Resource Kit, REG has also been included in the Windows 2000 Resource Kit.

SC.EXE

SC.EXE focuses on services. It can start, stop, pause, and continue services. Additionally, it can change a service's description. Querying a service for its status is also supported. Another type of query will show whether the service database is locked. If it's locked, SC will show which process locked it and how long it's been locked. Finally, you can control the status of the LastKnownGood configuration, which is a feature offered nowhere else.

Administrators may find SC useful because it can list the name of a service's executable. It can also show if the executable is shared with multiple services and can provide information on each of those services, such as its type and the options it supports.

Additional Utilities

To document each Resource Kit utility would require a chapter by itself. Certainly, most of the utilities are very worthwhile, but space prevents a full discussion of each. Therefore, a number of utilities are listed in Table 11.5. Rather than document each fully, this table simply describes the function of each. For full details on one of these or any Resource Kit utility, check out the Resource Kit's help file.

Operating System Features

Windows 2000 provides a number of important features within the OS that administrators may not be aware of. Each of these utilities enables you to simplify your administrative tasks in some way.

REG.EXE: A Shortcoming

Although REG works very well, it is missing one much-needed capability: It's unable to set permissions on the Registry. Unfortunately, no other Resource Kit utilities provide this function either. However, this feature is available in various third-party utilities.

Table 11.5 **Additional Resource Kit Utilities**

Utility	Description
DHCPCMD	Command line DHCP management
DNSCMD	Command line DNS management
PPTPPING	Tests PPTP functionality between subnets
RPCPING	Tests RPC functionality between Exchange Server and clients
SNMPUTILG	Graphical SNMP Query and Set utility
WSREMOTE	Telnet-like client and server
KSETUP	Kerberos setup utility for non-Windows 2000 Kerberos domain controllers
KTPASS	Allows non-Windows 2000 Kerberos services to provide authentication for AD
SHUTDOWN	Shuts down or reboots local or remote Windows 2000/NT machine (see Chapter 2)
SIDWALKER	Migrates machines from one domain to another by reconfiguring all ACLs (see Chapter 2)

The Secondary Logon Service

The Secondary Logon Service debuted with Windows 2000. Similar to the SU utility in Windows NT 4.0's Resource Kit and UNIX, it allows a user to perform tasks as an arbitrary user, without having to log off. A standard tenet of security is that administrators should have two accounts—one that is privileged and one that is not. As a rule, they should use the non-privileged account all the time, unless they need to perform an administrative task. By using the Secondary Logon Service, they no longer need to stop what they're doing, save documents, log out, and log in as an administrator. Instead, they simply start a privileged session within their current session.

The service is not exclusively used for logging on as an administrator. In fact, you can log in as any user, so long as you meet the following requirements:

- You must be able to provide the user's credentials, usually in the form of his or her password. (Administrators can't impersonate users without knowing the correct password.)

- The user must be able to log in locally. Often, normal users don't have rights to log in locally to servers.

- The application being launched must be accessible in the specified context. If file permissions or user rights are not high enough, the operation will fail.

302 Chapter 11 Simplifying Administration

Before you try to use the service, make sure it's started. If you find yourself using it frequently, you may want to set it to start automatically. The syntax for accessing the service is as follows:

```
runas /user:domain\account [application]
```

You will be prompted for the password, and if it's correct, the application will open. Specifying the application is optional; if it's left blank, a CMD prompt appears. To reduce confusion, the window's title will indicate that it's running in the other user's context in some cases. However, some applications don't support this functionality, in which case you must remember which windows have which context.

The service has one minor limitation: Due to the nature of the Explorer shell, certain programs (such as the Control Panel and Explorer itself) will not work by default. In order to work around this problem, you can use Task Manager to kill the shell process (EXPLORER.EXE) and then restart it using the service. Once you finish working in the other user context, kill the shell again and restart it in your own context.

Service Failure and Recovery

As part of Microsoft's focus on making Windows 2000 an enterprise-class operating system, it has introduced recovery options for services. When SERVICES.EXE discovers that a service has terminated unexpectedly, it can take one of four courses of action:

- Take no action
- Restart the service
- Run a file
- Reboot the computer

The system will also keep a count of the number of times the service fails. This count is reset after a configurable number of days. Depending on how many times the service has failed, the system can take different actions. Three different actions can be set: for the first failure, for the second failure, and for all subsequent failures.

Unmonitorable Services

SERVICES.EXE both monitors for service failures and provides certain services itself, such as the Alerter service. If SERVICES.EXE fails, it is unable to perform any recovery steps. As a result, none of the services offered by SERVICES itself can make use of the recovery procedures.

Instead of manually taking action to restart the service, the administrator can now give the system some intelligence to try to fix the problem itself. The first action to take should nearly always be to restart the service. The only time this shouldn't be a default for a service is if the service requires some sort of cleanup (of files, for example) prior to the restart. In this case, create a batch file of WSH script to perform the cleanup, and configure the machine to run that file. (Note that the file will need to restart the service as its last step.) Another use of the "run a file" capability is to run a program to notify an administrator of the problem by broadcasting a message, by sending an email, or via pager software.

Some service failures can only be fixed by rebooting the machine. This is usually the last step you should take, however, because the machine will be inaccessible during the reboot, and current connections will be terminated. If you want, you can configure a message that will be displayed onscreen when the system shuts down.

Most often, recovery attempts will follow this order: restart the service on the first failure, run a file after the second failure, and reboot after all subsequent failures. In some cases, rebooting may be the second or even the first action attempted. This will depend on the type of failure and the service affected.

Configuring these capabilities can often save users from downtime and allow administrators a full, uninterrupted night of sleep. However, be sure you're monitoring your systems for service failures. A problem could occur without your knowledge if the system is able to restart the service. Rather than depend on the system to recover, you should work with the service's vendor to determine a long-term solution that resolves the condition causing the problem.

III

Deploying Windows 2000

12

Windows 2000
Upgrade and Migration

Your transition to Windows 2000 should be carefully planned, rigorously tested, and (finally) smoothly executed. Moving from one operating system to the next without tripping over a few technical hurdles along the way can be a daunting task. This will be true whether you upgrade to Windows 2000 from Windows NT or Novell NetWare. This chapter covers the steps in an upgrade or migration to Windows 2000 from beginning to end. First, it details the upgrade from Windows NT to Windows 2000. This includes a step-by-step overview of the upgrade procedure, as well as upgrade scenarios from popular NT domain models to Windows 2000 and Active Directory. After covering the upgrade from NT, you will examine migrating to Windows 2000 from Novell NetWare. That section details the process for moving to Windows 2000 from NetWare 3.x, 4.x, or 5.0.

Upgrading to Windows 2000

The complexity of moving to Windows 2000 is not in the upgrade procedure itself. Memorizing the sequence of each dialog box presented by the Windows 2000 Setup Wizard will only get you so far. As every preceding chapter has stressed, your efforts are best spent planning how to get from where you are today to where you should be tomorrow (in the Windows 2000 time frame). Rolling out a world-class Windows 2000 network takes a whole lot of planning, coordination, and old-fashioned hard work. Thoroughly preparing you for this transition is the aim of this book.

This chapter is focused directly on the upgrade procedure itself. Upgrading your Windows NT Servers to Windows 2000 is a fairly straightforward and automated task. Like most other modern-day upgrade routines, this upgrade procedure is wizard driven and more or less hands free. Each of the supported upgrade paths to Windows 2000 is shown here. You can upgrade to Windows 2000 Server from NT Server version 3.51 or 4.0.

Previous Version	**Upgrade to...**
Windows NT 3.51 or 4.0 PDC	Windows 2000 Domain Controller
Windows NT 3.51 or 4.0 BDC	Windows 2000 Member Server or Windows 2000 Domain Controller
Windows NT 3.51 or 4.0 Member Server	Windows 2000 Member Server

This section details the primary steps in a Windows 2000 upgrade, which include:

- Planning for a safe Windows 2000 upgrade
- Running the Windows 2000 Setup Wizard
- Running the Active Directory Installation Wizard
- Running the Configure Server Wizard
- Validating the Windows 2000 upgrade

You should also review the final portion of the section "Upgrading Domains to Windows 2000." It lists several upgrade scenarios that can help you visualize the upgrade procedure from start to finish.

Planning for a Safe Windows 2000 Upgrade

You should take a few general precautions before upgrading any of your systems to Windows 2000. One safety measure you should definitely take is to make a full backup of the server you plan to upgrade. This provides you with a source for restoring the server's original configuration in the event of a failure. You should also develop a recovery strategy for the domain itself. This allows you to restore the account and policy information in your domain database if the upgrade to Windows 2000 fails.

In the course of upgrading an NT domain, the SAM database on your primary domain controller is converted to a partition in Active Directory. After a successful Windows 2000 upgrade, your domain controller then emulates the role of an NT 3.51 or 4.0 primary domain controller. This allows it to replicate any changes to backup domain controllers in the same domain. If the partition in Active Directory were to become corrupt, this corruption would be replicated to all backup domain controllers—rendering every domain controller in your domain useless. To guard against this kind of catastrophe, you should take one of two recommended precautions:

- Move a backup domain controller in the domain offline before you upgrade the primary domain controller.

- Move the primary domain controller offline to upgrade it to Windows 2000 in an isolated environment.

Figure 12.1 illustrates a Windows 2000 upgrade in progress using the first recommended precaution. The CHIBDC002 backup domain controller is offline during the upgrade of CHIPDC001 (the primary domain controller). If the upgrade of CHIPDC001 fails, CHIBDC002 can be moved back into production and promoted to primary status. Even if the upgrade of the CHICAGO domain is initially successful, the CHIBDC002 backup domain controller should remain offline for at least a week. This gives the administrative team a week to reverse the upgrade if they notice any problems.

You also have the option of moving your primary domain controller to an isolated network during its upgrade. This strategy is shown in Figure 12.2. The CHIPDC001 primary domain controller is taken offline and is upgraded to Windows 2000. The administrators of the CHICAGO domain wait until they are confident in the success of this upgrade before they move the server back into production. Once CHIPDC001 is back online, it replicates Active Directory as a flat database to the domain's backup domain controllers.

You need to make sure that your upgrade to Windows 2000 includes some measure of fault tolerance. At the very minimum, you need a way to restore each server to its original state. It is also recommended that you have a strategy in place for recovering your domain database.

Running the Windows 2000 Setup Wizard

To initiate the upgrade of an NT Server to Windows 2000, you must start the Windows 2000 Setup Wizard. This wizard is automatically invoked by autorun when you insert the Windows 2000 Server CD-ROM. You can also start the Setup Wizard by running WINNT32.EXE from the CD-ROM's i386 directory.

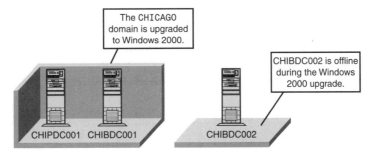

The CHICAGO domain is upgraded to Windows 2000.

CHIBDC002 is offline during the Windows 2000 upgrade.

CHIPDC001 CHIBDC001   CHIBDC002

Figure 12.1 Moving a backup domain controller offline before your upgrade offers you more flexibility than moving a primary domain controller to an isolated network.

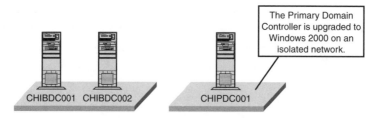

Figure 12.2   When you upgrade the primary domain controller in your domain on an isolated network, both backup domain controllers stay on the production network.

The purpose of the Setup Wizard is to guide you through the Windows 2000 upgrade. The upgrade from Windows NT to Windows 2000 occurs in several stages. These stages include:

1. The initial GUI mode phase of setup
2. The initial text mode phase of setup
3. The primary text mode phase of setup
4. The primary GUI mode phase of setup

Stage 1: The Initial GUI Mode Phase of Setup

The initial GUI mode phase of setup begins when you launch the Windows 2000 Setup Wizard for the first time. After you select **Upgrade to Windows 2000**, you will be prompted to accept the Windows 2000 license agreement. After that, a number of files are copied from the CD-ROM to your server's hard disk. These files allow your NT Server to boot into the initial text mode phase of setup. The default startup option in your server's BOOT.INI file is then changed to boot to the initial text mode phase of setup[1]. The Setup Wizard then automatically reboots the server.

Stage 2: The Initial Text Mode Phase of Setup

When the server comes back online, it reads the new default entry in its BOOT.INI file and begins the initial text mode phase of setup. This phase of setup is similar to text mode setup in Windows NT. Windows 2000 loads several familiar files at this stage, including NTLDR, NTDETECT.COM, and NTOSKRNL.EXE. This allows it to initialize essential file systems, drivers, and other devices. After enumerating and

---

1. Your original BOOT.INI file is backed up as BOOT.BAK.

loading these devices, the server's NTFS 4.0 partitions are converted to NTFS 5.0[2]. These partitions will be automatically converted without warning. The NTFS 4.0 to NTFS 5.0 conversion includes the entire partition, which consists of all logical drives formatted with NTFS 4.0.

Stage 3: The Primary Phase of Text Mode Setup

The primary phase of text mode setup begins after an automatic server reboot. In this phase of setup, a number of files are copied from the CD-ROM to your server. These are the core files that are required to install the Windows 2000 operating system. When the file copy operation is complete, the server's configuration is initialized and subsequently saved. The Setup Wizard then reboots the server for the third time.

Stage 4: The Primary Phase of GUI Mode Setup

At this point, the operating system loads into GUI mode for the first time. The Windows 2000 Setup Wizard then launches automatically. The Setup Wizard installs and detects various hardware devices, networking components, and other components required by the operating system. To finish, the wizard creates the Start Menu, registers components, saves settings, and removes temporary files used in the upgrade process. The upgrade of the operating system to Windows 2000 is now complete. However, before you can use the server in a production environment, one last reboot is required.

Running the Active Directory Installation Wizard

The Active Directory Installation Wizard launches automatically if you are upgrading a domain controller, but you can also start it by running DCPROMO.EXE from the `%systemroot%\system32` directory. It is worth noting that every Windows 2000 domain controller starts out as a member server. This represents quite a difference from the NT installation process, in which you must decide in advance what role your server will play. Before you install Active Directory, you should collect the information listed in Table 12.1.

In the sections that follow, you'll cover the following steps for installing Active Directory on a primary domain controller:

1. Creating a new Tree or a new child domain.

2. Creating a new Forest or joining an existing Forest.

3. Installing or configuring the Domain Name Service.

4. Specifying the full DNS name for the new domain.

---

2. The NTFS 5.0 file system is not optional for domain controllers in Windows 2000—it is strictly required to support the Windows 2000 system volume (SYSVOL). However, if there is an existing FAT partition, it will not be converted to NTFS 5.0, whether this FAT partition is the boot partition or the system partition. To access an NTFS 5.0 partition from Windows NT 4.0, you must apply Service Pack 4.

5. Setting the Active Directory database and log file locations.

6. Specifying the directory that is shared as the system volume.

7. Confirming your choices and starting the installation process.

8. Completing the Active Directory Installation Wizard.

Step 1: Creating a New Tree or New Child Domain

When you install Active Directory on a primary domain controller, its SAM database is converted to a partition in Active Directory. The first step in your installation will be to decide whether to create a new Tree or a new child domain. For this example, assume that this is the company's first Windows 2000 domain controller. Therefore, you will select **Create a New Domain Tree.**

Step 2: Creating a New Forest or Joining an Existing One

The next step is to decide whether to create a new Forest or join an existing one. If one or more Trees were present, you could join an existing Forest to share resources with other domains. Because no other Trees exist, select the **Create a New Forest of Domain Trees** option.

Step 3: Installing or Configuring the Domain Naming Service

Next, you must install or configure the Domain Name Service (DNS). If DNS had been previously set up, you would configure the server's TCP/IP settings with a valid DNS address. Assume, however, that DNS has not yet been installed. To move forward with your installation of Active Directory, select **No, There Are No DNS Servers on the Network. Install and Configure DNS on This Computer.**

Table 12.1 Information Required for the Active Directory Installation Wizard

Required Information	Example
Whether to create a new Tree or a new child domain	Domain will be installed as the root domain in a new Tree.
Whether to create a new Forest or to join an existing Forest	Domain will form a new Forest.
The full DNS name for the new domain	Domain name will be `chicago.mycompany.com`.
The location for the Active Directory database and log files	Active Directory database and log files will be stored in `c:\winnt\ntds`.
The location for the shared system volume	Shared system volume will be created in `c:\winnt\sysvol`.

Step 4: Specifying the Full DNS Name for the New Domain

Now you have to give your new domain a full DNS name. For more information on selecting an appropriate domain name, see Chapter 7, "Planning a Dynamic DNS Structure." The section "Creating DDNS Naming Standards" offers guidelines for naming Windows 2000 domains. For this example, name your new domain `chicago.mycompany.com`.

Step 5: Setting the Directory Database and Log Locations

For this step, you define where to store the Active Directory database and log files. The default selection is to store them in the `%systemroot%\ntds` folder. However, you should consider moving these files to a separate disk subsystem for enhanced performance. The disk subsystem you select for your Active Directory database should be optimized for random access. The log files, on the other hand, will be better off on a subsystem that is optimized for sequential access. For this example, stick with the default selection.

Step 6: Specifying the Directory for the System Volume

Your next task is to specify the shared folder that will be used for the Windows 2000 system volume. The default location for the SYSVOL share is the `%systemroot%\sysvol` folder. The only requirement for SYSVOL is that it be stored on a volume formatted with NTFS 5.0. The SYSVOL share contains files that are used to support every member of the domain, such as Group Policy files and logon scripts. For the sake of simplicity, select `c:\winnt\sysvol` as the directory for your SYSVOL share.

Step 7: Confirming Your Choices and Starting the Installation

When you finalize your selections, the Windows 2000 confirmation dialog box appears. This dialog box lists the choices you made while running the installation wizard, which include:

- The DNS name of your domain
- The NetBIOS name of your domain
- The Active Directory database location
- The Active Directory log file location
- The location of your shared SYSVOL folder

Verify that these selections are indeed correct, and then start the Active Directory installation routine. The wizard will alert you if any problems occur.

Step 8: Completing the Installation Wizard

If your installation is successful, you are presented with a final dialog box. This dialog box lets you know that the domain, `chicago.mycompany.com`, was created successfully. It also tells you that your domain controller has been placed in the default site, *Default-First-Site-Name*. After reviewing this dialog box, you can exit the wizard. The installation of Active Directory on your domain controller is now complete.

Running the Configure Server Wizard

The Configure Server Wizard provides a common interface for configuring a range of server settings. After installing Active Directory, you must reboot your server. The Configure Server Wizard is displayed automatically after this reboot. You can accomplish the following tasks from this easy-to-use interface:

- Registering your installation
- Configuring and managing Active Directory
- Installing and managing network services
- Creating and managing shared folders
- Installing and configuring printers
- Establishing and managing Web services
- Installing and managing clustering services
- Installing advanced Windows services

Of course, if you're not a fan of wizards, you can also install, manage, and configure these same services using the standard Windows 2000 user interface.

Validating the Windows 2000 Upgrade

You should get into the habit of validating an upgrade to Windows 2000 with a series of simple tests. These tests can help you verify that your server is in good working order. The validation processes included in the following sections are by no means comprehensive. These tests only verify whether or not the core components of your servers are functioning properly. These validation techniques are explored further in the following sections.

Testing Basic Connectivity

By running a few basic connectivity tests, you can confirm a server's ability to communicate on the network. The first test you should perform is a simple ping test. Attempt to ping another host on your network, as shown in the following example:

```
C:\>ping chidc002

Pinging chidc002.mycompany.com [205.231.234.55] with 32 bytes of data:

Reply from 205.231.234.55: bytes=32 time<10ms TTL=128
Reply from 205.231.234.55: bytes=32 time<10ms TTL=128
Reply from 205.231.234.55: bytes=32 time<10ms TTL=128
Reply from 205.231.234.55: bytes=32 time<10ms TTL=128

Ping statistics for 205.231.234.55:
    Packets: Sent = 4, Received = 4, Lost = 0 (0% loss),
Approximate round trip times in milli-seconds:
    Minimum = 0ms, Maximum =  0ms, Average =  0ms
```

If you have trouble pinging another host, your server's TCP/IP settings may be improperly configured. Verify the TCP/IP configuration of the server using `ipconfig`, as shown below:

```
C:\>ipconfig /all

Windows NT IP Configuration

        Host Name . . . . . . . . . : CHIDC001
        Primary Domain Name . . . . : chicago.mycompany.com
        Node Type . . . . . . . . . : Hybrid
        IP Routing Enabled. . . . . : No
        WINS Proxy Enabled. . . . . : No

Ethernet adapter Local Area Connection:

        Adapter Domain Name . . . . : chicago.mycompany.com
        DNS Servers . . . . . . . . : 205.231.234.57
        Description . . . . . . . . : 3Com 3C90x Ethernet Adapter
        Physical Address. . . . . . : 00-10-4B-93-C5-16
        DHCP Enabled. . . . . . . . : No
        Autoconfiguration Enabled . : Yes
        IP Address. . . . . . . . . : 205.231.234.57
        Subnet Mask . . . . . . . . : 255.255.255.0
        Default Gateway . . . . . . : 205.231.234.1
        Primary WINS Server . . . . : 205.231.234.55
```

The `ipconfig` command gives you a lot of useful information. It can usually help you get to the bottom of any connectivity problem. For example, if CHIDC001 were configured with the wrong DNS address, you'd know why your previous ping test failed.

If you're still having connectivity problems, you can perform more tests using `netdiag`. This handy utility from the Windows 2000 Resource Kit can be used to diagnose and fix a number of problems. The following example shows several tests you might want to try to help diagnose a connectivity problem:

```
netdiag /test:IpConfig       - IP config Test
netdiag /test:NetBTTransports        - NetBT transports Test
netdiag /test:IpLoopBk       - IP loopback ping Test
netdiag /test:DefGw          - Default gateway Test
netdiag /test:NbtNm          - NetBT name Test
netdiag /test:WINS          - WINS service Test
netdiag /test:DNS          - DNS Test
netdiag /test:Browser          - Redir and Browser Test
netdiag /test:Route          - Routing table Test
netdiag /test:Ndis          - Netcard queries Test
netdiag /test:Bindings       - Bindings Test
```

Testing Active Directory

You should also verify your installation of Active Directory. The success or failure of the installation is first indicated in the final dialog box of the Active Directory Installation Wizard. You should perform a few more simple tests to validate this installation routine. These include the following:

- Verify that the Active Directory database is created in the location you specified. The full path of this file is usually `%systemroot%\ntds\ntds.dit`.

- Launch the Directory Management tool to see if you can navigate through the Active Directory hierarchy.

- Verify that users, groups, and computers from your Windows NT domain are present in Active Directory.

- Check to see that the system volume was created in the location you specified. The default location for this volume is `%systemroot%\sysvol`.

Get in the habit of running through these simple tests each time you install Active Directory. The one time you find a serious problem will make up for the thirty times you don't.

Testing Dynamic DNS

You should perform another series of tests to see whether or not Dynamic DNS (DDNS) is functioning. Like the tests for Active Directory, the tests for validating DDNS are relatively straightforward. These include the following:

- Verify that you can resolve a host name to an IP address, as well as an IP address to a host name.

- Launch the DNS MMC snap-in to view the integrity of the DNS zone.

- Check to see whether the DNS zone is enabled for dynamic updates.

- Verify the forward and reverse lookup DNS zones for the domain.

- Check to see if LDAP SRV records are listed in the `%systemroot%\system32\config\netlogon.dns` file.

- Run a simple LDAP SRV record test with the following `nslookup` command:

```
C:\>nslookup
>set type=SRV
>ldap.tcp.chicago.mycompany.com

ldap.tcp.chicago.mycompany.com  SRV service location:
    priority    = 0
    weight      = 0
    port        = 389
    svr hostname    = chidc001.chicago.mycompany.com
chidc001.chicago.mycompany.com internet address = 205.231.234.57
```

These tests are just as important as those you run for Active Directory. Taking a little extra time to validate DNS services is well worth the effort.

Upgrading Domains to Windows 2000

This section looks at how several example companies would transition from Windows NT to Windows 2000. Just about every upgrade to Windows 2000 will be somewhat unique. Although many companies will share some of the same reasons for making their transition, each will have a peculiar dynamic that sets it apart from the crowd. This section makes an effort to capture a sampling of these dynamics by illustrating how four companies would upgrade to Windows 2000 using these different domain models:

- The single domain model
- The single master domain model
- The multi master domain model
- The complete trust domain model

The Single Domain Model

The single Windows NT 4.0 domain shown in Figure 12.3 supports the small office of Salt Creek Software. Several lead developers are responsible for the day-to-day administration of shared resources in the SALTCREEK domain. This small software company is moving to Windows 2000 to support its latest development efforts.

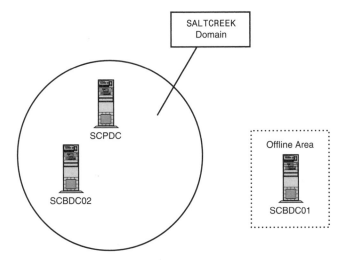

Figure 12.3   During the upgrade of the single NT 4.0 domain for Salt Creek Software, SCBDC01 is moved offline.

The company's administrators have carefully planned their transition to Windows 2000. Before the scheduled upgrade of the SALTCREEK domain, the integrity of their backup and restore process is verified. The two lead developers for the company have also selected and registered an appropriate domain name, saltcreeksoftware.com. Because the company is relatively small, an OU delegation plan was examined, but was not required.

The shared resources of Salt Creek Software will be centrally administered. The following steps outline the upgrade of the SALTCREEK domain to Windows 2000:

1. The company's administrators make a full backup of the SALTCREEK domain controllers (SCPDC, SCBDC01, and SCBDC02).

2. Before starting the upgrade, they take the SCBDC01 backup domain controller offline.

3. The Windows 2000 upgrade procedure is then run on the primary domain controller, SCPDC.

4. The administrators validate the upgrade to Windows 2000 by testing basic connectivity, Active Directory, and DDNS.

Figure 12.4 shows the saltcreeksoftware.com domain at this stage in the upgrade. SCPDC now emulates the role of an NT 4.0 primary domain controller. It replicates any updates it receives to SCBDC02. SCBDC01 is still offline.

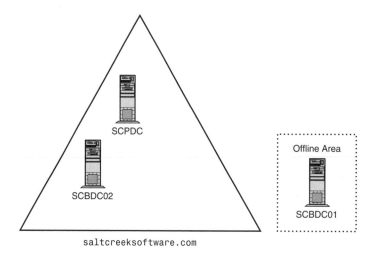

SCPDC

SCBDC02

Offline Area

SCBDC01

saltcreeksoftware.com

Figure 12.4 The saltcreeksoftware.com domain is now operating in mixed mode, and all changes in the domain are replicated to SCBDC02.

The company's administrators want to move the domain from mixed mode to native mode as soon as they can. When they are satisfied with the stability of SCPDC, they move SCBDC01 back into production. Both backup domain controllers are then upgraded to Windows 2000 the following weekend. This allows the company's administrators to switch the `saltcreeksoftware.com` domain to native mode operation. Once the domain is in native mode, replication between domain controllers is multi master, universal groups can be created, and all group accounts can be nested.

The Single Master Domain Model

Midwest Transit uses the single master domain model shown in Figure 12.5. This mid-sized tour bus operator has offices in Chicago and throughout the western suburbs. The administrators in the Chicago office have centralized the management of the company's users and groups. Administrators in each individual location—Westchester, Oakbrook, and Naperville—are responsible for managing the company's distributed resources.

The `CHITRANSIT` domain is the company's master domain. The company's three resource domains have been named for the locations they represent: `WESTCHESTER`, `OAKBROOK`, and `NAPERVILLE`. Midwest Transit will upgrade its single master domain model in several stages. The company's administrators have decided on a top-down approach, in which the master domain is upgraded to Windows 2000 before any of the resource domains.

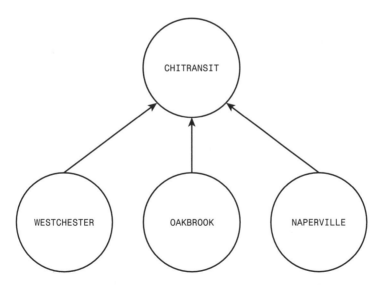

Figure 12.5 The `CHITRANSIT` domain in this single master domain model will be upgraded to Windows 2000 first.

The following steps outline Midwest Transit's upgrade of its master domain:

1. The backup and restore procedure is verified to make sure it is stable before-hand.

2. Before upgrading the primary domain controller, administrators take a backup domain controller offline.

3. The primary domain controller, `TRANSITPDC`, is then upgraded to Windows 2000 and Active Directory.

4. The administrators validate the upgrade procedure by testing basic connectivity, Active Directory, and DDNS.

Figure 12.6 shows the Midwest Transit network after the upgrade of the primary domain controller in its master domain to Windows 2000. The master domain now has two valid names on the wire: a NetBIOS name and a DNS name[3]. In addition, several other important characteristics of the Midwest Transit network should be noted:

■ The one-way trust relationships between the master domain and the resource domains are still valid.

■ Clients in the network can still authenticate to the master domain using NTLM.

---

3. The company formally registered the `midwest-transit.com` domain name with the InterNIC. If another company were to register `midwest-transit.com`, clients would have difficulty distinguishing between internal and external resources.

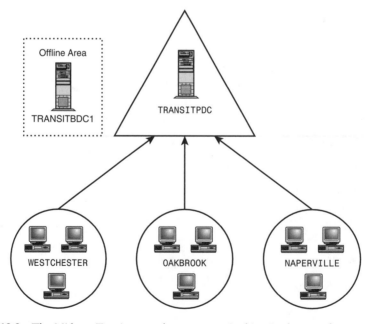

Figure 12.6   The Midwest Transit network can operate in this mixed state as long as necessary.

■ Single master replication occurs between `TRANSITPDC` and the NT 4.0 backup domain controllers in the master domain.

■ Every downlevel client sees the upgraded domain controller as an NT 4.0 primary domain controller.

No functionality, security, or performance is compromised by running Windows 2000 in the master domain and Windows NT in the resource domains. The company's users and administrators can continue to work normally even if the former master domain is switched to native mode.

The Multi Master Domain Model

The multi master domain model shown in Figure 12.7 supports decentralized administration for Nationwide Brokerage, a full-service brokerage house. As with most other companies dealing in stocks, mutual funds, and other investments, security is of great concern to Nationwide. The company's master domains represent areas of the business that are managed autonomously. One side of the brokerage house deals only in managed accounts, whereas the other side handles more than 300,000 self-directed accounts. The employees that oversee managed accounts and self-directed accounts never mingle. However, managerial and executive-level personnel often share research, profit and loss data, and analysis of broad trends in the overall market.

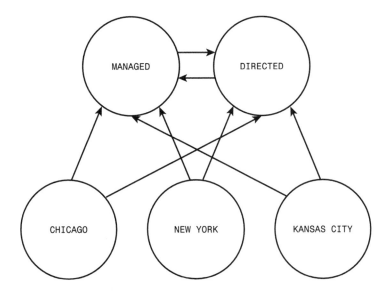

Figure 12.7 The current master domain model supports two autonomous entities: `MANAGED` and `DIRECTED`.

The administrators in each master domain have been working out a plan for Windows 2000 over the last six months. Their biggest fear is that their superiors will oppose streamlining the current domain model for perceived security reasons. The same administrative lines that exist today can be drawn by grouping the company's domains in a single Tree. This proposed design is shown in Figure 12.8. Instead of bickering over who becomes the root domain, the company's administrators have compromised. The root domain shown in Figure 12.8 is a "false root." No resources from either side of the brokerage house will be placed in the "false root" domain. Instead, a mix of administrators from both business lines will manage the root domain together. Both master user domains are then positioned to be subordinate to the root. Resource domains in each of the entities are then arranged and managed according to their requirements.

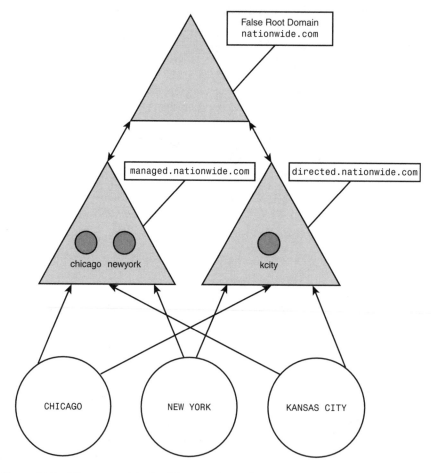

Figure 12.8 The proposed Active Directory design for Nationwide Brokerage calls for the elimination of the company's resource domains.

After several conference calls and scores of meetings, the executives and managers making decisions within Nationwide Brokerage approve the proposed design. The following upgrade plan is then established for the company's domains:

1. The "false root" will be created first.

2. The company's administrators will upgrade the master domains to Windows 2000.

3. Organizational units will be created in the former master domains to house resources from each of the resource domains.

4. The company's resource domains will be upgraded to Windows 2000 one-by-one until they've all been dissolved.

This configuration allows Nationwide Brokerage to maintain its current level of security, yet reduce the complexity of its domain structure.

The Complete Trust Domain Model

The complete trust domain model shown in Figure 12.9 is used by Bridgeworth Holdings, a real estate acquisitions and management conglomerate. In three short years, the company has acquired six properties in major metropolitan areas. Each property is managed independently by a small group of administrators. To share the company's resources, the administrators of Bridgeworth Holdings have created a web of two-way trust relationships.

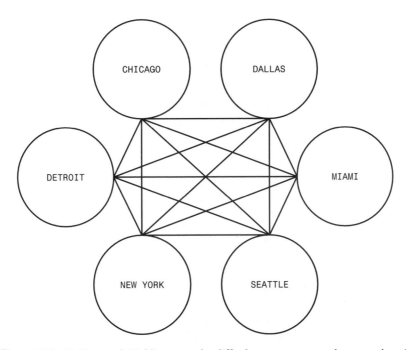

Figure 12.9   Bridgeworth Holdings uses the difficult-to-manage complete trust domain model.

The director of Bridgeworth Holdings has requested a more streamlined and manageable architecture. She is tired of the seemingly endless wait time required for administrative teams to coordinate and facilitate company-wide resource sharing. As a result of her request, the company's administrative teams work together to form the following upgrade plan:

- The NEWYORK domain that is now supporting the administrative offices in New York will be created as the root domain (bridgeworth.com).

- Every other domain in the company will be positioned directly beneath the root, as shown in Figure 12.10.

- Tree-wide administration will not be permitted, and policies will be defined only in individual domains.

Bridgeworth Holdings now has a more streamlined solution that doesn't interfere with the way it conducts business or manages its resources. The biggest benefit for companies using the complete trust model that upgrade to Windows 2000 is the ability to do away with the management of their trust relationships.

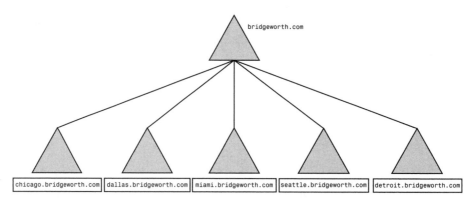

Figure 12.10   Moving its domains to a single Tree, the company no longer needs to manage a web of trusts.

Migrating to Windows 2000 Using the Directory Services Migration Tool

Microsoft provides a robust tool with Windows 2000 to help you migrate resources from Novell NetWare. Using the new Directory Service Migration Tool, you can migrate Bindery and NDS objects, as well as volumes from NetWare, to Windows 2000 and Active Directory. Making a case for the transition from NetWare to Windows 2000 is beyond the scope of this section. Instead, this section deals with the mechanics of the migration procedure itself.

The new Directory Service Migration Tool supports migration from NetWare versions 3.x, 4.x, and 5.0. This handy utility can be used to migrate information from the Bindery, NDS, and NetWare volumes to Windows 2000 and Active Directory. The migration from NetWare to Windows 2000 requires the following general steps:

1. Create and model a view from NetWare.

2. Configure a View to Active Directory.

3. Migrate NetWare volumes to Windows 2000.

Each of these steps is further detailed in the sections that follow.

Creating and Modeling a View from NetWare

The first step in a migration from NetWare to Windows 2000 is to collect information from the Bindery or from NDS[4]. This includes network objects such as users, groups, and/or organizational units. In the remainder of this section, you will walk through a migration from NetWare and NDS to Windows 2000 and Active Directory.

To start the migration, you launch the Directory Service Migration Tool. You then need to create a new project that will house your view from NetWare. For the purposes of this migration, assign this project the name NetWare 5 Migration. After you've established a project, you can create your View. In step 2 of 3 in the Discover Wizard, you will create your View of the NetWare NDS Tree.

When the discover process is finished, the objects from the naming context you selected in step 2 of 3 in the Discover Wizard are shown in your View. Your NetWare 5 Migration View contains the NDS Tree's organizational units, which house users and groups.

---

4. Versions 4.x or later of NetWare support Novell Directory Services (NDS). All other versions of NetWare store their objects, properties, and values in the Bindery (a flat database).

The ability to model information in a View before you configure it to Active Directory is one of the strengths of the Directory Service Migration Tool. You can now modify any object to suit your requirements before the migration. For example, you can add a user to a group or set options for creating new passwords. You can also create, delete, and move objects in the modeling phase and define how duplicate objects will merge. This capability is especially useful, because it allows you to modify the content and structure of your View before the migration. The modifications to your example View can include a hierarchical Domain DNS and OU structure to guide how your View is configured to Active Directory.

Configuring a View to Active Directory

When you finish working with the objects and general structure of your View from NetWare, you can configure it to Active Directory. You initiate the configuration process by selecting **Configure Objects to Active Directory**... from your View's drop-down context menu. This shows the source and destination containers for objects in the View.

When the pre-configure verification process is complete, you are asked to continue or cancel configuring the objects in your View to Active Directory. If you continue, a progress indicator appears as each object is created in Active Directory. Once the objects in your View have been created in Active Directory, you can exit the Directory Service Migration Tool.

You should then verify that each object in your View was created successfully. You can do this by launching the Windows 2000 Directory Management tool. The objects from the NDS Tree were migrated to your Windows 2000 domain. All of the users and groups from your NetWare server now exist in Active Directory.

Several rules govern how rights on objects in NDS convert to permissions in Active Directory. These rights-to-permissions mappings are shown in Table 12.2.

Advanced Options for Modeling a View

When modeling a View, you can closely control how passwords are assigned and how objects will merge. When you establish how passwords are created for users migrated to Active Directory, you have four options: Assign No Password, Assign a Random Password, Set Passwords to Users' Logon Names, and Assign Each User the Same Custom Password.

Your options for merging objects include: Append Multivalued Properties, Replace Multivalued Properties, and Replace Single Valued Properties.

Table 12.2   **Rights from NDS Versus Permissions in Active Directory**

NDS Object or Property Right	Active Directory Object or Property Permission
Supervisor object right	Equivalent to all permissions
Browse object right	Equivalent to the list object permission
Create object right	Equivalent to the create object permission
Delete object right	Equivalent to the delete object permission
Rename object right	Equivalent to the write property permission
Supervisor property right	Equivalent to all permissions
Compare property right	Equivalent to the read property permission
Read property right	Equivalent to the read property permission
Write property right	Equivalent to the write property permission

In addition, you need to be aware of another difference when migrating objects from NDS to Active Directory. NDS supports inherited rights filters (IRFs), which are used in NDS to block inheritable permissions from above. Because Active Directory does not support IRFs, the Directory Service Migration Tool migrates them using the following procedure:

1. It reads the NDS rights and then translates these rights into Windows 2000 permissions using the mappings shown in Table 12.2.

2. If the object being configured already exists, the tool changes its permissions from inherited to explicit.

3. Explicit permissions are combined with the permissions that were calculated in step 1.

4. The tool blocks all permissions inheritance from above.[5]

The Directory Service Migration Tool greatly simplifies migrating objects, properties, and their security attributes from NetWare to Windows 2000 and Active Directory.

Migrating NetWare Volumes to Windows 2000

You can also use the Directory Service Migration Tool to migrate files and their security attributes, as well as volume objects, from NetWare to Windows 2000. This migration process requires the following steps:

1. Right-click a volume object in your NetWare view and launch the File Migrate Wizard from the drop-down context menu.

2. When prompted, decide whether or not to migrate security attributes from the NetWare volume.

5. Notice that in Active Directory all permissions can be blocked from above, but individual permissions cannot.

3. Choose whether or not to migrate the files from the NetWare volume you've selected.

4. Specify the drive on your Windows 2000 server where the NetWare volume will be stored.

5. If you wish, change the share name that the Migration Wizard defined as a default on your Windows 2000 server in step 4.

6. Review the permissions that will be assigned to NetWare files that are migrated to your Windows 2000 file share.

7. The File Migrate Wizard creates the new share on your Windows 2000 server. After the share is created, the wizard completes the migration of the NetWare volume and all of its permissions.

After migrating the required volumes and permissions to Windows 2000, you can decommission your NetWare server. Users that once relied on the NetWare server can now access their resources from your newly created share.

13

Removing Resource Domains

WHEN YOU UPGRADE YOUR WINDOWS NT 3.x–4.0 domains to Windows 2000, you have the option of eliminating one or more of your existing resource domains. If you are currently using the single or multi master domain model, this can be a great opportunity to simplify and flatten your network. If you rely on the single domain model or the complete trust domain model, you shouldn't be concerned with removing resource domains; neither of those models has resource domains to eliminate. If this is not the case, however, you should strongly consider eliminating or reducing the number of your existing resource domains. To get rid of these domains, you can move their resources to organizational units in Active Directory.

Determining Which Resource Domains to Eliminate

To decide whether or not to eliminate a particular resource domain, examine your Active Directory design. Your design may call for fewer resource domains than your current domain model. If so, you should create a plan to eliminate them. For example, to meet the objectives of their Active Directory design, Thompson Oil plans to eliminate two of the three resource domains shown in Figure 13.1. This will help them simplify administration by reducing the number of current domains.

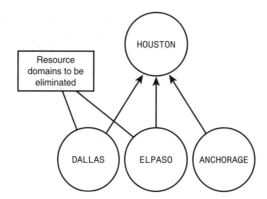

Figure 13.1   The ELPASO and DALLAS resource domains will be eliminated when Thompson Oil moves to Windows 2000. The ANCHORAGE domain will remain.

Many organizations will eliminate resource domains they created in NT 3.x–4.0 for reasons that would no longer be justified in Windows 2000. These resource domains were most often created to delegate administrative tasks or to comply with limits of the SAM. Establishing separate domains in Windows 2000 for either of these reasons is not valid.

For instance, it is no longer necessary to create a separate domain to delegate administrative tasks. Because Windows 2000 permits granular access control within domains, you can create organizational units instead. You also aren't forced to create separate domains to comply with limits of the SAM. Windows 2000 domains can be up to 17TB in size, and they can contain roughly 1,000,000 objects.

However, this does not necessarily mean that a single Windows 2000 domain can support all of an organization's needs. There are still many valid reasons for creating multiple Windows 2000 domains. These include the following:

- To support decentralized administration
- To isolate domain replication traffic
- To balance domain replication traffic
- To support multiple domain policies
- To address international differences
- To comply with internal political pressures

For more information on when to create multiple Windows 2000 domains, see Chapter 6, "Designing the Active Directory." The section "Determining When to Create a Domain" explains this in more detail. You should definitely not plan to remove a resource domain that is needed to meet any of these requirements.

For example, although the administrators of Thompson Oil would like to eliminate all three of their resource domains, they cannot. To support a unique password requirement in their Alaskan division, they need a second domain policy. Therefore, the `anchorage.thompsonoil.com` domain shown in Figure 13.2 must remain. The `DALLAS` and `ELPASO` domains can be eliminated, however. They were originally created to delegate administrative tasks to operations and help desk personnel. These same tasks can now be delegated at the organizational unit level instead.

Eliminating your company's resource domains is not always an all or nothing decision. You must closely evaluate the reasons that each particular resource domain exists in order to determine whether it should remain after your upgrade.

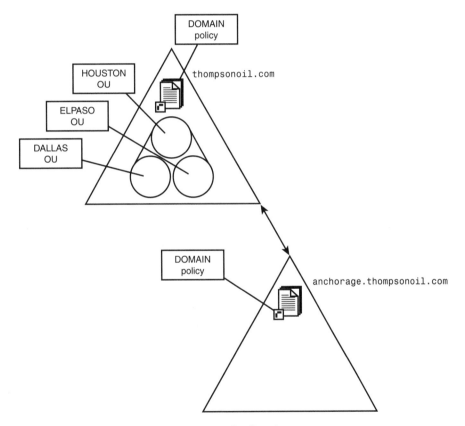

Figure 13.2   To support its unique password policy, the `anchorage.thompsonoil.com` resource domain remains separated from `thompsonoil.com` where organizational units now house resources from HOUSTON, ELPASO, and DALLAS.

Developing a Domain Upgrade Recovery Plan

After you determine the conditions under which you should eliminate a particular resource domain, you must carefully plan its removal to ensure that it is safe, predictable, and worth the effort. To move the resources from a resource domain to an organizational unit, you must first upgrade the domain from Windows NT to Windows 2000. However, before you upgrade any domain to Windows 2000, you should develop a sound recovery plan. This will give you a foolproof way of restoring the domain to its original state in the event of a serious problem. This section offers two alternatives for recovering a domain during your Windows 2000 upgrade:

- Taking a backup domain controller offline
- Upgrading an isolated primary domain controller

Taking a Backup Domain Controller Offline

You can preserve the state of a domain during an upgrade to Windows 2000 by moving one of the domain's backup domain controllers offline first. Safeguarding this backup domain controller gives you added insurance against potential problems in your upgrade.

Figure 13.3 shows this recovery strategy in more detail. The PACIFIC resource domain consists of a primary domain controller and two backup domain controllers (PACPDC01, PACBDC01, and PACBDC02). Before upgrading its domain to Windows 2000, the company's administrators take the PACBDC02 backup domain controller offline. During scheduled downtime, the domain's primary domain controller, PACPDC01, is then upgraded to Windows 2000. If the upgrade of PACPDC01 fails, it will be removed from the network and replaced by the company's offline backup domain controller. The offline backup domain controller, PACBDC02, will then be promoted to the role of primary domain controller.

Taking this sort of precaution before you upgrade a domain is often worthwhile. It is possible to corrupt the SAM on every backup domain controller if the upgrade of your primary domain controller fails. However, if you store a working backup domain controller offline, you have the option of promoting it to primary status in the event of a failure. That new primary domain controller would then hold the only Read/Write copy of the SAM. Any corruption in the domain would be eliminated when backup domain controllers synchronized with the SAM stored on your primary.

> **Should You Eliminate Your Resource Domains Before or After Your Upgrade to Windows 2000?**
>
> As you may remember, the topic of eliminating resource domains was also covered in Chapter 2, "Restructuring Downlevel Domains." That chapter offers strategies for preparing for Windows 2000 by restructuring or eliminating domains *before* your upgrade. This chapter, on the other hand, explains how to eliminate domains *after* your upgrade. If you're still trying to decide whether to remove a particular domain before or after your upgrade, see the section "Understanding Your Restructuring Options" in Chapter 2. It can make deciding when to eliminate domains a whole lot easier.

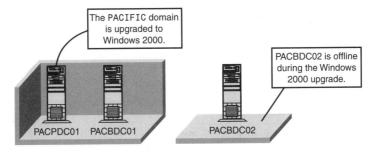

Figure 13.3 Moving a backup domain controller offline before your Windows 2000 upgrade
lets you preserve the state of the SAM if necessary.

Upgrading an Isolated Primary Domain Controller

You can also safely upgrade a domain by moving its primary domain controller to an
isolated network. This strategy is further detailed in Figure 13.4. Before upgrading the
NORTHWEST resource domain to Windows 2000, the company's administrators move the
primary domain controller to an isolated network. The primary domain controller is
then upgraded to Windows 2000. Because NWPDC01 is offline during the upgrade,
any problems that arise are confined to the isolated network. If the upgrade of
NWPDC01 fails, the company's administrators can promote one of their backup
domain controllers to primary status. If the upgrade goes well, the primary domain
controller is moved back to the production network.

It is worth noting that you should not promote a backup domain controller to a
primary unless the upgrade of your primary domain controller fails. If you promote a
backup domain controller beforehand and then make changes to the SAM, those
changes will be lost when you bring your Windows 2000 domain controller online.

Both of these strategies allow you to reverse the effects of a failed Windows 2000
upgrade. You can employ either recovery plan to bring a domain back to its original
state in the event of a serious problem.

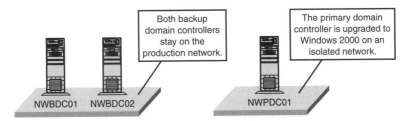

Figure 13.4 Upgrading the primary domain controller on an isolated network prevents
potential problems on the production network.

Preparing for Post-Upgrade Administration

The process of removing a resource domain, which you will walk through later on, involves moving resources in the domain to organizational units. Moving a resource such as a user, computer, or group to an organizational unit affects how it can be administered. For example, consider the administrators of resource domains in the single and multi master domain models. By default, these administrators can only create and manage user, group, and computer accounts in the resource domain itself. This changes after you move these resources to organizational units. Your former resource domain administrators can now be delegated the ability to create and manage user, group, or computer accounts in the entire organizational unit.

Therefore, another task that you should complete before upgrading to Windows 2000 concerns administration. You should carefully prepare for the administration of every resource that will move from a resource domain to an organizational unit. Your company should create a comprehensive post-upgrade administration plan. This plan must include details regarding how administrators in resource domains you plan to eliminate will perform everyday administration after your upgrade.

Moving resources from a resource domain to an organizational unit often benefits the former domain's administrators. You can then delegate the following tasks to former resource domain administrators:

- Completely control an organizational unit and all of its contents
- Create all child objects in an organizational unit
- Delete all child objects in an organizational unit
- Create user objects in an organizational unit
- Delete user objects in an organizational unit
- Modify the group memberships for user objects in an organizational unit
- Reset passwords for user objects in an organizational unit
- Create group objects in an organizational unit
- Delete group objects in an organizational unit
- Modify the member list for group objects in an organizational unit
- Create printer objects in an organizational unit
- Delete printer objects in an organizational unit

This list is quite lengthy, but it is not even close to being comprehensive. For more details on delegating administrative tasks in organizational units, see Chapter 6, "Designing the Active Directory." The section "Strategies for Delegating OU Administration" includes many more details, as well as recommendations for delegating administrative tasks. You should use that section to further define your post-upgrade administration plan.

Eliminating a Resource Domain

If you take the time to plan ahead, eliminating a resource domain will be relatively simple. By now you should have verified that your reasons for eliminating each resource domain are indeed valid. The details of your domain upgrade recovery plan should be clear, and your strategy for post-upgrade administration should be fully defined. With each of these essential requirements out of the way, you are well prepared to flatten and simplify your network.

To remove a resource domain, follow these steps:

1. Implement the domain upgrade recovery plan you've chosen in your master domain.
2. Upgrade the domain controllers in your master domain to Windows 2000.
3. Create one or more organizational units in your former master domain.
4. Implement the domain upgrade recovery plan you've chosen in your resource domain.
5. Upgrade the domain controllers in your resource domain to Windows 2000.
6. Move users and groups to organizational units in your former master domain.
7. Move member servers and workstations to your former master domain.
8. Shut down the domain controllers in your former resource domain.

The following sections walk you through each of these steps in great detail. Throughout these steps, you'll be studying the plans of a company called Northeast Publishing.

Step 1: Implementing a Recovery Plan in the Master Domain

To recuperate from a serious problem during your upgrade, you must implement your domain recovery plan. This plan must allow you to restore your domain to the state it was in before the upgrade.

The administrators of Northeast Publishing plan to eliminate the two resource domains shown in Figure 13.5. The company currently uses the single master domain model to manage its resources in Manchester, Boston, and Montpelier. The large office in Manchester is the company's center of operations. Boston and Montpelier are connected to Manchester over wide area links. To minimize disruption, Northeast Publishing plans to upgrade its master domain over a long weekend.

Before the domain is upgraded to Windows 2000, the NEBDC01 backup domain controller shown in Figure 13.5 is taken offline. This will enable the company's administrators to reverse the upgrade procedure in the event of a failure.

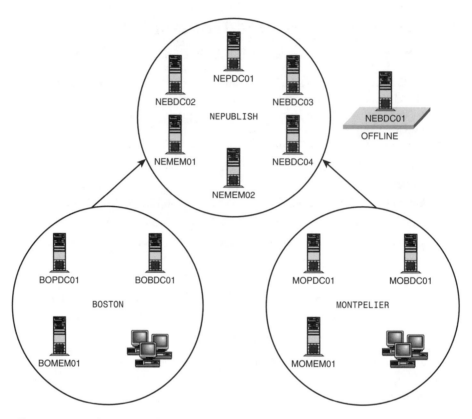

Figure 13.5 Before you take your backup domain controller offline, verify that replication in the master domain is up-to-date and check the quality of your most recent backup.

Step 2: Upgrading Domain Controllers in the Master Domain

The next step is to upgrade the domain controllers in your master domain. If this domain is the first in your enterprise to be upgraded, it will become the root domain in Active Directory. You must upgrade the primary domain controller in your master domain first. (If you need more details on the Windows 2000 upgrade procedure, see Chapter 12, "Windows 2000 Upgrade and Migration." It outlines the upgrade procedure from start to finish.)

After you upgrade the primary domain controller in your master domain, the domain operates in what is known as mixed mode. The former master domain and resource domains for Northeast Publishing are shown in Figure 13.6. The master domain is now the root domain in Active Directory. Its newly assigned name is nepublish.com. For downlevel compatibility, it also retains its NetBIOS name, NEPUBLISH.

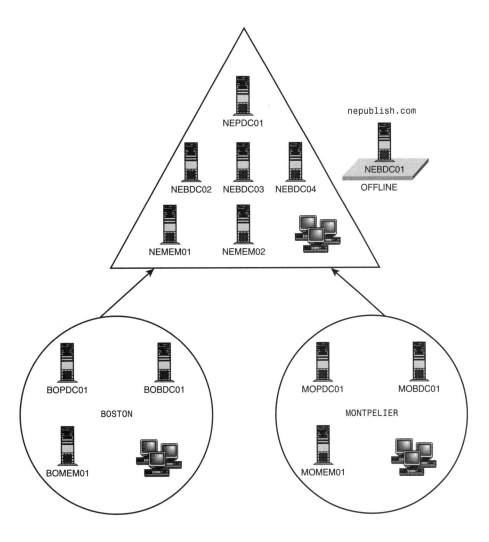

Figure 13.6 When a domain operates in mixed mode, it can support both downlevel computers and directory-enabled computers.

This mixed mode domain now has the following characteristics:

- The new Windows 2000 domain controller, NEPDC01, appears to all backup domain controllers and downlevel clients as an NT 3.x–4.0 primary domain controller.

- The upgraded primary domain controller uses single master replication to replicate its domain database to NEBDC02, NEBDC03, and NEBDC04. The NEBDC01 backup domain controller remains offline.

- Kerberos and NTLM are both supported for authentication in the domain. Downlevel computers continue to use NTLM. However, any directory-enabled clients in the domain, which include Windows 2000 computers and Windows 9x computers with the DSClient installed, have the option to use Kerberos.

- The former master domain now supports the creation of transitive trusts. However, any trust relationships that were created before the upgrade (such as the one-way trusts that were created to support each resource domain) are not converted. Further, while in mixed mode, transitive trusts are available only to directory-enabled computers.

- Structural elements, such as organizational units, can now be created in the former master domain (now the root domain in Active Directory). This allows administrators to arrange users, groups, and computers in the domain in a more intuitive hierarchy.

- The ability to read, write, and delete objects in Active Directory is available to all directory-enabled clients (with appropriate permissions). However, downlevel clients, such as those without the DSClient installed, continue to view and manage objects in the domain as if they existed in the NT 3.x–4.0 SAM.

Your former master domain must operate in mixed mode until all backup domain controllers in the domain have been upgraded. If the upgrade of your primary domain controller is a success, you can immediately begin this process. For example, after verifying that the upgrade of NEPDC01 is a success, the administrators of Northeast Publishing upgrade NEBDC01, NEBDC02, NEBDC03, and NEBDC04. The former master domain is then switched to native mode. The native mode domain now has the following traits:

- The domain now supports multi master replication between all domain controllers. This allows directory updates to occur at any domain controller in the domain. However, no downlevel domain controllers can be added to the domain after you switch it to native mode.

- The domain continues to advertise its existence using its NetBIOS name and its new DDNS name. This allows downlevel and directory-enabled computers to locate domain controllers in the domain for authentication purposes.

- The domain still supports both Kerberos and NTLM authentication. This lets domain controllers in the native mode domain authenticate both downlevel and directory-enabled computers.

- The trust relationships that were created in the domain before the upgrade remain intact. This includes the one-way trusts created to support the BOSTON and MONTPELIER resource domains.

- If a transitive trust relationship is created between the former master domain and another domain, that trust will be transitive for both downlevel and directory-enabled computers.

- The creation of universal groups and the nesting of groups is now supported in the domain.

Step 3: Creating OUs in the Upgraded Master Domain

You will need to create organizational units in your new Windows 2000 domain to store the resources from any resource domains you eliminate. To plan this structure, you need to closely examine your company's organizational and administrative requirements. For more details on creating organizational units, see Chapter 6, "Designing the Active Directory." The section "Planning an OU Structure" can help you decide when it is appropriate to create an organizational unit.

To move forward with the company's domain removal effort, the administrators of Northeast Publishing create the two organizational units shown in Figure 13.7.

Step 4: Implementing a Recovery Plan in the Resource Domain

Before you upgrade any domain controller in your resource domain, you should implement your recovery plan. Use the same kind of preventive measures you did when upgrading your master domain. This will allow you to reverse the upgrade process in the event of a failure. Both of the resource domains in the Northeast Publishing network are shown in Figure 13.8; however, the company's administrators have chosen a different recovery plan. Instead of moving a backup domain controller offline, they have settled on the second alternative. In each resource domain, they will upgrade the primary domain controller on an isolated network.

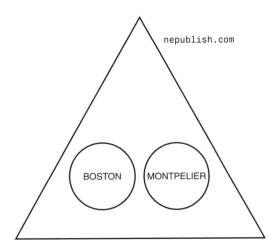

Figure 13.7   The resources in the BOSTON and MONTPELIER domains will eventually move to organizational units in nepublish.com.

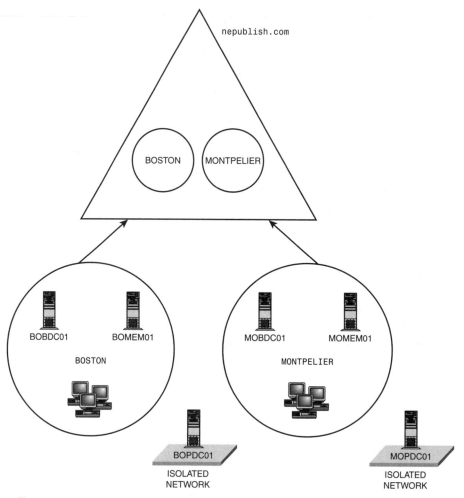

Figure 13.8 Upgrading BOPDC01 and MOPDC01 on isolated networks means that any problems in the upgrade remain isolated from production computers.

Step 5: Upgrading Domain Controllers in the Resource Domain

The next step is to upgrade the domain controllers in your resource domains. In the course of this upgrade, each resource domain must be created as a child domain in Active Directory. You can't upgrade a resource domain directly to an organizational unit in your former master domain.

The recovery plan for Northeast Publishing calls for the primary domain controllers in the BOSTON and MONTPELIER domains to be upgraded on isolated networks. After the success of these upgrades is verified, the BOPDC01 and MOPDC01 domain controllers are moved back into production. Figure 13.9 shows the new structure of the Northeast Publishing network.

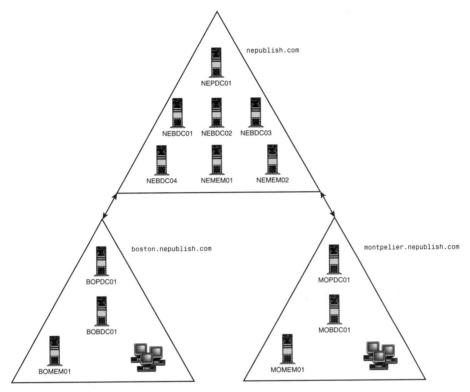

Figure 13.9 In this new structure, the former master domain, `nepublishing.com`, is the root domain in the company's Tree. The other two domains are subordinate to the root.

The company's administrators can now begin upgrading their backup domain controllers (BODC01 and MOBDC01). After they successfully upgrade BOBDC01 and MOBDC01, they can switch each resource domain from mixed to native mode.

Step 6: Moving Users and Groups to the Former Master Domain

With all of your domains in native mode, you can now move such resources as users and groups from your resource domains to organizational units. For long-time administrators of Microsoft networks, this feat will seem impossible. The root of disbelief in the minds of most administrators will be grounded in the fundamentals of security.

To implement access control for its objects, both Windows NT and Windows 2000 use access control lists (ACLs). These ACLs define an object's security properties. Listed in the ACL of every object are one or more access control entries (ACEs). ACEs define access rights to an object for particular users, groups, or special identities. An ACE is not the display name of a user or group, such as Thomas Jones or Accounting. Instead, an ACE is made of a string known as a security identifier (or SID).

The SID of a particular object always identifies the domain in which it was issued. To move a user from one NT 3.x–4.0 domain to another, you must re-create that user in the target domain. This newly created user will receive a new SID. When the user receives the new SID, all access permissions previously associated with the user are lost. This is not the case in Windows 2000 networks.

Figure 13.10 shows what happens when you move a user or group from one Windows 2000 domain to another. When you move an object to another Windows 2000 domain, it is always assigned a new SID. However, that object's original SID is retained in what is known as its SIDHistory property. This allows two or more SIDs to be associated with the object. With multiple SIDs, a user that you move to another domain can continue to access resources in his or her original domain.

Select user and group accounts from the former Northeast Publishing resource domains are moved to their respective organizational units through the UI. It is worth noting that you should not have to move many user and group accounts from resource domains. After all, the user accounts in the single and multi master models should reside in the master domains—not the resource domains.

Step 7: Moving Member Servers and Workstations to the Former Master Domain

You can now approach the task of moving your member servers and workstations to your former master domain. Moving a member server to your new domain will not affect a client's ability to find it. For example, a client that normally attaches to \\BOMEM01\APPS is able to connect to that share regardless of the server's domain membership. It doesn't matter if \\BOMEM01 belongs to the BOSTON domain or to the BOSTON organizational unit in nepublishing.com.

To move a server or workstation to your former master domain, you must modify its domain membership information, which you can do through the computer's Network Identification tab. You can also use the NETDOM.EXE utility from the NT 4.0 Resource Kit, as in the following command:

```
netdom.exe /domain:MasterDomain member %computername% /joindomain
```

Moving Large Numbers of Users and Groups to Another Windows 2000 Domain

In most cases, you will not have to move many users and groups from one Windows 2000 domain to another. However, if you are faced with this task, see the Windows 2000 Resource Kit. It contains several utilities that will make moving users and groups en masse a whole lot easier.

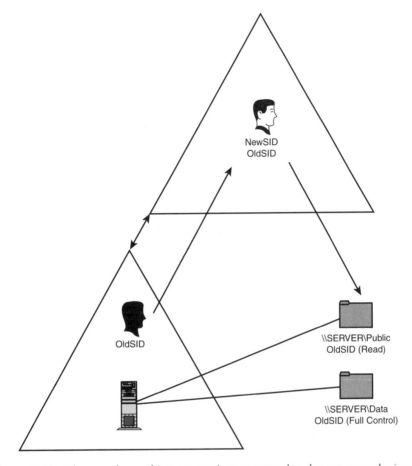

NewSID
OldSID

OldSID

\\SERVER\Public
OldSID (Read)

\\SERVER\Data
OldSID (Full Control)

Figure 13.10 The moved user object can continue to access data that was secured using the SID issued in its original domain.

Step 8: Shutting Down Domain Controllers in the Former Resource Domain

After moving your workstations and member servers to your former master domain, you can shut down domain controllers in your former resource domains. This is the final step in the domain removal process. After you decommission the domain controllers in your resource domains, you can use them for other purposes.

Figure 13.11 shows the state of the Northeast Publishing network after its two resource domains were removed. Notice that all the company's resources now reside in `nepublishing.com`. The post-upgrade administration plan for the company dictates that the management of resources in the BOSTON and MONTPELIER organizational units be delegated to the company's former resource domain administrators.

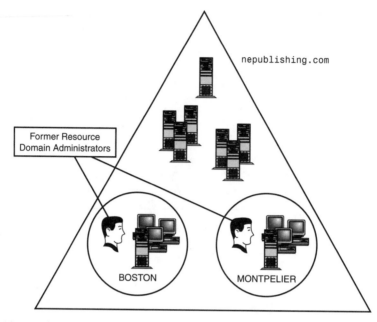

Figure 13.11 The users, groups, member servers, and workstations from the company's former resource domains are now managed in organizational units.

If you take the time to carefully plan the removal of your resource domains, simplifying and flattening your network can be a safe, predictable, and worthwhile process. Remember the time it takes to complete this process each time you consider creating another Windows 2000 domain. With the ability to leverage granular access control, you should never again be forced to create structure for the sake of structure itself.

14

Putting It All Together

BECAUSE EACH CHAPTER IN THIS BOOK has a unique focus, the requirements to meet each chapter's objectives are unique as well. The primary goal of *Planning for Windows 2000* is to give you the information you need to understand and meet these requirements. Your approach to carrying out the recommendations explained in these chapters will have a significant impact on your transition to Windows 2000. How well you prepare for Windows 2000, the focus of Part I, will greatly influence the success of your move from Windows NT to Windows 2000. Likewise, your approach to design, the focus of Part II, will have a significant bearing on the quality of services in your new Windows 2000 network. Finally, your understanding of the Windows 2000 upgrade procedure, detailed in Part III, will be extremely helpful during your implementation, although it will do you little good if you fail to take the time to adequately prepare beforehand. To carry out a successful Windows 2000 upgrade, you must plan ahead. Planning this transition, rather than the implementation itself, should be your primary focus.

This chapter includes a section for each preceding chapter and major topic in Parts I, II, and III. In each of this chapter's sections, you will find a series of checklists and planning templates. Each checklist is a "to do" list of requirements that you must carry out to meet the objectives in a particular chapter. This can include performing tasks such as planning a domain structure, forming a standard for authentication, or validating a Windows 2000 upgrade.

You will need to collect a fair amount of information to complete the majority of tasks presented in these checklists. This is precisely where the planning templates can help. Each planning template lists the information you must collect to complete a particular task. For example, some of the information that you must collect for the template for planning a domain structure includes the company's physical locations, the speed of its local and remote links, and the utilization of its local and remote links.

These checklists and templates are certainly not a replacement for the preceding thirteen chapters. They only specify which tasks to perform and what information to collect to meet a particular objective. To understand the significance of the data you collect, you must be familiar with the topic at hand. Hence, each checklist and template should be used in conjunction with its corresponding chapter.

Leading a transition to Windows 2000 using checklists and templates is a good start, but there remains room for improvement. Only the smallest of companies will be successful using this fairly basic approach. The amount of work that is required to move to Windows 2000 is substantial, to say the least. It's probably not too much of a stretch to say that this is one of the largest tasks on your plate this year. Simply put, to be successful you must run your transition to Windows 2000 as a project. You are much more likely to do well in this transition if you use a proven methodology with a track record of success. Most medium- and large-sized companies execute tasks such as this following a public or privately developed methodology.

Figure 14.1 shows the details of a very basic project methodology. Some of the tasks that are executed when following this methodology are listed beneath the boxes representing each major phase in the project. For example, in the Gather Requirements phase, the methodology dictates that you must determine the scope of the project requirements. It is worth noting that the methodologies that are used by leading companies and top IT consulting firms are much more detailed than this. If you work for an organization of considerable size, and you don't plan to use a structured methodology to transition to Windows 2000, we wish you a whole lot of luck[1].

Basic Project Methodology

Gather Requirements	Form Approach	Test Approach	Rollout
Determine the scope of project requirements	Develop approach to meet project requirements	Create lab for testing	Pilot approach in production environment
		Test approach in the lab	
Conduct meetings to further define the requirements	Create an acceptance test plan	Refine the approach and document any changes	Perform acceptance test plan against pilot
Inventory the environment	Document the approach		Refine approach if necessary
			Rollout

Figure 14.1   The four phases included in this basic project methodology must be completed in sequence.

1. If you have no methodology in place, but you would like to start using one, you can start with the Microsoft Solutions Framework, which is publicly available at www.microsoft.com.

Part I: Preparing for Windows 2000

Part I includes topics to help you prepare for your eventual transition. These include topics you should explore well in advance of your move to Windows 2000. You can use the following checklists and planning templates to meet the objectives in Part I:

- Restructuring Downlevel Domains
- Implementing Standards
- Assessing Critical Applications
- Removing NetBIOS

Checklist: Restructuring Downlevel Domains

✓ Determine the organization's current domain model.

✓ Evaluate options to restructure the organization's domains.

✓ Choose tools to use for the domain restructuring project.

✓ Move applications and services from domain controllers to member servers if required.

✓ Consolidate domains using the chosen tool set if required.

Determining the Current Domain Model

Information to Collect	Your Information
Organization uses the single domain model	
Organization uses the single master domain model	
Organization uses the multi master domain model	
Organization uses the complete trust domain model	
The number of master domains	
The names of master domains	
The number of resource domains	
The names of resource domains	

Evaluating Options to Restructure Domains

Information to Collect	Your Information
Does the current domain model match your plans for Active Directory?	
The number of domains to eliminate to match your plans for Active Directory	
Are applications or services running on domain controllers in any domains you plan to get rid of?	
Are the number of domains you plan to eliminate greater than thirty percent of your total domains?	

Choosing Tools to Use for Restructuring

Information to Collect	Your Information
Number and size (in MB) of domains to eliminate in your Windows 2000 upgrade	
Number of domain controllers from which applications and services will be moved	
Estimate for time to move applications and services from domain controllers to member servers	
Estimate for time to consolidate domains using resource kit utilities	
Estimate for time to consolidate domains using a third-party tool	
The cost to move applications and services from domain controllers to member servers	
The cost of a third-party domain consolidation tool	
The cost of time to consolidate domains using Resource Kit utilities	

Moving Applications and Services

Information to Collect	Your Information
Domain controller where application and/or service now resides	
Member server that application and/or service will move to	
Steps required to move application and/or service from domain controller to member server	
Back out procedures for the transition of application and/or service from domain controller to member server	
Acceptance test plan that signifies that your application and/or service migration is successful	

Combining Domains Before the Upgrade

Information to Collect	Your Information
Source domains (domains that will be eliminated)	
Target domains (domains that will house resources from the eliminated domain)	
Size of the SAM database in source domains	
Size of the SAM database in target domains	
Total size of SAM after source domains and target domains combine	
Is total SAM size greater than 40MB?	
Speed of network links between source and target domain locations if any exist	
Will network links be adversely affected when combining your source and target domains?	
Were source domains created to delegate certain administrative tasks?	
Will combining source domains with target domains break the current administrative model?	
Will you use resource kit utilities or a third-party tool to combine domains?	

Checklist: Implementing Standards

✓ Discover the current status of the enterprise computing environment.

✓ Establish standards for the computing environment.

✓ Document the standard.

✓ Bring the computing environment into compliance with the standard.

✓ Maintain the standard.

✓ Review and update the standard.

Discovering the Current Status

Information to Collect	Your Information
Tools to use when discovering current status	
Which inventory items will be used for a baseline in establishing standards?	
Does hardware inventory show systems that are not Windows 2000 compliant?	
Does software inventory raise any licensing issues?	
Can inventory be used for the purposes of asset management and loss prevention?	
Will an inventory be used for Y2K preparedness?	

Establishing Standards

Information to Collect	Your Information
Basic hardware standards (CPU, RAM, HD, NIC, and so on)	
Preferred hardware standards (CPU, RAM, HD, NIC, and so on)	
BIOS standards (APM/ACPI, Windows 2000 compliant, and so on)	
System driver standards (RAID, SCSI, NIC, and so on)	
Software standards (Office suite, database manager, Web browser, anti-virus, and so on)	
Service standards (service name, version, and so on)	
Service pack, hot fixes/patches standards (service pack and hot fix versions)	
Naming standards (domain names, computer names, user names, and so on)	

Information to Collect	Your Information
Network protocol standards (TCP/IP, IPX/SPX, NetBEUI, and so on)	
User rights and permissions standards	

Documenting the Standard

Information to Collect	Your Information
Required meetings to ratify enterprise computing standards within IT	
Meetings that are required with the enduser community to approve these standards	
Teams to create and review the standards document	

Implementing, Maintaining, and Updating Standards

Information to Collect	Your Information
Standards to implement	
Number and frequency of standards that will be implemented in parallel	
Impact of change to the computing environment	
Is there a formal change control process?	
Plan to track changes to computing environment if no formal change control process is in place	
Plan to periodically review the standard Strategy for updating the standard	

Checklist: Assessing Critical Applications

✓ Identify critical applications.

✓ Discover problem applications.

✓ Upgrade or replace problem applications.

Identifying Critical Applications

Information to Collect	Your Information
Critical application definition for company	
Critical application list	

Discovering Problem DOS Applications

Information to Collect	Your Information
DOS applications that access hardware directly	
DOS applications that rely on the FAT file system	
DOS applications with Y2K issues	
DOS applications that cannot run in a window	
DOS applications that do not understand the Windows NT or Windows 2000 security model	

Discovering Problem Windows 3.x Applications

Information to Collect	Your Information
Windows 3.x (16-bit) applications that require a VXD for hardware access	
Windows 3.x (16-bit) applications that require the FAT file system	
Windows 3.x (16-bit) applications with Y2K issues	
Windows 3.x (16-bit) applications that do not understand the Windows NT or Windows 2000 security model	
Windows 3.x (16-bit) applications that require a specific Windows 3.x driver	
Windows 3.x (16-bit) applications that are CPU intensive	

Discovering Problem Windows 9x Applications

Information to Collect	Your Information
Windows 9x applications that require a specific Windows 9x driver	
Windows 9x applications that do not understand the Windows NT or Windows 2000 security model	
Windows 9x applications written to Windows 9x Win32 API	
Windows 9x applications that store user settings in HKLM instead of HKCU, or machine settings in HKCU rather than HKLM	

Discovering Problem Windows NT Applications

Information to Collect	Your Information
Windows NT services whose function is performed by Windows 2000	
Windows NT system utilities (disk defragm enters, backup software, and so on)	
Windows NT applications operating in OS/2 or a POSIX environmental subsystem	

Checklist: Removing NetBIOS

✓ Determine which applications and machines use NetBIOS.

✓ Determine the impact on the network of changing these applications and/or machines.

✓ Determine whether to upgrade, replace, or retire NetBIOS applications and machines.

✓ Implement Dynamic DNS in the network.

✓ Move to Windows 2000 and implement plan to remove NetBIOS applications and services.

✓ Decommission WINS.

Transitioning from NetBIOS to DDNS

Information to Collect	Your Information
NetBIOS-dependent applications and services	
Will you upgrade, replace, or retire NetBIOS-dependent applications and services?	
Date to upgrade, replace, or retire NetBIOS applications and services	
NetBIOS-dependent operating systems	
Date to upgrade systems to Windows 2000	
Date to implement Dynamic DNS	
Date to decommission WINS	
Date to disable NBT on client computers	

Part II: Designing Windows 2000 Networks

Part II covers each important Windows 2000 design topic. The objectives that are raised in Part II can be met using the checklists and planning templates that follow:

- Designing the Active Directory
- Planning a Dynamic DNS Structure
- Forming TCP/IP Standards
- Estimating Hardware Needs
- Creating a Security Plan
- Simplifying Administration

Checklist: Designing the Active Directory

✓ Plan a domain structure.

✓ Plan an organizational unit structure.

✓ Plan a site structure.

Checklist: Planning a Domain Structure

✓ Examine the current operational environment.

✓ Explore the current physical environment.

✓ Identify the organization's administrative requirements.

✓ Determine when it is appropriate to create a domain.

✓ Organize domains into a Tree or Forest.

✓ Create a naming standard for domains.

Examining the Current Operational Environment

Information to Collect	Your Information
Is the organization operating locally, regionally, nationally, or internationally?	
Number of functional boundaries within the organization	
Functional boundary 1	
Functional boundary 2	
Functional boundary 3	
Functional boundary 4	
Functional boundary 5	
Functional boundary x	

Exploring the Current Physical Environment

Information to Collect	Your Information
Physical locations	
Number of employees in each physical location	
Average growth rate of the organization	
Speed of local network links	
TCP/IP subnets in use at each physical location	
Organization of links between physical locations	
Speed of links between physical locations	
Utilization (as a percentage) of local and remote network links	

Identifying Administrative Requirements

Information to Collect	Your Information
Locations using the centralized administrative model	
Locations using the decentralized administrative model	
Locations using the hybrid administrative model	

Determining When to Create a Domain

Information to Collect	Your Information
Domains required to support decentralized administration	
Domains required to isolate domain replication traffic	
Domains required to balance domain replication traffic	
Domains required to support multiple domain policies	
Domains required to address international differences	
Domains required to comply with political pressures	

Determining Whether to Create a Tree or Forest

Information to Collect	Your Information
Is the organization operating as a single entity or as multiple entities?	
Division 1 of a multi-entity organization	
Division 2 of a multi-entity organization	
Division 3 of a multi-entity organization	
Division x of a multi-entity organization	

Creating Naming Standards for Domains

Information to Collect	Your Information
Existing internal DNS name(s)	
Existing external DNS name(s)	
Will organization use different internal and external DNS names?	
Selection of internal DNS name (usually representative of corporate identity)	
Is chosen internal DNS name registered with the InterNIC?	

Information to Collect	Your Information
What will subdomains be based on (geopolitical boundaries, business units, departments, and so on)?	
Naming standard for subdomains	

Checklist: Planning an Organizational Unit Structure

✓ Determine when it is appropriate to create an organizational unit.

✓ Form a meaningful organizational unit hierarchy.

✓ Create a strategy for delegating organizational unit administration.

Determining When to Form an Organizational Unit

Information to Collect	Your Information
Organizational units required to delegate administration within a domain	
Organizational units required to separate users with unlike policy requirements	
Organizational units required to simplify the administration of similar resources	
Organizational units required to scope the visibility of objects	

Forming an Organizational Unit Hierarchy

Information to Collect	Your Information
Maximum number of levels allowed in an organizational unit structure	
What will organizational units represent (geopolitical boundaries, business units, departments, and so on)?	
Number of physical or functional divisions within a domain	
Division 1 of a domain	
Division 2 of a domain	
Division 3 of a domain	
Division x of a domain	
Divisions of a domain using centralized administration	

continues

Forming an Organizational Unit Hierarchy (Continued)

Information to Collect	Your Information
Divisions of a domain using decentralized administration	
Divisions of a domain using hybrid administration	
How will organizational units be structured (by location, function, both, and so on)?	

Forming a Plan for Delegating Administration

Information to Collect	Your Information
Organizational units in which you will delegate complete control	
Organizational units in which you will delegate control over objects of a specific type	
Organizational units in which you will delegate the ability to create and/or delete all object types	
Organizational units in which you will delegate the ability to create and/or delete objects of a specific type	
Organizational units in which you will delegate control over certain object properties	
Delegate specific delegated ability x to user _____.	
Delegate specific delegated ability x to user _____.	
Delegate specific delegated ability x to user _____.	
Delegate specific delegated ability x to user _____.	

Checklist: Planning a Site Structure

✓ Review the organization's physical environment.

✓ Examine the physical locations in the organization that exist in single domains.

✓ Define the organization's sites.

✓ Define the organization's site links.

✓ Determine a cost and replication schedule for site links.

✓ Create one or more site link bridges (optional).

Reviewing the Physical Environment

Information to Collect	Your Information
Locations where the organization has offices	
Speed of links in each office	
TCP/IP subnets that are used in each office	
The organization of links between offices	
Speed of links between offices	
Utilization (as a percentage) of local and remote links	

Examining Locations that Form Domains

Information to Collect	Your Information
Physical location 1	
Physical location 2	
Physical location 3	
Physical location 4	
Physical location x	

Defining Sites in an Organization

Information to Collect	Your Information
Areas of the network that require scheduled replication	
Areas of the network that require control over the logon process	
Areas of the network that require the identification of resources by proximity	
Naming convention for site objects	

Defining an Organization's Site Links

Information to Collect	Your Information
Physical links between each site	
Primary links between each site	
Secondary links between each site	
Site link object naming convention	

Determining a Schedule and Cost for Site Links

Information to Collect	Your Information
Site links over which replication must occur most frequently	
Site links over which replication must occur least frequently	
Site links over which replication must occur using the default replication schedule (every 3 hours, 24 hours a day, 7 days a week)	
Replication schedule for each site link (every x hours, x hours a day, x days a week)	
Cost for each site link (100 is the default)	

Creating Site Link Bridges (Optional)

Information to Collect	Your Information
Sites connected by secondary physical links	
Replication schedule and cost for secondary link	
Site links to be contained by site link bridge	
Total cost of site link bridge	
Naming convention for site link bridge objects	

Checklist: Planning a Dynamic DNS Structure

✓ Plan the Dynamic DNS namespace.

✓ Implement Windows 2000 in an environment with an established DNS namespace, if necessary.

✓ Create Dynamic DNS naming standards.

✓ Form a Dynamic DNS zone replication strategy.

✓ Integrate WINS and Dynamic DNS if necessary.

✓ Plan DHCP services if necessary.

Checklist: Planning the Dynamic DNS Namespace

✓ Plan Dynamic DNS (DDNS) namespace with the Active Directory namespace in mind.

✓ Plan the organization's topmost domain and subdomain names.

✓ Determine whether to use the same or different namespaces for internal and external resources.

Planning DDNS with Active Directory in Mind

Information to Collect	Your Information
DDNS domains that must be created to support Active Directory domains required for decentralized administration	
DDNS domains that must be created to mirror Active Directory domains needed to support multiple domain-level policies	
DDNS domains that must be created to support Active Directory domains required to address international differences	
DDNS domains that must be created to mirror Active Directory domains required to isolate replication traffic	
DDNS domains that must be created to support Active Directory domains needed to comply with political pressures	

Planning Top-Level and Subdomain Names

Information to Collect	Your Information
Name of organization	
Is organization divided internationally?	
If organization were grouped beneath a single DDNS domain, would that DDNS domain be excessively large?	
What will subdomain creation be based on (geopolitical boundaries, business units, divisions, the current IT support structure, and so on)?	
Will proposed subdomain structure be confusing to endusers?	
Will proposed DDNS domain structure match the organization's Active Directory structure?	

Determining Whether to Use the Same Internal & External Namespace

Information to Collect	Your Information
Does the organization currently support the same DNS namespace internally and externally?	
Name of current root domain in internal DNS namespace (if already present)	
Name of current root domain in external DNS namespace (if already present)	
Method for supporting name resolution for resources in environment using the same internal and external namespace (if required)	
Method for securing resources in organization using the same internal and external namespace (if required)	

Checklist: Implementing Windows 2000 in an Established DNS Environment

✓ Determine software and version number used on DNS servers forming the existing DNS namespace.

✓ Determine whether current DNS server software supports the DNS requirements of Active Directory.

✓ Form a plan to establish Windows 2000 in the existing DNS environment.

Determining Current DNS Software and Version

Information to Collect	Your Information
Existing DNS software	
Version of existing DNS software	
Is the same DNS software and version used throughout the organization?	
DNS software and version in location 1	
DNS software and version in location 2	
DNS software and version in location 3	
DNS software and version in location x	

Determining Whether Servers Support the DNS Requirements of Active Directory

Information to Collect	Your Information
Do current DNS servers support service (SRV) resource records as defined in RFC 2052 (required)?	
Do current DNS servers support dynamic update as defined in RFC 2136 (strongly suggested)?	
Do current DNS servers support incremental zone transfer as defined in RFC 1995 (optional)?	
Do current DNS servers support secure dynamic update as defined in RFC 2137 (optional)?	

Forming a Plan to Implement Windows 2000 in an Established DNS Environment

Information to Collect	Your Information
Will you create a separate Dynamic DNS namespace to implement Windows 2000?	
Will you create a delegated subdomain to implement Windows 2000?	
Will you upgrade or migrate existing DNS servers to implement Windows 2000?	

Checklist: Creating Dynamic DNS Naming Standards

✓ Choose a name for the organization's second level domain.

✓ Select names for the organization's subdomains.

Choosing a Second-Level Domain Name

Information to Collect	Your Information
Name of company	
Dynamic DNS name that is representative of the corporate identity	
Does Dynamic DNS name violate DNS naming standards (A-Z, a-z, 0-9, and -)?	
Is the domain name registered with the InterNIC?	
Will the domain name remain static?	

Selecting Appropriate Subdomain Names

Information to Collect	Your Information
What will subdomain names be based on (geopolitical boundaries, business units, divisions, and so on)?	
Are any subdomain names currently used as top-level domains, or other registered domain names?	
Are the subdomain names intuitive and friendly to endusers and administrators?	
Subdomain name 1	
Subdomain name 2	
Subdomain name 3	
Subdomain name x	

Checklist: Forming a DDNS Zone Replication Strategy

✓ Choose whether to replicate Dynamic DNS zone data using standard or Active Directory replication.

✓ Plan the location of primary, secondary, and caching-only servers if using standard replication.

Choosing Between Standard and Active Directory Replication

Information to Collect	Your Information
Is an existing standard zone replication topology in place?	
Reasons to choose standard over Active Directory integrated replication of zone data	
Reasons to choose Active Directory integrated replication over standard replication of zone data	

Planning a Standard Zone Replication Topology

Information to Collect	Your Information
Physical locations using DDNS services	
TCP/IP subnets in each location	
Links between physical locations	
Speed of local links	

Information to Collect	**Your Information**
Speed of remote links	
Utilization (as a percentage) of local and remote links	
Expected query traffic by location	
Location of primary server	
Locations for secondary servers	
Locations for caching-only servers	
Zone transfer frequency	
Plan for fault tolerance for the primary server in the event of a failure	

Integrating WINS and Dynamic DNS

Information to Collect	**Your Information**
Does organization without Windows 2000 DHCP servers need to support downlevel clients?	
Does organization wish to provide downlevel client name resolution services via DDNS and WINS for its Windows 2000 (or other DDNS-aware systems)?	
Do non-Microsoft operating systems need to query DDNS to resolve the names of downlevel clients?	

Planning DHCP Services

Information to Collect	**Your Information**
Number of DHCP servers required for fault tolerance	
Location of routers and number of IP subnets	
Link speed between network segments	
Number of scopes required	
Pool of addresses in each scope	
Pool of addresses to exclude from each scope	
Subnet mask of each scope	

continues

Planning DHCP Services (Continued)

Information to Collect	Your Information
Options for each scope, such as default gateway, WINS address, user class, and so on	
Lease duration for each scope	
Name of each scope	
Does organization have any multi-nets?	
Superscopes required to support multi-nets	
Scopes that belong to each superscope	
Reservations for each scope	

Checklist: Forming TCP/IP Standards

✓ Align TCP/IP addressing and Active Directory.

✓ Plan TCP/IP standards in a Windows 2000 environment.

Aligning TCP/IP Addressing with Active Directory

Information to Collect	Your Information
List the address ranges and subnet masks in use	
Correlate the address ranges and subnet masks according to entities, sites, regions, departments, and so on	
Is TCP/IP addressing scheme aligned with Active Directory (sites, site links, and site link bridges)?	
Is TCP/IP addressing scheme aligned with QoS policy?	
Is the TCP/IP addressing scheme aligned with IP Security policy?	
Is the TCP/IP addressing scheme aligned with 802.1p prioritization scheme?	
Is the TCP/IP addressing scheme aligned with CNS/AD?	

Planning TCP/IP Standards for Windows 2000

Information to Collect	Your Information
Plan for organization to use Microsoft QoS	
Plan for organization to use RSVP	
Plan for organization to use traffic control	
Plan for organization to use IP Security	
Plan for organization to use 802.1p	
Plan for organization to use CNS/AD or other DEN solution	

Checklist: Estimating Hardware Needs

✓ Analyze current systems to determine how they will perform on the Windows 2000 platform versus NT.

✓ Decide whether to upgrade or replace current systems that perform poorly under Windows 2000.

✓ Establish hardware requirements for new systems.

Analyzing Current Systems

Information to Collect	Your Information
CPU performance of current systems versus performance with Windows 2000	
Memory performance of current systems versus performance with Windows 2000	
Mass storage performance of current systems versus performance with Windows 2000	
Network performance of current systems versus performance with Windows 2000	

Upgrading or Replacing Systems

Information to Collect	Your Information
Cost of upgrade versus replacement	
Number of subsystems that require replacement	
Component(s) causing the performance bottleneck	
Warranty of upgraded subsystem versus replacement	

Forming Hardware Standards for Systems

Information to Collect   **Your Information**

CPU type, speed, cache, and number of CPUs for domain controllers

Memory size, speed, and fault tolerance level for domain controllers

Mass storage speed, interface type, fault tolerance level, and storage layout for domain controllers

Network interface type and speed for domain controllers

CPU type, speed, cache, and number of CPUs for file/print servers

Memory size, speed, and fault tolerance level for file/print servers

Mass storage speed, interface type, fault tolerance level, and storage layout for file/print servers

Network interface type and speed for file/print servers

CPU type, speed, cache, and number of CPUs for database servers

Memory size, speed, and fault tolerance level for database servers

Mass storage speed, interface type, fault tolerance level, and storage layout for database servers

Network interface type and speed for database servers

CPU type, speed, cache, and number of CPUs for Web/ftp servers

Memory size, speed, and fault tolerance level for Web/ftp servers

Mass storage speed, interface type, fault tolerance level, and storage layout for Web/ftp servers

Network interface type and speed for Web/ftp servers

CPU type, speed, cache, and number of CPUs for "number-cruncher" servers

Memory size, speed, and fault tolerance level for "number-cruncher" servers

Mass storage speed, interface type, fault tolerance level, and storage layout for "number-cruncher" servers

Information to Collect	Your Information
Network interface type, and speed for "number-cruncher" servers	
_____(additional component,such as fiber channel card type) for	
_____(server class, such as "nearline storage") servers	

Checklist: Creating a Security Plan

- ✓ Form a standard for secure authentication.
- ✓ Create a standard for securing the file system.
- ✓ Establish a standard for user rights.
- ✓ Create a standard for securing Active Directory.
- ✓ Form a standard for certificate services.

Checklist: Forming a Standard for Secure Authentication

- ✓ Standardize on core authentication protocols.
- ✓ Standardize on smart card authentication use.
- ✓ Standardize on the use of IP Security.
- ✓ Standardize on security policies.

Standardizing Core Authentication Protocols

Information to Collect	Your Information
Is organization required to support NTLM?	
Will organization phase out support for NTLM?	
Time frame for phase out of NTLM (if required)	
Kerberos configurable parameter standards	

Standardizing the Use of Smart Cards

Information to Collect	Your Information
Will organization require smart card services across the entire organization?	
Individual areas that require smart card authentication services (if required)	

continues

Standardizing the Use of Smart Cards (Continued)

Information to Collect	**Your Information**
Will organization or individual departments require smart cards for every logon?	
How often will PIN codes on smart cards be changed in an organization or in individual departments?	
What is the certificate revocation frequency for the organization or individual departments?	
What smart card vendor will be used by the organization or by individual departments?	

Standardizing the Use of IP Security

Information to Collect	**Your Information**
Does the organization need to use IP Security services across the entire organization?	
Individual areas that need to use IP Security services (if required)	
Predefined or custom IP Security policy that will be used across the organization or within individual departments	

Establishing Security Policy Standards

Information to Collect	**Your Information**
Password policy parameters	
Account policy settings	
User account property standards	
Security options parameters	

Checklist: Creating a Standard for Securing the File System

✓ Create permissions usage standards.

✓ Form file systems permissions standards.

✓ Create standards for use of the encrypting file system.

Creating Permissions Usage Standards

Information to Collect	**Your Information**
Files and folders on systems that have similar security requirements	
Groups of users to which permissions for files and folders will be granted	
Standard permissions for shared folders	

Forming File System Permissions Standards

Information to Collect	**Your Information**
Individual system classes	
Application and data permissions standards for system class 1	
Application and data permissions standards for system class 2	
Application and data permissions standards for system class x	
System class 1 permissions standards for OS-specific files and folders	
System class 2 permissions standards for OS-specific files and folders	
System class x permissions standards for OS-specific files and folders	
Template names for each system class	
Frequency of permissions audit for each system class	

Forming Standards for Using EFS

Information to Collect	**Your Information**
Will there be organization- or department-wide use of EFS?	
Will organization or department use EFS with only a user key pair?	
Will organization or department use EFS with a user key pair on a smart card?	

continues

Forming Standards for Using EFS (Continued)

Information to Collect	Your Information
Will organization or department use EFS with a user and recovery key pair?	
Will organization or department use EFS with a user and recovery key pair on a smart card?	

Establishing a Standard for User Rights

Information to Collect	Your Information
System classes in the organization (domain controllers, workstations, file servers, and so on)	
Privileges for system class 1	
Logon rights for system class 1	
Privileges for system class 2	
Logon rights for system class 2	
Privileges for system class x	
Logon rights for system class x	

Creating a Standard for Securing Active Directory

Information to Collect	Your Information
Lowest level in Active Directory where permissions will be assigned (container or object level)	
Container level in Active Directory where global, and decentralized security standards will be enforced	
Groups that will be assigned permissions to objects in Active Directory	
Whether or not the organization endorses the use of the Deny permission	
Accounts with sweeping control over Active Directory	
Audit plan for administrator level accounts	
Audit plan for Active Directory permissions	

Forming a Standard for Certificate Services

Information to Collect	Your Information
Requirement for certificate services	
Will organization use enterprise or standalone certificate authorities?	
Will organization use enterprise or standalone subordinate certificate authorities?	
Number of sites that require the ability to set policies and issue certificates	
Function and role of each certificate authority	
Certificate revocation and renewal standards	

Checklist: Simplifying Administration

✓ Form a plan for using Group Policy.

✓ Create a plan for using IntelliMirror.

✓ Build a strategy for the Distributed File System (DFS).

✓ Create a plan for using Automatic System Recovery (ASR).

✓ Develop a strategy for Windows Scripting Host (WSH).

✓ Create a plan for auditing events.

✓ Form a strategy for using Resource Kit utilities.

✓ Develop a plan for using operating system features.

Forming a Plan for Group Policy

Information to Collect	Your Information
Will different groups of users require different Group Policies?	
Organization-wide or department-level user settings in Group Policy	
Organization-wide or department-level computer settings in Group Policy	
How will organization support different groups with different policy requirements?	
How will Group Policy be managed (using the centralized, decentralized, task-based, or _____ administrative model)?	
Accounts with privileges to manage group policy objects	

Creating a Strategy for Using IntelliMirror

Information to Collect	Your Information
Do separate user groups need different IntelliMirror settings?	
Software installation settings for organization or for separate user groups	
User settings parameters for organization or for separate user groups	
User document management settings for organization or for separate user groups	

Building a Strategy for Using DFS

Information to Collect	Your Information
File shares and locations to form DFS Tree	
File shares that will require replicas	
Location and replication schedule for file share replicas	
Object name for DFS shares published in Active Directory	
Will the DFS root node be fault tolerant?	
Cache timeout settings for child nodes	
Frequency of running the `check status` command	
Naming convention for root and child DFS nodes	

Creating a Plan for Using ASR

Information to Collect	Your Information
Systems to be protected by Automatic System Recovery	
Frequency of Automatic System Recovery Saveset creation	
Location of Automatic System Recovery floppy disk and backup media	

Developing a Strategy for Using WSH

Information to Collect

Will organization use Windows Scripting Host for its logon and logoff scripts?

Will organization use Windows Scripting Host to create user accounts en masse?

Will organization use Windows Scripting Host for other purposes?

Your Information

Creating a Plan for Auditing Events

Information to Collect

Systems on which auditing will be enabled

Frequency of security log checks

Audit settings for Active Directory

Audit settings for the file system by computer (servers and workstations)

Other standard audit settings for areas such as account logon, account management, policy change, and so on

Your Information

Forming a Strategy for Using the Resource Kit

Information to Collect

Will organization standardize on the use of NETAFX.EXE?

Will organization standardize on the use of NETDIAG.EXE?

Will organization standardize on the use of LOGEVENT.EXE?

Will organization standardize on the use of NLTESTRK.EXE?

Will organization standardize on the use of REG.EXE?

Will organization standardize on the use of SC.EXE?

Will organization standardize on the use of any additional Resource Kit utilities?

Your Information

Developing a Plan for Using OS features

Information to Collect	Your Information
Will organization standardize on the use of the secondary logon service?	
Will organization standardize on service failure and recovery standards?	
Standard actions performed by service 1 upon failure	
Standard actions performed by service 2 upon failure	
Standard actions performed by service 3 upon failure	
Standard actions performed by service x upon failure	

Part III: Deploying Windows 2000

Part III details the Windows 2000 upgrade procedure and removing resource domains. The topics in this section include the following checklists and planning templates you can use to meet the objectives in Part III:

- Upgrade and migrate to Windows 2000
- Remove resource domains.

Checklist: Upgrading and Migrating to Windows 2000

✓ Plan the upgrade to Windows 2000 from Windows NT
✓ Plan a migration to Windows 2000 from NetWare

Checklist: Planning the Upgrade to Windows 2000

✓ Form a strategy for a safe Windows 2000 upgrade.
✓ Run the Windows 2000 Setup Wizard.
✓ Run the Active Directory Installation Wizard.
✓ Run the Server Configure Wizard.
✓ Validate the upgrade to Windows 2000.

Forming a Strategy for a Safe Upgrade

Information to Collect	Your Information
Name and operating system version of server to upgrade	

Information to Collect	Your Information
Time and date when full backup of server to be upgraded will be performed	
Recovery strategy for domain database (when upgrading domain controllers)	

Running the Windows 2000 Setup Wizard

Information to Collect	Your Information
Time, date, and success of last full backup	
Is domain recovery plan in place (if this is a domain controller)?	
Time and date for running the Setup Wizard	
Offline time window for the upgrade	
Does plan for backing out of the upgrade require more time than the offline time windows?	

Running the Active Directory Installation Wizard

Information to Collect	Your Information
Will you create a new Tree or a new child domain?	
Will you create a new Forest or join an existing one?	
The full DNS name of the new domain	
Location for the Active Directory database and log files be stored	
Location for the shared system volume	

Running the Server Configure Wizard

Information to Collect	Your Information
Registration information (licensing details)	
Additional configuration required for Active Directory	
Additional configuration required for network services	

continues

Running the Server Configure Wizard (Continued)

Information to Collect	Your Information
Additional configuration required for shared folders	
Additional configuration required for printers	
Additional configuration required for Web services	
Additional configuration required for clustering services	
Additional configuration required for any other Windows services	

Validating the Windows 2000 upgrade

Information to Collect	Your Information
Name and address of server on which validation will be performed	
Results of a simple ping test	
Connectivity problems isolated using `ipconfig`	
Additional connectivity issues uncovered by `netdiag`	
If domain controller, indication of success or failure for the installation Active Directory shown in the final installation dialog	
If domain controller, was the NTDS.DIT file found?	
If domain controller, did navigation of Active Directory fail or succeed?	
If domain controller, did all users and groups migrate from the old domain?	
If domain controller, was the system volume created?	
If running DDNS, can you resolve a host name to an IP address?	
If running DDNS, can you resolve an IP address to a host name?	
If running DDNS, were you able to view the contents of your DDNS zone using the DNS snap-in?	
If running DDNS, is DDNS enabled for dynamic updates?	

Information to Collect	Your Information
If running DDNS, were forward and reverse lookup zones created properly?	
If running DDNS, are LDAP SRV records listed in the NETLOGON.DNS file?	
If running DDNS, did the LDAP SRV record test using `nslookup` fail or succeed?	

Checklist: Planning a Migration to Windows 2000

- ✓ Create and model a view from NetWare.
- ✓ Configure the view to Active Directory.
- ✓ Migrate volumes from NetWare to Windows 2000.

Creating and Modeling a View from NetWare

Information to Collect	Your Information
Project name	
View name	
Naming context to discover	
Modeling requirements	
User or group level modeling	
Modeling performed on hierarchical structure	

Configuring a View to Active Directory

Information to Collect	Your Information
Source naming context	
Destination naming context	
Results of pre-verification configure process	
Errors (if any) during configure of objects and structure to Active Directory	
Were all objects migrated to Active Directory as expected?	

Migrating Volumes from NetWare to Windows 2000

Information to Collect	Your Information
Volumes to migrate from NetWare to Windows 2000	
Whether or not to migrate security information	
Whether or not to migrate files in volumes	
Share on Windows 2000 server for resources from NetWare	
Were all file and/or folder resources migrated from NetWare to Windows 2000?	
Are file and/or folder permissions correct?	

Checklist: Removing Resource Domains

✓ Determine whether it is appropriate to remove a resource domain.

✓ Plan the removal of a resource domain.

✓ Remove a resource domain during the upgrade to Windows 2000.

Determining Whether Resource Domains Should Be Removed

Information to Collect	Your Information
Is the resource domain required for decentralized administration?	
Is the resource domain needed to isolate replication traffic?	
Is the resource domain required to support unique domain policies?	
Is the resource domain needed to address international differences?	
Is the resource domain required to comply with political pressures?	

Planning for the Removal of a Resource Domain

Information to Collect   **Your Information**

Domain recovery strategy for the upgrade and
subsequent removal of the domain

Post-upgrade administration plan for group
account management

Post-upgrade administration plan for computer
account management

Post-upgrade administration plan for printer
management

Post-upgrade administration plan for server and
workstation management

Post-upgrade administration plan for any other
resources

Enhanced administrative control that will be
delegated, if any

Removing a Resource Domain During the Upgrade

Information to Collect   **Your Information**

Master domain name

Resource domain name

Backup plan for individual servers in the master
domain

Recovery plan for the master domain

Primary domain controller in master domain

Organizational units that will be created in master
domain for resources from the resource domain

Backup plan for individual servers in the resource
domain

Recovery plan for the resource domain

Primary domain controller in resource domain

Users to move from resource domain to OUs in
master domain

Groups to move from resource domain to OUs in
master domain

continues

Removing a Resource Domain During the Upgrade (Continued)

Information to Collect	Your Information
Member servers to move to master domain	
Workstations to move to master domain	
Time frame for shutting down domain controllers in the resource domain	

Glossary

Access Control Entry (ACE) An entry in the access control list of an object that defines the level of access to that object for a user or group.

Access Control List (ACL) A list associated with an object that contains access control entries.

Active Directory The directory service that is used to logically store and replicate resources in a Windows 2000 network.

asynchronous transfer mode (ATM) A standardized multiplexing and switching method that packetizes data, voice, and video simultaneously over high-bandwidth circuits using fixed-length cells.

Automatic System Recovery (ASR) A component of the NT backup utility that simplifies restoring a computer to its original state.

certificate A credential used to substantiate the origin, authenticity, and purpose of a public key to a user holding the matching private key in a key-pair.

certificate authority (CA) A service that is used to issue and manage public key certificates.

certificate revocation list (CRL) A list published by a certificate authority that contains certificates that are no longer valid for use.

class of service (CoS) A way to group common applications or users with similar service requirements into one of several broad service or priority classes.

convergence The time it takes for a change to be recognized throughout a portion of Active Directory.

cryptography A process that defines a secure method for transmitting data between entities.

delegation of authentication A process supported by Kerberos that lets a server impersonate a user's identity to establish a connection with another computer on that user's behalf.

disk quota The amount of disk space defined by an administrator that is allocated to a particular user.

Distributed File System (DFS) A service used to build a logical structure of file shares that exist on separate computers, which is presented to users and administrators in a single directory Tree.

domain local group A group that can contain users, universal groups, and global groups from any domain and other domain local groups from the same domain when that domain operates in native mode. When a domain local group is created in a mixed mode domain, users and global groups from any domain are allowed.

downlevel A term used to describe any client, server, domain, or network service that is based on Microsoft technology released prior to Windows 2000.

downlevel name registration A process performed by a Windows 2000 DHCP server to register the NetBIOS names of downlevel computers in DDNS.

dynamic disk A physical disk that can contain dynamic volumes.

Dynamic Domain Name System (DDNS) An update to the original DNS specification that allows name servers to accept dynamic updates.

Dynamic Host Configuration Protocol (DHCP) A TCP/IP service protocol that is used to automatically assign and configure the TCP/IP addresses of network clients.

dynamic update Rules that allow a name server to dynamically process updates for its entries.

dynamic volume A volume you can create, extend, or mirror without rebooting a Windows 2000 computer.

encapsulation The process in which a protocol specifies the interface for programs to communicate with it and then relies on lower level protocols to actually transport the information between machines.

Encrypting File System (EFS) The public key-based service that provides file and directory encryption capabilities to Windows 2000 computers.

Forest A structure created by domains in two or more Trees that share the same configuration, schema, and global catalog, but that do not share the same DNS namespace.

fully qualified domain name (FQDN) The concatenation of a host name and the name of that host's parent.

global catalog (GC) A partial replica of every partition in Active Directory that stores the values of objects most frequently used in search operations.

global group A group that can contain users and other global groups from the same domain when that domain is operating in native mode. If the global group is used in a mixed mode domain, only users from the same domain are allowed.

Group Policy   An object in Active Directory that can be used to centrally configure and maintain the settings on client computers.

IntelliMirror   A set of technologies built into Windows 2000 that enable a user's data, applications, and desktop settings to follow him or her on the network.

intersite replication   Directory replication traffic that occurs between sites.

intrasite replication   Directory replication traffic that occurs within a site.

IP Security (IPSec)   A framework of open standards that ensures secure communications over public networks like the Internet.

Kerberos   An identity-based security protocol used in Windows 2000 to authenticate users to network services.

Key Distribution Center (KDC) A service that runs on Windows 2000 domain controllers that issues and authenticates tickets for Kerberos clients.

Lightweight Directory Access Protocol (LDAP)   A lightweight version of the X.500 directory access protocol developed at MIT that is used to read, write, and search the Active Directory.

master user domain   A Windows NT 3.x–4.0 domain created to house and maintain a company's user accounts.

migration.dll   A .dll that can be used to automatically make changes to an application so that it becomes Windows 2000 compliant during a Windows 2000 upgrade.

mixed mode   The default mode a Windows 2000 domain operates in, which permits replication of the domain partition to NT 4.0 backup domain controllers.

name registration   The process used by a computer to reserve a NetBIOS name for its exclusive use.

name resolution   The process of transforming a name into a TCP/IP address.

namespace   Any context within which a name can be resolved to an actual object. Examples include the Domain Name System (DNS) and Active Directory.

native mode   The domain mode in which multi-master replication is enabled, nesting of groups is allowed, and support for replication to Windows NT 4.0 backup domain controllers is turned off.

Organizational Unit (OU)   A container object in Active Directory that is used to separate resources such as users, groups, and printers into one or more logical areas.

partition   A portion of the Active Directory namespace that contains all the objects in a particular domain.

policy-based networking   A set of rules that determines how various network services are performed.

public key cryptography   A cryptography method in which a pair of public and private keys are used to encrypt and decrypt data.

Quality of Service (QoS)   A set of standards used to assure the quality of data transmission on a network.

Request for Comment (RFC)   An evolving series of reports, proposals, and official standards that detail the functions within the TCP/IP protocol family.

resolver   Any network client that queries a DNS server for information.

resource domain   A domain used to house resources, such as files, printers, and applications, that is often managed by a separate set of administrators.

root domain   The uppermost domain in Active Directory.

schema   A definition of the object classes and attributes that can be stored in Active Directory.

scope   A range of TCP/IP addresses that are made available to network clients by a DHCP server.

second-level domain   A domain that exists in the DNS namespace below a top-level domain. For example, in mycompany.com, .com is a top-level domain, and mycompany is a second-level domain.

security identifier (SID)   A unique string that is used to identify each user and group account for security purposes.

site   An object in Active Directory that defines an area of good network connectivity.

site link   An object in Active Directory that defines a cost and schedule for the replication of directory traffic between two separate sites.

site link bridge   An object in Active Directory that can route directory replication traffic by using the costs and schedules defined in two or more site links.

smart card   A device the size of a credit card that securely stores user credentials, passwords, certificates, and other sensitive information.

subdomain   A domain in the DNS namespace that is located directly beneath another domain.

subnet   Portions of a wide area network (WAN) within which defined network bits designate a local area network (LAN).

superscope   A group of two or more child scopes defining several logical networks to be used on one physical network.

system volume   The shared directory on a Windows 2000 domain controller (named SYSVOL) that is used to store and replicate public domain data.

top-level domain   A domain that exists in the first tier of the DNS namespace, directly beneath ".", the unnamed root. Examples include .com, .edu, and .mil.

traffic control   A mechanism that reduces delay and latency while transmitting network traffic.

transitive trust   A trust relationship that is shared by domains. If a transitive trust is established between DOMAINA and DOMAINB, as well as between DOMAINB and DOMAINC, DOMAINA will also trust DOMAINC.

Tree   A hierarchy of Windows 2000 domains that share a contiguous namespace, configuration, schema, and global catalog.

universal group   A group that can contain users, other universal groups, and global groups from any domain, and that can be granted permissions in any domain that can be used only in domains operating in native mode.

Windows Internet Naming Service (WINS)   A NetBIOS name server that allows NetBIOS clients to locate resources on a TCP/IP network.

Windows Scripting Host (WSH)   A language-independent scripting host for Microsoft's 32-bit operating systems that provides out-of-the-box support for scripts created with VBScript or JavaScript.

zone A portion of the DNS namespace that consists either of a single domain or of a domain and several subdomains that can be managed by a separate authority.

Index

A

ABR (Available Bit Rate), 207

acceptance tests, performing, 71

access control, delegating (Active Directory), 252-253

Access Control Entry, *see* **ACE**

Access Control List, *see* **ACL**

access control standards
EFS, 247-248
establishing, 243
NTFS permissions
creating standards, 245
finalizing, 247
operating system-specific files and folders, securing, 246
Security Configuration & Analysis, 250
servers and workstations, classifying, 245

account domains, 9

account lockout policy, 236-237
Windows 2000 Professional, 261
Windows 2000 Server, 269

ACE (Access Control Entry), 6
Active Directory, 251

ACL (Access Control List), 6
Active Directory, 251

Active Directory, 4
access control, delegating, 252-253
ACE, 251
ACL, 6, 251
ASR, 288
auditing, 295
DCs, 214

DDNS, 182
planning, 360
designing, 354-356
DFS, 22, 286
domain structure, planning, 354
domains, 5-6
events, auditing, 293-294
Forests, 9
global catalog, 11-12
granular access control, 251
Group Policy, 278
ideal domain models, 38
IntelliMirror, 284
log files, storing, 313
NDS, moving, 326-327
object and property permissions, securing, 251
OUs, 7-8
partitions, 5
permissions, calculating, 253
policy, 30
Resource Kit utilities, 297
rights versus permissions, 326-327
schema, 5
securing, 251
security, 12
sites, 10-11
SRV RRs, 187
standard and special permissions, securing, 252
standards
creating, 371
security, 254
SYSVOL, shared folders, 313
TCP/IP addressing, aligning, 365-366
Trees, 9

J-K

L

M

M-nodes, NBT (name resolution types), 124

maintaining standards, 93, 98, 351

managing
Group Policy, 281-282
Windows 2000 standardization, 76

manual inventory, tools, 80

mass storage
replacing, 219
systems, examining, 216
upgrading, 219

master domains
domain controllers, upgrading, 336-338
member servers, moving, 342
moving, 341-342
organizational units, 339

master user domains, single master domain models, 34

member servers, moving
Domain Reconfiguration Tool, 68
Resource Kit utilities, 59

memory, 224
fault tolerance, 224-225
/MAXMEM switch, 216
replacing, 218
size of, 224
speed, 224
systems, examining, 215
upgrading, 218
see also cache

message services, RSVP, 208

methods, WSH, 291

Microsoft Certificate Services, public key cryptography, 17

Microsoft Certificate Services, *see* **Certificate Services**

Microsoft networks, DNS, 174

Microsoft standard templates, 246

Microsoft Systems Management Server, *see* **SMS**

migrating, *see* **moving**

migration plans, 69-71

mixed mode, domains, 6

mixed OS environments, establishing standards, 85

modeling, Views, 326
NetWare, 325, 377

models, determining domains, 347

monitors, 217

moving
applications, 348
applications before upgrading, 41-42
computer accounts
Domain Reconfiguration Tool, 66
Resource Kit utilities, 57-58
domain controllers
Domain Reconfiguration Tool, 66-68
Resource Kit utilities, 58-59
global groups
Domain Reconfiguration Tool, 63
Resource Kit utilities, 52
groups to master domains, 341-342
member servers
Domain Reconfiguration Tool, 68
to master domains, 342
Resource Kit utilities, 59
NetWare
to Windows 2000, 324-325
volumes, 327-328
resources, resource domains, 334
services, 348
to Windows 2000, 377-378
user accounts
Domain Reconfiguration Tool, 61-62
Resource Kit utilities, 51-52
users to master domains, 341-342
volumes from NetWare, 378
workstations
Domain Reconfiguration Tool, 68-69
to master domains, 342
Resource Kit utilities, 59-60

multi master domain models, upgrading, 321-323

multi-nets, 196

Implementing Exchange Server

TECHNICAL SOLUTIONS FOR DEPLOYING EXCHANGE SERVER IN THE ENTERPRISE

- Written by Hauger, Leon, and Wade III
- 1st Edition
- 400 pages
- $29.99
- ISBN: 1-56205-931-9

Trustworthy Advice

With over 300,000 seats of practical Exchange deployments between them, Hauger, Leon, and Wade are some of the foremost practitioners of Exchange design and implementation in the world. Professional trainers, they have also participated in the development of all three Microsoft Exchange Server MCSE exams. They have written this book to share their considerable insight and experience.

Technical and Comprehensive

The first book to satisfy the practical needs of those tasked with deploying Exchange, *Implementing Exchange Server* gives you a hands-on analysis of the most difficult aspects of creating an Exchange infrastructure. Focusing on architecture and connectivity, the authors illustrate how to effectively implement and run a robust, integrated system.

Implementing Exchange Server helps you analyze your current environment and create an Exchange architecture that complements that environment while meeting your business needs. It's the authoritative reference that provides you with uncommon consulting experience.

If you plan to deploy Microsoft Exchange Server, this book will show you how to:

- Develop the best Exchange solution for your company
- Provide reliable connectivity — between Exchange servers, and to the Internet
- Coexist with or migrate from the other popular messaging systems
- Integrate Exchange with your existing network and messaging system
- Optimize, monitor, and administer your Exchange organization
- Develop a Disaster Recovery plan
- Scale your solution — especially for the next version of Exchange

Advanced Information on Windows® Technologies

New Riders Books Offer Advice and Experience

LANDMARK
Rethinking Computer Books

The *Landmark* series from New Riders targets the distinct needs of the working computer professional by providing detailed and solution-oriented information on core technologies. We begin by partnering with authors who have unique depth of experience and the ability to speak to the needs of the practicing professional. Each book is then carefully reviewed at all stages to ensure it covers the most essential subjects in substantial depth, with great accuracy, and with ease of use in mind. These books speak to the practitioner – accurate information and trustworthy advice, at the right depth, at an attractive value.

ESSENTIAL REFERENCE
Smart, Like You

The *Essential Reference* series from New Riders provides answers when you know what you want to do but need to know how to do it. Each title skips extraneous material and assumes a strong base level of knowledge. These are indispensable books for the practitioner who wants to find specific features of a technology quickly and efficiently. Avoiding fluff and basic material, these books present solutions in an innovative, clean format – and at a great value.

MCSE CERTIFICATION
Engineered for Test Success

New Riders offers a complete line of test preparation materials to help you achieve your certification. With books like *MCSE Training Guide*, *TestPrep*, and *FastTrack*, and software like the acclaimed *MCSE Complete* and *Top Score*, New Riders offers comprehensive products built by experienced professionals who have passed the exams and instructed hundreds of candidates.

Windows NT Performance

By Mark Edmead and Paul Hinsberg
1st Edition
288 pages, $29.99
ISBN: 1-56205-942-4

Performance monitoring is a little like preventative medicine for the administrator: No one enjoys a checkup, but it's a good thing to do on a regular basis. This book helps you focus on the critical aspects of improving the performance of your NT system, showing you how to monitor the system, implement benchmarking, and tune your network. The book is organized by resource components, which makes it easy to use as a reference tool.

Windows NT Terminal Server

By Ted Harwood
1st Edition
416 pages, $29.99
ISBN: 1-56205-944-0

It's no surprise that most administration headaches revolve around integration with other networks and clients. This book addresses these types of real-world issues on a case-by-case basis, giving tools and advice on solving each problem. The author also offers the real nuts and bolts of thin client administration on multiple systems, covering such relevant issues as installation, configuration, network connection, management, and application distribution.

Windows NT Security

By Richard Puckett
1st Edition Summer 1999
600 pages, $29.99
ISBN: 1-56205-945-9

Swiss cheese. That's what some people say Windows NT security is like. And they may be right, because they only know what the NT documentation says about implementing security. Who has the time to research alternatives; play around with the features, service packs, hot fixes and add-on tools; and figure out what makes NT rock solid? Well, Richard Puckett does. He's been researching Windows NT Security for the University of Virginia for a while now, and he's got pretty good news. He's going to show you how to make NT secure in your environment, and we mean really secure.

Windows NT Network Management

By Anil Desai
1st Edition Spring 1999
400 pages, $34.99
ISBN: 1-56205-946-7

Administering a Windows NT network is kind of like trying to herd cats—an impossible task characterized by constant motion, exhausting labor and lots of hairballs. Author Anil Desai knows all about it—he's a consulting engineer for Sprint Paranet, and specializes in Windows NT implementation, integration and management. So we asked him to put together a concise manual of best practices, a book of tools and ideas that other administrators can turn to again and again in managing their own NT networks.

Planning for Windows 2000
By Eric K. Cone, Jon Boggs, and Sergio Perez
1st Edition Spring 1999
400 pages, $29.99
ISBN: 0-73570-048-6

Windows 2000 is poised to be one of the largest and most important software releases of the next decade, and you are charged with planning, testing, and deploying it in your enterprise. Are you ready? With this book, you will be. Planning for Windows 2000 lets you know what the upgrade hurdles will be, informs you how to clear them, guides you through effective Active Directory design, and presents you with detailed rollout procedures. The authors give you the benefit of their extensive experiences as Windows 2000 Rapid Deployment Program members, sharing problems and solutions they've encountered on the job.

MCSE Core NT Exams Essential Reference
By Matthew Shepker
1st Edition
256 pages, $19.99
ISBN: 0-7357-0006-0

You're sitting in the first session of your Networking Essentials class, the instructor starts talking about RAS, and you have no idea what that means. You think about raising your hand to ask about RAS, but you reconsider—you'd feel pretty foolish asking a question in front of all these people. You turn to your handy MCSE Core NT Exams Essential Reference and find a quick summary on Remote Access Services. Question answered. It's a couple months later and you're taking your Networking Essentials exam the next day. You're reviewing practice tests and you keep forgetting the maximum lengths for the various commonly used cable types. Once again, you turn to the MCSE Core NT Exams Essential Reference and find a table on cables, including all of the characteristics you need to memorize in order to pass the test.

BackOffice Titles

Implementing Exchange Server
By Doug Hauger, Marywynne Leon, and William C. Wade III
1st Edition
400 pages, $29.99
ISBN: 1-56205-931-9

If you're interested in connectivity and maintenance issues for Exchange Server, then this book is for you. Exchange's power lies in its ability to be connected to multiple email subsystems to create a "universal email backbone." It's not unusual to have several different and complex systems all connected via email gateways, including Lotus Notes or cc:Mail, Microsoft Mail, legacy mainframe systems, and Internet mail. This book covers all of the problems and issues associated with getting an integrated system running smoothly and addresses troubleshooting and diagnosis of email problems with an eye toward prevention and best practices.

Exchange Server Administration

By Janice K. Howd
1st Edition Spring 1999
400 pages, $34.99
ISBN: 0-7357-0081-8

OK, you've got your Exchange Server installed and connected, now what? Email administration is one of the most critical networking jobs, and Exchange can be particularly troublesome in large, heterogenous environments. So Janice Howd, a noted consultant and teacher with over a decade of email administration experience, has put together this advanced, concise handbook for daily, periodic, and emergency administration. With in-depth coverage of topics like managing disk resources, replication, and disaster recovery, this is the one reference book every Exchange administrator needs.

SQL Server System Administration

By Sean Baird, Chris Miller, et al.
1st Edition
352 pages, $29.99
ISBN: 1-56205-955-6

How often does your SQL Server go down during the day when everyone wants to access the data? Do you spend most of your time being a "report monkey" for your co-workers and bosses? *SQL Server System Administration* helps you keep data consistently available to your users. This book omits the introductory information. The authors don't spend time explaining queries and how they work. Instead, they focus on the information that you can't get anywhere else, like how to choose the correct replication topology and achieve high availability of information.

Internet Information Server Administration

By Kelli Adam, et. al.
1st Edition Fall 1999
300 pages, $29.99
ISBN: 0-73570-022-2

Are the new Internet technologies in Internet Information Server giving you headaches? Does protecting security on the Web take up all of your time? Then this is the book for you. With hands-on configuration training, advanced study of the new protocols in IIS, and detailed instructions on authenticating users with the new Certificate Server and implementing and managing the new e-commerce features, *Internet Information Server Administration* gives you the real-life solutions you need. This definitive resource also prepares you for the release of Windows 2000 by giving you detailed advice on working with Microsoft Management Console, which was first used by IIS.

SMS Administration

By Darshan Doshi and Michael Lubanski
1st Edition Winter 1999
350 pages, $34.99
ISBN: 0-7357-0082-6

Microsoft's new version of its Systems Management Server (SMS) is starting to turn heads. While complex, it's allowing administrators to lower their total cost of ownership and more efficiently manage clients, applications and support operations. So if your organization is using or implementing SMS, you'll need some expert advice. Wayne Koop and Brian Steck can help you get the most bang for your buck, with insight, expert tips, and real-world examples. Brian and Wayne are consultants specializing in SMS, having worked with Microsoft on one of the most complex SMS rollouts in the world, involving 32 countries, 15 languages, and thousands of clients.

Unix/Linux Titles

Solaris Essential Reference
By John Mulligan
1st Edition Spring 1999
350 pages, $19.99
ISBN: 0-7357-0230-7
Looking for the fastest, easiest way to find the Solaris command you need? Need a few pointers on shell scripting? How about advanced administration tips and sound, practical expertise on security issues? Are you looking for trustworthy information about available third-party software packages that will enhance your operating system? Author John Mulligan—creator of the popular Unofficial Guide to Solaris Web site (sun.icsnet.com)—delivers all that and more in one attractive, easy-to-use reference book. With clear and concise instructions on how to perform important administration and management tasks and key information on powerful commands and advanced topics, *Solaris Essential Reference* is the reference you need when you know what you want to do and you just need to know how.

Linux System Administration
By James T. Dennis
1st Edition Spring 1999
450 pages, $29.99
ISBN: 1-56205-934-3
As an administrator, you probably feel that most of your time and energy is spent in endless firefighting. If your network has become a fragile quilt of temporary patches and workarounds, then this book is for you. For example, have you had trouble sending or receiving your email lately? Are you looking for a way to keep your network running smoothly with enhanced performance? Are your users always hankering for more storage, more services, and more speed? *Linux System Administration* advises you on the many intricacies of maintaining a secure, stable system. In this definitive work, the author addresses all the issues related to system administration, from adding users and managing files permission to Internet services and Web hosting to recovery planning and security. This book fulfills the need for expert advice that will ensure a trouble-free Linux environment.

Linux Security
By John S. Flowers
1st Edition Spring 1999
400 pages, $29.99
ISBN: 0-7357-0035-4
New Riders is proud to offer the first book aimed specifically at Linux security issues. While there are a host of general UNIX security books, we thought it was time to address the practical needs of the Linux network. In this definitive work, author John Flowers takes a balanced approach to system security, from discussing topics like planning a secure environment to firewalls to utilizing security scripts. With comprehensive information on specific system compromises, and advice on how to prevent and repair them, this is one

book that every Linux administrator should have on the shelf.

Developing Linux Applications
By Eric Harlow
1st Edition
400 pages, $34.99
ISBN: 0-7357-0214-7

We all know that Linux is one of the most powerful and solid operating systems in existence. And as the success of Linux grows, there is an increasing interest in developing applications with graphical user interfaces that really take advantage of the power of Linux. In this book, software developer Eric Harlow gives you an indispensable development handbook focusing on the GTK+ toolkit. More than an overview on the elements of application or GUI design, this is a hands-on book that delves deeply into the technology. With in-depth material on the various GUI programming tools and loads of examples, this book's unique focus will give you the information you need to design and launch professional-quality applications.

Linux Essential Reference
By David "Hacksaw" Todd
1st Edition Summer 1999
400 pages, $19.99
ISBN: 0-7357-0852-5

This book is all about getting things done as quickly and efficiently as possible by providing a structured organization to the plethora of available Linux information. We can sum it up in one word: VALUE. This book has it all: concise instruction on how to perform key administration tasks; advanced information on configuration; shell scripting; hardware management; systems management; data tasks; automation; and tons of other useful information. All coupled with an unique navigational structure and a great price. This book truly provides groundbreaking information for the growing community of advanced Linux professionals.

Lotus Notes and Domino Titles

Domino System Administration
By Rob Kirkland
1st Edition Summer 1999
500 pages, $34.99
ISBN: 1-56205-948-3

Your boss has just announced that you will be upgrading to the newest version of Notes and Domino when it ships. As a Premium Lotus Business Partner, Lotus has offered a substantial price break to keep your company away from Microsoft's Exchange Server. How are you supposed to get this new system installed, configured, and rolled out to all your endusers? You understand how Lotus Notes works—you've been administering it for years. What you need is a concise, practical explanation about the new features, and how to make some of the advanced stuff really work. You need answers and solutions from someone like you, who has worked with the product for years, and understands what it is you need to know. *Domino System Administration* is the answer—the first book on Domino that attacks the technology at the professional level, with practical, hands-on assistance to get Domino running in your organization.

Lotus Notes and Domino Essential Reference

By Dave Hatter & Tim Bankes
1st Edition Spring 1999
500 pages, $24.99
ISBN: 0-7357-0007-9

You're in a bind because you've been asked to design and program a new database in Notes for an important client that will keep track of and itemize a myriad of inventory and shipping data. The client wants a user-friendly interface, without sacrificing speed or functionality. You are experienced (and could develop this app in your sleep), but feel that you need to take your talents to the next level. You need something to facilitate your creative and technical abilities, something to perfect your programming skills. Your answer is waiting for you: *Lotus Notes and Domino Essential Reference.* It's compact and simply designed. It's loaded with information. All the objects, classes, functions, and methods are listed. It shows you the object hierarchy and the overlaying relationship between each one. It's perfect for you. Problem solved.

Networking Titles

Cisco Router Configuration and Troubleshooting

By Mark Tripod
1st Edition
300 pages, $34.99
ISBN: 0-7357-0024-9

Want the real story on making your Cisco routers run like a dream? Why not pick up a copy of *Cisco Router Configuration and Troubleshooting* and see what Pablo Espinosa and Mark Tripod have to say? They're the folks responsible for making some of the largest sites on the Net scream, like Amazon.com, Hotmail, USAToday, Geocities, and Sony. In this book, they provide advanced configuration issues, sprinkled with advice and preferred practices. You won't see a general overview on TCP/IP—they talk about more meaty issues like security, monitoring, traffic management, and more. In the troubleshooting section, the authors provide a unique methodology and lots of sample problems to illustrate. By providing real-world insight and examples instead of rehashing Cisco's documentation, Pablo and Mark give network administrators information they can start using today.

Implementing and Troubleshooting LDAP

By Robert Lamothe
1st Edition Spring 1999
400 pages, $34.99
ISBN: 1-56205-947-5

While there is some limited information available about LDAP, most of it is RFCs, white papers, and books about programming LDAP into your networking applications. That leaves the people who most need information—administrators—out in the cold. What do you do if you need to know how to make LDAP work in your system? You ask Bob Lamothe. Bob is a UNIX administrator with hands-on experience in setting up a corporate-wide directory service using LDAP. Bob's book is NOT a guide to the protocol; rather, it is designed to be an aid to administrators to help them understand the most efficient way to structure, encrypt, authenticate, administer, and troubleshoot LDAP in a mixed network environment. The book shows you how to work with the major implementations of LDAP and get them to coexist.

Implementing Virtual Private Networks

By Tina Bird and Ted Stockwell
1st Edition Spring 1999
300 pages, $29.99
ISBN: 0-73570-047-8

Tired of looking for decent, practical, up-to-date information on virtual private networks? *Implementing Virtual Private Networks*, by noted authorities Dr. Tina Bird and Ted Stockwell, finally gives you what you need—an authoritative guide on the design, implementation, and maintenance of Internet-based access to private networks. This book focuses on real-world solutions, demonstrating how the choice of VPN architecture should align with an organization's business and technological requirements. Tina and Ted give you the information you need to determine whether a VPN is right for your organization, select the VPN that suits your needs, and design and implement the VPN you have chosen.

Understanding Data Communications, Sixth Edition

By Gilbert Held
6th Edition Summer 1999
500 pages, $34.99
ISBN: 0-7357-0036-2

Updated from the highly successful fifth edition, this book explains how data communications systems and their various hardware and software components work. Not an entry-level book, it approaches the material in a textbook format, addressing the complex issues involved in internetworking today. A great reference book for the experienced networking professional, written by noted networking authority, Gilbert Held.

Other Books By New Riders Press

Windows Technologies

Windows NT Network
Management 1-56205-946-7

Implementing Exchange Server
1-56205-931-9

SQL Server System Administration
1-56205-955-6

Windows NT DNS 1-56205-943-2

Windows NT Performance
Monitoring 1-56205-942-4

Windows NT Registry
1-56205-941-6

Windows NT TCP/IP
1-56205-887-8

Windows NT Terminal Server and
Citrix MetaFrame
1-56205-944-0

Certification

A+ Certification TestPrep
1-56205-892-4

A+ Certification Top Score Software
0-7357-0017-6

A+ Certification Training Guide
1-56205-896-7

A+ Complete v 1.1 0-7357-0045-1

A+ Fast Track 0-7357-0028-1

MCSE Essential Reference: Core
NT Exams 0-7357-0006-0

MCSD Fast Track: Visual Basic 6,
Exam 70-176 0-7357-0019-2

MCSE Fast Track: 6-in-1 Bundle
1-56205-909-2

MCSE Fast Track: Internet
Information Server 4
1-56205-936-X

MCSE Fast Track: Networking
Essentials 1-56205-939-4

MCSE Fast Track: TCP/IP
1-56205-937-8

MCSD Fast Track: Visual Basic 6,
Exam 70-175 0-7357-0018-4

MCSE Fast Track: Windows 98
0-7357-0016-8

MCSE Fast Track: Windows NT
Server 4 1-56205-935-1

MCSE Fast Track: Windows NT
Server 4 Enterprise
1-56205-940-8

MCSE Fast Track: Windows NT
Workstation 4 1-56205-938-6

MCSE Simulation Guide: Windows
NT Server 4 & Enterprise
1-56205-914-9

MCSE Simulation Guide: Windows
NT Workstation 4 1-56205-925-4

MCSE TestPrep: Core Exam Bundle,
2E 0-7357-0030-3

MCSE TestPrep: Networking
Essentials Second Edition
0-7357-0010-9

MCSE TestPrep: TCP/IP, Second
Edition 0-7357-0025-7

MCSE TestPrep: Windows 95
Second Edition 0-7357-0011-7

MCSE TestPrep: Windows 98
1-56205-922-X

MCSE TestPrep: Windows NT
Server 4 Enterprise Second Edition
0-7357-0009-5

MCSE TestPrep: Windows NT
Server 4 Second Edition
0-7357-0012-5

MCSE TestPrep: Windows NT
Workstation 4 Second Edition
0-7357-0008-7

MCSD TestPrep: Visual Basic 6
Exams 0-7357-0032-X

MCSE Training Guide: Core Exams
Bundle, Second Edition
1-56205-926-2

MCSE Training Guide: Networking
Essentials Second Edition
1-56205-919-X

MCSE Training Guide: TCP/IP
Second Edition 1-56205-920-3

MCSE Training Guide: Windows 98
1-56205-890-8

MCSE Training Guide: Windows
NT Server 4 Second Edition
1-56205-916-5

MCSE Training Guide: Windows
NT Server Enterprise Second
Edition 1-56205-917-3

MCSE Training Guide: Windows
NT Workstation 4 Second Edition
1-56205-918-1

MCSD Training Guide: Visual Basic
6 Exams 0-7357-0002-8

MCSE Top Score Software: Core
Exams 0-7357-0033-8

MCSE + Complete, v1.1
0-7897-1564-3

MCSE + Internet Complete, v1.2
0-7357-0072-9

Graphics

Inside 3D Studio MAX 2 Volume I
1-56205-857-6

Inside 3D Studio MAX 2 Volume II:
Modeling and Materials
1-56205-864-9

Inside 3D Studio MAX 2
Volume III: Animation
1-56205-865-7

Inside 3D Studio MAX 2 Resource
Kit 1-56205-953-X

Inside AutoCAD 14 Limited Edition
1-56205-898-3

Inside Softimage 3D 1-56205-885-1

HTML Web Magic, 2nd Edition
1-56830-475-7

Dynamic HTML Web Magic
1-56830-421-8

<Designing Web Graphics.3>
1-56205-949-1

Illustrator 8 Magic 1-56205-952-1

Inside trueSpace 4 1-56205-957-2

Inside Adobe Photoshop 5
1-56205-884-3

Inside Adobe Photoshop 5, Limited
Edition 1-56205-951-3

Photoshop 5 Artistry 1-56205-895-9

Photoshop 5 Type Magic
1-56830-465-X

Photoshop 5 Web Magic
1-56205-913-0

New Riders How to Contact Us

Visit Our Web Site

www.newriders.com

On our Web site you'll find information about our other books, authors, tables of contents, indexes, and book errata. You can also place orders for books through our Web site.

Email Us

Contact us at this address:

newriders@mcp.com

- If you have comments or questions about this book
- To report errors that you have found in this book
- If you have a book proposal to submit or are interested in writing for New Riders
- If you would like to have an author kit sent to you
- If you are an expert in a computer topic or technology and are interested in being a technical editor who reviews manuscripts for technical accuracy

slayton@mcp.com

- To find a distributor in your area, please contact our international department at the address above.

slayton@mcp.com

- For instructors from educational institutions who wish to preview New Riders books for classroom use. Email should include your name, title, school, department, address, phone number, office days/hours, text in use, and enrollment in the body of your text along with your request for desk/examination copies and/or additional information.

Write to Us

New Riders Publishing

201 W. 103rd St.

Indianapolis, IN 46290-1097

Call Us

Toll-free (800) 571-5840 + 9 +3657

If outside U.S. (317) 581-3500. Ask for New Riders.

Fax Us

(317) 581-4663

Fold here and tape to mail

New Riders Publishing
201 W. 103rd St.
Indianapolis, IN 46290

We Want to Know What You Think

To better serve you, we would like your opinion on the content and quality of this book. Please complete this card and mail it to us or fax it to 317-581-4663.

Name _____

Address _____

City_____State_____Zip _____

Phone _____

Email Address _____

Occupation _____

Operating System(s) that you use _____

What influenced your purchase of this book?
- ❏ Recommendation
- ❏ Cover Design
- ❏ Table of Contents
- ❏ Index
- ❏ Magazine Review
- ❏ Advertisement
- ❏ New Rider's Reputation
- ❏ Author Name

How would you rate the contents of this book?
- ❏ Excellent
- ❏ Very Good
- ❏ Good
- ❏ Fair
- ❏ Below Average
- ❏ Poor

How do you plan to use this book?
- ❏ Quick reference
- ❏ Self-training
- ❏ Classroom
- ❏ Other

What do you like most about this book?
Check all that apply.
- ❏ Content
- ❏ Writing Style
- ❏ Accuracy
- ❏ Examples
- ❏ Listings
- ❏ Design
- ❏ Index
- ❏ Page Count
- ❏ Price
- ❏ Illustrations

What do you like least about this book?
Check all that apply.
- ❏ Content
- ❏ Writing Style
- ❏ Accuracy
- ❏ Examples
- ❏ Listings
- ❏ Design
- ❏ Index
- ❏ Page Count
- ❏ Price
- ❏ Illustrations

What would be a useful follow-up book to this one for you?_____

Where did you purchase this book? _____

Can you name a similar book that you like better than this one, or one that is as good? Why?

_____

_____

How many New Riders books do you own? _____

What are your favorite computer books?_____

_____

What other titles would you like to see us develop? _____

Any comments for us? _____

_____

_____

_____

Planning for Windows 2000, 0-7357-0048-6

www.newriders.com • **Fax** 317-581-4663